LLEWE

2 · 0

ASTROLOGICAL

POCKET PLANNER

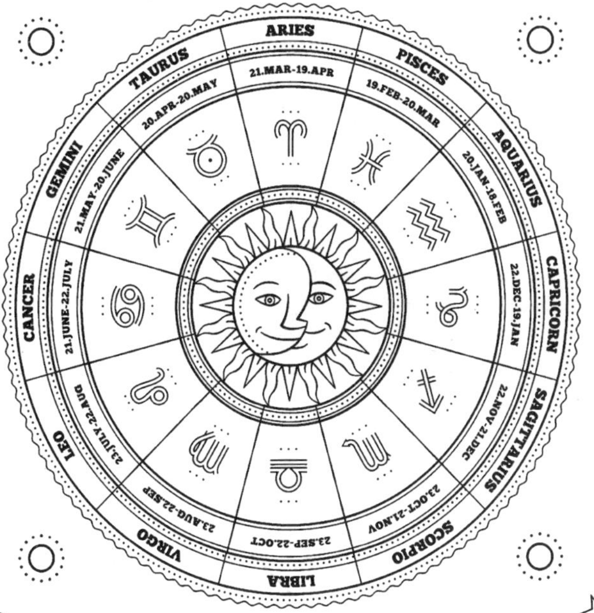

Daily Ephemeris & Aspectarian

2019-2021

ISBN-13: 978-0-7387-4941-9
Second Printing

Cover design by Shannon McKuhen
Designed by Susan Van Sant
Edited by Annie Burdick

A special thanks to Phoebe Aina Allen for astrological proofreading.

Astrological calculations compiled and programmed by Rique Pottenger based on the earlier work of Neil F. Michelsen. Reuse is prohibited.

Published by
LLEWELLYN WORLDWIDE LTD.
2143 Wooddale Drive
Woodbury, MN 55125-2989
www.llewellyn.com

Printed in the United States of America

Table of Contents

Mercury Retrograde 2020

	DATE	ET	PT			DATE	ET	PT
Mercury Retrograde	2/16	**7:54 pm**	4:54 pm	—	Mercury Direct	3/9	**11:49 pm**	8:49 pm
Mercury Retrograde	6/17		9:59 pm	—	Mercury Direct	7/12	**4:26 am**	1:26 am
Mercury Retrograde	6/18	**12:59 am**		—	Mercury Direct	7/12	**4:26 am**	1:26 am
Mercury Retrograde	10/13	**9:05 pm**	6:05 pm	—	Mercury Direct	11/3	**12:50 pm**	9:50 am

Moon Void-of-Course 2020

Times are listed in Eastern Time in this table only. All other information in the *Pocket Planner* is listed in both Eastern time and Pacific time. Refer to "Time Zone Conversions" on page 8 for changing to other time zones. Note: All times are corrected for Daylight Saving Time.

JANUARY

Last Aspect Date	Time	Moon Enters New Sign Date	Sign	Time
1	9:14 pm	1	♈	11:00 pm
3	8:18 pm	4	♉	11:15 am
6	7:08 am	6	♊	9:11 pm
8	5:16 pm	9	♋	3:43 am
10	6:58 pm	11	♌	7:16 am
13	8:42 am	13	♍	9:06 am
15	7:12 am	15	♎	10:43 am
17	7:58 am	17	♏	1:20 pm
19	4:22 pm	19	♐	5:41 pm
20	11:46 pm	22	♑	12:00 am
23	9:08 pm	24	♒	8:20 am
25	2:06 pm	26	♓	6:44 pm
28	8:08 pm	28	♈	6:51 am
31	10:10 am	31	♉	7:28 pm

FEBRUARY

Last Aspect Date	Time	Moon Enters New Sign Date	Sign	Time
3	6:28 am	3	♊	6:29 am
5	9:20 am	5	♋	2:03 pm
7	10:43 am	7	♌	5:45 pm
9	11:08 am	9	♍	6:39 pm
11	1:26 pm	11	♎	6:37 pm
13	4:40 pm	13	♏	7:37 pm
15	5:20 pm	15	♐	11:07 pm
18	4:03 am	18	♑	5:37 am
20	9:18 am	20	♒	2:42 pm
21	11:08 pm	23	♓	1:37 am
25	9:12 am	25	♈	1:47 pm
27	10:25 pm	28	♉	2:30 am

MARCH

Last Aspect Date	Time	Moon Enters New Sign Date	Sign	Time
1	10:52 am	1	♊	2:21 pm
3	9:20 pm	3	♋	11:25 pm
6	2:11 am	6	♌	4:27 am
8	4:12 am	8	♍	6:47 am
10	4:32 am	10	♎	6:03 am
12	4:12 am	12	♏	5:28 am
14	6:06 am	14	♐	7:09 am
16	5:34 am	16	♑	12:25 pm
18	8:48 pm	18	♒	9:16 pm
20	5:00 am	21	♓	8:33 am
23	10:51 am	23	♈	8:58 pm
26	3:16 am	26	♉	9:37 am
28	7:05 pm	28	♊	9:38 pm
30	11:10 am	31	♋	7:43 am

Moon Void-of-Course 2020 (cont.)

APRIL

Last Aspect Date	Time	Moon Enters New Sign Date	Sign	Time
2	12:49 pm	2	♌	2:26 pm
3	3:29 pm	4	♍	5:18 pm
6	9:29 am	6	♎	5:16 pm
8	8:50 am	8	♏	4:17 pm
10	3:35 pm	10	♐	4:35 pm
12	7:46 am	12	♑	8:05 pm
14	7:47 pm	15	♒	3:37 am
17	10:34 am	17	♓	2:29 pm
19	7:31 pm	20	♈	3:00 am
22	8:32 am	22	♉	3:36 pm
24	8:43 pm	25	♊	3:20 am
27	1:00 pm	27	♋	1:28 pm
29	3:29 pm	29	♌	9:06 pm

MAY

Last Aspect Date	Time	Moon Enters New Sign Date	Sign	Time
1	12:04 pm	2	♍	1:35 am
3	10:25 pm	4	♎	3:09 am
5	10:31 pm	6	♏	3:05 am
7	10:39 pm	8	♐	3:15 am
10	2:11 am	10	♑	5:39 am
12	6:30 am	12	♒	11:39 am
14	10:03 am	14	♓	9:24 pm
17	3:59 am	17	♈	9:36 am
19	4:33 pm	19	♉	10:10 pm
22	4:01 am	22	♊	9:36 am
24	7:09 am	24	♋	7:09 pm
26	9:06 pm	27	♌	2:33 am
28	9:30 am	29	♍	7:40 am
31	5:17 am	31	♎	10:38 am

JUNE

Last Aspect Date	Time	Moon Enters New Sign Date	Sign	Time
2	6:40 am	2	♏	12:06 pm
4	7:36 am	4	♐	1:17 pm
6	12:10 am	6	♑	3:44 pm
8	2:06 pm	8	♒	8:54 pm
10	10:35 am	11	♓	5:32 am
13	8:35 am	13	♈	5:03 pm
15	8:49 pm	16	♉	5:35 am
18	8:02 am	18	♊	5:00 pm
20	5:48 pm	21	♋	2:02 am
23	3:20 am	23	♌	8:33 am
24	1:34 am	25	♍	1:05 pm
27	4:02 pm	27	♎	4:16 pm
29	9:02 am	29	♏	6:48 pm

JULY

Last Aspect Date	Time	Moon Enters New Sign Date	Sign	Time
1	9:20 pm	1	♐	9:21 pm
3	9:06 am	4	♑	12:48 am
6	5:35 am	6	♒	6:08 am
7	12:37 am	8	♓	2:13 pm
10	11:49 pm	11	♈	1:06 am
13	11:54 am	13	♉	1:34 pm
15	11:21 pm	16	♊	1:19 am
17	5:14 pm	18	♋	10:24 am
20	1:55 pm	20	♌	4:16 pm
21	8:27 pm	22	♍	7:40 pm
24	7:08 pm	24	♎	9:54 pm
26	9:09 pm	27	♏	12:12 am
29	12:01 am	29	♐	3:25 am
30	8:08 pm	31	♑	7:58 am

AUGUST

Last Aspect Date	Time	Moon Enters New Sign Date	Sign	Time
2	9:59 am	2	♒	2:11 pm
4	5:45 pm	4	♓	10:28 pm
7	8:53 am	7	♈	9:05 am
9	3:50 pm	9	♉	9:28 pm
12	3:55 am	12	♊	9:46 am
14	7:19 am	14	♋	7:35 pm
16	7:59 pm	17	♌	1:38 am
19	1:38 am	19	♍	4:20 am
20	11:37 pm	21	♎	5:16 am
23	12:20 am	23	♏	6:16 am
25	2:27 am	25	♐	8:49 am
27	8:00 am	27	♑	1:37 pm
29	3:31 pm	29	♒	8:37 pm

SEPTEMBER

Last Aspect Date	Time	Moon Enters New Sign Date	Sign	Time
1	12:56 am	1	♓	5:34 am
3	10:34 am	3	♈	4:22 pm
6	12:45 am	6	♉	4:43 am
8	8:47 am	8	♊	5:28 pm
11	12:48 am	11	♋	4:23 am
13	8:05 am	13	♌	11:32 am
15	11:09 am	15	♍	2:37 pm
17	7:42 am	17	♎	2:56 pm
19	10:29 am	19	♏	2:33 pm
21	2:13 pm	21	♐	3:32 pm
23	1:31 pm	23	♑	7:16 pm
25	11:36 pm	26	♒	2:08 am
28	3:18 am	28	♓	11:34 am
30	1:30 pm	30	♈	10:47 pm

OCTOBER

Last Aspect Date	Time	Moon Enters New Sign Date	Sign	Time
3	1:47 am	3	♉	11:12 am
5	2:41 pm	6	♊	12:03 am
7	9:57 pm	8	♋	11:45 am
10	12:04 pm	10	♌	8:24 pm
12	10:29 am	13	♍	12:56 am
14	6:47 pm	15	♎	1:54 am
16	6:11 pm	17	♏	1:05 am
18	5:43 pm	19	♐	12:43 am
20	11:38 pm	21	♑	2:44 am
23	12:35 am	23	♒	8:17 am
24	5:54 pm	25	♓	5:18 pm
27	8:46 pm	28	♈	4:45 am
30	12:12 pm	30	♉	5:19 pm

NOVEMBER

Last Aspect Date	Time	Moon Enters New Sign Date	Sign	Time
1	9:29 pm	2	♊	5:00 am
4	8:49 am	4	♋	4:45 pm
6	8:27 pm	7	♌	2:18 am
9	6:05 am	9	♍	8:30 am
11	5:58 am	11	♎	11:09 am
13	6:32 am	13	♏	11:19 am
15	6:13 am	15	♐	10:47 am
17	2:55 am	17	♑	11:35 am
19	11:30 am	19	♒	3:25 pm
20	7:49 pm	21	♓	11:06 pm
24	5:44 am	24	♈	10:05 am
26	6:46 pm	26	♉	10:43 pm
29	7:48 am	29	♊	11:16 am
30	11:22 pm	12/1	♋	10:33 pm

DECEMBER

Last Aspect Date	Time	Moon Enters New Sign Date	Sign	Time
4	5:29 am	4	♌	7:53 am
5	5:28 pm	6	♍	2:46 pm
8	5:35 pm	8	♎	7:01 pm
10	7:56 pm	10	♏	8:59 pm
12	8:58 pm	12	♐	9:39 pm
14	11:17 am	14	♑	10:35 pm
17	12:34 am	17	♒	1:27 am
19	3:45 am	19	♓	7:39 am
21	5:25 am	21	♈	5:32 pm
23	5:51 pm	24	♉	5:55 am
26	6:32 am	26	♊	6:33 pm
28	10:01 pm	29	♋	5:28 am
31	5:45 am	31	♌	1:58 pm

How to Use the *Pocket Planner*

by Leslie Nielsen

This handy guide contains information that can be most valuable to you as you plan your daily activities. As you read through the first few pages, you can start to get a feel for how well organized this guide is.

Read the Symbol Key on the next page, which is rather like astrological shorthand. The characteristics of the planets can give you direction in planning your strategies. Much like traffic signs that signal "go," "stop," or even "caution," you can determine for yourself the most propitious time to get things done.

You'll find tables that show the dates when Mercury is retrograde (℞) or direct (**D**). Because Mercury deals with the exchange of information, a retrograde Mercury makes miscommunication more noticeable.

There's also a section dedicated to the times when the Moon is void-of-course (V/C). These are generally poor times to conduct business because activities begun during these times usually end badly or fail to get started. If you make an appointment during a void-of-course, you might save yourself a lot of aggravation by confirming the time and date later. The Moon is only void-of-course for 7 percent of the time when business is usually conducted during a normal workday (that is, 8:00 am to 5:00 pm). Sometimes, by waiting a matter of minutes or a few hours until the Moon has left the void-of-course phase, you have a much better chance to make action move more smoothly. Moon voids can also be used successfully to do routine activities or inner work, such as dream therapy or personal contemplation.

You'll find Moon phases, as well as each of the Moon's entries into a new sign. Times are expressed in Eastern time (in bold type) and Pacific time (in regular type). The New Moon time is generally best for beginning new activities, as the Moon is increasing in light and can offer the element of growth to our endeavors. When the Moon is Full, its illumination is greatest and we can see the results of our efforts. When it moves from the Full stage back to the New stage, it can best be used to reflect on our projects. If necessary, we can make corrections at the New Moon.

The section of "Planetary Stations" on page 9 will give you the times when the planets are changing signs or direction, thereby affording us opportunities for new starts.

The ephemeris in the back of your *Pocket Planner* can be very helpful to you. As you start to work with the ephemeris, you may notice that not all planets seem to be comfortable in every sign. Think of the planets as actors and the signs as the costumes they wear. Sometimes, costumes just itch. If you find this to be so for a certain time period, you may choose to delay your plans for a time or be more creative with the energies at hand.

As you turn to the daily pages, you'll find information about the Moon's sign, phase, and the time it changes phase. You'll find icons indicating the best days to plant and fish. Also, you will find times and dates when the planets and asteroids change signs and go either retrograde or direct, major holidays, a three-month calendar, and room to record your appointments.

This guide is a powerful tool. Make the most of it!

Symbol Key

Planets:	☉ Sun	⚳ Ceres	♄ Saturn
	☽ Moon	⚴ Pallas	⚷ Chiron
	☿ Mercury	⚵ Juno	♅ Uranus
	♀ Venus	⚶ Vesta	♆ Neptune
	♂ Mars	♃ Jupiter	♇ Pluto
Signs:	♈ Aries	♌ Leo	♐ Sagittarius
	♉ Taurus	♍ Virgo	♑ Capricorn
	♊ Gemini	♎ Libra	♒ Aquarius
	♋ Cancer	♏ Scorpio	♓ Pisces
Aspects:	☌ Conjunction (0°)	⚺ Semisextile (30°)	⚹ Sextile (60°)
	□ Square (90°)	△ Trine (120°)	
	⚻ Quincunx (150°)	☍ Opposition (180°)	
Motion:	℞ Retrograde	D Direct	

Best Days for Planting: 🌿 **Best Days for Fishing:** 🐟

World Map of Time Zones

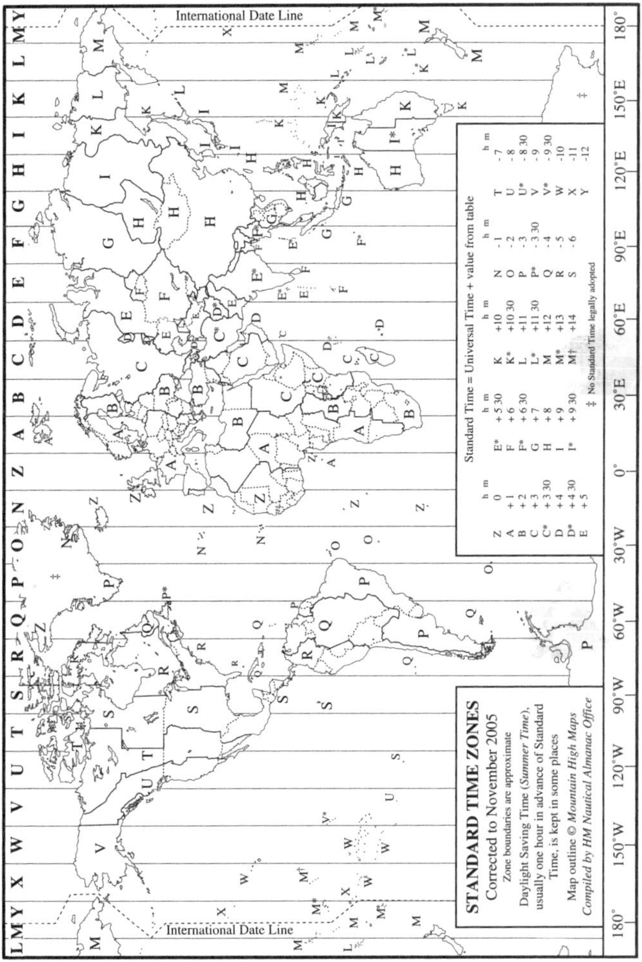
International Date Line
STANDARD TIME ZONES
Corrected to November 2005
Zone boundaries are approximate
Daylight Saving Time (Summer Time), usually one hour in advance of Standard Time, is kept in some places
Map outline © Mountain High Maps
Compiled by HM Nautical Almanac Office
Standard Time = Universal Time + value from table
Z 0
A +1
B +2
C +3
C* +3 30
D +4
D* +4 30
E +5
E* +5 30
F +6
F* +6 30
G +7
H +8
I +9
I* +9 30
K +10
K* +10 30
L +11
L* +11 30
M +12
M* +13
M† +14
N -1
O -2
P -3
P* -3 30
Q -4
R -5
S -6
T -7
U -8
U* -8 30
V -9
V* -9 30
W -10
X -11
Y -12
‡ No Standard Time legally adopted
180° 150°W 120°W 90°W 60°W 30°W 0° 30°E 60°E 90°E 120°E 150°E 180°

Time Zone Conversions

World Time Zones

Compared to Eastern Standard Time

( )	From Map	(Y)	Subtract 7 hours	(C*)	Add 8.5 hours
(S)	CST/Subtract 1 hour	(A)	Add 6 hours	(D*)	Add 9.5 hours
(R)	EST	(B)	Add 7 hours	(E*)	Add 10.5 hours
(Q)	Add 1 hour	(C)	Add 8 hours	(F*)	Add 11.5 hours
(P)	Add 2 hours	(D)	Add 9 hours	(I*)	Add 14.5 hours
(O)	Add 3 hours	(E)	Add 10 hours	(K*)	Add 15.5 hours
(N)	Add 4 hours	(F)	Add 11 hours	(L*)	Add 16.5 hours
(Z)	Add 5 hours	(G)	Add 12 hours	(M*)	Add 18 hours
(T)	MST/Subtract 2 hours	(H)	Add 13 hours	(P*)	Add 2.5 hours
(U)	PST/Subtract 3 hours	(I)	Add 14 hours	(U*)	Subtract 3.5 hours
(V)	Subtract 4 hours	(K)	Add 15 hours	(V*)	Subtract 4.5 hours
(W)	Subtract 5 hours	(L)	Add 16 hours		
(X)	Subtract 6 hours	(M)	Add 17 hours		

World Map of Time Zones is supplied by HM Nautical Almanac Office © Center for the Central Laboratory of the Research Councils. Note: This is not an official map. Countries change their time zones as they wish.

Planetary Stations for 2020

	JAN	FEB	MAR	APR	MAY	JUN	JUL	AUG	SEP	OCT	NOV	DEC
☿		2/16–3/9				6/18–7/12				10/13–11/3		
♀					5/13–6/25							
♂									9/9–11/13			
♃					5/14–9/12							
♄					5/11–9/29							
♅	–1/20							8/5–1/14/21				
♆						6/23–11/28						
♇				4/25–10/4								
⚷							7/11–12/15					
⚳							7/7–10/18					
⚴					5/17–9/5							
⚵		2/8–5/26										
⚶												

30 Monday

1st ♒
☽ V/C **5:24 am** 2:24 am
☽ enters ♓ **10:41 am** 7:41 am

31 Tuesday

1st ♓

New Year's Eve

1 Wednesday

1st ♓
☽ V/C **9:14 pm** 6:14 pm
☽ enters ♈ **11:00 pm** 8:00 pm

New Year's Day • Kwanzaa ends

2 Thursday

1st ♈
2nd Quarter **11:45 pm** 8:45 pm

Eastern time in bold type
Pacific time in medium type

3 Friday

2nd ♈

♂ enters ♐	**4:37 am**	1:37 am
☽ V/C	**8:18 pm**	5:18 pm

4 Saturday

2nd ♈

☽ enters ♉	**11:15 am**	8:15 am

5 Sunday

2nd ♉

December 2019

S	M	T	W	T	F	S
1	2	3	4	5	6	7
8	9	10	11	12	13	14
15	16	17	18	19	20	21
22	23	24	25	26	27	28
29	30	31				

January 2020

S	M	T	W	T	F	S
			1	2	3	4
5	6	7	8	9	10	11
12	13	14	15	16	17	18
19	20	21	22	23	24	25
26	27	28	29	30	31	

February 2020

S	M	T	W	T	F	S
						1
2	3	4	5	6	7	8
9	10	11	12	13	14	15
16	17	18	19	20	21	22
23	24	25	26	27	28	29

Eastern time in bold type
Pacific time in medium type

6 Monday

2nd ♉

☽ V/C	**7:08 am**	4:08 am
☽ enters ♊	**9:11 pm**	6:11 pm

7 Tuesday

2nd ♊

8 Wednesday

2nd ♊

☽ V/C	**5:16 pm**	2:16 pm

9 Thursday

2nd ♊

☽ enters ♋	**3:43 am**	12:43 am

Eastern time in bold type
Pacific time in medium type

10 Friday

2nd ♋
Full Moon **2:21 pm** 11:21 am
☽ V/C **6:58 pm** 3:58 pm
♅ D **8:48 pm** 5:48 pm

Lunar Eclipse 20° ♋ 00'

11 Saturday

3rd ♋
☽ enters ♌ **7:16 am** 4:16 am

12 Sunday

3rd ♌

December 2019

S	M	T	W	T	F	S
1	2	3	4	5	6	7
8	9	10	11	12	13	14
15	16	17	18	19	20	21
22	23	24	25	26	27	28
29	30	31				

January 2020

S	M	T	W	T	F	S
			1	2	3	4
5	6	7	8	9	10	11
12	13	14	15	16	17	18
19	20	21	22	23	24	25
26	27	28	29	30	31	

February 2020

S	M	T	W	T	F	S
						1
2	3	4	5	6	7	8
9	10	11	12	13	14	15
16	17	18	19	20	21	22
23	24	25	26	27	28	29

13 Monday

3rd ♌

☽ V/C	**8:42 am**	5:42 am
☽ enters ♍	**9:06 am**	6:06 am
♀ enters ♓	**1:39 pm**	10:39 am

14 Tuesday

3rd ♍

15 Wednesday

3rd ♍

☽ V/C	**7:12 am**	4:12 am
☽ enters ♎	**10:43 am**	7:43 am

16 Thursday

3rd ♎

☿ enters ♒	**1:31 pm**	10:31 am

Eastern time in bold type
Pacific time in medium type

17 Friday

3rd ♎

☽ V/C	**7:58 am**	4:58 am
4th Quarter	**7:58 am**	4:58 am
☽ enters ♏	**1:20 pm**	10:20 am

18 Saturday

4th ♏

♀ enters ♑	**5:33 am**	2:33 am

19 Sunday

4th ♏

☽ V/C	**4:22 pm**	1:22 pm
☽ enters ♐	**5:41 pm**	2:41 pm

December 2019

S	M	T	W	T	F	S
1	2	3	4	5	6	7
8	9	10	11	12	13	14
15	16	17	18	19	20	21
22	23	24	25	26	27	28
29	30	31				

January 2020

S	M	T	W	T	F	S
			1	2	3	4
5	6	7	8	9	10	11
12	13	14	15	16	17	18
19	20	21	22	23	24	25
26	27	28	29	30	31	

February 2020

S	M	T	W	T	F	S
						1
2	3	4	5	6	7	8
9	10	11	12	13	14	15
16	17	18	19	20	21	22
23	24	25	26	27	28	29

20 Monday

4th ♐
☉ enters ♒ **9:55 am** 6:55 am
☽ V/C **11:46 pm** 8:46 pm

Martin Luther King Jr. Day

21 Tuesday

4th ♐
☽ enters ♑ 9:00 pm

22 Wednesday

4th ♑
☽ enters ♑ **12:00 am**

23 Thursday

4th ♑
☽ V/C **9:08 pm** 6:08 pm

Eastern time in bold type
Pacific time in medium type

24 Friday

4th ♑
☽ enters ♒ **8:20 am** 5:20 am
New Moon **4:42 pm** 1:42 pm

25 Saturday

1st ♒
☽ V/C **2:06 pm** 11:06 am

Lunar New Year (Rat)

26 Sunday

1st ♒
☽ enters ♓ **6:44 pm** 3:44 pm

December 2019

S	M	T	W	T	F	S
1	2	3	4	5	6	7
8	9	10	11	12	13	14
15	16	17	18	19	20	21
22	23	24	25	26	27	28
29	30	31				

January 2020

S	M	T	W	T	F	S
			1	2	3	4
5	6	7	8	9	10	11
12	13	14	15	16	17	18
19	20	21	22	23	24	25
26	27	28	29	30	31	

February 2020

S	M	T	W	T	F	S
						1
2	3	4	5	6	7	8
9	10	11	12	13	14	15
16	17	18	19	20	21	22
23	24	25	26	27	28	29

27 Monday
1st ♓

28 Tuesday
1st ♓
☽ V/C **8:08 pm** 5:08 pm

29 Wednesday
1st ♓
☽ enters ♈ **6:51 am** 3:51 am

30 Thursday
1st ♈

Eastern time in bold type
Pacific time in medium type

31 Friday

1st ♈

⚳ enters ♒	**3:01 am**	12:01 am
☽ V/C	**10:10 am**	7:10 am
☽ enters ♉	**7:28 pm**	4:28 pm

1 Saturday

1st ♉

2nd Quarter **8:42 pm** 5:42 pm

2 Sunday

2nd ♉

Imbolc • Groundhog Day

January 2020

S	M	T	W	T	F	S
			1	2	3	4
5	6	7	8	9	10	11
12	13	14	15	16	17	18
19	20	21	22	23	24	25
26	27	28	29	30	31	

February 2020

S	M	T	W	T	F	S
						1
2	3	4	5	6	7	8
9	10	11	12	13	14	15
16	17	18	19	20	21	22
23	24	25	26	27	28	29

March 2020

S	M	T	W	T	F	S
1	2	3	4	5	6	7
8	9	10	11	12	13	14
15	16	17	18	19	20	21
22	23	24	25	26	27	28
29	30	31				

3 Monday

2nd ♉

☽ V/C	**6:28 am**	3:28 am
☽ enters ♊	**6:29 am**	3:29 am
☿ enters ♓	**6:37 am**	3:37 am

4 Tuesday

2nd ♊

5 Wednesday

2nd ♊

☽ V/C	**9:20 am**	6:20 am
☽ enters ♋	**2:03 pm**	11:03 am

6 Thursday

2nd ♋

Eastern time in bold type
Pacific time in medium type

7 Friday

2nd ♋

☽ V/C	**10:43 am**	7:43 am
♀ enters ♈	**3:02 pm**	12:02 pm
☽ enters ♌	**5:45 pm**	2:45 pm

8 Saturday

2nd ♌

⚵ ℞	**12:59 pm**	9:59 am
Full Moon		11:33 pm

9 Sunday

2nd ♌

Full Moon	**2:33 am**	
☽ V/C	**11:08 am**	8:08 am
☽ enters ♍	**6:39 pm**	3:39 pm

January 2020

S	M	T	W	T	F	S
			1	2	3	4
5	6	7	8	9	10	11
12	13	14	15	16	17	18
19	20	21	22	23	24	25
26	27	28	29	30	31	

February 2020

S	M	T	W	T	F	S
						1
2	3	4	5	6	7	8
9	10	11	12	13	14	15
16	17	18	19	20	21	22
23	24	25	26	27	28	29

March 2020

S	M	T	W	T	F	S
1	2	3	4	5	6	7
8	9	10	11	12	13	14
15	16	17	18	19	20	21
22	23	24	25	26	27	28
29	30	31				

Eastern time in bold type
Pacific time in medium type

10 Monday
3rd ♍

11 Tuesday
3rd ♍

☽ V/C **1:26 pm** 10:26 am

☽ enters ♎ **6:37 pm** 3:37 pm

12 Wednesday
3rd ♎

13 Thursday
3rd ♎

☽ V/C **4:40 pm** 1:40 pm

☽ enters ♏ **7:37 pm** 4:37 pm

Eastern time in bold type
Pacific time in medium type

14 Friday
3rd ♏

Valentine's Day

15 Saturday
3rd ♏

4th Quarter	**5:17 pm**	2:17 pm
☽ V/C	**5:20 pm**	2:20 pm
☽ enters ♐	**11:07 pm**	8:07 pm

16 Sunday
4th ♐

♂ enters ♑	**6:33 am**	3:33 am
☿ ℞	**7:54 pm**	4:54 pm

January 2020

S	M	T	W	T	F	S
			1	2	3	4
5	6	7	8	9	10	11
12	13	14	15	16	17	18
19	20	21	22	23	24	25
26	27	28	29	30	31	

February 2020

S	M	T	W	T	F	S
						1
2	3	4	5	6	7	8
9	10	11	12	13	14	15
16	17	18	19	20	21	22
23	24	25	26	27	28	29

March 2020

S	M	T	W	T	F	S
1	2	3	4	5	6	7
8	9	10	11	12	13	14
15	16	17	18	19	20	21
22	23	24	25	26	27	28
29	30	31				

Eastern time in bold type
Pacific time in medium type

17 Monday
4th ♐

Presidents' Day

18 Tuesday
4th ♐

☽ V/C	**4:03 am**	1:03 am
☽ enters ♑	**5:37 am**	2:37 am
☉ enters ♓	**11:57 pm**	8:57 pm

19 Wednesday
4th ♑

20 Thursday
4th ♑

☽ V/C	**9:18 am**	6:18 am
☽ enters ♒	**2:42 pm**	11:42 am

Eastern time in bold type
Pacific time in medium type

21 Friday

4th ♒
☽ V/C **11:08 pm** 8:08 pm

22 Saturday

4th ♒
☽ enters ♓ 10:37 pm

23 Sunday

4th ♒
☽ enters ♓ **1:37 am**
New Moon **10:32 am** 7:32 am

January 2020

S	M	T	W	T	F	S
			1	2	3	4
5	6	7	8	9	10	11
12	13	14	15	16	17	18
19	20	21	22	23	24	25
26	27	28	29	30	31	

February 2020

S	M	T	W	T	F	S
						1
2	3	4	5	6	7	8
9	10	11	12	13	14	15
16	17	18	19	20	21	22
23	24	25	26	27	28	29

March 2020

S	M	T	W	T	F	S
1	2	3	4	5	6	7
8	9	10	11	12	13	14
15	16	17	18	19	20	21
22	23	24	25	26	27	28
29	30	31				

Eastern time in bold type
Pacific time in medium type

24 Monday
1st ♓

25 Tuesday
1st ♓

☽ V/C	**9:12 am**	6:12 am
☽ enters ♈	**1:47 pm**	10:47 am

Mardi Gras (Fat Tuesday)

26 Wednesday
1st ♈

Ash Wednesday

27 Thursday
1st ♈

☽ V/C	**10:25 pm**	7:25 pm
☽ enters ♉		11:30 pm

Eastern time in bold type
Pacific time in medium type

28 Friday

1st ♈
☽ enters ♉ **2:30 am**

29 Saturday

1st ♉

1 Sunday

1st ♉
☽ V/C **10:52 am** 7:52 am
☽ enters ♊ **2:21 pm** 11:21 am

February 2020

S	M	T	W	T	F	S
						1
2	3	4	5	6	7	8
9	10	11	12	13	14	15
16	17	18	19	20	21	22
23	24	25	26	27	28	29

March 2020

S	M	T	W	T	F	S
1	2	3	4	5	6	7
8	9	10	11	12	13	14
15	16	17	18	19	20	21
22	23	24	25	26	27	28
29	30	31				

April 2020

S	M	T	W	T	F	S
			1	2	3	4
5	6	7	8	9	10	11
12	13	14	15	16	17	18
19	20	21	22	23	24	25
26	27	28	29	30		

2 Monday

1st ♊
2nd Quarter **2:57 pm** 11:57 am

3 Tuesday

2nd ♊
☽ V/C **9:20 pm** 6:20 pm
☽ enters ♋ **11:25 pm** 8:25 pm

4 Wednesday

2nd ♋
☿ enters ♒ **6:08 am** 3:08 am
♀ enters ♉ **10:07 pm** 7:07 pm

5 Thursday

2nd ♋
☽ V/C 11:11 pm

Eastern time in bold type
Pacific time in medium type

6 Friday

2nd ♋

☽ V/C	**2:11 am**	
☽ enters ♌	**4:27 am**	1:27 am

7 Saturday

2nd ♌

8 Sunday

2nd ♌

☽ V/C	**4:12 am**	12:12 am
☽ enters ♍	**6:47 am**	3:47 am

Daylight Saving Time begins at 2 am

February 2020

S	M	T	W	T	F	S
						1
2	3	4	5	6	7	8
9	10	11	12	13	14	15
16	17	18	19	20	21	22
23	24	25	26	27	28	29

March 2020

S	M	T	W	T	F	S
1	2	3	4	5	6	7
8	9	10	11	12	13	14
15	16	17	18	19	20	21
22	23	24	25	26	27	28
29	30	31				

April 2020

S	M	T	W	T	F	S
			1	2	3	4
5	6	7	8	9	10	11
12	13	14	15	16	17	18
19	20	21	22	23	24	25
26	27	28	29	30		

9 Monday

2nd ♍

Full Moon	**1:48 pm**	10:48 am
☿ D	**11:49 pm**	8:49 pm

10 Tuesday

3rd ♍

☽ V/C	**4:32 am**	1:32 am
☽ enters ♎	**6:03 am**	3:03 am

Purim

11 Wednesday

3rd ♎

12 Thursday

3rd ♎

☽ V/C	**4:12 am**	1:12 am
☽ enters ♏	**5:28 am**	2:28 am

Eastern time in bold type
Pacific time in medium type

13 Friday
3rd ♏

14 Saturday
3rd ♏
☽ V/C **6:06 am** 3:06 am
☽ enters ♐ **7:09 am** 4:09 am

15 Sunday
3rd ♐

February 2020

S	M	T	W	T	F	S
						1
2	3	4	5	6	7	8
9	10	11	12	13	14	15
16	17	18	19	20	21	22
23	24	25	26	27	28	29

March 2020

S	M	T	W	T	F	S
1	2	3	4	5	6	7
8	9	10	11	12	13	14
15	16	17	18	19	20	21
22	23	24	25	26	27	28
29	30	31				

April 2020

S	M	T	W	T	F	S
			1	2	3	4
5	6	7	8	9	10	11
12	13	14	15	16	17	18
19	20	21	22	23	24	25
26	27	28	29	30		

16 Monday

3rd ♐

☿ enters ♓	**3:42 am**	12:42 am
☽ V/C	**5:34 am**	2:34 am
4th Quarter	**5:34 am**	2:34 am
☽ enters ♑	**12:25 pm**	9:25 am

17 Tuesday

4th ♑

St. Patrick's Day

18 Wednesday

4th ♑

☽ V/C	**8:48 pm**	5:48 pm
☽ enters ♒	**9:16 pm**	6:16 pm

19 Thursday

4th ♒

☉ enters ♈	**11:50 pm**	8:50 pm

Ostara • Spring Equinox • Int'l Astrology Day

Eastern time in bold type
Pacific time in medium type

20 Friday

4th ≈
☽ V/C **5:00 am** 2:00 am
⚶ enters ♊ 10:10 pm

21 Saturday

4th ≈
⚶ enters ♊ **1:10 am**
☽ enters ♓ **8:33 am** 5:33 am
♄ enters ≈ **11:58 pm** 8:58 pm

22 Sunday

4th ♓

February 2020

S	M	T	W	T	F	S
						1
2	3	4	5	6	7	8
9	10	11	12	13	14	15
16	17	18	19	20	21	22
23	24	25	26	27	28	29

March 2020

S	M	T	W	T	F	S
1	2	3	4	5	6	7
8	9	10	11	12	13	14
15	16	17	18	19	20	21
22	23	24	25	26	27	28
29	30	31				

April 2020

S	M	T	W	T	F	S
			1	2	3	4
5	6	7	8	9	10	11
12	13	14	15	16	17	18
19	20	21	22	23	24	25
26	27	28	29	30		

Eastern time in bold type
Pacific time in medium type

23 Monday

4th ♓
☽ V/C **10:51 am** 7:51 am
☽ enters ♈ **8:58 pm** 5:58 pm

24 Tuesday

4th ♈
New Moon **5:28 am** 2:28 am

25 Wednesday

1st ♈

26 Thursday

1st ♈
☽ V/C **3:16 am** 12:16 am
☽ enters ♉ **9:37 am** 6:37 am

Eastern time in bold type
Pacific time in medium type

27 Friday

1st ♉

28 Saturday

1st ♉

☽ V/C	**7:05 pm**	4:05 pm
☽ enters ♊	**9:38 pm**	6:38 pm

29 Sunday

1st ♊

February 2020

S	M	T	W	T	F	S
						1
2	3	4	5	6	7	8
9	10	11	12	13	14	15
16	17	18	19	20	21	22
23	24	25	26	27	28	29

March 2020

S	M	T	W	T	F	S
1	2	3	4	5	6	7
8	9	10	11	12	13	14
15	16	17	18	19	20	21
22	23	24	25	26	27	28
29	30	31				

April 2020

S	M	T	W	T	F	S
			1	2	3	4
5	6	7	8	9	10	11
12	13	14	15	16	17	18
19	20	21	22	23	24	25
26	27	28	29	30		

Eastern time in bold type
Pacific time in medium type

30 Monday
1st ♊
☽ V/C **11:10 am** 8:10 am
♂ enters ♒ **3:43 pm** 12:43 pm

31 Tuesday
1st ♊
☽ enters ♋ **7:43 am** 4:43 am

1 Wednesday
1st ♋
2nd Quarter **6:21 am** 3:21 am

April Fools' Day (All Fools' Day—Pagan)

2 Thursday
2nd ♋
☽ V/C **12:49 pm** 9:49 am
☽ enters ♌ **2:26 pm** 11:26 am

3 Friday

2nd ♌
♀ enters ♊ **1:11 pm** 10:11 am
☽ V/C **3:29 pm** 12:29 pm

4 Saturday

2nd ♌
☽ enters ♍ **5:18 pm** 2:18 pm

5 Sunday

2nd ♍

Palm Sunday

March 2020

S	M	T	W	T	F	S
1	2	3	4	5	6	7
8	9	10	11	12	13	14
15	16	17	18	19	20	21
22	23	24	25	26	27	28
29	30	31				

April 2020

S	M	T	W	T	F	S
			1	2	3	4
5	6	7	8	9	10	11
12	13	14	15	16	17	18
19	20	21	22	23	24	25
26	27	28	29	30		

May 2020

S	M	T	W	T	F	S
					1	2
3	4	5	6	7	8	9
10	11	12	13	14	15	16
17	18	19	20	21	22	23
24	25	26	27	28	29	30
31						

6 Monday

2nd ♍

☽ V/C	**9:29 am**	6:29 am
☽ enters ♎	**5:16 pm**	2:16 pm

7 Tuesday

2nd ♎

Full Moon	**10:35 pm**	7:35 pm

8 Wednesday

3rd ♎

☽ V/C	**8:50 am**	5:50 am
☽ enters ♏	**4:17 pm**	1:17 pm

9 Thursday

3rd ♏

Passover begins (at sundown on April 8)

Eastern time in bold type
Pacific time in medium type

10 Friday

3rd ♏

☽ V/C	**3:35 pm**	12:35 pm
☽ enters ♐	**4:35 pm**	1:35 pm
☿ enters ♈		9:48 pm

Good Friday

11 Saturday

3rd ♐

☿ enters ♈ **12:48 am**

12 Sunday

3rd ♐

☽ V/C	**7:46 am**	4:46 am
☽ enters ♑	**8:05 pm**	5:05 pm

Easter

March 2020

S	M	T	W	T	F	S
1	2	3	4	5	6	7
8	9	10	11	12	13	14
15	16	17	18	19	20	21
22	23	24	25	26	27	28
29	30	31				

April 2020

S	M	T	W	T	F	S
			1	2	3	4
5	6	7	8	9	10	11
12	13	14	15	16	17	18
19	20	21	22	23	24	25
26	27	28	29	30		

May 2020

S	M	T	W	T	F	S
					1	2
3	4	5	6	7	8	9
10	11	12	13	14	15	16
17	18	19	20	21	22	23
24	25	26	27	28	29	30
31						

13 Monday

3rd ♑

14 Tuesday

3rd ♑

4th Quarter	**6:56 pm**	3:56 pm
☽ V/C	**7:47 pm**	4:47 pm

15 Wednesday

4th ♑

☽ enters ♒	**3:37 am**	12:37 am

16 Thursday

4th ♒

Passover ends

Eastern time in bold type
Pacific time in medium type

17 Friday

4th ♒

☽ V/C	**10:34 am**	7:34 am
☽ enters ♓	**2:29 pm**	11:29 am

Orthodox Good Friday

18 Saturday

4th ♓

19 Sunday

4th ♓

☉ enters ♉	**10:45 am**	7:45 am
☽ V/C	**7:31 pm**	4:31 pm

Orthodox Easter

March 2020

S	M	T	W	T	F	S
1	2	3	4	5	6	7
8	9	10	11	12	13	14
15	16	17	18	19	20	21
22	23	24	25	26	27	28
29	30	31				

April 2020

S	M	T	W	T	F	S
			1	2	3	4
5	6	7	8	9	10	11
12	13	14	15	16	17	18
19	20	21	22	23	24	25
26	27	28	29	30		

May 2020

S	M	T	W	T	F	S
					1	2
3	4	5	6	7	8	9
10	11	12	13	14	15	16
17	18	19	20	21	22	23
24	25	26	27	28	29	30
31						

Eastern time in bold type
Pacific time in medium type

20 Monday

4th ♓
☽ enters ♈ **3:00 am** 12:00 am

21 Tuesday

4th ♈

22 Wednesday

4th ♈
☽ V/C **8:32 am** 5:32 am
☽ enters ♉ **3:36 pm** 12:36 pm
New Moon **10:26 pm** 7:26 pm

Earth Day

23 Thursday

1st ♉
⚳ enters ♓ **4:20 pm** 1:20 pm

Ramadan begins

24 Friday

1st ♉

☽ V/C	**8:43 pm**	5:43 pm

25 Saturday

1st ♉

☽ enters ♊	**3:20 am**	12:20 am
♇ ℞	**2:54 pm**	11:54 am

26 Sunday

1st ♊

March 2020

S	M	T	W	T	F	S
1	2	3	4	5	6	7
8	9	10	11	12	13	14
15	16	17	18	19	20	21
22	23	24	25	26	27	28
29	30	31				

April 2020

S	M	T	W	T	F	S
			1	2	3	4
5	6	7	8	9	10	11
12	13	14	15	16	17	18
19	20	21	22	23	24	25
26	27	28	29	30		

May 2020

S	M	T	W	T	F	S
					1	2
3	4	5	6	7	8	9
10	11	12	13	14	15	16
17	18	19	20	21	22	23
24	25	26	27	28	29	30
31						

Eastern time in bold type
Pacific time in medium type

27 Monday

1st ♊

☽ V/C	**1:00 pm**	10:00 am
☽ enters ♋	**1:28 pm**	10:28 am
☿ enters ♉	**3:53 pm**	12:53 pm

28 Tuesday

1st ♋

29 Wednesday

1st ♋

☽ V/C	**3:29 pm**	12:29 pm
♀ enters ♒	**8:29 pm**	5:29 pm
☽ enters ♌	**9:06 pm**	6:06 pm

30 Thursday

1st ♌

2nd Quarter	**4:38 pm**	1:38 pm

1 Friday

2nd ♌
☽ V/C **12:04 pm** 9:04 am
☽ enters ♍ 10:35 pm

Beltane

2 Saturday

2nd ♌
☽ enters ♍ **1:35 am**

3 Sunday

2nd ♍
☽ V/C **10:25 pm** 7:25 pm

April 2020

S	M	T	W	T	F	S
			1	2	3	4
5	6	7	8	9	10	11
12	13	14	15	16	17	18
19	20	21	22	23	24	25
26	27	28	29	30		

May 2020

S	M	T	W	T	F	S
					1	2
3	4	5	6	7	8	9
10	11	12	13	14	15	16
17	18	19	20	21	22	23
24	25	26	27	28	29	30
31						

June 2020

S	M	T	W	T	F	S
	1	2	3	4	5	6
7	8	9	10	11	12	13
14	15	16	17	18	19	20
21	22	23	24	25	26	27
28	29	30				

Eastern time in bold type
Pacific time in medium type

4 Monday

2nd ♍
☽ enters ♎ **3:09 am** 12:09 am

5 Tuesday

2nd ♎
☽ V/C **10:31 pm** 7:31 pm

Cinco de Mayo

6 Wednesday

2nd ♎
☽ enters ♏ **3:05 am** 12:05 am

7 Thursday

2nd ♏
Full Moon **6:45 am** 3:45 am
☽ V/C **10:39 pm** 7:39 pm

Eastern time in bold type
Pacific time in medium type

8 Friday

3rd ♏
☽ enters ♐ **3:15 am** 12:15 am

9 Saturday

3rd ♐
☽ V/C 11:11 pm

10 Sunday

3rd ♐
☽ V/C **2:11 am**
☽ enters ♑ **5:39 am** 2:39 am
♄ ℞ 9:09 pm

Mother's Day

April 2020

S	M	T	W	T	F	S
			1	2	3	4
5	6	7	8	9	10	11
12	13	14	15	16	17	18
19	20	21	22	23	24	25
26	27	28	29	30		

May 2020

S	M	T	W	T	F	S
					1	2
3	4	5	6	7	8	9
10	11	12	13	14	15	16
17	18	19	20	21	22	23
24	25	26	27	28	29	30
31						

June 2020

S	M	T	W	T	F	S
	1	2	3	4	5	6
7	8	9	10	11	12	13
14	15	16	17	18	19	20
21	22	23	24	25	26	27
28	29	30				

11 Monday

3rd ♑

♄ ℞	**12:09 am**	
☿ enters ♊	**5:58 pm**	2:58 pm

12 Tuesday

3rd ♑

☽ V/C	**6:30 am**	3:30 am
☽ enters ♒	**11:39 am**	8:39 am
♂ enters ♓		9:17 pm
♀ ℞		11:45 pm

13 Wednesday

3rd ♒

♂ enters ♓	**12:17 am**	
♀ ℞	**2:45 am**	

14 Thursday

3rd ♒

☽ V/C	**10:03 am**	7:03 am
4th Quarter	**10:03 am**	7:03 am
♃ ℞	**10:32 am**	7:32 am
☽ enters ♓	**9:24 pm**	6:24 pm

Eastern time in bold type
Pacific time in medium type

15 Friday
4th ♓

16 Saturday
4th ♓

17 Sunday
4th ♓

☽ V/C	**3:59 am**	12:59 am
⚴ ℞	**4:29 am**	1:29 am
☽ enters ♈	**9:36 am**	6:36 am

April 2020

S	M	T	W	T	F	S
			1	2	3	4
5	6	7	8	9	10	11
12	13	14	15	16	17	18
19	20	21	22	23	24	25
26	27	28	29	30		

May 2020

S	M	T	W	T	F	S
					1	2
3	4	5	6	7	8	9
10	11	12	13	14	15	16
17	18	19	20	21	22	23
24	25	26	27	28	29	30
31						

June 2020

S	M	T	W	T	F	S
	1	2	3	4	5	6
7	8	9	10	11	12	13
14	15	16	17	18	19	20
21	22	23	24	25	26	27
28	29	30				

18 Monday
4th ♈

19 Tuesday
4th ♈

☽ V/C **4:33 pm** 1:33 pm

☽ enters ♉ **10:10 pm** 7:10 pm

20 Wednesday
4th ♉

☉ enters ♊ **9:49 am** 6:49 am

21 Thursday
4th ♉

Eastern time in bold type
Pacific time in medium type

22 Friday

4th ♉

☽ V/C	**4:01 am**	1:01 am
☽ enters ♊	**9:36 am**	6:36 am
New Moon	**1:39 pm**	10:39 am

23 Saturday

1st ♊

Ramadan ends

24 Sunday

1st ♊

☽ V/C	**7:09 am**	4:09 am
☽ enters ♋	**7:09 pm**	4:09 pm

April 2020

S	M	T	W	T	F	S
			1	2	3	4
5	6	7	8	9	10	11
12	13	14	15	16	17	18
19	20	21	22	23	24	25
26	27	28	29	30		

May 2020

S	M	T	W	T	F	S
					1	2
3	4	5	6	7	8	9
10	11	12	13	14	15	16
17	18	19	20	21	22	23
24	25	26	27	28	29	30
31						

June 2020

S	M	T	W	T	F	S
	1	2	3	4	5	6
7	8	9	10	11	12	13
14	15	16	17	18	19	20
21	22	23	24	25	26	27
28	29	30				

Eastern time in bold type
Pacific time in medium type

25 Monday

1st ♋

Memorial Day

26 Tuesday

1st ♋

☽ V/C	**9:06 pm**	6:06 pm
⚵ D	**10:51 pm**	7:51 pm
☽ enters ♌		11:33 pm

27 Wednesday

1st ♋

☽ enters ♌ **2:33 am**

28 Thursday

1st ♌

☽ V/C	**9:30 am**	6:30 am
☿ enters ♋	**2:09 pm**	11:09 am

Eastern time in bold type
Pacific time in medium type

29 Friday

1st ♌

☽ enters ♍	**7:40 am**	4:40 am
2nd Quarter	**11:30 pm**	8:30 pm

Shavuot (begins at sundown on May 28)

30 Saturday

2nd ♍

31 Sunday

2nd ♍

☽ V/C	**5:17 am**	2:17 am
☽ enters ♎	**10:38 am**	7:38 am

April 2020

S	M	T	W	T	F	S
			1	2	3	4
5	6	7	8	9	10	11
12	13	14	15	16	17	18
19	20	21	22	23	24	25
26	27	28	29	30		

May 2020

S	M	T	W	T	F	S
					1	2
3	4	5	6	7	8	9
10	11	12	13	14	15	16
17	18	19	20	21	22	23
24	25	26	27	28	29	30
31						

June 2020

S	M	T	W	T	F	S
	1	2	3	4	5	6
7	8	9	10	11	12	13
14	15	16	17	18	19	20
21	22	23	24	25	26	27
28	29	30				

Eastern time in bold type
Pacific time in medium type

1 Monday

2nd ♎

2 Tuesday

2nd ♎

☽ V/C	**6:40 am**	3:40 am
☽ enters ♏	**12:06 pm**	9:06 am
⚳ enters ♑	**8:55 pm**	5:55 pm

3 Wednesday

2nd ♏

⚶ enters ♋	**2:55 pm**	11:55 am

4 Thursday

2nd ♏

☽ V/C	**7:36 am**	4:36 am
☽ enters ♐	**1:17 pm**	10:17 am

5 Friday

2nd ♐

Full Moon	**3:12 pm**	12:12 pm
☽ V/C		9:10 pm

Lunar Eclipse 15 ° ♐ 34'

6 Saturday

3rd ♐

☽ V/C	**12:10 am**	
☽ enters ♑	**3:44 pm**	12:44 pm

7 Sunday

3rd ♑

May 2020

S	M	T	W	T	F	S
					1	2
3	4	5	6	7	8	9
10	11	12	13	14	15	16
17	18	19	20	21	22	23
24	25	26	27	28	29	30
31						

June 2020

S	M	T	W	T	F	S
	1	2	3	4	5	6
7	8	9	10	11	12	13
14	15	16	17	18	19	20
21	22	23	24	25	26	27
28	29	30				

July 2020

S	M	T	W	T	F	S
			1	2	3	4
5	6	7	8	9	10	11
12	13	14	15	16	17	18
19	20	21	22	23	24	25
26	27	28	29	30	31	

8 Monday

3rd ♑

☽ V/C **2:06 pm** 11:06 am

☽ enters ♒ **8:54 pm** 5:54 pm

9 Tuesday

3rd ♒

10 Wednesday

3rd ♒

☽ V/C **10:35 am** 7:35 am

11 Thursday

3rd ♒

☽ enters ♓ **5:32 am** 2:32 am

Eastern time in bold type
Pacific time in medium type

12 Friday

3rd ♓
4th Quarter 11:24 pm

13 Saturday

3rd ♓

4th Quarter	**2:24 am**	
☽ V/C	**8:45 am**	5:45 am
☽ enters ♈	**5:03 pm**	2:03 pm

14 Sunday

4th ♈

Flag Day

May 2020

S	M	T	W	T	F	S
					1	2
3	4	5	6	7	8	9
10	11	12	13	14	15	16
17	18	19	20	21	22	23
24	25	26	27	28	29	30
31						

June 2020

S	M	T	W	T	F	S
	1	2	3	4	5	6
7	8	9	10	11	12	13
14	15	16	17	18	19	20
21	22	23	24	25	26	27
28	29	30				

July 2020

S	M	T	W	T	F	S
			1	2	3	4
5	6	7	8	9	10	11
12	13	14	15	16	17	18
19	20	21	22	23	24	25
26	27	28	29	30	31	

Eastern time in bold type
Pacific time in medium type

15 Monday

4th ♈
☽ V/C **8:49 pm** 5:49 pm

16 Tuesday

4th ♈
☽ enters ♉ **5:35 am** 2:35 am

17 Wednesday

4th ♉
☿ ℞ 9:59 pm

18 Thursday

4th ♉
☿ ℞ **12:59 am**
☽ V/C **8:02 am** 5:02 am
☽ enters ♊ **5:00 pm** 2:00 pm

Eastern time in bold type
Pacific time in medium type

19 Friday

4th ♊

20 Saturday

4th ♊

☉ enters ♋	**5:44 pm**	2:44 pm
☽ V/C	**5:48 pm**	2:48 pm
☽ enters ♋		11:02 pm
New Moon		11:41 pm

Litha • Summer Solstice

21 Sunday

4th ♊

☽ enters ♋	**2:02 am**
New Moon	**2:41 am**

Father's Day • Solar Eclipse 0 ° ♋ 21'

May 2020

S	M	T	W	T	F	S
					1	2
3	4	5	6	7	8	9
10	11	12	13	14	15	16
17	18	19	20	21	22	23
24	25	26	27	28	29	30
31						

June 2020

S	M	T	W	T	F	S
	1	2	3	4	5	6
7	8	9	10	11	12	13
14	15	16	17	18	19	20
21	22	23	24	25	26	27
28	29	30				

July 2020

S	M	T	W	T	F	S
			1	2	3	4
5	6	7	8	9	10	11
12	13	14	15	16	17	18
19	20	21	22	23	24	25
26	27	28	29	30	31	

Eastern time in bold type
Pacific time in medium type

22 Monday

1st ♋
♆ ℞ 9:32 pm

23 Tuesday

1st ♋
♆ ℞ **12:32 am**
☽ V/C **3:20 am** 12:20 am
☽ enters ♌ **8:33 am** 5:33 am
☽ V/C 10:34 pm

24 Wednesday

1st ♌
☽ V/C **1:34 am**
♀ D 11:48 pm

25 Thursday

1st ♌
♀ D **2:48 am**
☽ enters ♍ **1:05 pm** 10:05 am

Eastern time in bold type
Pacific time in medium type

26 Friday
1st ♍

27 Saturday
1st ♍

☽ V/C	**4:02 pm**	1:02 pm
☽ enters ♎	**4:16 pm**	1:16 pm
♂ enters ♈	**9:45 pm**	6:45 pm

28 Sunday
1st ♎

2nd Quarter	**4:16 am**	1:16 am

May 2020

S	M	T	W	T	F	S
					1	2
3	4	5	6	7	8	9
10	11	12	13	14	15	16
17	18	19	20	21	22	23
24	25	26	27	28	29	30
31						

June 2020

S	M	T	W	T	F	S
	1	2	3	4	5	6
7	8	9	10	11	12	13
14	15	16	17	18	19	20
21	22	23	24	25	26	27
28	29	30				

July 2020

S	M	T	W	T	F	S
			1	2	3	4
5	6	7	8	9	10	11
12	13	14	15	16	17	18
19	20	21	22	23	24	25
26	27	28	29	30	31	

Eastern time in bold type
Pacific time in medium type

29 Monday

2nd ♎
☽ V/C **9:02 am** 6:02 am
☽ enters ♏ **6:48 pm** 3:48 pm

30 Tuesday

2nd ♏

1 Wednesday

2nd ♏
♄ enters ♑ **7:39 pm** 4:39 pm
☽ V/C **9:20 pm** 6:20 pm
☽ enters ♐ **9:21 pm** 6:21 pm

2 Thursday

2nd ♐

Eastern time in bold type
Pacific time in medium type

3 Friday

2nd ♐
☽ V/C **9:06 am** 6:06 am
☽ enters ♑ 9:48 pm

4 Saturday

2nd ♐
☽ enters ♑ **12:48 am**
Full Moon 9:44 pm

Independence Day

5 Sunday

2nd ♑
Full Moon **12:44 am**

Lunar Eclipse 13 ° ♑ 38'

June 2020

S	M	T	W	T	F	S
	1	2	3	4	5	6
7	8	9	10	11	12	13
14	15	16	17	18	19	20
21	22	23	24	25	26	27
28	29	30				

July 2020

S	M	T	W	T	F	S
			1	2	3	4
5	6	7	8	9	10	11
12	13	14	15	16	17	18
19	20	21	22	23	24	25
26	27	28	29	30	31	

August 2020

S	M	T	W	T	F	S
						1
2	3	4	5	6	7	8
9	10	11	12	13	14	15
16	17	18	19	20	21	22
23	24	25	26	27	28	29
30	31					

Eastern time in bold type
Pacific time in medium type

6 Monday

3rd ♑

☽ V/C	**5:35 am**	2:35 am
☽ enters ♒	**6:08 am**	3:08 am
⚳ ℞		9:01 pm
☽ V/C		9:37 pm

7 Tuesday

3rd ♒

⚳ ℞	**12:01 am**	
☽ V/C	**12:37 am**	

8 Wednesday

3rd ♒

☽ enters ♓	**2:13 pm**	11:13 am

9 Thursday

3rd ♓

Eastern time in bold type
Pacific time in medium type

10 Friday

3rd ♓
☽ V/C **11:49 pm** 8:49 pm
☽ enters ♈ 10:06 pm

11 Saturday

3rd ♓
☽ enters ♈ **1:06 am**
⚷ ℞ **5:09 pm** 2:09 pm

12 Sunday

3rd ♈
☿ D **4:26 am** 1:26 am
4th Quarter **7:29 pm** 4:29 pm

June 2020

S	M	T	W	T	F	S
	1	2	3	4	5	6
7	8	9	10	11	12	13
14	15	16	17	18	19	20
21	22	23	24	25	26	27
28	29	30				

July 2020

S	M	T	W	T	F	S
			1	2	3	4
5	6	7	8	9	10	11
12	13	14	15	16	17	18
19	20	21	22	23	24	25
26	27	28	29	30	31	

August 2020

S	M	T	W	T	F	S
						1
2	3	4	5	6	7	8
9	10	11	12	13	14	15
16	17	18	19	20	21	22
23	24	25	26	27	28	29
30	31					

13 Monday

4th ♈
☽ V/C **11:54 am** 8:54 am
☽ enters ♉ **1:34 pm** 10:34 am

14 Tuesday

4th ♉

15 Wednesday

4th ♉
☽ V/C **11:21 pm** 8:21 pm
☽ enters ♊ 10:19 pm

16 Thursday

4th ♉
☽ enters ♊ **1:19 am**

Eastern time in bold type
Pacific time in medium type

17 Friday

4th ♊
☽ V/C **5:14 pm** 2:14 pm

18 Saturday

4th ♊
☽ enters ♋ **10:24 am** 7:24 am

19 Sunday

4th ♋

June 2020

S	M	T	W	T	F	S
	1	2	3	4	5	6
7	8	9	10	11	12	13
14	15	16	17	18	19	20
21	22	23	24	25	26	27
28	29	30				

July 2020

S	M	T	W	T	F	S
			1	2	3	4
5	6	7	8	9	10	11
12	13	14	15	16	17	18
19	20	21	22	23	24	25
26	27	28	29	30	31	

August 2020

S	M	T	W	T	F	S
						1
2	3	4	5	6	7	8
9	10	11	12	13	14	15
16	17	18	19	20	21	22
23	24	25	26	27	28	29
30	31					

Eastern time in bold type
Pacific time in medium type

20 Monday

4th ♋

New Moon	**1:33 pm**	10:33 am
☽ V/C	**1:55 pm**	10:55 am
☽ enters ♌	**4:16 pm**	1:16 pm

21 Tuesday

1st ♌

☽ V/C	**8:27 pm**	5:27 pm

22 Wednesday

1st ♌

☉ enters ♌	**4:37 am**	1:37 am
☽ enters ♍	**7:40 pm**	4:40 pm

23 Thursday

1st ♍

Eastern time in bold type
Pacific time in medium type

24 Friday

1st ♍

☽ V/C	**7:08 pm**	4:08 pm
☽ enters ♎	**9:54 pm**	6:54 pm

25 Saturday

1st ♎

26 Sunday

1st ♎

☽ V/C	**9:09 pm**	6:09 pm
☽ enters ♏		9:12 pm

June 2020

S	M	T	W	T	F	S
	1	2	3	4	5	6
7	8	9	10	11	12	13
14	15	16	17	18	19	20
21	22	23	24	25	26	27
28	29	30				

July 2020

S	M	T	W	T	F	S
			1	2	3	4
5	6	7	8	9	10	11
12	13	14	15	16	17	18
19	20	21	22	23	24	25
26	27	28	29	30	31	

August 2020

S	M	T	W	T	F	S
						1
2	3	4	5	6	7	8
9	10	11	12	13	14	15
16	17	18	19	20	21	22
23	24	25	26	27	28	29
30	31					

Eastern time in bold type
Pacific time in medium type

27 Monday

1st ♎
☽ enters ♏ **12:12 am**
2nd Quarter **8:33 am** 5:33 am

28 Tuesday

2nd ♏
☽ V/C 9:01 pm

29 Wednesday

2nd ♏
☽ V/C **12:01 am**
☽ enters ♐ **3:25 am** 12:25 am

30 Thursday

2nd ♐
☽ V/C **8:08 pm** 5:08 pm

Eastern time in bold type
Pacific time in medium type

31 Friday
2nd ♐
☽ enters ♑ **7:58 am** 4:58 am

1 Saturday
2nd ♑

Lammas

2 Sunday
2nd ♑
☽ V/C **9:59 am** 6:59 am
☽ enters ♒ **2:11 pm** 11:11 am

July 2020

S	M	T	W	T	F	S
			1	2	3	4
5	6	7	8	9	10	11
12	13	14	15	16	17	18
19	20	21	22	23	24	25
26	27	28	29	30	31	

August 2020

S	M	T	W	T	F	S
						1
2	3	4	5	6	7	8
9	10	11	12	13	14	15
16	17	18	19	20	21	22
23	24	25	26	27	28	29
30	31					

September 2020

S	M	T	W	T	F	S
		1	2	3	4	5
6	7	8	9	10	11	12
13	14	15	16	17	18	19
20	21	22	23	24	25	26
27	28	29	30			

Eastern time in bold type
Pacific time in medium type

3 Monday

2nd ♒

Full Moon	**1:59 am**	8:59 am

4 Tuesday

3rd ♒

☽ V/C	**5:45 pm**	2:45 pm
☽ enters ♓	**10:28 pm**	7:28 pm
☿ enters ♌	**11:32 pm**	8:32 pm

5 Wednesday

3rd ♓

6 Thursday

3rd ♓

Eastern time in bold type
Pacific time in medium type

7 Friday

3rd ♓
☽ V/C **8:53 am** 5:53 am
☽ enters ♈ **9:05 am** 6:05 am
♀ enters ♋ **11:21 am** 8:21 am

8 Saturday

3rd ♈

9 Sunday

3rd ♈
☽ V/C **3:50 pm** 12:50 pm
☽ enters ♉ **9:28 pm** 6:28 pm

July 2020

S	M	T	W	T	F	S
			1	2	3	4
5	6	7	8	9	10	11
12	13	14	15	16	17	18
19	20	21	22	23	24	25
26	27	28	29	30	31	

August 2020

S	M	T	W	T	F	S
						1
2	3	4	5	6	7	8
9	10	11	12	13	14	15
16	17	18	19	20	21	22
23	24	25	26	27	28	29
30	31					

September 2020

S	M	T	W	T	F	S
		1	2	3	4	5
6	7	8	9	10	11	12
13	14	15	16	17	18	19
20	21	22	23	24	25	26
27	28	29	30			

10 Monday

3rd ♉

11 Tuesday

3rd ♉

⚴ enters ♌	**7:17 am**	4:17 am
4th Quarter	**12:45 pm**	9:45 am

12 Wednesday

4th ♉

☽ V/C	**3:55 am**	12:55 am
☽ enters ♊	**9:46 am**	6:46 am

13 Thursday

4th ♊

Eastern time in bold type
Pacific time in medium type

14 Friday

4th ♊

☽ V/C	**7:19 am**	4:19 am
☽ enters ♋	**7:35 pm**	4:35 pm

15 Saturday

4th ♋

♅ ℞	**10:25 am**	7:25 am

16 Sunday

4th ♋

☽ V/C	**7:59 pm**	4:59 pm
☽ enters ♌		10:38 pm

July 2020

S	M	T	W	T	F	S
			1	2	3	4
5	6	7	8	9	10	11
12	13	14	15	16	17	18
19	20	21	22	23	24	25
26	27	28	29	30	31	

August 2020

S	M	T	W	T	F	S
						1
2	3	4	5	6	7	8
9	10	11	12	13	14	15
16	17	18	19	20	21	22
23	24	25	26	27	28	29
30	31					

September 2020

S	M	T	W	T	F	S
		1	2	3	4	5
6	7	8	9	10	11	12
13	14	15	16	17	18	19
20	21	22	23	24	25	26
27	28	29	30			

Eastern time in bold type
Pacific time in medium type

17 Monday

4th ♋
☽ enters ♌ **1:38 am**

18 Tuesday

4th ♌
New Moon **10:42 pm** 7:42 pm
☽ V/C 10:38 pm

19 Wednesday

1st ♌
☽ V/C **1:38 am**
☽ enters ♍ **4:20 am** 1:20 am
☿ enters ♍ **9:30 pm** 6:30 pm

20 Thursday

1st ♍
☽ V/C **11:37 pm** 8:37 pm

Islamic New Year (begins at sundown on August 19)

21 Friday

1st ♍
☽ enters ♎ **5:16 am** 2:16 am

22 Saturday

1st ♎
☉ enters ♍ **11:45 am** 8:45 am
☽ V/C 9:20 pm

23 Sunday

1st ♎
☽ V/C **12:20 am**
☽ enters ♏ **6:16 am** 3:16 am

July 2020

S	M	T	W	T	F	S
			1	2	3	4
5	6	7	8	9	10	11
12	13	14	15	16	17	18
19	20	21	22	23	24	25
26	27	28	29	30	31	

August 2020

S	M	T	W	T	F	S
						1
2	3	4	5	6	7	8
9	10	11	12	13	14	15
16	17	18	19	20	21	22
23	24	25	26	27	28	29
30	31					

September 2020

S	M	T	W	T	F	S
		1	2	3	4	5
6	7	8	9	10	11	12
13	14	15	16	17	18	19
20	21	22	23	24	25	26
27	28	29	30			

Eastern time in bold type
Pacific time in medium type

24 Monday

1st ♏

☽ V/C		11:27 pm

25 Tuesday

1st ♏

☽ V/C	**2:27 am**	
☽ enters ♐	**8:49 am**	5:49 am
2nd Quarter	**1:58 pm**	10:58 am

26 Wednesday

2nd ♐

27 Thursday

2nd ♐

☽ V/C	**8:00 am**	5:00 am
☽ enters ♑	**1:37 pm**	10:37 am

Eastern time in bold type
Pacific time in medium type

28 Friday

2nd ♑

29 Saturday

2nd ♑

☽ V/C	**3:31 pm**	12:31 pm
☽ enters ♒	**8:37 pm**	5:37 pm

30 Sunday

2nd ♒

July 2020

S	M	T	W	T	F	S
			1	2	3	4
5	6	7	8	9	10	11
12	13	14	15	16	17	18
19	20	21	22	23	24	25
26	27	28	29	30	31	

August 2020

S	M	T	W	T	F	S
						1
2	3	4	5	6	7	8
9	10	11	12	13	14	15
16	17	18	19	20	21	22
23	24	25	26	27	28	29
30	31					

September 2020

S	M	T	W	T	F	S
		1	2	3	4	5
6	7	8	9	10	11	12
13	14	15	16	17	18	19
20	21	22	23	24	25	26
27	28	29	30			

31 Monday

2nd ♒

☽ V/C 9:56 pm

1 Tuesday

2nd ♒

☽ V/C **12:56 am**

☽ enters ♓ **5:34 am** 2:34 am

Full Moon 10:22 pm

2 Wednesday

2nd ♓

Full Moon **1:22 am**

3 Thursday

3rd ♓

☽ V/C **10:34 am** 7:34 am

☽ enters ♈ **4:22 pm** 1:22 pm

4 Friday
3rd ♈

5 Saturday
3rd ♈

☿ enters ♎	**3:46 pm**	12:46 pm
⚴ D	**9:06 pm**	6:06 pm
☽ V/C		9:45 pm

6 Sunday
3rd ♈

☽ V/C	**12:45 am**	
♀ enters ♌	**3:22 am**	12:22 am
☽ enters ♉	**4:43 am**	1:43 am

August 2020

S	M	T	W	T	F	S
						1
2	3	4	5	6	7	8
9	10	11	12	13	14	15
16	17	18	19	20	21	22
23	24	25	26	27	28	29
30	31					

September 2020

S	M	T	W	T	F	S
		1	2	3	4	5
6	7	8	9	10	11	12
13	14	15	16	17	18	19
20	21	22	23	24	25	26
27	28	29	30			

October 2020

S	M	T	W	T	F	S
				1	2	3
4	5	6	7	8	9	10
11	12	13	14	15	16	17
18	19	20	21	22	23	24
25	26	27	28	29	30	31

Eastern time in bold type
Pacific time in medium type

7 Monday
3rd ♉

Labor Day

8 Tuesday
3rd ♉

☽ V/C	**8:47 am**	5:47 am
☽ enters ♊	**5:28 pm**	2:28 pm

9 Wednesday
3rd ♊

♂ ℞	**6:22 pm**	3:22 pm

10 Thursday
3rd ♊

4th Quarter	**5:26 am**	2:26 am
☽ V/C		9:48 pm

Eastern time in bold type
Pacific time in medium type

11 Friday

4th ♊
☽ V/C **12:48 am**
☽ enters ♋ **4:23 am** 1:23 am

12 Saturday

4th ♋
♃ D **8:41 pm** 5:41 pm

13 Sunday

4th ♋
☽ V/C **8:05 am** 5:05 am
☽ enters ♌ **11:32 am** 8:32 am

August 2020

S	M	T	W	T	F	S
						1
2	3	4	5	6	7	8
9	10	11	12	13	14	15
16	17	18	19	20	21	22
23	24	25	26	27	28	29
30	31					

September 2020

S	M	T	W	T	F	S
		1	2	3	4	5
6	7	8	9	10	11	12
13	14	15	16	17	18	19
20	21	22	23	24	25	26
27	28	29	30			

October 2020

S	M	T	W	T	F	S
				1	2	3
4	5	6	7	8	9	10
11	12	13	14	15	16	17
18	19	20	21	22	23	24
25	26	27	28	29	30	31

Eastern time in bold type
Pacific time in medium type

14 Monday
4th ♌

15 Tuesday
4th ♌
☽ V/C **11:09 am** 8:09 am
☽ enters ♍ **2:37 pm** 11:37 am

16 Wednesday
4th ♍

17 Thursday
4th ♍
New Moon **7:00 am** 4:00 am
☽ V/C **7:42 am** 4:42 am
☽ enters ♎ **2:56 pm** 11:56 am

18 Friday
1st ♎

19 Saturday
1st ♎
☽ V/C **10:29 am** 7:29 am
☽ enters ♏ **2:33 pm** 11:33 am

Rosh Hashanah (begins at sundown on Sept. 18)

20 Sunday
1st ♏
⚵ enters ♏ **7:19 am** 4:19 am

August 2020

S	M	T	W	T	F	S
						1
2	3	4	5	6	7	8
9	10	11	12	13	14	15
16	17	18	19	20	21	22
23	24	25	26	27	28	29
30	31					

September 2020

S	M	T	W	T	F	S
		1	2	3	4	5
6	7	8	9	10	11	12
13	14	15	16	17	18	19
20	21	22	23	24	25	26
27	28	29	30			

October 2020

S	M	T	W	T	F	S
				1	2	3
4	5	6	7	8	9	10
11	12	13	14	15	16	17
18	19	20	21	22	23	24
25	26	27	28	29	30	31

Eastern time in bold type
Pacific time in medium type

21 Monday

1st ♏

☽ V/C	**2:13 pm**	11:13 am
☽ enters ♐	**3:32 pm**	12:32 pm

UN International Day of Peace

22 Tuesday

1st ♐

☉ enters ♎	**9:31 am**	6:31 am

Mabon • Fall Equinox

23 Wednesday

1st ♐

☽ V/C	**1:31 pm**	10:31 am
☽ enters ♑	**7:16 pm**	4:16 pm
2nd Quarter	**9:55 pm**	6:55 pm

24 Thursday

2nd ♑

Eastern time in bold type
Pacific time in medium type

25 Friday

2nd ♑
☽ V/C **11:36 pm** 8:36 pm
☽ enters ♒ 11:08 pm

26 Saturday

2nd ♑
☽ enters ♒ **2:08 am**

27 Sunday

2nd ♒
⚳ enters ♒ **3:08 am** 12:08 am
☿ enters ♏ **3:41 am** 12:41 am

August 2020

S	M	T	W	T	F	S
						1
2	3	4	5	6	7	8
9	10	11	12	13	14	15
16	17	18	19	20	21	22
23	24	25	26	27	28	29
30	31					

September 2020

S	M	T	W	T	F	S
		1	2	3	4	5
6	7	8	9	10	11	12
13	14	15	16	17	18	19
20	21	22	23	24	25	26
27	28	29	30			

October 2020

S	M	T	W	T	F	S
				1	2	3
4	5	6	7	8	9	10
11	12	13	14	15	16	17
18	19	20	21	22	23	24
25	26	27	28	29	30	31

Eastern time in bold type
Pacific time in medium type

28 Monday

2nd ♒
☽ V/C **3:18 am** 12:18 am
☽ enters ♓ **11:34 am** 8:34 am
♄ D 10:11 pm

Yom Kippur (begins at sundown on Sept. 27)

29 Tuesday

2nd ♓
♄ D **1:11 am**

30 Wednesday

2nd ♓
☽ V/C **1:30 pm** 10:30 am
☽ enters ♈ **10:47 pm** 7:47 pm

1 Thursday

2nd ♈
Full Moon **5:05 pm** 2:05 pm

Eastern time in bold type
Pacific time in medium type

2 Friday

3rd ♈
♀ enters ♍ **4:48 pm** 1:48 pm
☽ V/C 10:47 pm

3 Saturday

3rd ♈
☽ V/C **1:47 am**
☽ enters ♉ **11:12 am** 8:12 am

Sukkot (begins at sundown on Oct. 2)

4 Sunday

3rd ♉
♇ D **9:32 am** 6:32 am

September 2020

S	M	T	W	T	F	S
		1	2	3	4	5
6	7	8	9	10	11	12
13	14	15	16	17	18	19
20	21	22	23	24	25	26
27	28	29	30			

October 2020

S	M	T	W	T	F	S
				1	2	3
4	5	6	7	8	9	10
11	12	13	14	15	16	17
18	19	20	21	22	23	24
25	26	27	28	29	30	31

November 2020

S	M	T	W	T	F	S
1	2	3	4	5	6	7
8	9	10	11	12	13	14
15	16	17	18	19	20	21
22	23	24	25	26	27	28
29	30					

Eastern time in bold type
Pacific time in medium type

5 Monday

3rd ♉
☽ V/C **2:41 pm** 11:41 am
☽ enters ♊ 9:03 pm

6 Tuesday

3rd ♉
☽ enters ♊ **12:03 am**

7 Wednesday

3rd ♊
☽ V/C **9:57 pm** 6:57 pm

8 Thursday

3rd ♊
☽ enters ♋ **11:45 am** 8:45 am

Eastern time in bold type
Pacific time in medium type

9 Friday

3rd ♋
4th Quarter **8:40 pm** 5:40 pm

Sukkot ends

10 Saturday

4th ♋
☽ V/C **12:04 pm** 9:04 am
☽ enters ♌ **8:24 pm** 5:24 pm

11 Sunday

4th ♌

September 2020

S	M	T	W	T	F	S
		1	2	3	4	5
6	7	8	9	10	11	12
13	14	15	16	17	18	19
20	21	22	23	24	25	26
27	28	29	30			

October 2020

S	M	T	W	T	F	S
				1	2	3
4	5	6	7	8	9	10
11	12	13	14	15	16	17
18	19	20	21	22	23	24
25	26	27	28	29	30	31

November 2020

S	M	T	W	T	F	S
1	2	3	4	5	6	7
8	9	10	11	12	13	14
15	16	17	18	19	20	21
22	23	24	25	26	27	28
29	30					

Eastern time in bold type
Pacific time in medium type

12 Monday

4th ♌
☽ V/C **10:29 am** 7:29 am
☽ enters ♍ 9:56 pm

Columbus Day • Indigenous Peoples' Day

13 Tuesday

4th ♌
☽ enters ♍ **12:56 am**
☿ ℞ **9:05 pm** 6:05 pm

14 Wednesday

4th ♍
☽ V/C **6:47 pm** 3:47 pm
☽ enters ♎ 10:54 pm

15 Thursday

4th ♍
☽ enters ♎ **1:54 am**

Eastern time in bold type
Pacific time in medium type

16 Friday

4th ♎

New Moon	**3:31 pm**	12:31 pm
☽ V/C	**6:11 pm**	3:11 pm
☽ enters ♏		10:05 pm

17 Saturday

1st ♎

☽ enters ♏	**1:05 am**	

18 Sunday

1st ♏

⚳ D	**12:59 pm**	9:59 am
☽ V/C	**5:43 pm**	2:43 pm
☽ enters ♐		9:43 pm

September 2020

S	M	T	W	T	F	S
		1	2	3	4	5
6	7	8	9	10	11	12
13	14	15	16	17	18	19
20	21	22	23	24	25	26
27	28	29	30			

October 2020

S	M	T	W	T	F	S
				1	2	3
4	5	6	7	8	9	10
11	12	13	14	15	16	17
18	19	20	21	22	23	24
25	26	27	28	29	30	31

November 2020

S	M	T	W	T	F	S
1	2	3	4	5	6	7
8	9	10	11	12	13	14
15	16	17	18	19	20	21
22	23	24	25	26	27	28
29	30					

19 Monday

1st ♏
☽ enters ♐ **12:43 am**

20 Tuesday

1st ♐
☽ V/C **11:38 pm** 8:38 pm
☽ enters ♑ 11:44 pm

21 Wednesday

1st ♐
☽ enters ♑ **2:44 am**

22 Thursday

1st ♑
⚵ enters ♍ **3:38 am** 12:38 am
☉ enters ♏ **7:00 pm** 4:00 pm
☽ V/C 9:35 pm

23 Friday

1st ♑︎
☽ V/C **12:35 am**
☽ enters ♒︎ **8:17 am** 5:17 am
2nd Quarter **9:23 am** 6:23 am

24 Saturday

2nd ♒︎
☽ V/C **5:54 pm** 2:54 pm

25 Sunday

2nd ♒︎
☽ enters ♓︎ **5:18 pm** 2:18 pm

September 2020

S	M	T	W	T	F	S
		1	2	3	4	5
6	7	8	9	10	11	12
13	14	15	16	17	18	19
20	21	22	23	24	25	26
27	28	29	30			

October 2020

S	M	T	W	T	F	S
				1	2	3
4	5	6	7	8	9	10
11	12	13	14	15	16	17
18	19	20	21	22	23	24
25	26	27	28	29	30	31

November 2020

S	M	T	W	T	F	S
1	2	3	4	5	6	7
8	9	10	11	12	13	14
15	16	17	18	19	20	21
22	23	24	25	26	27	28
29	30					

26 Monday
2nd ♓

27 Tuesday
2nd ♓

☽ V/C	**8:46 pm**	5:46 pm
☿ enters ♎	**9:33 pm**	6:33 pm
♀ enters ♎	**9:41 pm**	6:41 pm

28 Wednesday
2nd ♓

☽ enters ♈	**4:45 am**	1:45 am

29 Thursday
2nd ♈

Eastern time in bold type
Pacific time in medium type

30 Friday

2nd ♈

☽ V/C	**12:12 pm**	9:12 am
☽ enters ♉	**5:19 pm**	2:19 pm

31 Saturday

2nd ♉

Full Moon	**10:49 am**	7:49 am

Halloween • Samhain

1 Sunday

3rd ♉

☽ V/C	**9:29 pm**	6:29 pm

Daylight Saving Time ends at 2 am • All Saints' Day

October 2020

S	M	T	W	T	F	S
				1	2	3
4	5	6	7	8	9	10
11	12	13	14	15	16	17
18	19	20	21	22	23	24
25	26	27	28	29	30	31

November 2020

S	M	T	W	T	F	S
1	2	3	4	5	6	7
8	9	10	11	12	13	14
15	16	17	18	19	20	21
22	23	24	25	26	27	28
29	30					

December 2020

S	M	T	W	T	F	S
		1	2	3	4	5
6	7	8	9	10	11	12
13	14	15	16	17	18	19
20	21	22	23	24	25	26
27	28	29	30	31		

2 Monday

3rd ♉
☽ enters ♊ **5:00 am** 2:00 am

3 Tuesday

3rd ♊
☿ D **12:50 pm** 9:50 am

Election Day (general)

4 Wednesday

3rd ♊
☽ V/C **8:49 am** 5:49 am
☽ enters ♋ **4:45 pm** 1:45 pm

5 Thursday

3rd ♋

Eastern time in bold type
Pacific time in medium type

6 Friday

3rd ♋
☽ V/C **8:27 pm** 5:27 pm
☽ enters ♌ 11:18 pm

7 Saturday

3rd ♋
☽ enters ♌ **2:18 am**

8 Sunday

3rd ♌
4th Quarter **8:46 am** 5:46 am

October 2020

S	M	T	W	T	F	S
				1	2	3
4	5	6	7	8	9	10
11	12	13	14	15	16	17
18	19	20	21	22	23	24
25	26	27	28	29	30	31

November 2020

S	M	T	W	T	F	S
1	2	3	4	5	6	7
8	9	10	11	12	13	14
15	16	17	18	19	20	21
22	23	24	25	26	27	28
29	30					

December 2020

S	M	T	W	T	F	S
		1	2	3	4	5
6	7	8	9	10	11	12
13	14	15	16	17	18	19
20	21	22	23	24	25	26
27	28	29	30	31		

9 Monday

4th ♌
☽ V/C **6:05 am** 3:05 am
☽ enters ♍ **8:30 am** 5:30 am
⚳ enters ♓ **9:48 am** 6:48 am

10 Tuesday

4th ♍
☿ enters ♏ **4:55 pm** 1:55 pm

11 Wednesday

4th ♍
☽ V/C **5:58 am** 2:58 am
☽ enters ♎ **11:09 am** 8:09 am

Veterans Day

12 Thursday

4th ♎

Eastern time in bold type
Pacific time in medium type

13 Friday

4th ♎

☽ V/C	**6:32 am**	3:32 am
☽ enters ♏	**11:19 am**	8:19 am
♂ D	**7:36 pm**	4:36 pm

14 Saturday

4th ♏

New Moon		9:07 pm

15 Sunday

4th ♏

New Moon	**12:07 am**	
☽ V/C	**6:13 am**	3:13 am
☽ enters ♐	**10:47 am**	7:47 am

October 2020

S	M	T	W	T	F	S
				1	2	3
4	5	6	7	8	9	10
11	12	13	14	15	16	17
18	19	20	21	22	23	24
25	26	27	28	29	30	31

November 2020

S	M	T	W	T	F	S
1	2	3	4	5	6	7
8	9	10	11	12	13	14
15	16	17	18	19	20	21
22	23	24	25	26	27	28
29	30					

December 2020

S	M	T	W	T	F	S
		1	2	3	4	5
6	7	8	9	10	11	12
13	14	15	16	17	18	19
20	21	22	23	24	25	26
27	28	29	30	31		

Eastern time in bold type
Pacific time in medium type

16 Monday
1st ♐
☽ V/C 11:55 pm

17 Tuesday
1st ♐
☽ V/C **2:55 am**
☽ enters ♑ **11:35 am** 8:35 am

18 Wednesday
1st ♑

19 Thursday
1st ♑
☽ V/C **11:30 am** 8:30 am
☽ enters ♒ **3:25 pm** 12:25 pm

Eastern time in bold type
Pacific time in medium type

20 Friday

1st ♒
☽ V/C **7:49 pm** 4:49 pm

21 Saturday

1st ♒
♀ enters ♏ **8:22 am** 5:22 am
☉ enters ♐ **3:40 pm** 12:40 pm
☽ enters ♓ **11:06 pm** 8:06 pm
2nd Quarter **11:45 pm** 8:45 pm

22 Sunday

2nd ♓

October 2020

S	M	T	W	T	F	S
				1	2	3
4	5	6	7	8	9	10
11	12	13	14	15	16	17
18	19	20	21	22	23	24
25	26	27	28	29	30	31

November 2020

S	M	T	W	T	F	S
1	2	3	4	5	6	7
8	9	10	11	12	13	14
15	16	17	18	19	20	21
22	23	24	25	26	27	28
29	30					

December 2020

S	M	T	W	T	F	S
		1	2	3	4	5
6	7	8	9	10	11	12
13	14	15	16	17	18	19
20	21	22	23	24	25	26
27	28	29	30	31		

Eastern time in bold type
Pacific time in medium type

23 Monday
2nd ♓

24 Tuesday
2nd ♓

☽ V/C	**5:44 am**	2:44 am
☽ enters ♈	**10:05 am**	7:05 am

25 Wednesday
2nd ♈

26 Thursday
2nd ♈

☽ V/C	**6:46 pm**	3:46 pm
☽ enters ♉	**10:43 pm**	7:43 pm

Thanksgiving Day

Eastern time in bold type
Pacific time in medium type

27 Friday
2nd ♉

28 Saturday
2nd ♉

♆ D **7:36 pm** 4:36 pm

29 Sunday
2nd ♉

☽ V/C **7:48 am** 4:48 am

☽ enters ♊ **11:16 am** 8:16 am

October 2020

S	M	T	W	T	F	S
				1	2	3
4	5	6	7	8	9	10
11	12	13	14	15	16	17
18	19	20	21	22	23	24
25	26	27	28	29	30	31

November 2020

S	M	T	W	T	F	S
1	2	3	4	5	6	7
8	9	10	11	12	13	14
15	16	17	18	19	20	21
22	23	24	25	26	27	28
29	30					

December 2020

S	M	T	W	T	F	S
		1	2	3	4	5
6	7	8	9	10	11	12
13	14	15	16	17	18	19
20	21	22	23	24	25	26
27	28	29	30	31		

30 Monday

2nd ♊

Full Moon	**4:30 am**	1:30 am
☽ V/C	**11:22 pm**	8:22 pm

Lunar Eclipse 8 ° ♊ 38'

1 Tuesday

3rd ♊

☿ enters ♐	**2:51 pm**	11:51 am
☽ enters ♋	**10:33 pm**	7:33 pm

2 Wednesday

3rd ♋

3 Thursday

3rd ♋

Eastern time in bold type
Pacific time in medium type

4 Friday

3rd ♋
☽ V/C **5:29 am** 2:29 am
☽ enters ♌ **7:53 am** 4:53 am

5 Saturday

3rd ♌
☽ V/C **5:28 pm** 2:28 pm

6 Sunday

3rd ♌
☽ enters ♍ **2:46 pm** 11:46 am

November 2020

S	M	T	W	T	F	S
1	2	3	4	5	6	7
8	9	10	11	12	13	14
15	16	17	18	19	20	21
22	23	24	25	26	27	28
29	30					

December 2020

S	M	T	W	T	F	S
		1	2	3	4	5
6	7	8	9	10	11	12
13	14	15	16	17	18	19
20	21	22	23	24	25	26
27	28	29	30	31		

January 2021

S	M	T	W	T	F	S
					1	2
3	4	5	6	7	8	9
10	11	12	13	14	15	16
17	18	19	20	21	22	23
24	25	26	27	28	29	30
31						

7 Monday

3rd ♍

♀ enters ♒	**7:14 am**	4:14 am
4th Quarter	**7:37 pm**	4:37 pm

8 Tuesday

4th ♍

☽ V/C	**5:35 pm**	2:35 pm
☽ enters ♎	**7:01 pm**	4:01 pm

9 Wednesday

4th ♎

10 Thursday

4th ♎

☽ V/C	**7:56 pm**	4:56 pm
☽ enters ♏	**8:59 pm**	5:59 pm

Eastern time in bold type
Pacific time in medium type

11 Friday
4th ♏

Hanukkah begins (at sundown on Dec. 10)

12 Saturday
4th ♏

☽ V/C	**8:58 pm**	5:58 pm
☽ enters ♐	**9:39 pm**	6:39 pm

13 Sunday
4th ♐

November 2020

S	M	T	W	T	F	S
1	2	3	4	5	6	7
8	9	10	11	12	13	14
15	16	17	18	19	20	21
22	23	24	25	26	27	28
29	30					

December 2020

S	M	T	W	T	F	S
		1	2	3	4	5
6	7	8	9	10	11	12
13	14	15	16	17	18	19
20	21	22	23	24	25	26
27	28	29	30	31		

January 2021

S	M	T	W	T	F	S
					1	2
3	4	5	6	7	8	9
10	11	12	13	14	15	16
17	18	19	20	21	22	23
24	25	26	27	28	29	30
31						

14 Monday

4th ♐

☽ V/C	**11:17 am**	8:17 am
New Moon	**11:17 am**	8:17 am
☽ enters ♑	**10:35 pm**	7:35 pm

Solar Eclipse 23 ° ♐ 08'

15 Tuesday

1st ♑

♀ enters ♐	**11:21 am**	8:21 am
⚷ D	**5:17 pm**	2:17 pm

16 Wednesday

1st ♑

♄ enters ♒		9:04 pm
☽ V/C		9:34 pm
☽ enters ♒		10:27 pm

17 Thursday

1st ♑

♄ enters ♒	**12:04 am**
☽ V/C	**12:34 am**
☽ enters ♒	**1:27 am**

Eastern time in bold type
Pacific time in medium type

18 Friday

1st ♒

⚵ enters ♐ **12:25 pm** 9:25 am

Hanukkah ends

19 Saturday

1st ♒

☽ V/C **3:45 am** 12:45 am

☽ enters ♓ **7:39 am** 4:39 am

♃ enters ♒ **8:07 am** 5:07 am

20 Sunday

1st ♓

☿ enters ♑ **6:07 pm** 3:07 pm

November 2020

S	M	T	W	T	F	S
1	2	3	4	5	6	7
8	9	10	11	12	13	14
15	16	17	18	19	20	21
22	23	24	25	26	27	28
29	30					

December 2020

S	M	T	W	T	F	S
		1	2	3	4	5
6	7	8	9	10	11	12
13	14	15	16	17	18	19
20	21	22	23	24	25	26
27	28	29	30	31		

January 2021

S	M	T	W	T	F	S
					1	2
3	4	5	6	7	8	9
10	11	12	13	14	15	16
17	18	19	20	21	22	23
24	25	26	27	28	29	30
31						

Eastern time in bold type
Pacific time in medium type

21 Monday

1st ♓

☉ enters ♑	**5:02 am**	2:02 am
☽ V/C	**5:25 am**	2:25 am
☽ enters ♈	**5:32 pm**	2:32 pm
2nd Quarter	**6:41 pm**	3:41 pm

Yule • Winter Solstice

22 Tuesday

2nd ♈

23 Wednesday

2nd ♈

☽ V/C	**5:51 pm**	2:51 pm

24 Thursday

2nd ♈

☽ enters ♉	**5:55 am**	2:55 am

Christmas Eve

Eastern time in bold type
Pacific time in medium type

25 Friday
2nd ♉

Christmas Day

26 Saturday
2nd ♉

☽ V/C	**6:32 am**	3:32 am
☽ enters ♊	**6:33 pm**	3:33 pm

Kwanzaa Begins

27 Sunday
2nd ♊

November 2020

S	M	T	W	T	F	S
1	2	3	4	5	6	7
8	9	10	11	12	13	14
15	16	17	18	19	20	21
22	23	24	25	26	27	28
29	30					

December 2020

S	M	T	W	T	F	S
		1	2	3	4	5
6	7	8	9	10	11	12
13	14	15	16	17	18	19
20	21	22	23	24	25	26
27	28	29	30	31		

January 2021

S	M	T	W	T	F	S
					1	2
3	4	5	6	7	8	9
10	11	12	13	14	15	16
17	18	19	20	21	22	23
24	25	26	27	28	29	30
31						

28 Monday

2nd ♊

☽ V/C	**10:01 pm**	7:01 pm

29 Tuesday

2nd ♊

☽ enters ♋	**5:28 am**	2:28 am
Full Moon	**10:28 pm**	7:28 pm

30 Wednesday

3rd ♋

31 Thursday

3rd ♋

☽ V/C	**8:45 am**	5:45 am
☽ enters ♌	**1:58 pm**	10:58 am

New Year's Eve

Eastern time in bold type
Pacific time in medium type

The Year 2021

January

S	M	T	W	T	F	S
					1	2
3	4	5	6	7	8	9
10	11	12	13	14	15	16
17	18	19	20	21	22	23
24	25	26	27	28	29	30
31						

February

S	M	T	W	T	F	S
	1	2	3	4	5	6
7	8	9	10	11	12	13
14	15	16	17	18	19	20
21	22	23	24	25	26	27
28						

March

S	M	T	W	T	F	S
	1	2	3	4	5	6
7	8	9	10	11	12	13
14	15	16	17	18	19	20
21	22	23	24	25	26	27
28	29	30	31			

April

S	M	T	W	T	F	S
				1	2	3
4	5	6	7	8	9	10
11	12	13	14	15	16	17
18	19	20	21	22	23	24
25	26	27	28	29	30	

May

S	M	T	W	T	F	S
						1
2	3	4	5	6	7	8
9	10	11	12	13	14	15
16	17	18	19	20	21	22
23	24	25	26	27	28	29
30	31					

June

S	M	T	W	T	F	S
		1	2	3	4	5
6	7	8	9	10	11	12
13	14	15	16	17	18	19
20	21	22	23	24	25	26
27	28	29	30			

July

S	M	T	W	T	F	S
				1	2	3
4	5	6	7	8	9	10
11	12	13	14	15	16	17
18	19	20	21	22	23	24
25	26	27	28	29	30	31

August

S	M	T	W	T	F	S
1	2	3	4	5	6	7
8	9	10	11	12	13	14
15	16	17	18	19	20	21
22	23	24	25	26	27	28
29	30	31				

September

S	M	T	W	T	F	S
			1	2	3	4
5	6	7	8	9	10	11
12	13	14	15	16	17	18
19	20	21	22	23	24	25
26	27	28	29	30		

October

S	M	T	W	T	F	S
					1	2
3	4	5	6	7	8	9
10	11	12	13	14	15	16
17	18	19	20	21	22	23
24	25	26	27	28	29	30
31						

November

S	M	T	W	T	F	S
	1	2	3	4	5	6
7	8	9	10	11	12	13
14	15	16	17	18	19	20
21	22	23	24	25	26	27
28	29	30				

December

S	M	T	W	T	F	S
			1	2	3	4
5	6	7	8	9	10	11
12	13	14	15	16	17	18
19	20	21	22	23	24	25
26	27	28	29	30	31	

JANUARY 2019

☽ Last Aspect / ☽ Ingress

day	ET / hr:mn / PT		asp	sign	day	ET / hr:mn / PT	
1	**5:26 pm**	2:26 pm	☌ ♀	♐	2	**3:58 am**	12:58 am
4	**12:41 pm**	9:41 am	☌ ☿	♑	4	**1:55 pm**	10:55 am
6		10:20 pm	⚹ ♀	♒	6		10:46 pm
7	**1:20 am**		⚹ ♀	♒	7	**1:46 am**	
9	**11:53 am**	8:53 am	⚹ ♅	♓	9	**2:44 pm**	11:44 am
11	**9:25 am**	6:25 am	⚹ ☉	♈	12	**3:18 am**	12:18 am
14	**10:56 am**	7:56 am	☌ ♅	♉	14	**1:31 pm**	10:31 am
16	**1:34 pm**	10:34 am	△ ☉	♊	16	**8:00 pm**	5:00 pm
18	**8:32 pm**	5:32 pm	⚹ ♅	♋	18	**10:44 pm**	7:44 pm
20	**8:50 pm**	5:50 pm	□ ♅	♌	20	**10:54 pm**	7:54 pm
22	**8:19 pm**	5:19 pm	△ ♅	♍	22	**10:22 pm**	7:22 pm
24	**8:50 am**	5:50 am	△ ♇	♎	24	**11:02 pm**	8:02 pm
26		9:21 pm	☍ ♅	♏	26		11:31 pm
27	**12:21 am**		☍ ♅	♏	27	**2:31 am**	
28	**5:39 pm**	2:39 pm	⚹ ♇	♐	29	**9:33 am**	6:33 am
31	**5:33 pm**	2:33 pm	△ ♅	♑	31	**7:47 pm**	4:47 pm

☽ Phases & Eclipses

phase	day	ET / hr:mn / PT	
New Moon	5	**8:28 pm**	5:28 pm
● (eclipse)	5	15° ♑ 25'	
2nd Quarter	13		10:46 pm
2nd Quarter	14	**1:46 am**	
Full Moon	20		9:16 pm
Full Moon	21	**12:16 am**	
● (eclipse)	20/21	0° ♌ 52'	
4th Quarter	27	**4:10 pm**	1:10 pm

Planet Ingress

		day	ET / hr:mn / PT	
☿	♑	4	**10:40 pm**	7:40 pm
♀	♐	7	**6:18 am**	3:18 am
☉	♒	20	**4:00 am**	1:00 am
☿	♒	23		9:49 pm
☿	♒	24	**12:49 am**	
⚳	♒	25	**1:08 pm**	10:08 am

Planetary Motion

		day	ET / hr:mn / PT	
♅	D	6	**3:27 pm**	12:27 pm

1 TUESDAY
☽ ⚹ ♇ **10:19 am** 7:19 am
☽ ☌ ♀ **5:26 pm** 2:26 pm
☽ ⚺ ☿ **7:09 pm** 4:09 pm
☉ ☌ ♄ 9:50 pm
☽ ⚻ ♅ 10:20 pm

2 WEDNESDAY
☉ ☌ ♄ **12:50 am**
☽ ⚻ ♅ **1:20 am**
☽ △ ♂ **5:41 am** 2:41 am
☉ ⚺ ♃ **3:49 pm** 12:49 pm
☽ ⚺ ♄ 11:13 pm

3 THURSDAY
☽ ⚺ ♄ **2:13 am**
☽ ☌ ♃ **3:23 am** 12:23 am
☽ ⚺ ☉ **4:13 am** 1:13 am
☽ □ ♆ **7:00 am** 4:00 am
☽ ⚺ ♇ **7:43 pm** 4:43 pm
☿ △ ♅ 9:13 pm

4 FRIDAY
☿ △ ♅ **12:13 am**
☽ ⚺ ♀ **8:04 am** 5:04 am
☽ △ ♅ **11:10 am** 8:10 am
☽ ☌ ☿ **12:41 pm** 9:41 am
☉ ⚹ ♆ **2:57 pm** 11:57 am
☽ □ ♂ **7:05 pm** 4:05 pm

5 SATURDAY
☽ ☌ ♄ **1:32 pm** 10:32 am
☽ ⚺ ♃ **3:12 pm** 12:12 pm
☽ ⚹ ♆ **6:01 pm** 3:01 pm
☽ ☌ ☉ **8:28 pm** 5:28 pm
♀ ⚻ ♅ **9:28 pm** 6:28 pm

6 SUNDAY
☽ ☌ ♇ **7:12 am** 4:12 am
☽ □ ♅ **10:56 pm** 7:56 pm
☽ ⚹ ♀ 10:20 pm

7 MONDAY
☽ ⚹ ♀ **1:20 am**
☽ ⚺ ☿ **9:12 am** 6:12 am
☽ ⚹ ♂ **10:42 am** 7:42 am
☽ ⚺ ♄ 11:34 pm

8 TUESDAY
☽ ⚺ ♄ **2:34 am**
☽ ⚹ ♃ **4:44 am** 1:44 am
☿ □ ♂ **5:05 am** 2:05 am
☽ ⚺ ♆ **6:39 am** 3:39 am
☽ ⚺ ☉ **2:46 pm** 11:46 am
☽ ⚺ ♇ **8:07 pm** 5:07 pm

9 WEDNESDAY
☽ ⚹ ♅ **11:53 am** 8:53 am
☽ □ ♀ **8:09 pm** 5:09 pm

10 THURSDAY
☽ ⚺ ♂ **3:25 am** 12:25 am
☽ ⚹ ☿ **7:16 am** 4:16 am
☽ ⚹ ♄ **4:13 pm** 1:13 pm
☽ □ ♃ **6:48 pm** 3:48 pm
☽ ☌ ♆ **7:47 pm** 4:47 pm

11 FRIDAY
☉ ☌ ♇ **6:38 am** 3:38 am
☽ ⚹ ♇ **9:11 am** 6:11 am
☽ ⚹ ☉ **9:25 am** 6:25 am
☽ ⚺ ♅ 9:32 pm

12 SATURDAY
☽ ⚺ ♅ **12:32 am**
☽ △ ♀ **2:20 pm** 11:20 am
☽ ☌ ♂ **7:12 pm** 4:12 pm

13 SUNDAY
☽ □ ☿ **4:05 am** 1:05 am
☽ □ ♄ **4:36 am** 1:36 am
☽ △ ♃ **7:31 am** 4:31 am
☽ ⚺ ♆ **7:36 am** 4:36 am
☿ ☌ ♄ **8:31 am** 5:31 am
♃ □ ♆ **1:58 pm** 10:58 am
☽ □ ♇ **8:28 pm** 5:28 pm
☽ □ ☉ 10:46 pm

14 MONDAY
☽ □ ☉ **1:46 am**
☿ ⚹ ♆ **8:13 am** 5:13 am
☿ ⚺ ♃ **10:30 am** 7:30 am
☽ ☌ ♅ **10:56 am** 7:56 am

15 TUESDAY
☽ ⚻ ♀ **5:05 am** 2:05 am
☽ ⚺ ♂ **7:39 am** 4:39 am
☽ △ ♄ **1:50 pm** 10:50 am
☽ ⚹ ♆ **4:15 pm** 1:15 pm
☽ ⚻ ♃ **4:54 pm** 1:54 pm
☽ △ ☿ **8:30 pm** 5:30 pm

16 WEDNESDAY
☽ △ ♇ **4:17 am** 1:17 am
☽ △ ☉ **1:34 pm** 10:34 am
☽ ⚺ ♅ **5:38 pm** 2:38 pm

17 THURSDAY
☽ ☍ ♀ **2:54 pm** 11:54 am
☽ ⚹ ♂ **3:32 pm** 12:32 pm
☽ ⚻ ♄ **7:02 pm** 4:02 pm
☽ □ ♆ **8:56 pm** 5:56 pm
☽ ☍ ♃ **10:10 pm** 7:10 pm

18 FRIDAY
☽ ⚻ ☿ **7:19 am** 4:19 am
☽ ⚻ ♇ **8:10 am** 5:10 am
♀ △ ♂ **11:49 am** 8:49 am
☿ ☌ ♇ **3:03 pm** 12:03 pm
☉ □ ♅ **8:31 pm** 5:31 pm
☽ ⚹ ♅ **8:32 pm** 5:32 pm
☽ ⚻ ☉ **8:32 pm** 5:32 pm

19 SATURDAY
☽ □ ♂ **7:28 pm** 4:28 pm
☽ ⚻ ♀ **8:24 pm** 5:24 pm
☽ ☍ ♄ **8:48 pm** 5:48 pm
☽ △ ♆ **10:19 pm** 7:19 pm
☽ ⚻ ♃ 9:02 pm
♀ ⚺ ♄ 11:29 pm

20 SUNDAY
☽ ⚻ ♃ **12:02 am**
♀ ⚺ ♄ **2:29 am**
☽ ☍ ♇ **9:01 am** 6:01 am
☽ ☍ ☿ **1:56 pm** 10:56 am
☽ □ ♅ **8:50 pm** 5:50 pm
♀ □ ♆ **11:15 pm** 8:15 pm
☽ ☍ ☉ 9:16 pm

21 MONDAY
☽ ☍ ☉ **12:16 am**
♂ □ ♄ **6:48 am** 3:48 am
☽ ⚻ ♄ **8:47 pm** 5:47 pm
☽ △ ♂ **9:19 pm** 6:19 pm
☽ ⚻ ♆ **10:00 pm** 7:00 pm
☽ △ ♀ **11:43 pm** 8:43 pm
☽ △ ♃ 9:12 pm

22 TUESDAY
☽ △ ♃ **12:12 am**
♀ ☌ ♃ **7:26 am** 4:26 am
☽ ⚻ ♇ **8:36 am** 5:36 am
♂ ⚺ ♆ **1:13 pm** 10:13 am
☽ ⚻ ☿ **7:07 pm** 4:07 pm
☽ △ ♅ **8:19 pm** 5:19 pm

23 WEDNESDAY
☽ ⚻ ☉ **3:11 am** 12:11 am
☿ □ ♅ **6:13 am** 3:13 am
☽ △ ♄ **8:56 pm** 5:56 pm
☽ ☍ ♆ **9:55 pm** 6:55 pm
☽ ⚻ ♂ **11:25 pm** 8:25 pm
☽ □ ♃ 9:41 pm

24 THURSDAY
☽ □ ♃ **12:41 am**
☽ □ ♀ **3:27 am** 12:27 am
☽ △ ♇ **8:50 am** 5:50 am
☽ ⚻ ♅ **8:57 pm** 5:57 pm
☽ △ ☿ 10:56 pm

25 FRIDAY
☽ △ ☿ **1:56 am**
☽ △ ☉ **7:48 am** 4:48 am
♂ △ ♃ **12:53 pm** 9:53 am
☽ □ ♄ **11:10 pm** 8:10 pm
☽ ⚻ ♆ **11:55 pm** 8:55 pm

26 SATURDAY
☽ ⚹ ♃ **3:23 am** 12:23 am
☽ ☍ ♂ **3:56 am** 12:56 am
☽ ⚹ ♀ **10:03 am** 7:03 am
☽ □ ♇ **11:30 am** 8:30 am
☽ ☍ ♅ 9:21 pm

27 SUNDAY
☽ ☍ ♅ **12:21 am**
♀ ⚺ ♇ **4:32 am** 1:32 am
☽ □ ☿ **12:59 pm** 9:59 am
☽ □ ☉ **4:10 pm** 1:10 pm

28 MONDAY
☽ ⚹ ♄ **4:46 am** 1:46 am
☽ △ ♆ **5:14 am** 2:14 am
☽ ⚺ ♃ **9:35 am** 6:35 am
☽ ⚻ ♂ **12:21 pm** 9:21 am
☽ ⚹ ♇ **5:39 pm** 2:39 pm
☽ ⚺ ♀ **9:05 pm** 6:05 pm

29 TUESDAY
☽ ⚻ ♅ **7:19 am** 4:19 am
☉ ☌ ☿ **9:52 pm** 6:52 pm

30 WEDNESDAY
☽ ⚹ ☉ **5:04 am** 2:04 am
☽ ⚹ ☿ **5:32 am** 2:32 am
☽ ⚺ ♄ **1:59 pm** 10:59 am
☽ □ ♆ **2:06 pm** 11:06 am
☽ ☌ ♃ **7:23 pm** 4:23 pm
☽ △ ♂ 9:50 pm

31 THURSDAY
☽ △ ♂ **12:50 am**
☽ ⚺ ♇ **3:14 am** 12:14 am
♄ ⚹ ♆ **9:15 am** 6:15 am
☽ ☌ ♀ **12:35 pm** 9:35 am
☽ △ ♅ **5:33 pm** 2:33 pm

Eastern time in bold type
Pacific time in medium type

JANUARY 2019

DATE	SID.TIME	SUN	MOON	NODE	MERCURY	VENUS	MARS	JUPITER	SATURN	URANUS	NEPTUNE	PLUTO	CERES	PALLAS	JUNO	VESTA	CHIRON
1 T	6 41 26	10 ♑ 15 24	12 ♏ 22	26 ♋ 52 ℞	23 ♐ 51	23 ♏ 30	29 ♓ 56	11 ♐ 46	11 ♑ 23	28 ♈ 37 ℞	14 ♓ 05	20 ♑ 36	21 ♏ 00	21 ♎ 32	20 ♉ 37	14 ♒ 28	28 ♓ 08
2 W	6 45 22	11 16 34	25 15	26 50	25 19	24 29	0 ♈ 36	11 59	11 30	28 37	14 06	20 38	21 23	21 49	20 41	14 57	28 09
3 Th	6 49 19	12 17 45	7 ♐ 53	26 48	26 48	25 28	1 17	12 11	11 37	28 36	14 07	20 40	21 46	22 06	20 46	15 26	28 11
4 F	6 53 15	13 18 55	20 20	26 45	28 17	26 28	1 57	12 24	11 44	28 36	14 09	20 42	22 09	22 23	20 52	15 56	28 12
5 Sa	6 57 12	14 20 06	2 ♑ 35	26 44	29 46	27 29	2 38	12 36	11 51	28 36	14 10	20 44	22 32	22 40	20 58	16 25	28 13
6 Su	7 1 8	15 21 17	14 41	26 43	1 ♑ 16	28 30	3 18	12 49	11 58	28 36 D	14 11	20 46	22 55	22 56	21 05	16 55	28 15
7 M	7 5 5	16 22 28	26 39	26 43 D	2 47	29 31	3 58	13 01	12 05	28 36	14 13	20 48	23 18	23 12	21 12	17 24	28 16
8 T	7 9 1	17 23 39	8 ♒ 31	26 43	4 18	0 ♐ 33	4 39	13 13	12 12	28 36	14 14	20 50	23 40	23 28	21 20	17 54	28 18
9 W	7 12 58	18 24 49	20 19	26 44	5 49	1 35	5 19	13 25	12 19	28 36	14 16	20 52	24 03	23 44	21 28	18 23	28 20
10 Th	7 16 55	19 25 59	2 ♓ 06	26 44	7 21	2 37	6 00	13 37	12 26	28 36	14 17	20 54	24 25	23 59	21 37	18 53	28 21
11 F	7 20 51	20 27 09	13 55	26 45	8 53	3 40	6 41	13 50	12 33	28 36	14 19	20 56	24 47	24 14	21 46	19 22	28 23
12 Sa	7 24 48	21 28 18	25 51	26 46	10 26	4 43	7 21	14 02	12 40	28 37	14 20	20 58	25 09	24 29	21 56	19 52	28 25
13 Su	7 28 44	22 29 26	7 ♈ 56	26 46	11 59	5 46	8 02	14 14	12 47	28 37	14 22	21 00	25 31	24 44	22 06	20 22	28 27
14 M	7 32 41	23 30 34	20 16	26 46 ℞	13 32	6 50	8 42	14 25	12 55	28 37	14 23	21 02	25 53	24 58	22 17	20 51	28 28
15 T	7 36 37	24 31 42	2 ♉ 55	26 46	15 06	7 54	9 23	14 37	13 02	28 38	14 25	21 04	26 15	25 12	22 28	21 21	28 30
16 W	7 40 34	25 32 48	15 57	26 46	16 41	8 58	10 03	14 49	13 09	28 38	14 26	21 06	26 36	25 25	22 40	21 51	28 32
17 Th	7 44 30	26 33 54	29 26	26 46 D	18 16	10 03	10 44	15 01	13 15	28 39	14 28	21 08	26 58	25 39	22 52	22 20	28 34
18 F	7 48 27	27 34 59	13 ♊ 21	26 46	19 51	11 08	11 25	15 12	13 22	28 39	14 30	21 10	27 19	25 52	23 05	22 50	28 36
19 Sa	7 52 24	28 36 04	27 44	26 46	21 28	12 13	12 05	15 24	13 29	28 40	14 32	21 12	27 40	26 04	23 18	23 20	28 38
20 Su	7 56 20	29 37 07	12 ♋ 29	26 47 ℞	23 04	13 18	12 46	15 35	13 36	28 41	14 33	21 14	28 02	26 17	23 31	23 49	28 41
21 M	8 0 17	0 ♒ 38 11	27 32	26 47	24 41	14 24	13 27	15 47	13 43	28 41	14 35	21 16	28 22	26 29	23 45	24 19	28 43
22 T	8 4 13	1 39 13	12 ♌ 43	26 46	26 19	15 29	14 07	15 58	13 50	28 42	14 37	21 18	28 43	26 40	23 59	24 49	28 45
23 W	8 8 10	2 40 15	27 53	26 46	27 57	16 36	14 48	16 09	13 57	28 43	14 39	21 20	29 04	26 52	24 13	25 18	28 47
24 Th	8 12 6	3 41 16	12 ♍ 52	26 45	29 36	17 42	15 29	16 20	14 04	28 44	14 40	21 22	29 24	27 03	24 28	25 48	28 49
25 F	8 16 3	4 42 16	27 34	26 44	1 ♒ 15	18 48	16 09	16 31	14 11	28 45	14 42	21 24	29 45	27 13	24 44	26 18	28 52
26 Sa	8 19 59	5 43 16	11 ♎ 52	26 44	2 55	19 55	16 50	16 42	14 17	28 46	14 44	21 26	0 ♐ 05	27 24	24 59	26 48	28 54
27 Su	8 23 56	6 44 15	25 45	26 43 D	4 36	21 02	17 30	16 53	14 24	28 47	14 46	21 28	0 25	27 34	25 16	27 17	28 57
28 M	8 27 53	7 45 14	9 ♏ 12	26 43	6 17	22 09	18 11	17 04	14 31	28 48	14 48	21 30	0 45	27 43	25 32	27 47	28 59
29 T	8 31 49	8 46 13	22 15	26 43	7 59	23 17	18 52	17 15	14 38	28 49	14 50	21 32	1 05	27 52	25 49	28 17	29 02
30 W	8 35 46	9 47 10	4 ♐ 58	26 44	9 42	24 24	19 32	17 25	14 44	28 50	14 52	21 34	1 24	28 01	26 06	28 47	29 04
31 Th	8 39 42	10 48 07	17 24	26 45	11 25	25 32	20 13	17 36	14 51	28 51	14 54	21 36	1 44	28 10	26 23	29 16	29 07

EPHEMERIS CALCULATED FOR 12 MIDNIGHT GREENWICH MEAN TIME. ALL OTHER DATA AND FACING ASPECTARIAN PAGE IN **EASTERN TIME (BOLD)** AND PACIFIC TIME (REGULAR).

FEBRUARY 2019

☽ Last Aspect day	ET / hr:mn / PT		asp	☽ Ingress sign	day	ET / hr:mn / PT	
3	**5:53 am**	2:53 am	□♅	♒	3	**8:03 am**	5:03 am
5	**6:59 pm**	3:59 pm	⚹♅	♓	5	**9:02 pm**	6:02 pm
7	**5:14 pm**	2:14 pm	⚹♇	♈	8	**9:34 am**	6:34 am
10	**6:48 pm**	3:48 pm	☌♅	♉	10	**8:28 pm**	5:28 pm
12	**5:26 pm**	2:26 pm	□☉	♊	13	**4:32 am**	1:32 am
15	**7:48 am**	4:48 am	⚹♅	♋	15	**9:03 am**	6:03 am
17	**9:17 am**	6:17 am	□♅	♌	17	**10:21 am**	7:21 am
19	**8:51 am**	5:51 am	△♅	♍	19	**9:47 am**	6:47 am
20	**8:52 pm**	5:52 pm	△♇	♎	21	**9:17 am**	6:17 am
23	**10:11 am**	7:11 am	☍♅	♏	23	**10:56 am**	7:56 am
25	**7:14 am**	4:14 am	⚹♀	♐	25	**4:19 pm**	1:19 pm
27		10:17 pm	△♅	♑	27		10:48 pm
28	**1:17 am**		△♅	♑	28	**1:48 am**	

☽ Phases & Eclipses phase	day	ET / hr:mn / PT	
New Moon	4	**4:04 pm**	1:04 pm
2nd Quarter	12	**5:26 pm**	2:26 pm
Full Moon	19	**10:54 am**	7:54 am
4th Quarter	26	**6:28 am**	3:28 am

Planet Ingress		day	ET / hr:mn / PT	
⚶	♓	1	**6:04 am**	3:04 am
♀	♑	3	**5:29 pm**	2:29 pm
☿	♓	10	**5:51 am**	2:51 am
⚵	♊	10	**11:21 pm**	8:21 pm
♂	♉	14	**5:51 am**	2:51 am
⚷	♈	18	**4:10 am**	1:10 am
☉	♓	18	**6:04 pm**	3:04 pm

Planetary Motion		day	ET / hr:mn / PT	
⚴	℞	18	**11:40 am**	8:40 am

1 FRIDAY
☿ ⚺ ♆ **7:49 pm** 4:49 pm
☿ ⚺ ♄ **9:25 pm** 6:25 pm
☽ ⚺ ☉ **9:37 pm** 6:37 pm
♂ □ ♇ **10:20 pm** 7:20 pm
☽ ⚹ ♆ 10:41 pm
☽ ☌ ♄ 10:57 pm
☽ ⚺ ☿ 11:41 pm

2 SATURDAY
☽ ⚹ ♆ **1:41 am**
☽ ☌ ♄ **1:57 am**
☽ ⚺ ☿ **2:41 am**
☽ ⚺ ♃ **7:51 am** 4:51 am
☽ ☌ ♇ **3:14 pm** 12:14 pm
☽ □ ♂ **4:12 pm** 1:12 pm
♀ △ ♅ **6:41 pm** 3:41 pm

3 SUNDAY
☽ □ ♅ **5:53 am** 2:53 am
☽ ⚺ ♀ **7:03 am** 4:03 am
☿ ⚹ ♃ **4:54 pm** 1:54 pm
☉ ⚺ ♆ **11:00 pm** 8:00 pm

4 MONDAY
☉ ⚺ ♄ **6:09 am** 3:09 am
☽ ⚺ ♆ **2:38 pm** 11:38 am
☽ ⚺ ♄ **3:17 pm** 12:17 pm
☽ ☌ ☉ **4:04 pm** 1:04 pm
☽ ⚹ ♃ **9:35 pm** 6:35 pm
☽ ☌ ☿ 11:11 pm

5 TUESDAY
☽ ☌ ☿ **2:11 am**
☽ ⚺ ♇ **4:18 am** 1:18 am
☽ ⚹ ♂ **8:49 am** 5:49 am
☿ ⚺ ♇ **4:24 pm** 1:24 pm
☽ ⚹ ♅ **6:59 pm** 3:59 pm
☽ ⚹ ♀ 11:33 pm

6 WEDNESDAY
☽ ⚹ ♀ **2:33 am**

7 THURSDAY
☽ ☌ ♆ **3:43 am** 12:43 am
☽ ⚹ ♄ **4:44 am** 1:44 am
☽ ⚺ ☉ **10:37 am** 7:37 am
☽ □ ♃ **11:16 am** 8:16 am
☽ ⚹ ♇ **5:14 pm** 2:14 pm
☉ ⚹ ♃ **7:32 pm** 4:32 pm
☿ ⚹ ♂ **8:24 pm** 5:24 pm
☽ ⚺ ♂ 10:11 pm
☽ ⚺ ☿ 10:43 pm

8 FRIDAY
☽ ⚺ ♂ **1:11 am**
☽ ⚺ ☿ **1:43 am**
☽ ⚺ ♅ **7:41 am** 4:41 am
☽ □ ♀ **9:21 pm** 6:21 pm

9 SATURDAY
☽ ⚺ ♆ **3:45 pm** 12:45 pm
☽ □ ♄ **5:06 pm** 2:06 pm
☿ ⚹ ♅ **5:53 pm** 2:53 pm
☽ △ ♃ **11:42 pm** 8:42 pm

10 SUNDAY
☽ ⚹ ☉ **3:39 am** 12:39 am
☽ □ ♇ **4:51 am** 1:51 am
☽ ☌ ♂ **3:48 pm** 12:48 pm
☉ ⚺ ♇ **6:36 pm** 3:36 pm
☽ ☌ ♅ **6:48 pm** 3:48 pm
☽ ⚹ ☿ **10:57 pm** 7:57 pm

11 MONDAY
☽ △ ♀ **1:39 pm** 10:39 am
☽ ⚹ ♆ 10:31 pm

12 TUESDAY
☽ ⚹ ♆ **1:31 am**
☽ △ ♄ **3:05 am** 12:05 am
☽ ⚻ ♃ **9:36 am** 6:36 am
☽ △ ♇ **1:54 pm** 10:54 am
☽ □ ☉ **5:26 pm** 2:26 pm
♂ ☌ ♅ 10:21 pm

13 WEDNESDAY
♂ ☌ ♅ **1:21 am**
☽ ⚺ ♅ **3:05 am** 12:05 am
☽ ⚺ ♂ **3:10 am** 12:10 am
☽ □ ☿ **3:36 pm** 12:36 pm
☽ ⚻ ♀ 10:49 pm

14 THURSDAY
☽ ⚻ ♀ **1:49 am**
☽ □ ♆ **7:56 am** 4:56 am
☽ ⚻ ♄ **9:40 am** 6:40 am
☽ ☍ ♃ **3:56 pm** 12:56 pm
☽ ⚻ ♇ **7:30 pm** 4:30 pm
☽ △ ☉ 11:49 pm

15 FRIDAY
☽ △ ☉ **2:49 am**
☽ ⚹ ♅ **7:48 am** 4:48 am
☽ ⚹ ♂ **10:24 am** 7:24 am
☽ △ ☿ 11:39 pm

16 SATURDAY
☽ △ ☿ **2:39 am**
☽ ☍ ♀ **9:23 am** 6:23 am
☽ △ ♆ **10:48 am** 7:48 am
☽ ☍ ♄ **12:40 pm** 9:40 am
☽ ⚻ ♃ **6:42 pm** 3:42 pm
☽ ☍ ♇ **9:39 pm** 6:39 pm

17 SUNDAY
♀ ⚹ ♆ **3:44 am** 12:44 am
☽ ⚻ ☉ **8:03 am** 5:03 am
☽ □ ♅ **9:17 am** 6:17 am
☽ □ ♂ **1:57 pm** 10:57 am
☉ ⚹ ♅ 11:55 pm

18 MONDAY
☉ ⚹ ♅ **2:55 am**
♀ ☌ ♄ **5:52 am** 2:52 am
☽ ⚻ ☿ **9:18 am** 6:18 am
☽ ⚻ ♆ **11:03 am** 8:03 am
☽ ⚻ ♄ **1:01 pm** 10:01 am
☽ ⚻ ♀ **1:34 pm** 10:34 am
☽ △ ♃ **7:00 pm** 4:00 pm
☽ ⚻ ♇ **9:30 pm** 6:30 pm
☿ ☌ ♆ 10:37 pm

19 TUESDAY
☿ ☌ ♆ **1:37 am**
☽ △ ♅ **8:51 am** 5:51 am
☽ ☍ ☉ **10:54 am** 7:54 am
☽ △ ♂ **3:31 pm** 12:31 pm
☿ ⚹ ♄ **9:39 pm** 6:39 pm

20 WEDNESDAY
☽ ☍ ♆ **10:22 am** 7:22 am
☽ △ ♄ **12:32 pm** 9:32 am
☽ ☍ ☿ **2:11 pm** 11:11 am
☽ △ ♀ **4:45 pm** 1:45 pm
☽ □ ♃ **6:41 pm** 3:41 pm
☽ △ ♇ **8:52 pm** 5:52 pm

21 THURSDAY
☽ ⚻ ♅ **8:27 am** 5:27 am
☽ ⚻ ☉ **1:53 pm** 10:53 am
☽ ⚻ ♂ **5:27 pm** 2:27 pm
♀ ⚺ ♃ **8:44 pm** 5:44 pm

22 FRIDAY
☽ ⚻ ♆ **10:52 am** 7:52 am
☽ □ ♄ **1:20 pm** 10:20 am
☿ □ ♃ **3:40 pm** 12:40 pm
☽ ⚹ ♃ **7:56 pm** 4:56 pm
☽ ⚻ ☿ **8:21 pm** 5:21 pm
☽ □ ♀ **9:46 pm** 6:46 pm
☽ □ ♇ **9:52 pm** 6:52 pm
♀ ☌ ♇ **10:53 pm** 7:53 pm

23 SATURDAY
☽ ☍ ♅ **10:11 am** 7:11 am
☿ ⚹ ♇ **12:18 pm** 9:18 am
☽ △ ☉ **7:44 pm** 4:44 pm
☽ ☍ ♂ **10:12 pm** 7:12 pm

24 SUNDAY
☽ △ ♆ **2:29 pm** 11:29 am
☽ ⚹ ♄ **5:21 pm** 2:21 pm
☽ ⚺ ♃ 9:37 pm
☽ ⚹ ♇ 11:18 pm

25 MONDAY
☽ ⚺ ♃ **12:37 am**
☽ ⚹ ♇ **2:18 am**
☽ △ ☿ **6:14 am** 3:14 am
☽ ⚹ ♀ **7:14 am** 4:14 am
☽ ⚻ ♅ **3:40 pm** 12:40 pm

26 TUESDAY
☽ □ ☉ **6:28 am** 3:28 am
☽ ⚻ ♂ **7:32 am** 4:32 am
☽ □ ♆ **10:15 pm** 7:15 pm
☽ ⚺ ♄ 10:35 pm

27 WEDNESDAY
☽ ⚺ ♄ **1:35 am**
☽ ☌ ♃ **9:33 am** 6:33 am
☽ ⚺ ♇ **10:55 am** 7:55 am
☽ □ ☿ **8:11 pm** 5:11 pm
☉ ⚹ ♂ **9:33 pm** 6:33 pm
☽ ⚺ ♀ **10:09 pm** 7:09 pm
☽ △ ♅ 10:17 pm

28 THURSDAY
☽ △ ♅ **1:17 am**
☽ △ ♂ **9:26 pm** 6:26 pm
☽ ⚹ ☉ **10:09 pm** 7:09 pm

Eastern time in bold type
Pacific time in medium type

FEBRUARY 2019

DATE	SID.TIME	SUN	MOON	NODE	MERCURY	VENUS	MARS	JUPITER	SATURN	URANUS	NEPTUNE	PLUTO	CERES	PALLAS	JUNO	VESTA	CHIRON
1 F	8 43 39	11 ♒ 49 04	29 ♐ 36	26 ♋ 47	13 ♒ 09	26 ♐ 40	20 ♈ 54	17 ♐ 46	14 ♑ 57	28 ♈ 52	14 ♓ 56	21 ♑ 38	2 ♐ 03	28 ♎ 18	26 ♉ 41	29 ♒ 46	29 ♓ 09
2 Sa	8 47 35	12 49 59	11 ♑ 38	26 48	14 54	27 48	21 34	17 56	15 04	28 54	14 58	21 40	2 22	28 25	26 59	0 ♓ 16	29 12
3 Su	8 51 32	13 50 54	23 33	26 48 ℞	16 39	28 56	22 15	18 07	15 11	28 55	15 00	21 42	2 41	28 32	27 18	0 46	29 15
4 M	8 55 28	14 51 47	5 ♒ 24	26 48	18 25	0 ♑ 04	22 56	18 17	15 17	28 57	15 02	21 43	2 59	28 39	27 37	1 16	29 17
5 T	8 59 25	15 52 40	17 12	26 47	20 12	1 13	23 36	18 27	15 24	28 58	15 04	21 45	3 18	28 46	27 56	1 45	29 20
6 W	9 3 22	16 53 31	29 00	26 45	21 59	2 21	24 17	18 37	15 30	28 59	15 06	21 47	3 36	28 52	28 15	2 15	29 23
7 Th	9 7 18	17 54 21	10 ♓ 50	26 41	23 46	3 30	24 57	18 47	15 36	29 01	15 08	21 49	3 55	28 57	28 35	2 45	29 26
8 F	9 11 15	18 55 09	22 44	26 38	25 34	4 39	25 38	18 56	15 43	29 03	15 10	21 51	4 12	29 02	28 55	3 15	29 29
9 Sa	9 15 11	19 55 56	4 ♈ 44	26 34	27 22	5 48	26 19	19 06	15 49	29 04	15 12	21 53	4 30	29 07	29 15	3 45	29 32
10 Su	9 19 8	20 56 42	16 53	26 30	29 11	6 57	26 59	19 15	15 55	29 06	15 14	21 55	4 48	29 11	29 35	4 14	29 34
11 M	9 23 4	21 57 26	29 14	26 27	1 ♓ 00	8 07	27 40	19 25	16 01	29 08	15 16	21 56	5 05	29 15	29 56	4 44	29 37
12 T	9 27 1	22 58 09	11 ♉ 51	26 25 D	2 48	9 16	28 21	19 34	16 08	29 09	15 18	21 58	5 22	29 19	0 ♊ 17	5 14	29 40
13 W	9 30 57	23 58 50	24 46	26 25	4 36	10 25	29 01	19 43	16 14	29 11	15 20	22 00	5 39	29 22	0 39	5 44	29 43
14 Th	9 34 54	24 59 30	8 ♊ 04	26 25	6 24	11 35	29 42	19 52	16 20	29 13	15 23	22 02	5 56	29 24	1 00	6 13	29 46
15 F	9 38 51	26 00 07	21 46	26 27	8 12	12 45	0 ♉ 22	20 01	16 26	29 15	15 25	22 04	6 13	29 26	1 22	6 43	29 49
16 Sa	9 42 47	27 00 43	5 ♋ 55	26 28	9 58	13 55	1 03	20 10	16 32	29 17	15 27	22 05	6 29	29 28	1 44	7 13	29 53
17 Su	9 46 44	28 01 18	20 29	26 29 ℞	11 43	15 04	1 43	20 19	16 38	29 19	15 29	22 07	6 45	29 29	2 06	7 43	29 56
18 M	9 50 40	29 01 50	5 ♌ 25	26 29	13 26	16 14	2 24	20 27	16 44	29 21	15 31	22 09	7 01	29 29 ℞	2 29	8 12	29 59
19 T	9 54 37	0 ♓ 02 21	20 36	26 27	15 07	17 25	3 04	20 35	16 49	29 23	15 34	22 10	7 17	29 29	2 51	8 42	0 ♈ 02
20 W	9 58 33	1 02 51	5 ♍ 52	26 24	16 45	18 35	3 45	20 44	16 55	29 25	15 36	22 12	7 32	29 29	3 14	9 12	0 05
21 Th	10 2 30	2 03 18	21 04	26 19	18 20	19 45	4 25	20 52	17 01	29 27	15 38	22 14	7 48	29 28	3 37	9 41	0 08
22 F	10 6 26	3 03 44	6 ♎ 01	26 13	19 52	20 55	5 06	21 00	17 06	29 30	15 40	22 15	8 03	29 27	4 01	10 11	0 12
23 Sa	10 10 23	4 04 09	20 35	26 08	21 19	22 06	5 46	21 08	17 12	29 32	15 42	22 17	8 17	29 25	4 24	10 41	0 15
24 Su	10 14 20	5 04 33	4 ♏ 41	26 03	22 41	23 16	6 26	21 16	17 18	29 34	15 45	22 19	8 32	29 22	4 48	11 10	0 18
25 M	10 18 16	6 04 55	18 18	26 00	23 57	24 27	7 07	21 23	17 23	29 37	15 47	22 20	8 46	29 19	5 12	11 40	0 21
26 T	10 22 13	7 05 15	1 ♐ 27	25 58 D	25 07	25 38	7 47	21 31	17 29	29 39	15 49	22 22	9 00	29 16	5 36	12 10	0 25
27 W	10 26 9	8 05 35	14 10	25 58	26 10	26 49	8 28	21 38	17 34	29 41	15 51	22 23	9 14	29 12	6 00	12 39	0 28
28 Th	10 30 6	9 05 52	26 33	25 59	27 06	27 59	9 08	21 45	17 39	29 44	15 54	22 25	9 28	29 08	6 25	13 09	0 31

EPHEMERIS CALCULATED FOR 12 MIDNIGHT GREENWICH MEAN TIME. ALL OTHER DATA AND FACING ASPECTARIAN PAGE IN **EASTERN TIME (BOLD)** AND PACIFIC TIME (REGULAR).

MARCH 2019

☽ Last Aspect day	ET / hr:mn	PT	asp	☽ Ingress sign	day	ET / hr:mn	PT
2	**1:47 pm**	10:47 am	□♅	♒	2	**2:06 pm**	11:06 am
5	**3:05 am**	12:05 am	✶♅	♓	5	**3:11 am**	12:11 am
7	**2:08 pm**	11:08 am	☌☿	♈	7	**3:27 pm**	12:27 pm
9	**12:14 pm**	9:14 am	△♃	♉	9		11:10 pm
9	**12:14 pm**	9:14 am	△♃	♉	10	**3:10 am**	
12	**5:31 am**	2:31 am	✶☿	♊	12	**11:48 am**	8:48 am
14	**8:30 am**	5:30 am	□☿	♋	14	**5:49 pm**	2:49 pm
16	**2:03 pm**	11:03 am	△☉	♌	16	**8:57 pm**	5:57 pm
18	**11:19 am**	8:19 am	△♃	♍	18	**9:41 pm**	6:41 pm
20	**11:22 am**	8:22 am	□♃	♎	20	**9:28 pm**	6:28 pm
22	**2:10 pm**	11:10 am	△♀	♏	22	**10:16 pm**	7:16 pm
24	**10:24 pm**	7:24 pm	□♀	♐	24		11:06 pm
24	**10:24 pm**	7:24 pm	□♀	♐	25	**2:06 am**	
26	**10:37 pm**	7:37 pm	☌♃	♑	27	**10:07 am**	7:07 am
29	**8:05 pm**	5:05 pm	△♂	♒	29	**9:46 pm**	6:46 pm
31	**11:02 pm**	8:02 pm	✶♃	♓	4/1	**10:48 am**	7:48 am

☽ Phases & Eclipses phase	day	ET / hr:mn	PT
New Moon	6	**11:04 am**	8:04 am
2nd Quarter	14	**6:27 am**	3:27 am
Full Moon	20	**9:43 pm**	6:43 pm
4th Quarter	27		9:10 pm
4th Quarter	28	**12:10 am**	

Planet Ingress		day	ET / hr:mn	PT
♀	♒	1	**11:45 am**	8:45 am
♅	♉	6	**3:26 am**	12:26 am
☉	♈	20	**5:58 pm**	2:58 pm
♀	♓	26	**3:43 pm**	12:43 pm
♂	♊	30		11:12 pm
♂	♊	31	**2:12 am**	

Planetary Motion		day	ET / hr:mn	PT
☿	℞	5	**1:19 pm**	10:19 am
☿	D	28	**9:59 am**	6:59 am

1 FRIDAY

♀□♅	**7:32 am**	4:32 am
☽✶♆	**9:39 am**	6:39 am
☽☌♄	**1:23 pm**	10:23 am
☽⚺♃	**9:52 pm**	6:52 pm
☽☌♇	**10:49 pm**	7:49 pm

2 SATURDAY

☽✶☿	**11:55 am**	8:55 am
☽□♅	**1:47 pm**	10:47 am
☽☌♀	**5:03 pm**	2:03 pm

3 SUNDAY

☽□♂	**1:54 pm**	10:54 am
☽⚺☉	**4:37 pm**	1:37 pm
☽⚺♆	**10:49 pm**	7:49 pm
☽⚺♄		11:49 pm

4 MONDAY

☽⚺♄	**2:49 am**	
☽✶♃	**11:30 am**	8:30 am
☽⚺♇	**12:00 pm**	9:00 am
☽⚺☿		11:26 pm

5 TUESDAY

☽⚺☿	**2:26 am**	
☽✶♅	**3:05 am**	12:05 am
☽⚺♀	**12:54 pm**	9:54 am

6 WEDNESDAY

☽✶♂	**6:26 am**	3:26 am
☽☌☉	**11:04 am**	8:04 am
☽☌♆	**11:47 am**	8:47 am
☽✶♄	**3:58 pm**	12:58 pm
☉☌♆	**8:00 pm**	5:00 pm
☽□♃		9:37 pm
☽✶♇		9:41 pm

7 THURSDAY

☽□♃	**12:37 am**	
☽✶♇	**12:41 am**	
♃⚺♇	**11:33 am**	8:33 am
☽☌☿	**2:08 pm**	11:08 am
☽⚺♅	**3:35 pm**	12:35 pm

8 FRIDAY

☽✶♀	**7:29 am**	4:29 am
☽⚺♂	**9:31 pm**	6:31 pm
☽⚺♆	**11:28 pm**	8:28 pm
☉✶♄		11:10 pm

9 SATURDAY

☉✶♄	**2:10 am**	
☽□♄	**3:44 am**	12:44 am
☽⚺☉	**3:52 am**	12:52 am
☽□♇	**11:56 am**	8:56 am
☽△♃	**12:14 pm**	9:14 am
☽⚺☿	**10:46 pm**	7:46 pm
☽☌♅		11:31 pm

10 SUNDAY

☽☌♅	**3:31 am**	
♂✶♆	**12:20 pm**	9:20 am
☽□♀		9:45 pm

11 MONDAY

☽□♀	**12:45 am**	
☽✶♆	**10:18 am**	7:18 am
☽☌♂	**11:27 am**	8:27 am
☽△♄	**2:34 pm**	11:34 am
☽✶☉	**7:13 pm**	4:13 pm
☽△♇	**10:13 pm**	7:13 pm
☽⚻♃	**10:49 pm**	7:49 pm

12 TUESDAY

☽✶☿	**5:31 am**	2:31 am
☽⚺♅	**12:20 pm**	9:20 am

13 WEDNESDAY

☉✶♇	**10:29 am**	7:29 am
☽△♀	**1:58 pm**	10:58 am
☽□♆	**5:44 pm**	2:44 pm
☉□♃	**9:29 pm**	6:29 pm
☽⚺♂	**9:34 pm**	6:34 pm
☽⚻♄	**9:57 pm**	6:57 pm

14 THURSDAY

☽⚻♇	**5:00 am**	2:00 am
☽☍♃	**5:50 am**	2:50 am
♂△♄	**6:02 am**	3:02 am
☽□☉	**6:27 am**	3:27 am
☽□☿	**8:30 am**	5:30 am
☽✶♅	**6:31 pm**	3:31 pm
☉☌☿	**9:48 pm**	6:48 pm

15 FRIDAY

♀⚺♆	**9:11 am**	6:11 am
☿□♃	**7:17 pm**	4:17 pm
☽△♆	**10:18 pm**	7:18 pm
☽⚻♀	**11:28 pm**	8:28 pm
☽☍♄		11:24 pm

16 SATURDAY

☽☍♄	**2:24 am**	
☽✶♂	**4:22 am**	1:22 am
☽☍♇	**8:53 am**	5:53 am
☽△☿	**8:54 am**	5:54 am
☿✶♇	**9:08 am**	6:08 am
☽⚻♃	**9:54 am**	6:54 am
☽△☉	**2:03 pm**	11:03 am
☽□♅	**9:47 pm**	6:47 pm

17 SUNDAY

♀⚺♄	**12:09 pm**	9:09 am
☿✶♂	**11:23 pm**	8:23 pm
☽⚻♆		9:07 pm

18 MONDAY

☽⚻♆	**12:07 am**	
☽⚻♄	**4:08 am**	1:08 am
☽☍♀	**5:27 am**	2:27 am
☽⚻☿	**7:14 am**	4:14 am
☽□♂	**8:06 am**	5:06 am
☽⚻♇	**10:10 am**	7:10 am
☽△♃	**11:19 am**	8:19 am
☽⚻☉	**6:33 pm**	3:33 pm
☿⚺♀	**6:56 pm**	3:56 pm
☽△♅	**10:40 pm**	7:40 pm

19 TUESDAY

☽☍♆		9:13 pm

20 WEDNESDAY

☽☍♆	**12:13 am**	
☽△♄	**4:15 am**	1:15 am
☽☍☿	**4:35 am**	1:35 am
♂△♇	**7:41 am**	4:41 am
☽⚻♀	**9:29 am**	6:29 am
☽△♇	**10:04 am**	7:04 am
☽△♂	**10:10 am**	7:10 am
☿✶♄	**10:27 am**	7:27 am
☽□♃	**11:22 am**	8:22 am
♀⚺♇	**4:54 pm**	1:54 pm
☽☍☉	**9:43 pm**	6:43 pm
☽⚻♅	**10:36 pm**	7:36 pm

21 THURSDAY

♀□♂	**4:07 am**	1:07 am
♀✶♃	**10:17 am**	7:17 am
☉⚺♅	**11:48 am**	8:48 am
♂⚻♃	**3:43 pm**	12:43 pm
☽⚻♆		9:26 pm
☽⚻☿		11:35 pm

22 FRIDAY

☽⚻♆	**12:26 am**	
☽⚻☿	**2:35 am**	
☽□♄	**4:39 am**	1:39 am
☽□♇	**10:29 am**	7:29 am
☽✶♃	**11:59 am**	8:59 am
☽⚻♂	**12:52 pm**	9:52 am
☽△♀	**2:10 pm**	11:10 am
☽☍♅	**11:38 pm**	8:38 pm
☽⚻☉		11:09 pm

23 SATURDAY

☽⚻☉	**2:09 am**	
☽△♆		11:50 pm

24 SUNDAY

☽△♆	**2:50 am**	
☽△☿	**3:10 am**	12:10 am
☽✶♄	**7:25 am**	4:25 am
☿☌♆	**1:28 pm**	10:28 am
☽✶♇	**1:30 pm**	10:30 am
☽⚺♃	**3:15 pm**	12:15 pm
☽☍♂	**6:38 pm**	3:38 pm
☽□♀	**10:24 pm**	7:24 pm

25 MONDAY

☽⚻♅	**3:46 am**	12:46 am
☽△☉	**10:30 am**	7:30 am

26 TUESDAY

☽□☿	**8:01 am**	5:01 am
☽□♆	**9:07 am**	6:07 am
☽⚺♄	**2:10 pm**	11:10 am
☽⚺♇	**8:35 pm**	5:35 pm
☽☌♃	**10:37 pm**	7:37 pm

27 WEDNESDAY

☽⚻♂	**5:10 am**	2:10 am
☽✶♀	**12:06 pm**	9:06 am
☽△♅	**12:10 pm**	9:10 am
♀✶♅	**12:45 pm**	9:45 am
☽□☉		9:10 pm

28 THURSDAY

☽□☉	**12:10 am**	
☽✶☿	**5:48 pm**	2:48 pm
☽✶♆	**7:33 pm**	4:33 pm
☽☌♄		10:00 pm

29 FRIDAY

☽☌♄	**1:00 am**	
☽☌♇	**7:35 am**	4:35 am
☽⚺♃	**9:53 am**	6:53 am
☽△♂	**8:05 pm**	5:05 pm
☽□♅		9:10 pm

30 SATURDAY

☽□♅	**12:10 am**	
☽⚺♀	**6:36 am**	3:36 am
☽✶☉	**5:53 pm**	2:53 pm

31 SUNDAY

☽⚺☿	**7:17 am**	4:17 am
☽⚺♆	**8:30 am**	5:30 am
☽⚺♄	**2:06 pm**	11:06 am
☽⚺♇	**8:36 pm**	5:36 pm
☽✶♃	**11:02 pm**	8:02 pm

Eastern time in bold type
Pacific time in medium type

MARCH 2019

DATE	SID.TIME	SUN	MOON	NODE	MERCURY	VENUS	MARS	JUPITER	SATURN	URANUS	NEPTUNE	PLUTO	CERES	PALLAS	JUNO	VESTA	CHIRON
1 F	10 34 2	10 ♓ 06 09	8 ♑ 39	26 ♋ 01	27 ♓ 54	29 ♑ 10	9 ♉ 48	21 ♐ 52	17 ♑ 44	29 ♈ 46	15 ♓ 56	22 ♑ 26	9 ♐ 41	29 ♎ 03 ℞	6 ♊ 49	13 ♓ 38	0 ♈ 35
2 Sa	10 37 59	11 06 24	20 35	26 02 ℞	28 33	0 ♒ 21	10 29	21 59	17 50	29 49	15 58	22 28	9 54	28 57	7 14	14 08	0 38
3 Su	10 41 55	12 06 37	2 ♒ 24	26 02	29 03	1 33	11 09	22 06	17 55	29 51	16 01	22 29	10 07	28 52	7 39	14 37	0 42
4 M	10 45 52	13 06 49	14 11	26 00	29 24	2 44	11 49	22 13	18 00	29 54	16 03	22 31	10 19	28 45	8 04	15 07	0 45
5 T	10 49 49	14 06 58	25 58	25 56	29 36 ℞	3 55	12 30	22 19	18 05	29 56	16 05	22 32	10 31	28 38	8 29	15 37	0 48
6 W	10 53 45	15 07 07	7 ♓ 49	25 49	29 39	5 06	13 10	22 25	18 10	29 59	16 07	22 34	10 43	28 31	8 55	16 06	0 52
7 Th	10 57 42	16 07 13	19 45	25 40	29 32	6 17	13 50	22 32	18 14	0 ♉ 02	16 10	22 35	10 55	28 23	9 20	16 35	0 55
8 F	11 1 38	17 07 17	1 ♈ 47	25 31	29 16	7 29	14 30	22 38	18 19	0 04	16 12	22 36	11 06	28 14	9 46	17 05	0 59
9 Sa	11 5 35	18 07 20	13 58	25 20	28 52	8 40	15 10	22 44	18 24	0 07	16 14	22 38	11 17	28 05	10 12	17 34	1 02
10 Su	11 9 31	19 07 20	26 17	25 10	28 20	9 52	15 51	22 49	18 28	0 10	16 16	22 39	11 28	27 56	10 38	18 04	1 06
11 M	11 13 28	20 07 18	8 ♉ 48	25 02	27 41	11 03	16 31	22 55	18 33	0 13	16 19	22 40	11 39	27 46	11 04	18 33	1 09
12 T	11 17 24	21 07 15	21 30	24 56	26 56	12 15	17 11	23 00	18 38	0 16	16 21	22 41	11 49	27 35	11 30	19 03	1 13
13 W	11 21 21	22 07 09	4 ♊ 27	24 52	26 06	13 26	17 51	23 05	18 42	0 18	16 23	22 43	11 59	27 24	11 56	19 32	1 16
14 Th	11 25 17	23 07 01	17 41	24 50 D	25 12	14 38	18 31	23 10	18 46	0 21	16 26	22 44	12 08	27 13	12 23	20 01	1 20
15 F	11 29 14	24 06 51	1 ♋ 15	24 50	24 16	15 50	19 11	23 15	18 50	0 24	16 28	22 45	12 17	27 01	12 49	20 30	1 23
16 Sa	11 33 11	25 06 38	15 09	24 51 ℞	23 18	17 01	19 51	23 20	18 55	0 27	16 30	22 46	12 26	26 49	13 16	21 00	1 27
17 Su	11 37 7	26 06 23	29 26	24 51	22 21	18 13	20 31	23 25	18 59	0 30	16 32	22 47	12 35	26 36	13 43	21 29	1 30
18 M	11 41 4	27 06 06	14 ♌ 03	24 50	21 25	19 25	21 11	23 29	19 03	0 33	16 35	22 48	12 43	26 23	14 10	21 58	1 34
19 T	11 45 0	28 05 47	28 57	24 46	20 31	20 37	21 51	23 33	19 07	0 36	16 37	22 49	12 51	26 09	14 37	22 27	1 37
20 W	11 48 57	29 05 26	14 ♍ 00	24 39	19 41	21 49	22 31	23 37	19 11	0 39	16 39	22 50	12 59	25 55	15 04	22 57	1 41
21 Th	11 52 53	0 ♈ 05 02	29 05	24 30	18 55	23 01	23 11	23 41	19 14	0 42	16 41	22 51	13 06	25 41	15 31	23 26	1 45
22 F	11 56 50	1 04 36	14 ♎ 01	24 20	18 14	24 13	23 51	23 45	19 18	0 45	16 44	22 52	13 13	25 26	15 58	23 55	1 48
23 Sa	12 0 46	2 04 09	28 38	24 10	17 38	25 25	24 31	23 48	19 22	0 48	16 46	22 53	13 20	25 11	16 26	24 24	1 52
24 Su	12 4 43	3 03 39	12 ♏ 51	24 01	17 08	26 37	25 11	23 52	19 25	0 52	16 48	22 54	13 26	24 56	16 53	24 53	1 55
25 M	12 8 40	4 03 08	26 35	23 53	16 44	27 49	25 51	23 55	19 29	0 55	16 50	22 55	13 32	24 40	17 21	25 22	1 59
26 T	12 12 36	5 02 35	9 ♐ 50	23 48	16 25	29 01	26 31	23 58	19 32	0 58	16 52	22 56	13 37	24 24	17 48	25 51	2 02
27 W	12 16 33	6 02 00	22 39	23 45	16 13	0 ♓ 13	27 11	24 01	19 35	1 01	16 55	22 57	13 43	24 07	18 16	26 20	2 06
28 Th	12 20 29	7 01 24	5 ♑ 04	23 45 D	16 07 D	1 25	27 50	24 03	19 38	1 04	16 57	22 58	13 48	23 50	18 44	26 49	2 09
29 F	12 24 26	8 00 45	17 12	23 45 ℞	16 06	2 37	28 30	24 06	19 41	1 07	16 59	22 59	13 52	23 33	19 12	27 18	2 13
30 Sa	12 28 22	9 00 05	29 08	23 45	16 11	3 49	29 10	24 08	19 44	1 11	17 01	22 59	13 56	23 16	19 40	27 46	2 16
31 Su	12 32 19	9 59 23	10 ♒ 56	23 43	16 22	5 02	29 50	24 10	19 47	1 14	17 03	23 00	14 00	22 58	20 08	28 15	2 20

EPHEMERIS CALCULATED FOR 12 MIDNIGHT GREENWICH MEAN TIME. ALL OTHER DATA AND FACING ASPECTARIAN PAGE IN **EASTERN TIME (BOLD)** AND PACIFIC TIME (REGULAR).

APRIL 2019

☽ Last Aspect day	ET / hr:mn / PT	asp	☽ Ingress sign	day	ET / hr:mn / PT
3/31	**11:02 pm** 8:02 pm	✶ ♃	♓	1	**10:48 am** 7:48 am
3	**11:36 am** 8:36 am	□ ♃	♈	3	**10:56 pm** 7:56 pm
5	**10:15 pm** 7:15 pm	△ ♃	♉	6	**9:06 am** 6:06 am
8	**4:29 am** 1:29 am	△ ♇	♊	8	**5:15 pm** 2:15 pm
10	**1:27 pm** 10:27 am	☍ ♃	♋	10	**11:31 pm** 8:31 pm
12	**7:33 pm** 4:33 pm	△ ☿	♌	13	**3:50 am** 12:50 am
14	**9:38 pm** 6:38 pm	△ ☉	♍	15	**6:14 am** 3:14 am
16	9:29 pm	☍ ♀	♎	17	**7:22 am** 4:22 am
17	**12:29 am**	☍ ♀	♎	17	**7:22 am** 4:22 am
19	**7:12 am** 4:12 am	☍ ☉	♏	19	**8:41 am** 5:41 am
20	9:00 pm	✶ ♇	♐	21	**11:59 am** 8:59 am
21	**12:00 am**	✶ ♇	♐	21	**11:59 am** 8:59 am
23	**7:44 am** 4:44 am	☌ ♃	♑	23	**6:50 pm** 3:50 pm
25	**3:48 pm** 12:48 pm	☌ ♇	♒	26	**5:27 am** 2:27 am
28	**5:44 am** 2:44 am	✶ ♃	♓	28	**6:11 pm** 3:11 pm
30	**5:57 pm** 2:57 pm	□ ♃	♈	5/1	**6:24 am** 3:24 am

☽ Phases & Eclipses phase	day	ET / hr:mn / PT
New Moon	5	**4:50 am** 1:50 am
2nd Quarter	12	**3:06 pm** 12:06 pm
Full Moon	19	**7:12 am** 4:12 am
4th Quarter	26	**6:18 pm** 3:18 pm

Planet Ingress		day	ET / hr:mn / PT
⚶	♈	3	**11:28 am** 8:28 am
☿	♈	16	11:01 pm
☿	♈	17	**2:01 am**
☉	♉	20	**4:55 am** 1:55 am
♀	♈	20	**12:11 pm** 9:11 am
⚵	♋	20	**12:38 pm** 9:38 am

Planetary Motion		day	ET / hr:mn / PT
⚳	℞	8	9:35 pm
⚳	℞	9	**12:35 am**
♃	℞	10	**1:01 pm** 10:01 am
♇	℞	24	**2:48 pm** 11:48 am
♄	℞	29	**8:54 pm** 5:54 pm

1 MONDAY
☽ □ ♂ **12:44 pm** 9:44 am
☽ ✶ ♅ **1:30 pm** 10:30 am
☽ ☌ ♀ 11:31 pm

2 TUESDAY
☽ ☌ ♀ **2:31 am**
♂ ⚺ ♅ **3:29 am** 12:29 am
☿ ☌ ♆ **5:36 am** 2:36 am
☽ ⚺ ☉ **12:20 pm** 9:20 am
☽ ☌ ♆ **9:25 pm** 6:25 pm
☽ ☌ ☿ **9:58 pm** 6:58 pm
☽ ✶ ♄ 11:58 pm

3 WEDNESDAY
☽ ✶ ♄ **2:58 am**
☽ ✶ ♇ **9:09 am** 6:09 am
☽ □ ♃ **11:36 am** 8:36 am
☽ ⚺ ♅ 10:50 pm

4 THURSDAY
☽ ⚺ ♅ **1:50 am**
☽ ✶ ♂ **4:16 am** 1:16 am
☽ ⚺ ♀ **8:41 pm** 5:41 pm

5 FRIDAY
☽ ☌ ☉ **4:50 am** 1:50 am
☽ ⚺ ♆ **8:38 am** 5:38 am
☽ ⚺ ☿ **11:48 am** 8:48 am
☽ □ ♄ **2:02 pm** 11:02 am
☽ □ ♇ **7:51 pm** 4:51 pm
☽ △ ♃ **10:15 pm** 7:15 pm

6 SATURDAY
☽ ☌ ♅ **12:09 pm** 9:09 am
☽ ⚺ ♂ **5:26 pm** 2:26 pm

7 SUNDAY
☿ ✶ ♄ **5:17 am** 2:17 am
☉ ⚺ ♆ **6:11 am** 3:11 am
☽ ✶ ♀ **12:04 pm** 9:04 am
☽ ✶ ♆ **5:46 pm** 2:46 pm
☽ ⚺ ☉ **6:42 pm** 3:42 pm
☽ △ ♄ **10:59 pm** 7:59 pm
☽ ✶ ☿ 9:04 pm

8 MONDAY
☽ ✶ ☿ **12:04 am**
☽ △ ♇ **4:29 am** 1:29 am
☽ ⚻ ♃ **6:49 am** 3:49 am
☽ ⚺ ♅ **8:26 pm** 5:26 pm

9 TUESDAY
☽ ☌ ♂ **4:16 am** 1:16 am
☽ □ ♀ 9:51 pm
☽ □ ♆ 9:58 pm
♀ ☌ ♆ 11:13 pm

10 WEDNESDAY
☽ □ ♀ **12:51 am**
☽ □ ♆ **12:58 am**
♀ ☌ ♆ **2:13 am**
☉ □ ♄ **4:47 am** 1:47 am
☽ ⚻ ♄ **6:01 am** 3:01 am
☽ ✶ ☉ **6:06 am** 3:06 am
☽ □ ☿ **10:43 am** 7:43 am

☽ ⚻ ♇ **11:13 am** 8:13 am
☽ ☍ ♃ **1:27 pm** 10:27 am
☿ ✶ ♇ **5:45 pm** 2:45 pm
☽ ✶ ♅ 11:49 pm

11 THURSDAY
☽ ✶ ♅ **2:49 am**
☽ ⚺ ♂ **12:53 pm** 9:53 am
☿ □ ♃ 9:18 pm

12 FRIDAY
☿ □ ♃ **12:18 am**
☽ △ ♆ **6:15 am** 3:15 am
☽ △ ♀ **11:05 am** 8:05 am
☽ ☍ ♄ **11:05 am** 8:05 am
♀ ✶ ♄ **11:08 am** 8:08 am
☽ □ ☉ **3:06 pm** 12:06 pm
☽ ☍ ♇ **4:01 pm** 1:01 pm
☽ ⚻ ♃ **6:07 pm** 3:07 pm
☽ △ ☿ **7:33 pm** 4:33 pm

13 SATURDAY
☉ □ ♇ **4:07 am** 1:07 am
☽ □ ♅ **7:14 am** 4:14 am
☽ ✶ ♂ **7:13 pm** 4:13 pm

14 SUNDAY
☽ ⚻ ♆ **9:31 am** 6:31 am
☉ △ ♃ **9:41 am** 6:41 am
☽ ⚻ ♄ **2:10 pm** 11:10 am
☽ ⚻ ♀ **6:45 pm** 3:45 pm
☽ ⚻ ♇ **6:50 pm** 3:50 pm
♀ ✶ ♇ **7:52 pm** 4:52 pm

☽ △ ♃ **8:49 pm** 5:49 pm
☽ △ ☉ **9:38 pm** 6:38 pm
☽ ⚻ ☿ 11:22 pm

15 MONDAY
☽ ⚻ ☿ **2:22 am**
☽ △ ♅ **9:42 am** 6:42 am
♀ □ ♃ **7:15 pm** 4:15 pm
☽ □ ♂ **11:28 pm** 8:28 pm

16 TUESDAY
☽ ☍ ♆ **11:09 am** 8:09 am
☽ △ ♄ **3:40 pm** 12:40 pm
☽ △ ♇ **8:10 pm** 5:10 pm
☽ □ ♃ **10:03 pm** 7:03 pm
☽ ☍ ♀ 9:29 pm
☽ ⚻ ☉ 11:25 pm

17 WEDNESDAY
☽ ☍ ♀ **12:29 am**
☽ ⚻ ☉ **2:25 am**
☽ ☍ ☿ **7:51 am** 4:51 am
☽ ⚻ ♅ **11:00 am** 8:00 am
☽ △ ♂ 11:46 pm

18 THURSDAY
☽ △ ♂ **2:46 am**
☽ ⚻ ♆ **12:17 pm** 9:17 am
☽ □ ♄ **4:48 pm** 1:48 pm
☽ □ ♇ **9:18 pm** 6:18 pm
☿ ⚺ ♅ **10:17 pm** 7:17 pm
☽ ✶ ♃ **11:07 pm** 8:07 pm

19 FRIDAY
☽ ⚻ ♀ **6:09 am** 3:09 am
☽ ☍ ☉ **7:12 am** 4:12 am
☽ ☍ ♅ **12:35 pm** 9:35 am
☽ ⚻ ☿ **1:56 pm** 10:56 am

20 SATURDAY
☽ ⚻ ♂ **7:05 am** 4:05 am
☽ △ ♆ **2:39 pm** 11:39 am
☽ ✶ ♄ **7:20 pm** 4:20 pm
☽ ✶ ♇ 9:00 pm
☽ ⚺ ♃ 10:47 pm

21 SUNDAY
☽ ✶ ♇ **12:00 am**
☽ ⚺ ♃ **1:47 am**
☽ △ ♀ **2:19 pm** 11:19 am
☽ ⚻ ☉ **2:23 pm** 11:23 am
☽ ⚻ ♅ **4:21 pm** 1:21 pm
☉ ⚺ ♀ **6:19 pm** 3:19 pm
☽ △ ☿ **11:18 pm** 8:18 pm

22 MONDAY
♀ ⚺ ♅ **2:03 pm** 11:03 am
☽ ☍ ♂ **2:35 pm** 11:35 am
☉ ☌ ♅ **7:07 pm** 4:07 pm
☽ □ ♆ **8:03 pm** 5:03 pm
☽ ⚺ ♄ 10:00 pm

23 TUESDAY
☽ ⚺ ♄ **1:00 am**
☽ ⚺ ♇ **5:58 am** 2:58 am
☽ ☌ ♃ **7:44 am** 4:44 am
☽ △ ♅ **11:46 pm** 8:46 pm
☽ △ ☉ 11:02 pm

24 WEDNESDAY
☽ △ ☉ **2:02 am**
☽ □ ♀ **3:12 am** 12:12 am
☽ □ ☿ **2:14 pm** 11:14 am
☽ ⚻ ♂ 11:35 pm

25 THURSDAY
☽ ⚻ ♂ **2:35 am**
☽ ✶ ♆ **5:22 am** 2:22 am
☽ ☌ ♄ **10:33 am** 7:33 am
☽ ☌ ♇ **3:48 pm** 12:48 pm
☽ ⚺ ♃ **5:28 pm** 2:28 pm

26 FRIDAY
☽ □ ♅ **10:57 am** 7:57 am
☽ □ ☉ **6:18 pm** 3:18 pm
☽ ✶ ♀ **8:58 pm** 5:58 pm

27 SATURDAY
♂ □ ♆ **9:03 am** 6:03 am
☽ ✶ ☿ **10:35 am** 7:35 am
☽ ⚺ ♆ **5:42 pm** 2:42 pm
☽ △ ♂ **6:11 pm** 3:11 pm
☽ ⚺ ♄ **10:55 pm** 7:55 pm

28 SUNDAY
☽ ⚺ ♇ **4:16 am** 1:16 am
☽ ✶ ♃ **5:44 am** 2:44 am
☽ ✶ ♅ 9:02 pm

29 MONDAY
☽ ✶ ♅ **12:02 am**
☽ ✶ ☉ **12:34 pm** 9:34 am
☿ ⚺ ♆ **4:08 pm** 1:08 pm
☽ ⚺ ♀ **4:44 pm** 1:44 pm

30 TUESDAY
☽ ☌ ♆ **6:33 am** 3:33 am
☽ ⚺ ☿ **8:47 am** 5:47 am
☽ □ ♂ **10:22 am** 7:22 am
☽ ✶ ♄ **11:34 am** 8:34 am
☽ ✶ ♇ **4:48 pm** 1:48 pm
☽ □ ♃ **5:57 pm** 2:57 pm
☿ ✶ ♂ 11:37 pm

Eastern time in bold type
Pacific time in medium type

APRIL 2019

DATE	SID.TIME	SUN	MOON	NODE	MERCURY	VENUS	MARS	JUPITER	SATURN	URANUS	NEPTUNE	PLUTO	CERES	PALLAS	JUNO	VESTA	CHIRON
1 M	12 36 15	10 ♈ 58 40	22 ♒ 43	23 ♋ 40 ℞	16 ♓ 38	6 ♓ 14	0 ♊ 29	24 ♐ 12	19 ♑ 50	1 ♉ 17	17 ♓ 05	23 ♑ 01	14 ♐ 03	22 ♎ 41 ℞	20 ♊ 36	28 ♓ 44	2 ♈ 23
2 T	12 40 12	11 57 54	4 ♓ 32	23 34	16 59	7 26	1 09	24 14	19 53	1 20	17 07	23 01	14 06	22 23	21 04	29 13	2 27
3 W	12 44 9	12 57 06	16 27	23 25	17 24	8 39	1 49	24 15	19 56	1 24	17 10	23 02	14 09	22 05	21 32	29 42	2 31
4 Th	12 48 5	13 56 17	28 31	23 14	17 54	9 51	2 28	24 17	19 58	1 27	17 12	23 03	14 11	21 46	22 00	0 ♈ 10	2 34
5 F	12 52 2	14 55 26	10 ♈ 44	23 00	18 28	11 03	3 08	24 18	20 01	1 30	17 14	23 03	14 13	21 28	22 29	0 39	2 37
6 Sa	12 55 58	15 54 32	23 09	22 46	19 07	12 16	3 48	24 19	20 03	1 34	17 16	23 04	14 14	21 09	22 57	1 07	2 41
7 Su	12 59 55	16 53 37	5 ♉ 44	22 33	19 49	13 28	4 27	24 20	20 05	1 37	17 18	23 04	14 15	20 51	23 26	1 36	2 44
8 M	13 3 51	17 52 39	18 31	22 21	20 35	14 41	5 07	24 20	20 07	1 40	17 20	23 05	14 16	20 32	23 54	2 05	2 48
9 T	13 7 48	18 51 39	1 ♊ 30	22 12	21 24	15 53	5 46	24 21	20 09	1 44	17 22	23 05	14 16 ℞	20 13	24 23	2 33	2 51
10 W	13 11 44	19 50 37	14 39	22 06	22 16	17 06	6 26	24 21 ℞	20 11	1 47	17 24	23 06	14 16	19 55	24 51	3 01	2 55
11 Th	13 15 41	20 49 33	28 01	22 03	23 12	18 18	7 06	24 21	20 13	1 51	17 26	23 06	14 16	19 36	25 20	3 30	2 58
12 F	13 19 37	21 48 27	11 ♋ 36	22 02	24 10	19 31	7 45	24 21	20 15	1 54	17 28	23 07	14 15	19 17	25 49	3 58	3 02
13 Sa	13 23 34	22 47 18	25 26	22 02	25 11	20 43	8 25	24 21	20 17	1 57	17 30	23 07	14 13	18 59	26 17	4 27	3 05
14 Su	13 27 31	23 46 07	9 ♌ 30	22 01	26 15	21 56	9 04	24 20	20 19	2 01	17 32	23 07	14 12	18 40	26 46	4 55	3 08
15 M	13 31 27	24 44 54	23 50	21 59	27 22	23 08	9 43	24 19	20 20	2 04	17 34	23 08	14 10	18 22	27 15	5 23	3 12
16 T	13 35 24	25 43 38	8 ♍ 22	21 55	28 31	24 21	10 23	24 18	20 21	2 08	17 35	23 08	14 07	18 04	27 44	5 51	3 15
17 W	13 39 20	26 42 20	23 02	21 48	29 42	25 33	11 02	24 17	20 23	2 11	17 37	23 08	14 04	17 45	28 13	6 19	3 18
18 Th	13 43 17	27 41 00	7 ♎ 44	21 38	0 ♈ 55	26 46	11 41	24 16	20 24	2 15	17 39	23 08	14 01	17 27	28 42	6 48	3 22
19 F	13 47 13	28 39 38	22 22	21 27	2 11	27 58	12 21	24 15	20 25	2 18	17 41	23 09	13 57	17 10	29 11	7 16	3 25
20 Sa	13 51 10	29 38 14	6 ♏ 46	21 15	3 29	29 11	13 00	24 13	20 26	2 21	17 43	23 09	13 53	16 52	29 40	7 44	3 28
21 Su	13 55 6	0 ♉ 36 48	20 50	21 05	4 49	0 ♈ 24	13 39	24 11	20 27	2 25	17 45	23 09	13 49	16 35	0 ♋ 09	8 12	3 32
22 M	13 59 3	1 35 20	4 ♐ 31	20 56	6 11	1 36	14 19	24 09	20 28	2 28	17 46	23 09	13 44	16 17	0 38	8 40	3 35
23 T	14 3 0	2 33 50	17 46	20 49	7 35	2 49	14 58	24 07	20 29	2 32	17 48	23 09	13 39	16 01	1 07	9 07	3 38
24 W	14 6 56	3 32 19	0 ♑ 37	20 46	9 01	4 02	15 37	24 05	20 29	2 35	17 50	23 09 ℞	13 33	15 44	1 36	9 35	3 41
25 Th	14 10 53	4 30 47	13 05	20 44 D	10 28	5 14	16 16	24 02	20 30	2 39	17 52	23 09	13 27	15 28	2 05	10 03	3 44
26 F	14 14 49	5 29 12	25 16	20 44 ℞	11 58	6 27	16 55	23 59	20 30	2 42	17 53	23 09	13 21	15 12	2 35	10 31	3 47
27 Sa	14 18 46	6 27 36	7 ♒ 14	20 44	13 30	7 40	17 35	23 56	20 31	2 46	17 55	23 09	13 14	14 56	3 04	10 58	3 51
28 Su	14 22 42	7 25 59	19 05	20 44	15 03	8 53	18 14	23 53	20 31	2 49	17 57	23 09	13 07	14 41	3 33	11 26	3 54
29 M	14 26 39	8 24 19	0 ♓ 54	20 41	16 38	10 05	18 53	23 50	20 31	2 52	17 58	23 09	13 00	14 26	4 02	11 54	3 57
30 T	14 30 35	9 22 39	12 46	20 37	18 15	11 18	19 32	23 47	20 31 ℞	2 56	18 00	23 09	12 52	14 11	4 31	12 21	4 00

EPHEMERIS CALCULATED FOR 12 MIDNIGHT GREENWICH MEAN TIME. ALL OTHER DATA AND FACING ASPECTARIAN PAGE IN **EASTERN TIME (BOLD)** AND PACIFIC TIME (REGULAR).

MAY 2019

☽ Last Aspect day	ET / hr:mn / PT		asp	☽ Ingress sign	day	ET / hr:mn / PT	
4/30	**5:57 pm**	2:57 pm	□♃	♈	1	**6:24 am**	3:24 am
3	**4:47 am**	1:47 am	☌☿	♉	3	**4:18 pm**	1:18 pm
5	**11:10 am**	8:10 am	△♇	♊	5	**11:40 pm**	8:40 pm
7	**7:50 pm**	4:50 pm	☌♂	♋	8	**5:06 am**	2:06 am
9	**10:06 pm**	7:06 pm	□♀	♌	10	**9:14 am**	6:14 am
12	**8:24 am**	5:24 am	⚹♂	♍	12	**12:22 pm**	9:22 am
14	**1:19 pm**	10:19 am	□♂	♎	14	**2:51 pm**	11:51 am
16	**5:37 am**	2:37 am	□♇	♏	16	**5:26 pm**	2:26 pm
18	**5:11 pm**	2:11 pm	☍☉	♐	18	**9:21 pm**	6:21 pm
20	**1:05 pm**	10:05 am	☌♃	♑	21	**3:56 am**	12:56 am
22	**11:58 pm**	8:58 pm	☌♇	♒	23	**1:49 pm**	10:49 am
25	**8:51 am**	5:51 am	⚹♃	♓	25		11:08 pm
25	**8:51 am**	5:51 am	⚹♃	♓	26	**2:08 am**	
27		9:21 pm	⚹♇	♈	28	**2:32 pm**	11:32 am
28	**12:21 am**		⚹♇	♈	28	**2:32 pm**	11:32 am
30	**11:08 am**	8:08 am	□♇	♉	30		9:43 pm
30	**11:08 am**	8:08 am	□♇	♉	31	**12:43 am**	

☽ Phases & Eclipses phase	day	ET / hr:mn / PT	
New Moon	4	**6:45 pm**	3:45 pm
2nd Quarter	11	**9:12 pm**	6:12 pm
Full Moon	18	**5:11 pm**	2:11 pm
4th Quarter	26	**12:34 pm**	9:34 am

Planet Ingress		day	ET / hr:mn / PT	
☿	♉	6	**2:25 pm**	11:25 am
♀	♉	15	**5:46 am**	2:46 am
♂	♋	15	**11:09 pm**	8:09 pm
☉	♊	21	**3:59 am**	12:59 am
☿	♊	21	**6:52 am**	3:52 am

Planetary Motion		day	ET / hr:mn / PT	
♀	D	30	**10:52 pm**	7:52 pm

1 WEDNESDAY
☿ ⚹ ♂ **2:37 am**
☿ □ ♄ **4:50 am** 1:50 am
♂ ⚻ ♄ **8:17 am** 5:17 am
☽ ⚺ ♅ **12:22 pm** 9:22 am

2 THURSDAY
☽ ⚺ ☉ **5:17 am** 2:17 am
☽ ☌ ♀ **10:39 am** 7:39 am
☽ ⚺ ♆ **5:36 pm** 2:36 pm
☿ □ ♇ **5:51 pm** 2:51 pm
☽ □ ♄ **10:17 pm** 7:17 pm
☿ △ ♃ **11:59 pm** 8:59 pm
☽ ⚹ ♂ 9:22 pm

3 FRIDAY
☽ ⚹ ♂ **12:22 am**
☽ □ ♇ **3:17 am** 12:17 am
☽ △ ♃ **4:06 am** 1:06 am
☽ ☌ ☿ **4:47 am** 1:47 am
☽ ☌ ♅ **10:15 pm** 7:15 pm

4 SATURDAY
☽ ☌ ☉ **6:45 pm** 3:45 pm
☽ ⚺ ♀ 10:06 pm
☽ ⚹ ♆ 11:02 pm

5 SUNDAY
☽ ⚺ ♀ **1:06 am**
☽ ⚹ ♆ **2:02 am**
☽ △ ♄ **6:22 am** 3:22 am
♂ ⚻ ♇ **8:29 am** 5:29 am
☽ △ ♇ **11:10 am** 8:10 am
♀ ⚺ ♆ **11:18 am** 8:18 am
☽ ⚺ ♂ **11:19 am** 8:19 am
☽ ⚻ ♃ **11:41 am** 8:41 am
♂ ☍ ♃ **5:57 pm** 2:57 pm
☽ ⚺ ☿ **9:18 pm** 6:18 pm

6 MONDAY
☽ ⚺ ♅ **5:37 am** 2:37 am

7 TUESDAY
☽ ⚺ ☉ **5:20 am** 2:20 am
☽ □ ♆ **8:15 am** 5:15 am
♀ □ ♄ **9:26 am** 6:26 am
☽ ⚻ ♄ **12:18 pm** 9:18 am
☽ ⚹ ♀ **12:35 pm** 9:35 am
☽ ⚻ ♇ **4:58 pm** 1:58 pm
☽ ☍ ♃ **5:11 pm** 2:11 pm
☽ ☌ ♂ **7:50 pm** 4:50 pm

8 WEDNESDAY
☿ ☌ ♅ **10:23 am** 7:23 am
☽ ⚹ ♅ **11:07 am** 8:07 am
☽ ⚹ ☿ **11:13 am** 8:13 am
☉ ⚹ ♆ **10:52 pm** 7:52 pm

9 THURSDAY
♃ ⚺ ♇ **6:30 am** 3:30 am
☽ △ ♆ **12:55 pm** 9:55 am
♀ △ ♃ **12:56 pm** 9:56 am
♀ □ ♇ **1:20 pm** 10:20 am
☽ ⚹ ☉ **1:57 pm** 10:57 am
☽ ☍ ♄ **4:44 pm** 1:44 pm
☽ ⚻ ♃ **9:15 pm** 6:15 pm
☽ ☍ ♇ **9:20 pm** 6:20 pm
☽ □ ♀ **10:06 pm** 7:06 pm
☽ ⚺ ♂ 11:43 pm

10 FRIDAY
☽ ⚺ ♂ **2:43 am**
☽ □ ♅ **3:19 pm** 12:19 pm
☽ □ ☿ **11:33 pm** 8:33 pm

11 SATURDAY
☉ △ ♄ **5:19 am** 2:19 am
☽ ⚻ ♆ **4:29 pm** 1:29 pm
☽ ⚻ ♄ **8:06 pm** 5:06 pm
☽ □ ☉ **9:12 pm** 6:12 pm
☽ △ ♃ 9:16 pm
☽ ⚻ ♇ 9:38 pm

12 SUNDAY
☽ △ ♃ **12:16 am**
☽ ⚻ ♇ **12:38 am**
☽ △ ♀ **6:14 am** 3:14 am
☽ ⚹ ♂ **8:24 am** 5:24 am
☽ △ ♅ **6:33 pm** 3:33 pm

13 MONDAY
☽ △ ☿ **10:48 am** 7:48 am
☉ ⚻ ♃ **2:27 pm** 11:27 am
☽ ☍ ♆ **7:14 pm** 4:14 pm
☽ △ ♄ **10:39 pm** 7:39 pm
☉ △ ♇ **11:07 pm** 8:07 pm
☽ □ ♃ 11:32 pm

14 TUESDAY
☽ □ ♃ **2:32 am**
☽ △ ♇ **3:12 am** 12:12 am
☽ △ ☉ **3:30 am** 12:30 am
♀ ⚹ ♂ **9:58 am** 6:58 am
☽ □ ♂ **1:19 pm** 10:19 am
☽ ⚻ ♀ **1:28 pm** 10:28 am
☽ ⚻ ♅ **9:11 pm** 6:11 pm

15 WEDNESDAY
☿ ⚹ ♆ **9:20 pm** 6:20 pm
☽ ⚻ ♆ **9:44 pm** 6:44 pm
☽ ⚻ ☿ **9:48 pm** 6:48 pm
☽ □ ♄ 10:00 pm

16 THURSDAY
☽ □ ♄ **1:00 am**
☽ ⚹ ♃ **4:39 am** 1:39 am
☽ □ ♇ **5:37 am** 2:37 am
☽ ⚻ ☉ **9:39 am** 6:39 am
☽ △ ♂ **6:18 pm** 3:18 pm
☿ △ ♄ **7:09 pm** 4:09 pm
☽ ☍ ♀ **8:47 pm** 5:47 pm
☽ ☍ ♅ 9:04 pm

17 FRIDAY
☽ ☍ ♅ **12:04 am**
☿ ⚻ ♃ **5:49 pm** 2:49 pm
☽ △ ♆ 10:02 pm
☿ △ ♇ 10:48 pm

18 SATURDAY
☽ △ ♆ **1:02 am**
☿ △ ♇ **1:48 am**
☽ ⚹ ♄ **4:15 am** 1:15 am
☽ ⚺ ♃ **7:43 am** 4:43 am
☽ ⚹ ♇ **9:04 am** 6:04 am
☽ ☍ ☿ **10:26 am** 7:26 am
♀ ☌ ♅ **12:17 pm** 9:17 am
☽ ☍ ☉ **5:11 pm** 2:11 pm
☽ ⚻ ♂ 9:52 pm

19 SUNDAY
☽ ⚻ ♂ **12:52 am**
☽ ⚻ ♅ **4:28 am** 1:28 am
☽ ⚻ ♀ **6:00 am** 3:00 am

20 MONDAY
☽ □ ♆ **6:32 am** 3:32 am
☽ ⚺ ♄ **9:43 am** 6:43 am
☽ ☌ ♃ **1:05 pm** 10:05 am
☽ ⚺ ♇ **2:54 pm** 11:54 am

21 TUESDAY
☽ ⚻ ☿ **3:20 am** 12:20 am
☽ ⚻ ☉ **3:56 am** 12:56 am
☉ ☌ ☿ **9:07 am** 6:07 am
☽ ☍ ♂ **10:35 am** 7:35 am
☽ △ ♅ **11:43 am** 8:43 am
☽ △ ♀ **6:58 pm** 3:58 pm

22 WEDNESDAY
♂ ⚹ ♅ **10:46 am** 7:46 am
☽ ⚹ ♆ **3:14 pm** 12:14 pm
☽ ☌ ♄ **6:23 pm** 3:23 pm
☽ ⚺ ♃ **9:36 pm** 6:36 pm
☽ ☌ ♇ **11:58 pm** 8:58 pm

23 THURSDAY
☿ ⚺ ♅ **5:05 am** 2:05 am
☿ ⚺ ♂ **12:04 pm** 9:04 am
☽ △ ☉ **6:49 pm** 3:49 pm
☽ □ ♅ **10:17 pm** 7:17 pm
☽ ⚻ ♂ 9:07 pm
☽ △ ☿ 11:01 pm

24 FRIDAY
☽ ⚻ ♂ **12:07 am**
☽ △ ☿ **2:01 am**
☽ □ ♀ **12:17 pm** 9:17 am
☽ ⚺ ♆ 11:54 pm

25 SATURDAY
☽ ⚺ ♆ **2:54 am**
☽ ⚺ ♄ **5:54 am** 2:54 am
☽ ⚹ ♃ **8:51 am** 5:51 am
☽ ⚺ ♇ **11:48 am** 8:48 am
☉ ⚺ ♅ **4:40 pm** 1:40 pm

26 SUNDAY
☽ ⚹ ♅ **11:02 am** 8:02 am
☽ □ ☉ **12:34 pm** 9:34 am
☽ △ ♂ **4:07 pm** 1:07 pm

27 MONDAY
☽ □ ☿ **4:07 am** 1:07 am
☽ ⚹ ♀ **7:52 am** 4:52 am
☽ ☌ ♆ **3:39 pm** 12:39 pm
☽ ⚹ ♄ **6:22 pm** 3:22 pm
☽ □ ♃ **8:54 pm** 5:54 pm
☽ ⚹ ♇ 9:21 pm

28 TUESDAY
☽ ⚹ ♇ **12:21 am**
☽ ⚺ ♅ **11:29 pm** 8:29 pm
☿ ⚺ ♀ 9:01 pm

29 WEDNESDAY
☿ ⚺ ♀ **12:01 am**
☽ ⚹ ☉ **5:51 am** 2:51 am
☽ □ ♂ **7:30 am** 4:30 am
☿ □ ♆ **9:22 pm** 6:22 pm
☽ ⚺ ♀ 10:53 pm
☽ ⚺ ♆ 11:56 pm

30 THURSDAY
☽ ⚺ ♀ **1:53 am**
☽ ⚺ ♆ **2:56 am**
☽ ⚹ ☿ **4:03 am** 1:03 am
☽ □ ♄ **5:16 am** 2:16 am
☽ △ ♃ **7:21 am** 4:21 am
☽ □ ♇ **11:08 am** 8:08 am
☿ ⚻ ♄ **11:19 am** 8:19 am
♀ ⚹ ♆ **12:50 pm** 9:50 am
☿ ☍ ♃ **11:12 pm** 8:12 pm

31 FRIDAY
☽ ☌ ♅ **9:26 am** 6:26 am
♀ △ ♄ **11:26 am** 8:26 am
☉ ⚺ ♂ **6:02 pm** 3:02 pm
☽ ⚹ ♂ **7:49 pm** 4:49 pm
☽ ⚺ ☉ **7:52 pm** 4:52 pm
☿ ⚻ ♇ **11:14 pm** 8:14 pm

Eastern time in bold type
Pacific time in medium type

MAY 2019

DATE	SID.TIME	SUN	MOON	NODE	MERCURY	VENUS	MARS	JUPITER	SATURN	URANUS	NEPTUNE	PLUTO	CERES	PALLAS	JUNO	VESTA	CHIRON
1 W	14 34 32	10♉20 56	24♓45	20♋30℞	19♈54	12♈31	20♊11	23♐43℞	20♑31℞	2♉59	18♓01	23♑09℞	12♐44℞	13♎57℞	5♋01	12♈49	4♈03
2 Th	14 38 29	11 19 12	6♈56	20 20	21 35	13 44	20 50	23 39	20 31	3 03	18 03	23 08	12 36	13 43	5 30	13 16	4 06
3 F	14 42 25	12 17 27	19 19	20 09	23 17	14 56	21 29	23 35	20 31	3 06	18 04	23 08	12 27	13 30	5 59	13 43	4 09
4 Sa	14 46 22	13 15 40	1♉58	19 57	25 02	16 09	22 08	23 31	20 30	3 10	18 06	23 08	12 18	13 17	6 29	14 11	4 12
5 Su	14 50 18	14 13 51	14 51	19 46	26 48	17 22	22 47	23 27	20 30	3 13	18 07	23 08	12 08	13 04	6 58	14 38	4 15
6 M	14 54 15	15 12 00	27 59	19 36	28 36	18 35	23 26	23 22	20 29	3 16	18 09	23 07	11 59	12 52	7 27	15 05	4 17
7 T	14 58 11	16 10 08	11♊19	19 28	0♉26	19 48	24 05	23 18	20 29	3 20	18 10	23 07	11 49	12 40	7 57	15 32	4 20
8 W	15 2 8	17 08 14	24 50	19 23	2 17	21 00	24 44	23 13	20 28	3 23	18 12	23 07	11 38	12 29	8 26	15 59	4 23
9 Th	15 6 4	18 06 18	8♋30	19 21 D	4 11	22 13	25 23	23 08	20 27	3 27	18 13	23 06	11 28	12 18	8 56	16 26	4 26
10 F	15 10 1	19 04 21	22 20	19 20	6 06	23 26	26 02	23 03	20 26	3 30	18 14	23 06	11 17	12 08	9 25	16 53	4 29
11 Sa	15 13 58	20 02 21	6♌17	19 21	8 03	24 39	26 41	22 58	20 25	3 33	18 16	23 05	11 06	11 58	9 54	17 20	4 31
12 Su	15 17 54	21 00 20	20 21	19 21℞	10 02	25 52	27 20	22 53	20 24	3 37	18 17	23 05	10 55	11 49	10 24	17 47	4 34
13 M	15 21 51	21 58 16	4♍31	19 21	12 03	27 05	27 58	22 47	20 23	3 40	18 18	23 04	10 43	11 40	10 53	18 14	4 37
14 T	15 25 47	22 56 11	18 47	19 18	14 05	28 17	28 37	22 41	20 22	3 43	18 20	23 04	10 31	11 32	11 23	18 41	4 39
15 W	15 29 44	23 54 04	3♎04	19 13	16 09	29 30	29 16	22 36	20 20	3 46	18 21	23 03	10 19	11 24	11 52	19 07	4 42
16 Th	15 33 40	24 51 55	17 20	19 06	18 15	0♉43	29 55	22 30	20 19	3 50	18 22	23 03	10 07	11 16	12 22	19 34	4 44
17 F	15 37 37	25 49 44	1♏31	18 58	20 22	1 56	0♋34	22 24	20 17	3 53	18 23	23 02	9 55	11 09	12 51	20 00	4 47
18 Sa	15 41 33	26 47 32	15 30	18 50	22 30	3 09	1 12	22 18	20 16	3 56	18 24	23 01	9 42	11 03	13 20	20 27	4 49
19 Su	15 45 30	27 45 19	29 14	18 42	24 39	4 22	1 51	22 12	20 14	3 59	18 25	23 01	9 30	10 57	13 50	20 53	4 52
20 M	15 49 27	28 43 04	12♐40	18 35	26 50	5 35	2 30	22 05	20 12	4 03	18 26	23 00	9 17	10 51	14 19	21 19	4 54
21 T	15 53 23	29 40 48	25 45	18 31	29 01	6 48	3 09	21 59	20 10	4 06	18 27	22 59	9 04	10 46	14 49	21 46	4 56
22 W	15 57 20	0♊38 30	8♑30	18 28 D	1♊12	8 01	3 47	21 52	20 08	4 09	18 28	22 59	8 51	10 42	15 18	22 12	4 59
23 Th	16 1 16	1 36 12	20 56	18 28	3 24	9 14	4 26	21 46	20 06	4 12	18 29	22 58	8 38	10 38	15 48	22 38	5 01
24 F	16 5 13	2 33 52	3♒07	18 29	5 35	10 27	5 05	21 39	20 04	4 15	18 30	22 57	8 25	10 34	16 17	23 04	5 03
25 Sa	16 9 9	3 31 32	15 06	18 30	7 46	11 39	5 43	21 32	20 02	4 18	18 31	22 56	8 11	10 31	16 46	23 30	5 05
26 Su	16 13 6	4 29 10	26 59	18 31℞	9 57	12 52	6 22	21 25	19 59	4 22	18 32	22 55	7 58	10 29	17 16	23 56	5 08
27 M	16 17 2	5 26 47	8♓49	18 32	12 07	14 05	7 00	21 18	19 57	4 25	18 33	22 55	7 45	10 26	17 45	24 22	5 10
28 T	16 20 59	6 24 23	20 43	18 30	14 15	15 18	7 39	21 11	19 54	4 28	18 34	22 54	7 31	10 25	18 15	24 47	5 12
29 W	16 24 56	7 21 59	2♈46	18 27	16 23	16 31	8 17	21 04	19 52	4 31	18 34	22 53	7 18	10 24	18 44	25 13	5 14
30 Th	16 28 52	8 19 33	15 00	18 23	18 28	17 44	8 56	20 56	19 49	4 34	18 35	22 52	7 04	10 23	19 13	25 39	5 16
31 F	16 32 49	9 17 06	27 30	18 17	20 32	18 57	9 35	20 49	19 46	4 37	18 36	22 51	6 51	10 23D	19 43	26 04	5 18

EPHEMERIS CALCULATED FOR 12 MIDNIGHT GREENWICH MEAN TIME. ALL OTHER DATA AND FACING ASPECTARIAN PAGE IN **EASTERN TIME (BOLD)** AND PACIFIC TIME (REGULAR).

JUNE 2019

☽ Last Aspect day	ET / hr:mn	PT	asp	☽ Ingress sign	day	ET / hr:mn	PT
1	**6:53 pm**	3:53 pm	△♇	♊	2	**7:48 am**	4:48 am
4	**11:42 am**	8:42 am	☌☿	♋	4	**12:17 pm**	9:17 am
6	**10:10 am**	7:10 am	✶♀	♌	6	**3:16 pm**	12:16 pm
8	**5:23 pm**	2:23 pm	□♀	♍	8	**5:45 pm**	2:45 pm
10	**8:01 am**	5:01 am	△♇	♎	10	**8:29 pm**	5:29 pm
12	**11:15 am**	8:15 am	□♇	♏	12		9:02 pm
12	**11:15 am**	8:15 am	□♇	♏	13	**12:02 am**	
14	**3:46 pm**	12:46 pm	✶♇	♐	15	**5:03 am**	2:03 am
17	**4:31 am**	1:31 am	☍☉	♑	17	**12:13 pm**	9:13 am
19	**7:19 am**	4:19 am	☍☿	♒	19	**10:01 pm**	7:01 pm
21	**10:02 am**	7:02 am	✶♃	♓	22	**10:01 am**	7:01 am
24	**7:10 pm**	4:10 pm	△☿	♈	24	**10:38 pm**	7:38 pm
27	**3:51 am**	12:51 am	□♂	♉	27	**9:32 am**	6:32 am
29	**2:38 pm**	11:38 am	✶♂	♊	29	**5:09 pm**	2:09 pm

☽ Phases & Eclipses phase	day	ET / hr:mn	PT
New Moon	3	**6:02 am**	3:02 am
2nd Quarter	9		10:59 pm
2nd Quarter	10	**1:59 am**	
Full Moon	17	**4:31 am**	1:31 am
4th Quarter	25	**5:46 am**	2:46 am

Planet Ingress		day	ET / hr:mn	PT
☿	♋	4	**4:05 pm**	1:05 pm
♀	♊	8	**9:37 pm**	6:37 pm
⚴	♉	9	**5:55 am**	2:55 am
⚵	♌	20	**10:37 pm**	7:37 pm
☉	♋	21	**11:54 am**	8:54 am
☿	♌	26	**8:19 pm**	5:19 pm

Planetary Motion		day	ET / hr:mn	PT
♆	R	21	**10:36 am**	7:36 am

1 SATURDAY				
♀⚻♃	**5:20**	**am**	2:20	am
☽✶♆	**11:15**	**am**	8:15	am
☽△♄	**1:12**	**pm**	10:12	am
☽⚻♃	**2:52**	**pm**	11:52	am
☽☌♀	**3:55**	**pm**	12:55	pm
☽△♇	**6:53**	**pm**	3:53	pm
☽⚺☿	**10:22**	**pm**	7:22	pm
2 SUNDAY				
☽⚺♅	**4:15**	**pm**	1:15	pm
♀△♇	**11:42**	**pm**	8:42	pm
3 MONDAY				
☽⚺♂	**4:34**	**am**	1:34	am
☽☌☉	**6:02**	**am**	3:02	am
☽□♆	**4:39**	**pm**	1:39	pm
☽⚻♄	**6:17**	**pm**	3:17	pm
☽☍♃	**7:35**	**pm**	4:35	pm
☽⚻♇	**11:50**	**pm**	8:50	pm
☽⚺♀			11:11	pm
4 TUESDAY				
☽⚺♀	**2:11**	**am**		
☽☌☿	**11:42**	**am**	8:42	am
☽✶♅	**8:36**	**pm**	5:36	pm
5 WEDNESDAY				
☽☌♂	**10:48**	**am**	7:48	am
☽⚺☉	**1:31**	**pm**	10:31	am
☽△♆	**8:06**	**pm**	5:06	pm
☽☍♄	**9:28**	**pm**	6:28	pm
☽⚻♃	**10:28**	**pm**	7:28	pm
6 THURSDAY				
☽☍♇	**3:00**	**am**	12:00	am
☽✶♀	**10:10**	**am**	7:10	am
☽⚺☿	**10:09**	**pm**	7:09	pm
☽□♅	**11:37**	**pm**	8:37	pm
7 FRIDAY				
☿✶♅	**10:16**	**am**	7:16	am
☽⚺♂	**3:50**	**pm**	12:50	pm
☽✶☉	**7:47**	**pm**	4:47	pm
☽⚻♆	**10:42**	**pm**	7:42	pm
☽⚻♄	**11:50**	**pm**	8:50	pm
☽△♃			9:35	pm
8 SATURDAY				
☽△♃	**12:35**	**am**		
☽⚻♇	**5:28**	**am**	2:28	am
☽□♀	**5:23**	**pm**	2:23	pm
☽△♅			11:16	pm
9 SUNDAY				
☽△♅	**2:16**	**am**		
☽✶☿	**7:33**	**am**	4:33	am
☉□♆	**3:34**	**pm**	12:34	pm
☽✶♂	**8:45**	**pm**	5:45	pm
☽☍♆			10:17	pm
☽□☉			10:59	pm
☽△♄			11:12	pm
☽□♃			11:42	pm
10 MONDAY				
☽☍♆	**1:17**	**am**		
☽□☉	**1:59**	**am**		
☽△♄	**2:12**	**am**		
☽□♃	**2:42**	**am**		
☉⚻♄	**5:04**	**am**	2:04	am
☽△♇	**8:01**	**am**	5:01	am
☉☍♃	**11:28**	**am**	8:28	am
☽△♀			9:55	pm
11 TUESDAY				
☽△♀	**12:55**	**am**		
☽⚻♅	**5:15**	**am**	2:15	am
☽□☿	**5:03**	**pm**	2:03	pm
☽□♂			11:19	pm
12 WEDNESDAY				
☽□♂	**2:19**	**am**		
☽⚻♆	**4:29**	**am**	1:29	am
☽□♄	**5:11**	**am**	2:11	am
☽✶♃	**5:27**	**am**	2:27	am
☽△☉	**8:57**	**am**	5:57	am
☽□♇	**11:15**	**am**	8:15	am
13 THURSDAY				
♀⚺♅	**4:41**	**am**	1:41	am
☽☍♅	**9:11**	**am**	6:11	am
☽⚻♀	**9:36**	**am**	6:36	am
☉⚻♇	**5:45**	**pm**	2:45	pm
♂△♆			11:11	pm
14 FRIDAY				
♂△♆	**2:11**	**am**		
☽△☿	**3:33**	**am**	12:33	am
☽△♆	**8:53**	**am**	5:53	am
☽△♂	**9:13**	**am**	6:13	am
☽✶♄	**9:21**	**am**	6:21	am
☽⚺♃	**9:22**	**am**	6:22	am
♂☍♄	**11:50**	**am**	8:50	am
♂⚻♃	**11:53**	**am**	8:53	am
♃⚺♄	**12:28**	**pm**	9:28	am
☽✶♇	**3:46**	**pm**	12:46	pm
☽⚻☉	**5:29**	**pm**	2:29	pm
15 SATURDAY				
☽⚻♅	**2:41**	**pm**	11:41	am
☽☍♀	**8:23**	**pm**	5:23	pm
16 SUNDAY				
☿△♆	**7:43**	**am**	4:43	am
☿⚻♃	**8:02**	**am**	5:02	am
☿☍♄	**10:00**	**am**	7:00	am
♃□♆	**11:22**	**am**	8:22	am
☽☌♃	**3:09**	**pm**	12:09	pm
☽□♆	**3:11**	**pm**	12:11	pm
☽⚺♄	**3:23**	**pm**	12:23	pm
☽⚻☿	**4:02**	**pm**	1:02	pm
☽⚻♂	**6:19**	**pm**	3:19	pm
☽⚺♇	**10:15**	**pm**	7:15	pm
17 MONDAY				
☽☍☉	**4:31**	**am**	1:31	am
☽△♅	**10:29**	**pm**	7:29	pm
18 TUESDAY				
♄✶♆	**7:47**	**am**	4:47	am
☽⚻♀	**10:17**	**am**	7:17	am
☿☌♂	**12:04**	**pm**	9:04	am
☽⚺♃	**11:22**	**pm**	8:22	pm
☽☌♄	**11:53**	**pm**	8:53	pm
☽✶♆	**11:59**	**pm**	8:59	pm
19 WEDNESDAY				
☽☍♂	**6:22**	**am**	3:22	am
☿☍♇	**6:56**	**am**	3:56	am
☽☌♇	**7:17**	**am**	4:17	am
☽☍☿	**7:19**	**am**	4:19	am
☽⚻☉	**6:48**	**pm**	3:48	pm
♂☍♇	**11:26**	**pm**	8:26	pm
20 THURSDAY				
☽□♅	**8:56**	**am**	5:56	am
21 FRIDAY				
☽△♀	**3:42**	**am**	12:42	am
☽✶♃	**10:02**	**am**	7:02	am
☽⚺♄	**10:52**	**am**	7:52	am
☽⚺♆	**11:17**	**am**	8:17	am
☽⚺♇	**6:44**	**pm**	3:44	pm
☽⚻♂	**9:16**	**pm**	6:16	pm
☽⚻☿			10:06	pm
22 SATURDAY				
☽⚻☿	**1:06**	**am**		
☽△☉	**11:57**	**am**	8:57	am
☽✶♅	**9:25**	**pm**	6:25	pm
23 SUNDAY				
♀☍♃	**12:45**	**pm**	9:45	am
☽□♃	**10:03**	**pm**	7:03	pm
♀⚻♄	**10:32**	**pm**	7:32	pm
☽✶♄	**11:09**	**pm**	8:09	pm
☽□♀	**11:14**	**pm**	8:14	pm
☽☌♆	**11:55**	**pm**	8:55	pm
24 MONDAY				
♀□♆	**5:58**	**am**	2:58	am
☽✶♇	**7:17**	**am**	4:17	am
☽△♂	**1:22**	**pm**	10:22	am
☽△☿	**7:10**	**pm**	4:10	pm
25 TUESDAY				
☽□☉	**5:46**	**am**	2:46	am
☽⚺♅	**10:03**	**am**	7:03	am
26 WEDNESDAY				
☽△♃	**9:20**	**am**	6:20	am
☽□♄	**10:38**	**am**	7:38	am
☽⚺♆	**11:42**	**am**	8:42	am
☽✶♀	**5:38**	**pm**	2:38	pm
☽□♇	**6:43**	**pm**	3:43	pm
27 THURSDAY				
☽□♂	**3:51**	**am**	12:51	am
♀⚻♇	**4:20**	**am**	1:20	am
☽□☿	**10:23**	**am**	7:23	am
☉✶♅	**1:45**	**pm**	10:45	am
☽☌♅	**8:34**	**pm**	5:34	pm
☽✶☉	**9:06**	**pm**	6:06	pm
28 FRIDAY				
☽⚻♃	**5:55**	**pm**	2:55	pm
☽△♄	**7:20**	**pm**	4:20	pm
☽✶♆	**8:38**	**pm**	5:38	pm
29 SATURDAY				
☽△♇	**3:08**	**am**	12:08	am
☽⚺♀	**8:01**	**am**	5:01	am
☽✶♂	**2:38**	**pm**	11:38	am
☽✶☿	**8:51**	**pm**	5:51	pm
30 SUNDAY				
☽⚺♅	**3:38**	**am**	12:38	am
☽⚺☉	**8:09**	**am**	5:09	am
☽☍♃	**11:06**	**pm**	8:06	pm
☽⚻♄			9:34	pm
☽□♆			11:03	pm

Eastern time in bold type
Pacific time in medium type

JUNE 2019

DATE	SID.TIME	SUN	MOON	NODE	MERCURY	VENUS	MARS	JUPITER	SATURN	URANUS	NEPTUNE	PLUTO	CERES	PALLAS	JUNO	VESTA	CHIRON
1 Sa	16 36 45	10 ♊ 14 39	10 ♉ 19	18 ♋ 11 ℞	22 ♊ 34	20 ♉ 10	10 ♋ 13	20 ♐ 42 ℞	19 ♑ 43 ℞	4 ♉ 40	18 ♓ 37	22 ♑ 50 ℞	6 ♐ 38 ℞	10 ♎ 23	20 ♋ 12	26 ♈ 29	5 ♈ 20
2 Su	16 40 42	11 12 11	23 26	18 05	24 33	21 24	10 52	20 34	19 41	4 43	18 37	22 49	6 24	10 23	20 42	26 55	5 22
3 M	16 44 38	12 09 42	6 ♊ 52	17 59	26 31	22 37	11 30	20 27	19 38	4 46	18 38	22 48	6 11	10 24	21 11	27 20	5 23
4 T	16 48 35	13 07 12	20 34	17 55	28 26	23 50	12 09	20 19	19 34	4 48	18 38	22 47	5 58	10 26	21 40	27 45	5 25
5 W	16 52 31	14 04 40	4 ♋ 30	17 53 D	0 ♋ 18	25 03	12 47	20 12	19 31	4 51	18 39	22 46	5 45	10 28	22 10	28 10	5 27
6 Th	16 56 28	15 02 08	18 36	17 52	2 08	26 16	13 26	20 04	19 28	4 54	18 39	22 45	5 32	10 30	22 39	28 35	5 29
7 F	17 0 25	15 59 35	2 ♌ 49	17 53	3 56	27 29	14 04	19 57	19 25	4 57	18 40	22 44	5 19	10 33	23 08	29 00	5 30
8 Sa	17 4 21	16 57 01	17 04	17 54	5 41	28 42	14 42	19 49	19 22	5 00	18 40	22 43	5 07	10 36	23 38	29 25	5 32
9 Su	17 8 18	17 54 25	1 ♍ 20	17 56	7 23	29 55	15 21	19 41	19 18	5 02	18 41	22 42	4 54	10 40	24 07	29 50	5 33
10 M	17 12 14	18 51 48	15 34	17 56 ℞	9 03	1 ♊ 08	15 59	19 34	19 15	5 05	18 41	22 40	4 42	10 44	24 36	0 ♉ 14	5 35
11 T	17 16 11	19 49 10	29 43	17 56	10 40	2 21	16 38	19 26	19 11	5 08	18 42	22 39	4 30	10 49	25 05	0 39	5 36
12 W	17 20 7	20 46 31	13 ♎ 46	17 55	12 14	3 34	17 16	19 18	19 08	5 10	18 42	22 38	4 18	10 53	25 35	1 03	5 38
13 Th	17 24 4	21 43 51	27 40	17 52	13 45	4 48	17 54	19 11	19 04	5 13	18 42	22 37	4 06	10 59	26 04	1 28	5 39
14 F	17 28 0	22 41 10	11 ♏ 25	17 49	15 14	6 01	18 33	19 03	19 00	5 16	18 43	22 36	3 55	11 04	26 33	1 52	5 40
15 Sa	17 31 57	23 38 28	24 57	17 45	16 40	7 14	19 11	18 55	18 57	5 18	18 43	22 34	3 44	11 10	27 02	2 16	5 41
16 Su	17 35 54	24 35 46	8 ♐ 16	17 42	18 03	8 27	19 49	18 48	18 53	5 21	18 43	22 33	3 33	11 17	27 31	2 40	5 43
17 M	17 39 50	25 33 02	21 19	17 39	19 24	9 40	20 28	18 40	18 49	5 23	18 43	22 32	3 22	11 24	28 00	3 04	5 44
18 T	17 43 47	26 30 19	4 ♑ 07	17 37	20 41	10 53	21 06	18 33	18 45	5 26	18 43	22 31	3 12	11 31	28 30	3 28	5 45
19 W	17 47 43	27 27 34	16 40	17 37 D	21 56	12 07	21 44	18 25	18 41	5 28	18 43	22 29	3 01	11 38	28 59	3 52	5 46
20 Th	17 51 40	28 24 49	28 59	17 37	23 07	13 20	22 22	18 18	18 37	5 31	18 43	22 28	2 51	11 46	29 28	4 16	5 47
21 F	17 55 36	29 22 04	11 ♒ 06	17 38	24 16	14 33	23 01	18 10	18 33	5 33	18 43 ℞	22 27	2 42	11 54	29 57	4 39	5 48
22 Sa	17 59 33	0 ♋ 19 19	23 03	17 40	25 21	15 46	23 39	18 03	18 29	5 35	18 43	22 26	2 33	12 03	0 ♌ 26	5 03	5 49
23 Su	18 3 30	1 16 33	4 ♓ 56	17 41	26 24	17 00	24 17	17 56	18 25	5 37	18 43	22 24	2 23	12 12	0 55	5 26	5 50
24 M	18 7 26	2 13 47	16 47	17 42	27 23	18 13	24 55	17 49	18 21	5 40	18 43	22 23	2 15	12 21	1 24	5 49	5 51
25 T	18 11 23	3 11 00	28 41	17 43 ℞	28 18	19 26	25 34	17 41	18 17	5 42	18 43	22 22	2 06	12 30	1 53	6 12	5 51
26 W	18 15 19	4 08 14	10 ♈ 44	17 43	29 11	20 39	26 12	17 34	18 13	5 44	18 43	22 20	1 58	12 40	2 22	6 35	5 52
27 Th	18 19 16	5 05 28	22 59	17 42	29 59	21 53	26 50	17 27	18 08	5 46	18 43	22 19	1 51	12 50	2 51	6 58	5 53
28 F	18 23 12	6 02 42	5 ♉ 30	17 41	0 ♌ 44	23 06	27 28	17 20	18 04	5 48	18 43	22 17	1 43	13 01	3 20	7 21	5 53
29 Sa	18 27 9	6 59 55	18 22	17 40	1 26	24 20	28 07	17 13	18 00	5 50	18 43	22 16	1 36	13 11	3 49	7 44	5 54
30 Su	18 31 5	7 57 09	1 ♊ 36	17 38	2 03	25 33	28 45	17 07	17 56	5 52	18 42	22 15	1 29	13 22	4 18	8 06	5 54

EPHEMERIS CALCULATED FOR 12 MIDNIGHT GREENWICH MEAN TIME. ALL OTHER DATA AND FACING ASPECTARIAN PAGE IN **EASTERN TIME (BOLD)** AND PACIFIC TIME (REGULAR).

JULY 2019

☽ Last Aspect / ☽ Ingress

day	ET / hr:mn / PT		asp	sign	day	ET / hr:mn / PT	
1	**5:48 pm**	2:48 pm	☌ ♀	♋	1	**9:24 pm**	6:24 pm
3	**10:25 am**	7:25 am	☍ ♇	♌	3	**11:19 pm**	8:19 pm
4		11:24 pm	△ ♃	♍	5		9:25 pm
5	**2:24 am**		△ ♃	♍	6	**12:25 am**	
7	**12:50 pm**	9:50 am	△ ♇	♎	7		11:07 pm
7	**12:50 pm**	9:50 am	△ ♇	♎	8	**2:07 am**	
9	**3:36 pm**	12:36 pm	□ ♇	♏	10	**5:29 am**	2:29 am
11	**8:28 pm**	5:28 pm	✶ ♇	♐	12	**11:05 am**	8:05 am
13	**9:30 pm**	6:30 pm	□ ♆	♑	14	**7:05 pm**	4:05 pm
16	**5:38 pm**	2:38 pm	☍ ☉	♒	17	**5:19 am**	2:19 am
18	**11:53 am**	8:53 am	✶ ♃	♓	19	**5:19 pm**	2:19 pm
22	**4:34 am**	1:34 am	△ ☉	♈	22	**6:02 am**	3:02 am
24	**10:48 am**	7:48 am	□ ☿	♉	24	**5:42 pm**	2:42 pm
26		9:28 pm	✶ ♀	♊	26		11:29 pm
27	**12:28 am**		✶ ♀	♊	27	**2:29 am**	
28	**11:24 am**	8:24 am	□ ♆	♋	29	**7:31 am**	4:31 am
30	**11:32 pm**	8:32 pm	☌ ☿	♌	31	**9:18 am**	6:18 am

☽ Phases & Eclipses

phase	day	ET / hr:mn / PT	
New Moon	2	**3:16 pm**	12:16 pm
(solar eclipse)	2	10° ♋	38'
2nd Quarter	9	**6:55 am**	3:55 am
Full Moon	16	**5:38 pm**	2:38 pm
(lunar eclipse)	16	24° ♑	04'
4th Quarter	24	**9:18 pm**	6:18 pm
New Moon	31	**11:12 pm**	8:12 pm

Planet Ingress

		day	ET / hr:mn / PT	
♂	♌	1	**7:19 pm**	4:19 pm
♀	♋	3	**11:18 am**	8:18 am
☿	♋	19	**3:06 am**	12:06 am
☉	♌	22	**10:50 pm**	7:50 pm
♀	♌	27	**9:54 pm**	6:54 pm

Planetary Motion

		day	ET / hr:mn / PT	
☿	℞	7	**7:14 pm**	4:14 pm
⚷	℞	8	**7:40 pm**	4:40 pm
⚳	D	17	**3:06 pm**	12:06 pm
☿	D	31	**11:58 pm**	8:58 pm

1 MONDAY
☽ ⚻ ♄ **12:34 am**
☽ □ ♆ **2:03 am**
☽ ⚻ ♇ **8:06 am** 5:06 am
☽ ☌ ♀ **5:48 pm** 2:48 pm
☽ ⚺ ♂ **9:30 pm** 6:30 pm
☽ ⚺ ☿ 11:50 pm

2 TUESDAY
☽ ⚺ ☿ **2:50 am**
☽ ✶ ♅ **7:27 am** 4:27 am
☽ ☌ ☉ **3:16 pm** 12:16 pm
☽ ⚻ ♃ 10:29 pm

3 WEDNESDAY
☽ ⚻ ♃ **1:29 am**
☽ ☍ ♄ **3:01 am** 12:01 am
☽ △ ♆ **4:40 am** 1:40 am
☽ ☍ ♇ **10:25 am** 7:25 am
☽ ⚺ ♀ 9:25 pm
☽ ☌ ♂ 10:41 pm

4 THURSDAY
☽ ⚺ ♀ **12:25 am**
☽ ☌ ♂ **1:41 am**
☽ ☌ ☿ **5:50 am** 2:50 am
☽ □ ♅ **9:11 am** 6:11 am
☽ ⚺ ☉ **8:10 pm** 5:10 pm
☽ △ ♃ 11:24 pm

5 FRIDAY
☽ △ ♃ **2:24 am**
☽ ⚻ ♄ **4:02 am** 1:02 am
☽ ⚻ ♆ **5:53 am** 2:53 am
♀ ⚺ ♂ **6:32 am** 3:32 am
☽ ⚻ ♇ **11:30 am** 8:30 am

6 SATURDAY
☽ ⚺ ♂ **5:01 am** 2:01 am
☽ ✶ ♀ **6:00 am** 3:00 am
☽ ⚺ ☿ **7:36 am** 4:36 am
☽ △ ♅ **10:24 am** 7:24 am
☽ ✶ ☉ 9:49 pm
☿ ⚺ ♀ 11:26 pm

7 SUNDAY
☽ ✶ ☉ **12:49 am**
☿ ⚺ ♀ **2:26 am**
☽ □ ♃ **3:20 am** 12:20 am
☽ △ ♄ **5:04 am** 2:04 am
☽ ☍ ♆ **7:11 am** 4:11 am
☽ △ ♇ **12:50 pm** 9:50 am

8 MONDAY
☽ ✶ ♂ **9:09 am** 6:09 am
☽ ✶ ☿ **9:37 am** 6:37 am
♀ ✶ ♅ **11:32 am** 8:32 am
☉ ⚻ ♃ **11:48 am** 8:48 am
☽ ⚻ ♅ **12:28 pm** 9:28 am
☽ □ ♀ **12:33 pm** 9:33 am
☿ ☌ ♂ **6:27 pm** 3:27 pm

9 TUESDAY
☽ ✶ ♃ **5:30 am** 2:30 am
☽ □ ☉ **6:55 am** 3:55 am
☽ □ ♄ **7:22 am** 4:22 am
☽ ⚻ ♆ **9:47 am** 6:47 am
☉ ☍ ♄ **1:07 pm** 10:07 am
☽ □ ♇ **3:36 pm** 12:36 pm

10 WEDNESDAY
☽ □ ☿ **12:48 pm** 9:48 am
☽ □ ♂ **3:20 pm** 12:20 pm
☽ ☍ ♅ **4:21 pm** 1:21 pm
☽ △ ♀ **9:29 pm** 6:29 pm
☉ △ ♆ 9:31 pm

11 THURSDAY
☉ △ ♆ **12:31 am**
☽ ⚺ ♃ **9:40 am** 6:40 am
☽ ✶ ♄ **11:42 am** 8:42 am
♂ □ ♅ **2:01 pm** 11:01 am
☽ △ ♆ **2:28 pm** 11:28 am
☽ △ ☉ **3:33 pm** 12:33 pm
☽ ✶ ♇ **8:28 pm** 5:28 pm

12 FRIDAY
☽ △ ☿ **5:33 pm** 2:33 pm
☽ ⚻ ♅ **10:33 pm** 7:33 pm
☽ △ ♂ 9:10 pm

13 SATURDAY
☽ △ ♂ **12:10 am**
☽ ⚻ ♀ **9:30 am** 6:30 am
☽ ☌ ♃ **4:11 pm** 1:11 pm
☽ ⚺ ♄ **6:21 pm** 3:21 pm
☽ □ ♆ **9:30 pm** 6:30 pm

14 SUNDAY
☽ ⚻ ☉ **3:08 am** 12:08 am
☽ ⚺ ♇ **3:44 am** 12:44 am
☉ ☍ ♇ **10:51 am** 7:51 am
☽ ⚻ ☿ **11:53 pm** 8:53 pm

15 MONDAY
☽ △ ♅ **7:08 am** 4:08 am
☽ ⚻ ♂ **11:44 am** 8:44 am
☽ ☍ ♀ 9:42 pm
☽ ⚺ ♃ 10:01 pm

16 TUESDAY
☽ ☍ ♀ **12:42 am**
☽ ⚺ ♃ **1:01 am**
☽ ☌ ♄ **3:18 am** 12:18 am
♀ ⚻ ♃ **3:44 am** 12:44 am
☽ ✶ ♆ **6:52 am** 3:52 am
☽ ☌ ♇ **1:16 pm** 10:16 am
☽ ☍ ☉ **5:38 pm** 2:38 pm
♀ ☍ ♄ 10:34 pm

17 WEDNESDAY
♀ ☍ ♄ **1:34 am**
☽ ☍ ☿ **7:39 am** 4:39 am
☽ □ ♅ **5:54 pm** 2:54 pm
☽ ☍ ♂ 10:50 pm

18 THURSDAY
☽ ☍ ♂ **1:50 am**
☽ ✶ ♃ **11:53 am** 8:53 am
♀ △ ♆ **2:03 pm** 11:03 am
☽ ⚺ ♄ **2:15 pm** 11:15 am
☽ ⚺ ♆ **6:13 pm** 3:13 pm
☽ ⚻ ♀ **6:42 pm** 3:42 pm
☽ ⚺ ♇ 9:45 pm

19 FRIDAY
☽ ⚺ ♇ **12:45 am**
☽ ⚻ ☉ **10:33 am** 7:33 am
☽ ⚻ ☿ **4:33 pm** 1:33 pm

20 SATURDAY
☽ ✶ ♅ **6:16 am** 3:16 am
☽ ⚻ ♂ **5:39 pm** 2:39 pm
☽ □ ♃ 9:06 pm
☽ ✶ ♄ 11:28 pm

21 SUNDAY
☽ □ ♃ **12:06 am**
☽ ✶ ♄ **2:28 am**
♀ ☍ ♇ **4:32 am** 1:32 am
☽ ☌ ♆ **6:46 am** 3:46 am
☉ ☌ ☿ **8:34 am** 5:34 am
☽ ✶ ♇ **1:18 pm** 10:18 am
☽ △ ♀ **2:20 pm** 11:20 am
☽ △ ☿ 10:58 pm

22 MONDAY
☽ △ ☿ **1:58 am**
☽ △ ☉ **4:34 am** 1:34 am
☽ ⚺ ♅ **7:01 pm** 4:01 pm

23 TUESDAY
☽ △ ♂ **9:34 am** 6:34 am
☽ △ ♃ **12:14 pm** 9:14 am
☽ □ ♄ **2:31 pm** 11:31 am
☽ ⚺ ♆ **6:59 pm** 3:59 pm
☽ □ ♇ 10:20 pm

24 WEDNESDAY
☽ □ ♇ **1:20 am**
☽ □ ♀ **9:12 am** 6:12 am
☽ □ ☿ **10:48 am** 7:48 am
☿ ☌ ♀ **8:26 pm** 5:26 pm
☽ □ ☉ **9:18 pm** 6:18 pm

25 THURSDAY
☽ ☌ ♅ **6:17 am** 3:17 am
♂ △ ♃ **8:23 am** 5:23 am
☽ ⚻ ♃ **10:24 pm** 7:24 pm
☽ □ ♂ **11:12 pm** 8:12 pm
☽ △ ♄ 9:29 pm

26 FRIDAY
☽ △ ♄ **12:29 am**
☽ ✶ ♆ **4:59 am** 1:59 am
☽ △ ♇ **10:57 am** 7:57 am
☽ ✶ ☿ **5:44 pm** 2:44 pm
♂ ⚻ ♄ **10:41 pm** 7:41 pm
☽ ✶ ♀ 9:28 pm

27 SATURDAY
☽ ✶ ♀ **12:28 am**
☽ ✶ ☉ **10:16 am** 7:16 am
☽ ⚺ ♅ **2:20 pm** 11:20 am

28 SUNDAY
☽ ☍ ♃ **5:08 am** 2:08 am
☽ ⚻ ♄ **7:00 am** 4:00 am
☽ ✶ ♂ **8:45 am** 5:45 am
☽ □ ♆ **11:24 am** 8:24 am
☽ ⚻ ♇ **4:57 pm** 1:57 pm
☽ ⚺ ☿ **9:55 pm** 6:55 pm

29 MONDAY
☽ ⚺ ♀ **10:44 am** 7:44 am
☽ ⚺ ☉ **6:34 pm** 3:34 pm
☽ ✶ ♅ **6:37 pm** 3:37 pm
☉ □ ♅ **7:14 pm** 4:14 pm

30 TUESDAY
☽ ⚻ ♃ **8:17 am** 5:17 am
☽ ☍ ♄ **9:57 am** 6:57 am
☽ ⚺ ♂ **2:09 pm** 11:09 am
☽ △ ♆ **2:15 pm** 11:15 am
♂ ⚻ ♆ **4:09 pm** 1:09 pm
☽ ☍ ♇ **7:27 pm** 4:27 pm
☽ ☌ ☿ **11:32 pm** 8:32 pm

31 WEDNESDAY
☽ ☌ ♀ **4:51 pm** 1:51 pm
☽ □ ♅ **7:54 pm** 4:54 pm
☽ ☌ ☉ **11:12 pm** 8:12 pm

Eastern time in bold type
Pacific time in medium type

JULY 2019

DATE	SID.TIME	SUN	MOON	NODE	MERCURY	VENUS	MARS	JUPITER	SATURN	URANUS	NEPTUNE	PLUTO	CERES	PALLAS	JUNO	VESTA	CHIRON
1 M	18 35 2	8 ♋ 54 23	15 ♊ 12	17 ♋ 37 ℞	2 ♌ 36	26 ♊ 46	29 ♋ 23	17 ♐ 00 ℞	17 ♑ 51 ℞	5 ♉ 54	18 ♓ 42 ℞	22 ♑ 13 ℞	1 ♐ 23 ℞	13 ♎ 34	4 ♌ 46	8 ♉ 28	5 ♈ 55
2 T	18 38 59	9 51 37	29 11	17 37	3 06	28 00	0 ♌ 01	16 53	17 47	5 56	18 42	22 12	1 17	13 45	5 15	8 51	5 55
3 W	18 42 55	10 48 50	13 ♋ 28	17 36D	3 31	29 13	0 39	16 47	17 43	5 58	18 41	22 10	1 11	13 57	5 44	9 13	5 55
4 Th	18 46 52	11 46 04	27 59	17 36	3 51	0 ♋ 27	1 17	16 41	17 38	6 00	18 41	22 09	1 06	14 10	6 13	9 35	5 56
5 F	18 50 48	12 43 18	12 ♌ 38	17 37	4 07	1 40	1 56	16 34	17 34	6 02	18 41	22 08	1 01	14 22	6 42	9 57	5 56
6 Sa	18 54 45	13 40 31	27 18	17 37	4 19	2 54	2 34	16 28	17 29	6 04	18 40	22 06	0 57	14 35	7 10	10 19	5 56
7 Su	18 58 41	14 37 44	11 ♍ 54	17 37	4 26 ℞	4 07	3 12	16 22	17 25	6 05	18 40	22 05	0 52	14 48	7 39	10 40	5 56
8 M	19 2 38	15 34 57	26 21	17 38	4 28	5 21	3 50	16 16	17 21	6 07	18 39	22 03	0 49	15 01	8 08	11 02	5 56 ℞
9 T	19 6 34	16 32 09	10 ♎ 35	17 38 ℞	4 25	6 34	4 28	16 11	17 16	6 09	18 39	22 02	0 45	15 15	8 36	11 23	5 56
10 W	19 10 31	17 29 21	24 33	17 38D	4 18	7 48	5 06	16 05	17 12	6 10	18 38	22 00	0 42	15 29	9 05	11 44	5 56
11 Th	19 14 28	18 26 33	8 ♏ 16	17 38	4 06	9 01	5 44	16 00	17 07	6 12	18 37	21 59	0 39	15 43	9 34	12 05	5 56
12 F	19 18 24	19 23 45	21 42	17 38	3 50	10 15	6 23	15 54	17 03	6 13	18 37	21 57	0 37	15 57	10 02	12 26	5 56
13 Sa	19 22 21	20 20 58	4 ♐ 52	17 38	3 29	11 28	7 01	15 49	16 58	6 15	18 36	21 56	0 35	16 11	10 31	12 47	5 56
14 Su	19 26 17	21 18 10	17 47	17 38	3 04	12 42	7 39	15 44	16 54	6 16	18 35	21 54	0 33	16 26	10 59	13 08	5 56
15 M	19 30 14	22 15 22	0 ♑ 29	17 39	2 36	13 56	8 17	15 39	16 50	6 18	18 35	21 53	0 32	16 41	11 28	13 28	5 55
16 T	19 34 10	23 12 34	12 58	17 39 ℞	2 04	15 09	8 55	15 34	16 45	6 19	18 34	21 52	0 31	16 56	11 56	13 48	5 55
17 W	19 38 7	24 09 47	25 16	17 39	1 29	16 23	9 33	15 30	16 41	6 20	18 33	21 50	0 31 D	17 12	12 25	14 08	5 55
18 Th	19 42 3	25 07 00	7 ♒ 25	17 39	0 51	17 36	10 11	15 25	16 37	6 21	18 32	21 49	0 31	17 27	12 53	14 28	5 54
19 F	19 46 0	26 04 14	19 25	17 38	0 12	18 50	10 49	15 21	16 32	6 23	18 32	21 47	0 31	17 43	13 21	14 48	5 54
20 Sa	19 49 57	27 01 28	1 ♓ 20	17 37	29 ♋ 31	20 04	11 27	15 17	16 28	6 24	18 31	21 46	0 32	17 59	13 50	15 08	5 53
21 Su	19 53 53	27 58 42	13 11	17 35	28 50	21 18	12 05	15 13	16 24	6 25	18 30	21 44	0 33	18 16	14 18	15 27	5 53
22 M	19 57 50	28 55 58	25 02	17 34	28 09	22 31	12 43	15 09	16 19	6 26	18 29	21 43	0 34	18 32	14 46	15 47	5 52
23 T	20 1 46	29 53 13	6 ♈ 56	17 32	27 29	23 45	13 21	15 06	16 15	6 27	18 28	21 41	0 36	18 49	15 15	16 06	5 51
24 W	20 5 43	0 ♌ 50 30	18 58	17 31	26 51	24 59	13 59	15 02	16 11	6 28	18 27	21 40	0 38	19 06	15 43	16 25	5 51
25 Th	20 9 39	1 47 48	1 ♉ 11	17 31 D	26 15	26 13	14 38	14 59	16 07	6 29	18 26	21 39	0 40	19 23	16 11	16 44	5 50
26 F	20 13 36	2 45 06	13 40	17 31	25 41	27 26	15 16	14 56	16 03	6 30	18 25	21 37	0 43	19 40	16 39	17 02	5 49
27 Sa	20 17 32	3 42 26	26 28	17 32	25 12	28 40	15 54	14 53	15 58	6 31	18 24	21 36	0 46	19 57	17 07	17 21	5 48
28 Su	20 21 29	4 39 46	9 ♊ 41	17 33	24 47	29 54	16 32	14 50	15 54	6 31	18 23	21 34	0 49	20 15	17 35	17 39	5 47
29 M	20 25 26	5 37 08	23 18	17 35	24 26	1 ♌ 08	17 10	14 47	15 50	6 32	18 22	21 33	0 53	20 33	18 03	17 57	5 46
30 T	20 29 22	6 34 30	7 ♋ 22	17 36 ℞	24 11	2 22	17 48	14 45	15 46	6 33	18 21	21 31	0 57	20 51	18 31	18 15	5 45
31 W	20 33 19	7 31 53	21 50	17 36	24 01	3 36	18 26	14 43	15 42	6 33	18 20	21 30	1 02	21 09	18 59	18 32	5 44

EPHEMERIS CALCULATED FOR 12 MIDNIGHT GREENWICH MEAN TIME. ALL OTHER DATA AND FACING ASPECTARIAN PAGE IN **EASTERN TIME (BOLD)** AND PACIFIC TIME (REGULAR).

AUGUST 2019

☽ Last Aspect day	ET / hr:mn / PT		asp	☽ Ingress sign	day	ET / hr:mn / PT	
1	**4:48 pm**	1:48 pm	☌ ♂	♍	2	**9:20 am**	6:20 am
3		9:27 pm	⚹ ☿	♎	4	**9:30 am**	6:30 am
4	**12:27 am**		⚹ ☿	♎	4	**9:30 am**	6:30 am
6	**3:36 am**	12:36 am	□ ☿	♏	6	**11:31 am**	8:31 am
8	**10:58 am**	7:58 am	△ ☿	♐	8	**4:35 pm**	1:35 pm
10	**3:50 pm**	12:50 pm	△ ♂	♑	10		9:50 pm
10	**3:50 pm**	12:50 pm	△ ♂	♑	11	**12:50 am**	
12	**6:11 pm**	3:11 pm	☌ ♇	♒	13	**11:35 am**	8:35 am
15	**9:02 pm**	6:02 pm	☍ ♂	♓	15	**11:49 pm**	8:49 pm
17	**6:35 pm**	3:35 pm	⚹ ♇	♈	18	**12:33 pm**	9:33 am

☽ Last Aspect day	ET / hr:mn / PT		asp	☽ Ingress sign	day	ET / hr:mn / PT	
20		9:06 pm	△ ♀	♉	20		9:37 pm
21	**12:06 am**		△ ♀	♉	21	**12:37 am**	
22	**5:33 pm**	2:33 pm	△ ♇	♊	23	**10:34 am**	7:34 am
24		11:58 pm	⚹ ☿	♋	25	**5:05 pm**	2:05 pm
25	**2:58 am**		⚹ ☿	♋	25	**5:05 pm**	2:05 pm
27	**4:55 am**	1:55 am	☍ ♇	♌	27	**7:53 pm**	4:53 pm
28	**8:07 pm**	5:07 pm	△ ♃	♍	29	**7:57 pm**	4:57 pm
31	**4:46 am**	1:46 am	△ ♇	♎	31	**7:08 pm**	4:08 pm

☽ Phases & Eclipses phase	day	ET / hr:mn / PT	
2nd Quarter	7	**1:31 pm**	10:31 am
Full Moon	15	**8:29 am**	5:29 am
4th Quarter	23	**10:56 am**	7:56 am
New Moon	30	**6:37 am**	3:37 am

Planet Ingress		day	ET / hr:mn / PT	
☿	♌	11	**3:46 pm**	12:46 pm
♂	♍	17		10:18 pm
♂	♍	18	**1:18 am**	
♀	♍	21	**5:06 am**	2:06 am
☉	♍	23	**6:02 am**	3:02 am
⚵	♍	23	**8:00 pm**	5:00 pm
⚴	♏	26	**4:56 am**	1:56 am
☿	♍	29	**3:48 am**	12:48 am

Planetary Motion		day	ET / hr:mn / PT	
♃	D	11	**9:37 am**	6:37 am
♅	R℞	11	**10:27 pm**	7:27 pm

1 THURSDAY
☽ △ ♃ **8:53 am** 5:53 am
☽ ⚻ ♄ **10:23 am** 7:23 am
☽ ⚻ ♆ **2:41 pm** 11:41 am
☽ ☌ ♂ **4:48 pm** 1:48 pm
☽ ⚻ ♇ **7:44 pm** 4:44 pm
☽ ⚺ ☿ **11:47 pm** 8:47 pm

2 FRIDAY
♀ □ ♅ **6:00 am** 3:00 am
☽ △ ♅ **7:50 pm** 4:50 pm
☽ ⚺ ♀ **9:03 pm** 6:03 pm
☽ ⚺ ☉ 11:20 pm

3 SATURDAY
☽ ⚺ ☉ **2:20 am**
☽ □ ♃ **8:39 am** 5:39 am
☽ △ ♄ **10:03 am** 7:03 am
☽ ☍ ♆ **2:30 pm** 11:30 am
☽ ⚺ ♂ **6:50 pm** 3:50 pm
☽ △ ♇ **7:35 pm** 4:35 pm
☽ ⚹ ☿ 9:27 pm

4 SUNDAY
☽ ⚹ ☿ **12:27 am**
♂ ⚻ ♇ **11:59 am** 8:59 am
☽ ⚻ ♅ **8:17 pm** 5:17 pm
☽ ⚹ ♀ 11:00 pm

5 MONDAY
☽ ⚹ ♀ **2:00 am**
☽ ⚹ ☉ **6:25 am** 3:25 am
☽ ⚹ ♃ **9:27 am** 6:27 am
☽ □ ♄ **10:46 am** 7:46 am
☽ ⚻ ♆ **3:33 pm** 12:33 pm
☽ □ ♇ **8:51 pm** 5:51 pm
☽ ⚹ ♂ **10:26 pm** 7:26 pm

6 TUESDAY
☽ □ ☿ **3:36 am** 12:36 am
☽ ☍ ♅ **10:55 pm** 7:55 pm

7 WEDNESDAY
☉ △ ♃ **3:31 am** 12:31 am
☽ □ ♀ **10:01 am** 7:01 am
☽ ⚺ ♃ **12:48 pm** 9:48 am
☽ □ ☉ **1:31 pm** 10:31 am
☽ ⚹ ♄ **2:02 pm** 11:02 am
☽ △ ♆ **7:15 pm** 4:15 pm
☉ ⚻ ♄ **8:24 pm** 5:24 pm
☽ ⚹ ♇ 9:53 pm

8 THURSDAY
☽ ⚹ ♇ **12:53 am**
☽ □ ♂ **5:16 am** 2:16 am
☽ △ ☿ **10:58 am** 7:58 am
♀ △ ♃ **4:28 pm** 1:28 pm

9 FRIDAY
♀ ⚻ ♄ **4:24 am** 1:24 am
☽ ⚻ ♅ **4:43 am** 1:43 am
☽ ☌ ♃ **7:25 pm** 4:25 pm
☽ ⚺ ♄ **8:30 pm** 5:30 pm
☽ △ ♀ **10:19 pm** 7:19 pm
☽ △ ☉ 9:39 pm
☽ □ ♆ 11:12 pm

10 SATURDAY
☽ △ ☉ **12:39 am**
☽ □ ♆ **2:12 am**
☽ ⚺ ♇ **8:09 am** 5:09 am
☽ △ ♂ **3:50 pm** 12:50 pm
☉ ⚻ ♆ **8:44 pm** 5:44 pm
☽ ⚻ ☿ **11:24 pm** 8:24 pm

11 SUNDAY
☽ △ ♅ **1:37 pm** 10:37 am
♀ ⚻ ♆ **1:43 pm** 10:43 am

12 MONDAY
☽ ⚺ ♃ **5:00 am** 2:00 am
☽ ☌ ♄ **5:53 am** 2:53 am
☽ ⚹ ♆ **11:58 am** 8:58 am
☽ ⚻ ♀ **2:31 pm** 11:31 am
☽ ⚻ ☉ **3:24 pm** 12:24 pm
☽ ☌ ♇ **6:11 pm** 3:11 pm

13 TUESDAY
☽ ⚻ ♂ **5:30 am** 2:30 am
☽ ☍ ☿ **4:33 pm** 1:33 pm
☽ □ ♅ 9:47 pm
☉ ☌ ♀ 11:07 pm
♀ ⚻ ♇ 11:08 pm
☉ ⚻ ♇ 11:08 pm

14 WEDNESDAY
☽ □ ♅ **12:47 am**
☉ ☌ ♀ **2:07 am**
♀ ⚻ ♇ **2:08 am**
☉ ⚻ ♇ **2:08 am**
☽ ⚹ ♃ **4:37 pm** 1:37 pm
☽ ⚺ ♄ **5:15 pm** 2:15 pm
☽ ⚺ ♆ **11:37 pm** 8:37 pm

15 THURSDAY
☽ ⚺ ♇ **6:00 am** 3:00 am
☽ ☍ ☉ **8:29 am** 5:29 am
☽ ☍ ♀ **9:16 am** 6:16 am
☽ ☍ ♂ **9:02 pm** 6:02 pm

16 FRIDAY
☿ □ ♅ **1:07 pm** 10:07 am
☽ ⚹ ♅ **1:11 pm** 10:11 am
☽ ⚻ ☿ **1:12 pm** 10:12 am

17 SATURDAY
☽ □ ♃ **5:17 am** 2:17 am
☽ ⚹ ♄ **5:36 am** 2:36 am
☽ ☌ ♆ **12:08 pm** 9:08 am
☽ ⚹ ♇ **6:35 pm** 3:35 pm
☽ ⚻ ☉ 11:32 pm

18 SUNDAY
☽ ⚻ ☉ **2:32 am**
☽ ⚻ ♀ **5:02 am** 2:02 am
☽ ⚻ ♂ **1:11 pm** 10:11 am
☽ ⚺ ♅ 10:51 pm

19 MONDAY
☽ ⚺ ♅ **1:51 am**
♃ ⚺ ♄ **10:47 am** 7:47 am
☽ △ ☿ **11:41 am** 8:41 am
☽ □ ♄ **5:56 pm** 2:56 pm
☽ △ ♃ **5:58 pm** 2:58 pm
☽ ⚺ ♆ 9:30 pm

20 TUESDAY
☽ ⚺ ♆ **12:30 am**
☽ □ ♇ **6:53 am** 3:53 am
☽ △ ☉ **8:01 pm** 5:01 pm
☽ △ ♀ 9:06 pm

21 WEDNESDAY
☽ △ ♀ **12:06 am**
☿ ⚻ ♄ **4:26 am** 1:26 am
☽ △ ♂ **4:33 am** 1:33 am
☿ △ ♃ **6:05 am** 3:05 am
☽ ☌ ♅ **1:33 pm** 10:33 am

22 THURSDAY
☽ △ ♄ **4:57 am** 1:57 am
☽ ⚻ ♃ **5:21 am** 2:21 am
☽ □ ☿ **9:22 am** 6:22 am
☽ ⚹ ♆ **11:23 am** 8:23 am
☽ △ ♇ **5:33 pm** 2:33 pm
☿ ⚻ ♆ **10:26 pm** 7:26 pm

23 FRIDAY
☽ □ ☉ **10:56 am** 7:56 am
☽ □ ♀ **4:17 pm** 1:17 pm
☽ □ ♂ **5:19 pm** 2:19 pm
☽ ⚺ ♅ **10:48 pm** 7:48 pm

24 SATURDAY
♀ ☌ ♂ **1:05 pm** 10:05 am
☽ ⚻ ♄ **1:12 pm** 10:12 am
☽ ☍ ♃ **1:53 pm** 10:53 am
☿ ⚻ ♇ **2:14 pm** 11:14 am
☽ □ ♆ **7:18 pm** 4:18 pm
☽ ⚻ ♇ 10:06 pm
☽ ⚹ ☿ 11:58 pm

25 SUNDAY
☽ ⚻ ♇ **1:06 am**
☽ ⚹ ☿ **2:58 am**
☽ ⚹ ☉ **9:33 pm** 6:33 pm
☽ ⚹ ♂ 10:59 pm

26 MONDAY
☽ ⚹ ♂ **1:59 am**
☽ ⚹ ♀ **3:44 am** 12:44 am
☽ ⚹ ♅ **4:27 am** 1:27 am
♀ △ ♅ **11:38 am** 8:38 am
☽ ☍ ♄ **5:45 pm** 2:45 pm
☽ ⚻ ♃ **6:42 pm** 3:42 pm
☽ △ ♆ **11:28 pm** 8:28 pm

27 TUESDAY
☽ ☍ ♇ **4:55 am** 1:55 am
☽ ⚺ ☿ **2:52 pm** 11:52 am

28 WEDNESDAY
☽ ⚺ ☉ **3:36 am** 12:36 am
☽ ⚺ ♂ **6:28 am** 3:28 am
☽ □ ♅ **6:29 am** 3:29 am
♂ △ ♅ **6:53 am** 3:53 am
☽ ⚺ ♀ **10:26 am** 7:26 am
☽ ⚻ ♄ **6:57 pm** 3:57 pm
☽ △ ♃ **8:07 pm** 5:07 pm
☽ ⚻ ♆ 9:23 pm

29 THURSDAY
☽ ⚻ ♆ **12:23 am**
☽ ⚻ ♇ **5:35 am** 2:35 am
☽ ☌ ☿ **10:22 pm** 7:22 pm
☉ △ ♅ **11:14 pm** 8:14 pm

30 FRIDAY
☽ △ ♅ **6:09 am** 3:09 am
☽ ☌ ☉ **6:37 am** 3:37 am
☽ ☌ ♂ **8:15 am** 5:15 am
☽ ☌ ♀ **2:13 pm** 11:13 am
☽ △ ♄ **6:14 pm** 3:14 pm
☽ □ ♃ **7:39 pm** 4:39 pm
☽ ☍ ♆ **11:35 pm** 8:35 pm

31 SATURDAY
☽ △ ♇ **4:46 am** 1:46 am

Eastern time in bold type
Pacific time in medium type

AUGUST 2019

DATE	SID.TIME	SUN	MOON	NODE	MERCURY	VENUS	MARS	JUPITER	SATURN	URANUS	NEPTUNE	PLUTO	CERES	PALLAS	JUNO	VESTA	CHIRON
1 Th	20 37 15	8♌29 18	6♌38	17♋35 R℞	23♋57 D	4♌50	19♌04	14♐41 R℞	15♑38 R℞	6♉34	18♓19 R℞	21♑29 R℞	1♐06	21♎27	19♌27	18♉50	5♈43 R℞
2 F	20 41 12	9 26 43	21 38	17 33	23 59	6 04	19 42	14 39	15 35	6 34	18 17	21 27	1 12	21 46	19 55	19 07	5 42
3 Sa	20 45 8	10 24 08	6♍41	17 31	24 07	7 18	20 20	14 37	15 31	6 35	18 16	21 26	1 17	22 04	20 23	19 24	5 40
4 Su	20 49 5	11 21 35	21 40	17 28	24 22	8 32	20 58	14 36	15 27	6 35	18 15	21 25	1 23	22 23	20 51	19 41	5 39
5 M	20 53 1	12 19 02	6♎25	17 25	24 43	9 46	21 36	14 34	15 23	6 36	18 14	21 23	1 29	22 42	21 19	19 58	5 38
6 T	20 56 58	13 16 30	20 52	17 22	25 11	11 00	22 14	14 33	15 20	6 36	18 12	21 22	1 35	23 01	21 47	20 14	5 37
7 W	21 0 55	14 13 58	4♏55	17 21 D	25 45	12 14	22 53	14 32	15 16	6 36	18 11	21 21	1 42	23 20	22 14	20 30	5 35
8 Th	21 4 51	15 11 27	18 35	17 20	26 26	13 28	23 31	14 31	15 12	6 37	18 10	21 19	1 49	23 40	22 42	20 46	5 34
9 F	21 8 48	16 08 57	1♐52	17 21	27 13	14 42	24 09	14 31	15 09	6 37	18 09	21 18	1 56	23 59	23 10	21 02	5 32
10 Sa	21 12 44	17 06 28	14 49	17 23	28 07	15 56	24 47	14 31	15 06	6 37	18 07	21 17	2 04	24 19	23 37	21 17	5 31
11 Su	21 16 41	18 04 00	27 29	17 24	29 06	17 10	25 25	14 30 D	15 02	6 37	18 06	21 15	2 12	24 39	24 05	21 32	5 29
12 M	21 20 37	19 01 33	9♑54	17 25 R℞	0♌12	18 24	26 03	14 30	14 59	6 37 R℞	18 04	21 14	2 20	24 59	24 32	21 47	5 27
13 T	21 24 34	19 59 06	22 08	17 26	1 24	19 38	26 41	14 30	14 56	6 37	18 03	21 13	2 28	25 19	25 00	22 02	5 26
14 W	21 28 30	20 56 41	4♒13	17 24	2 41	20 52	27 19	14 31	14 53	6 37	18 02	21 12	2 37	25 39	25 27	22 17	5 24
15 Th	21 32 27	21 54 16	16 12	17 21	4 03	22 07	27 57	14 31	14 50	6 37	18 00	21 10	2 46	26 00	25 55	22 31	5 22
16 F	21 36 24	22 51 53	28 06	17 17	5 31	23 21	28 35	14 32	14 47	6 37	17 59	21 09	2 55	26 20	26 22	22 45	5 20
17 Sa	21 40 20	23 49 31	9♓58	17 11	7 03	24 35	29 13	14 33	14 44	6 36	17 57	21 08	3 05	26 41	26 50	22 59	5 19
18 Su	21 44 17	24 47 11	21 49	17 04	8 40	25 49	29 52	14 34	14 41	6 36	17 56	21 07	3 15	27 02	27 17	23 12	5 17
19 M	21 48 13	25 44 51	3♈42	16 57	10 21	27 03	0♍30	14 35	14 38	6 36	17 54	21 06	3 25	27 23	27 44	23 25	5 15
20 T	21 52 10	26 42 34	15 37	16 51	12 05	28 18	1 08	14 37	14 35	6 35	17 53	21 05	3 35	27 44	28 11	23 38	5 13
21 W	21 56 6	27 40 17	27 40	16 45	13 53	29 32	1 46	14 38	14 33	6 35	17 51	21 04	3 46	28 05	28 39	23 51	5 11
22 Th	22 0 3	28 38 03	9♉52	16 42	15 44	0♍46	2 24	14 40	14 30	6 34	17 50	21 02	3 57	28 26	29 06	24 03	5 09
23 F	22 3 59	29 35 50	22 19	16 40 D	17 37	2 00	3 02	14 42	14 28	6 34	17 48	21 01	4 08	28 47	29 33	24 15	5 07
24 Sa	22 7 56	0♍33 39	5♊03	16 40	19 31	3 15	3 40	14 45	14 25	6 33	17 47	21 00	4 19	29 09	0♍00	24 27	5 05
25 Su	22 11 53	1 31 30	18 09	16 41	21 28	4 29	4 19	14 47	14 23	6 33	17 45	20 59	4 31	29 30	0 27	24 38	5 03
26 M	22 15 49	2 29 22	1♋40	16 42	23 25	5 43	4 57	14 49	14 21	6 32	17 44	20 58	4 43	29 52	0 54	24 50	5 00
27 T	22 19 46	3 27 16	15 38	16 43 R℞	25 24	6 58	5 35	14 52	14 19	6 31	17 42	20 57	4 55	0♏14	1 21	25 00	4 58
28 W	22 23 42	4 25 12	0♌04	16 42	27 22	8 12	6 13	14 55	14 16	6 31	17 40	20 56	5 07	0 36	1 48	25 11	4 56
29 Th	22 27 39	5 23 10	14 54	16 39	29 21	9 26	6 51	14 58	14 14	6 30	17 39	20 55	5 19	0 58	2 15	25 21	4 54
30 F	22 31 35	6 21 09	0♍02	16 34	1♍20	10 41	7 29	15 01	14 13	6 29	17 37	20 54	5 32	1 20	2 42	25 31	4 51
31 Sa	22 35 32	7 19 10	15 18	16 28	3 19	11 55	8 08	15 05	14 11	6 28	17 36	20 54	5 45	1 42	3 08	25 41	4 49

EPHEMERIS CALCULATED FOR 12 MIDNIGHT GREENWICH MEAN TIME. ALL OTHER DATA AND FACING ASPECTARIAN PAGE IN **EASTERN TIME (BOLD)** AND PACIFIC TIME (REGULAR).

SEPTEMBER 2019

☽ Last Aspect				☽ Ingress			
day	ET / hr:mn	PT	asp	sign day	ET / hr:mn	PT	
2	**4:34 am**	1:34 am	□♇	♏ 2	**7:35 pm**	4:35 pm	
4	**6:58 am**	3:58 am	✶♇	♐ 4	**11:08 pm**	8:08 pm	
6	**12:03 pm**	9:03 am	□♀	♑ 7	**6:37 am**	3:37 am	
9	**4:30 am**	1:30 am	△♀	♒ 9	**5:24 pm**	2:24 pm	
10		10:22 pm	✶♃	♓ 12	**5:52 am**	2:52 am	
11	**1:22 am**		✶♃	♓ 12	**5:52 am**	2:52 am	
13		9:33 pm	☍☉	♈ 14	**6:32 pm**	3:32 pm	
14	**12:33 am**		☍☉	♈ 14	**6:32 pm**	3:32 pm	
16	**12:03 pm**	9:03 am	□♇	♉ 17	**6:31 am**	3:31 am	
19	**9:57 am**	6:57 am	△☉	♊ 19	**4:58 pm**	1:58 pm	
21	**10:41 pm**	7:41 pm	□☉	♋ 21		9:50 pm	
21	**10:41 pm**	7:41 pm	□☉	♋ 22	**12:50 am**		
23	**6:05 pm**	3:05 pm	✶♂	♌ 24	**5:19 am**	2:19 am	
25	**12:14 pm**	9:14 am	✶☿	♍ 26	**6:37 am**	3:37 am	
27	**11:58 pm**	8:58 pm	☌♂	♎ 28	**6:03 am**	3:03 am	
29	**10:06 pm**	7:06 pm	☌☿	♏ 30	**5:42 am**	2:42 am	

☽ Phases & Eclipses			
phase	day	ET / hr:mn	PT
2nd Quarter	5	**11:10 pm**	8:10 pm
Full Moon	13		9:33 pm
Full Moon	14	**12:33 am**	
4th Quarter	21	**10:41 pm**	7:41 pm
New Moon	28	**2:26 pm**	11:26 am

Planet Ingress			
	day	ET / hr:mn	PT
☿ ♎	14	**3:14 am**	12:14 am
♀ ♎	14	**9:43 am**	6:43 am
☉ ♎	23	**3:50 am**	12:50 am

Planetary Motion				
		day	ET / hr:mn	PT
♄	D	18	**4:47 am**	1:47 am
♇	R℞	23	**11:43 pm**	8:43 pm

1 SUNDAY

☽⚺☿	**4:39 am**	1:39 am
☽⚻♅	**5:22 am**	2:22 am
☽⚺☉	**9:09 am**	6:09 am
☽⚺♂	**9:39 am**	6:39 am
☿△♅	**10:11 am**	7:11 am
♀△♄	**2:49 pm**	11:49 am
☽□♄	**5:40 pm**	2:40 pm
☽⚺♀	**5:56 pm**	2:56 pm
☽✶♃	**7:24 pm**	4:24 pm
☽⚻♆	**11:10 pm**	8:10 pm

2 MONDAY

☽□♇	**4:34 am**	1:34 am
☉☌♂	**6:42 am**	3:42 am
♀□♃	**12:26 pm**	9:26 am

3 TUESDAY

☽☍♅	**6:18 am**	3:18 am
☿☌♂	**11:40 am**	8:40 am
☽✶♂	**1:12 pm**	10:12 am
☽✶☿	**1:21 pm**	10:21 am
☽✶☉	**1:58 pm**	10:58 am
☽✶♄	**7:18 pm**	4:18 pm
☽⚺♃	**9:28 pm**	6:28 pm
☉☌☿	**9:40 pm**	6:40 pm
☽✶♀		9:32 pm
☽△♆		10:09 pm

4 WEDNESDAY

☽✶♀	**12:32 am**	
☽△♆	**1:09 am**	
☽✶♇	**6:58 am**	3:58 am
♀☍♆	**7:26 am**	4:26 am

5 THURSDAY

☿△♄	**8:37 am**	5:37 am
☽⚻♅	**10:36 am**	7:36 am
☽□♂	**8:49 pm**	5:49 pm
☽□☉	**11:10 pm**	8:10 pm
☽⚺♄		9:36 pm

6 FRIDAY

☽⚺♄	**12:36 am**	
☿□♃	**3:11 am**	12:11 am
☽☌♃	**3:20 am**	12:20 am
☽□☿	**3:21 am**	12:21 am
☽□♆	**6:53 am**	3:53 am
☽□♀	**12:03 pm**	9:03 am
☽⚺♇	**1:12 pm**	10:12 am
☉△♄	**5:56 pm**	2:56 pm
♀△♇	**11:46 pm**	8:46 pm

7 SATURDAY

☿☍♆	**3:18 am**	12:18 am
☽△♅	**6:47 pm**	3:47 pm

8 SUNDAY

☽△♂	**8:53 am**	5:53 am
☽☌♄	**9:42 am**	6:42 am
☉□♃	**11:27 am**	8:27 am
☽⚺♃	**1:04 pm**	10:04 am
☽△☉	**1:11 pm**	10:11 am
☽✶♆	**4:18 pm**	1:18 pm
☽△☿	**11:02 pm**	8:02 pm
☽☌♇	**11:03 pm**	8:03 pm
☿△♇	**11:09 pm**	8:09 pm
♂△♄		9:14 pm

9 MONDAY

♂△♄	**12:14 am**	
☽△♀	**4:30 am**	1:30 am

10 TUESDAY

☉☍♆	**3:24 am**	12:24 am
☽□♅	**5:57 am**	2:57 am
☽⚺♄	**9:25 pm**	6:25 pm
☽⚻♂		9:02 pm
☽✶♃		10:22 pm

11 WEDNESDAY

☽⚻♂	**12:02 am**	
☽✶♃	**1:22 am**	
☽⚺♆	**4:08 am**	1:08 am
☽⚻☉	**6:24 am**	3:24 am
☽⚺♇	**11:08 am**	8:08 am
☽⚻☿	**9:58 pm**	6:58 pm
☽⚻♀	**11:47 pm**	8:47 pm

12 THURSDAY

♂□♃	**5:06 am**	2:06 am
☽✶♅	**6:27 pm**	3:27 pm

13 FRIDAY

☽✶♄	**10:04 am**	7:04 am
☿☌♀	**11:11 am**	8:11 am
☽□♃	**2:35 pm**	11:35 am
☉△♇	**3:42 pm**	12:42 pm
☽☍♂	**4:12 pm**	1:12 pm
☽☌♆	**4:43 pm**	1:43 pm
☽✶♇	**11:49 pm**	8:49 pm
☽☍☉		9:33 pm
♂☍♆		10:25 pm

14 SATURDAY

☽☍☉	**12:33 am**	
♂☍♆	**1:25 am**	
☽☍♀	**7:34 pm**	4:34 pm
☽☍☿	**9:08 pm**	6:08 pm

15 SUNDAY

☽⚺♅	**6:55 am**	3:55 am
☽□♄	**10:29 pm**	7:29 pm

16 MONDAY

☽△♃	**3:29 am**	12:29 am
☽⚺♆	**4:57 am**	1:57 am
☽⚻♂	**7:58 am**	4:58 am
☽□♇	**12:03 pm**	9:03 am
☽⚻☉	**6:06 pm**	3:06 pm

17 TUESDAY

☽⚻♀	**2:21 pm**	11:21 am
☿⚻♅	**4:57 pm**	1:57 pm
☽☌♅	**6:31 pm**	3:31 pm
☽⚻☿	**6:46 pm**	3:46 pm

18 WEDNESDAY

☽△♄	**9:52 am**	6:52 am
☽⚻♃	**3:15 pm**	12:15 pm
☽✶♆	**4:02 pm**	1:02 pm
☽△♂	**10:20 pm**	7:20 pm
☽△♇	**11:02 pm**	8:02 pm

19 THURSDAY

♀⚻♅	**6:27 am**	3:27 am
☽△☉	**9:57 am**	6:57 am
♂△♇	**11:53 am**	8:53 am

20 FRIDAY

☽⚺♅	**4:24 am**	1:24 am
☽△♀	**6:50 am**	3:50 am
☽△☿	**1:24 pm**	10:24 am
☽⚻♄	**7:16 pm**	4:16 pm
☽☍♃		9:54 pm
☽□♆		10:02 pm

21 SATURDAY

☽☍♃	**12:54 am**	
☽□♆	**1:02 am**	
☽⚻♇	**7:47 am**	4:47 am
☽□♂	**10:05 am**	7:05 am
♃□♆	**12:44 pm**	9:44 am
☽□☉	**10:41 pm**	7:41 pm

22 SUNDAY

☽✶♅	**11:31 am**	8:31 am
☿□♄	**12:19 pm**	9:19 am
☽□♀	**7:30 pm**	4:30 pm
☽☍♄		10:39 pm

23 MONDAY

☽☍♄	**1:39 am**	
☽□☿	**3:23 am**	12:23 am
☽△♆	**6:55 am**	3:55 am
☽⚻♃	**7:22 am**	4:22 am
☽☍♇	**1:21 pm**	10:21 am
☽✶♂	**6:05 pm**	3:05 pm

24 TUESDAY

☽✶☉	**7:12 am**	4:12 am
☿⚻♆	**9:57 am**	6:57 am
☽□♅	**3:12 pm**	12:12 pm
☿✶♃	**5:01 pm**	2:01 pm

25 WEDNESDAY

☽✶♀	**3:35 am**	12:35 am
☽⚻♄	**4:35 am**	1:35 am
☽⚻♆	**9:25 am**	6:25 am
☽△♃	**10:21 am**	7:21 am
☽✶☿	**12:14 pm**	9:14 am
♀□♄	**3:20 pm**	12:20 pm
☽⚻♇	**3:32 pm**	12:32 pm
☽⚺♂	**10:15 pm**	7:15 pm

26 THURSDAY

☽⚺☉	**11:50 am**	8:50 am
☽△♅	**3:53 pm**	12:53 pm
☿□♇	**7:52 pm**	4:52 pm

27 FRIDAY

☽△♄	**4:50 am**	1:50 am
☽⚺♀	**8:08 am**	5:08 am
☽☍♆	**9:21 am**	6:21 am
☽□♃	**10:45 am**	7:45 am
☽△♇	**3:20 pm**	12:20 pm
☽⚺☿	**5:29 pm**	2:29 pm
♀⚻♆	**10:50 pm**	7:50 pm
☽☌♂	**11:58 pm**	8:58 pm

28 SATURDAY

☽☌☉	**2:26 pm**	11:26 am
☽⚻♅	**3:05 pm**	12:05 pm
♀✶♃	**7:41 pm**	4:41 pm
☉⚻♅		9:14 pm

29 SUNDAY

☉⚻♅	**12:14 am**	
☽□♄	**4:08 am**	1:08 am
☽⚻♆	**8:33 am**	5:33 am
☽✶♃	**10:27 am**	7:27 am
☽☌♀	**11:38 am**	8:38 am
☽□♇	**2:40 pm**	11:40 am
☽☌☿	**10:06 pm**	7:06 pm
☽⚺♂		10:36 pm

30 MONDAY

☽⚺♂	**1:36 am**	
☽☍♅	**2:56 pm**	11:56 am
☽⚺☉	**5:48 pm**	2:48 pm
♀□♇		9:18 pm

Eastern time in bold type
Pacific time in medium type

SEPTEMBER 2019

DATE	SID.TIME	SUN	MOON	NODE	MERCURY	VENUS	MARS	JUPITER	SATURN	URANUS	NEPTUNE	PLUTO	CERES	PALLAS	JUNO	VESTA	CHIRON
1 Su	22 39 28	8 ♍ 17 13	0 ♎ 33	16 ♋ 20 ℞	5 ♍ 17	13 ♍ 10	8 ♍ 46	15 ♐ 08	14 ♑ 09 ℞	6 ♉ 27 ℞	17 ♓ 34 ℞	20 ♑ 53 ℞	5 ♐ 58	2 ♏ 04	3 ♍ 35	25 ♉ 50	4 ♈ 47 ℞
2 M	22 43 25	9 15 16	15 35	16 12	7 15	14 24	9 24	15 12	14 08	6 26	17 32	20 52	6 12	2 27	4 02	25 59	4 44
3 T	22 47 22	10 13 22	0 ♏ 15	16 06	9 12	15 38	10 02	15 16	14 06	6 25	17 31	20 51	6 25	2 49	4 28	26 07	4 42
4 W	22 51 18	11 11 29	14 29	16 01	11 07	16 53	10 41	15 20	14 05	6 24	17 29	20 50	6 39	3 12	4 55	26 15	4 40
5 Th	22 55 15	12 09 37	28 14	15 58	13 02	18 07	11 19	15 25	14 03	6 23	17 27	20 49	6 53	3 34	5 21	26 23	4 37
6 F	22 59 11	13 07 46	11 ♐ 32	15 57 D	14 56	19 22	11 57	15 29	14 02	6 22	17 26	20 49	7 08	3 57	5 48	26 31	4 35
7 Sa	23 3 8	14 05 58	24 25	15 57	16 49	20 36	12 35	15 34	14 01	6 21	17 24	20 48	7 22	4 20	6 14	26 38	4 32
8 Su	23 7 4	15 04 10	6 ♑ 57	15 58 ℞	18 41	21 51	13 14	15 38	14 00	6 19	17 22	20 47	7 37	4 43	6 41	26 45	4 30
9 M	23 11 1	16 02 24	19 14	15 58	20 32	23 05	13 52	15 43	13 59	6 18	17 21	20 46	7 51	5 06	7 07	26 51	4 27
10 T	23 14 57	17 00 40	1 ♒ 18	15 57	22 22	24 19	14 30	15 49	13 58	6 17	17 19	20 46	8 06	5 29	7 33	26 57	4 25
11 W	23 18 54	17 58 57	13 15	15 53	24 10	25 34	15 09	15 54	13 57	6 16	17 17	20 45	8 22	5 52	7 59	27 03	4 22
12 Th	23 22 51	18 57 16	25 08	15 47	25 57	26 48	15 47	15 59	13 57	6 14	17 16	20 45	8 37	6 15	8 26	27 08	4 20
13 F	23 26 47	19 55 37	6 ♓ 59	15 39	27 43	28 03	16 25	16 05	13 56	6 13	17 14	20 44	8 53	6 39	8 52	27 13	4 17
14 Sa	23 30 44	20 53 59	18 50	15 28	29 29	29 17	17 03	16 11	13 56	6 11	17 13	20 43	9 08	7 02	9 18	27 17	4 14
15 Su	23 34 40	21 52 23	0 ♈ 43	15 15	1 ♎ 12	0 ♎ 32	17 42	16 17	13 55	6 10	17 11	20 43	9 24	7 25	9 44	27 21	4 12
16 M	23 38 37	22 50 49	12 40	15 03	2 55	1 46	18 20	16 23	13 55	6 08	17 09	20 42	9 40	7 49	10 10	27 25	4 09
17 T	23 42 33	23 49 17	24 42	14 51	4 37	3 01	18 59	16 29	13 55	6 06	17 08	20 42	9 57	8 13	10 36	27 28	4 06
18 W	23 46 30	24 47 47	6 ♉ 50	14 41	6 18	4 15	19 37	16 35	13 55 D	6 05	17 06	20 41	10 13	8 36	11 01	27 31	4 04
19 Th	23 50 26	25 46 19	19 07	14 33	7 57	5 30	20 15	16 42	13 55	6 03	17 04	20 41	10 29	9 00	11 27	27 33	4 01
20 F	23 54 23	26 44 53	1 ♊ 36	14 28	9 36	6 44	20 54	16 48	13 55	6 01	17 03	20 41	10 46	9 24	11 53	27 35	3 58
21 Sa	23 58 19	27 43 30	14 19	14 25	11 14	7 59	21 32	16 55	13 55	6 00	17 01	20 40	11 03	9 48	12 19	27 37	3 56
22 Su	0 2 16	28 42 09	27 20	14 24 D	12 50	9 14	22 11	17 02	13 55	5 58	16 59	20 40	11 20	10 12	12 44	27 38	3 53
23 M	0 6 13	29 40 50	10 ♋ 43	14 25 ℞	14 26	10 28	22 49	17 09	13 56	5 56	16 58	20 40	11 37	10 36	13 10	27 39	3 50
24 T	0 10 9	0 ♎ 39 33	24 31	14 24	16 01	11 43	23 28	17 16	13 56	5 54	16 56	20 39	11 55	11 00	13 35	27 39 ℞	3 48
25 W	0 14 6	1 38 19	8 ♌ 45	14 23	17 34	12 57	24 06	17 24	13 57	5 52	16 55	20 39	12 12	11 24	14 01	27 39	3 45
26 Th	0 18 2	2 37 07	23 24	14 18	19 07	14 12	24 44	17 31	13 57	5 50	16 53	20 39	12 30	11 48	14 26	27 38	3 42
27 F	0 21 59	3 35 57	8 ♍ 24	14 11	20 39	15 26	25 23	17 39	13 58	5 48	16 52	20 39	12 48	12 12	14 51	27 37	3 39
28 Sa	0 25 55	4 34 49	23 37	14 02	22 10	16 41	26 02	17 47	13 59	5 46	16 50	20 38	13 06	12 37	15 17	27 36	3 37
29 Su	0 29 52	5 33 43	8 ♎ 52	13 51	23 40	17 56	26 40	17 55	14 00	5 44	16 48	20 38	13 24	13 01	15 42	27 34	3 34
30 M	0 33 48	6 32 39	23 58	13 40	25 09	19 10	27 19	18 03	14 01	5 42	16 47	20 38	13 42	13 25	16 07	27 32	3 31

EPHEMERIS CALCULATED FOR 12 MIDNIGHT GREENWICH MEAN TIME. ALL OTHER DATA AND FACING ASPECTARIAN PAGE IN **EASTERN TIME (BOLD)** AND PACIFIC TIME (REGULAR).

OCTOBER 2019

☽ Last Aspect day	ET / hr:mn / PT	asp	☽ Ingress sign day	ET / hr:mn / PT
2	**5:46 am** 2:46 am	✶♂	♐ 2	**7:44 am** 4:44 am
4	**3:34 am** 12:34 am	✶♀	♑ 4	**1:43 pm** 10:43 am
6	**7:25 pm** 4:25 pm	□♀	♒ 6	**11:42 pm** 8:42 pm
8	**2:27 pm** 11:27 am	✶♃	♓ 9	**12:05 pm** 9:05 am
11	**5:55 am** 2:55 am	✶♇	♈ 11	9:46 pm
11	**5:55 am** 2:55 am	✶♇	♈ 12	**12:46 am**
13	**5:59 pm** 2:59 pm	□♇	♉ 14	**12:24 pm** 9:24 am
16	**4:37 am** 1:37 am	△♇	♊ 16	**10:30 pm** 7:30 pm
18	**10:14 pm** 7:14 pm	△☉	♋ 19	**6:43 am** 3:43 am
21	**8:39 am** 5:39 am	□☉	♌ 21	**12:29 pm** 9:29 am
23	**5:14 am** 2:14 am	□☿	♍ 23	**3:29 pm** 12:29 pm
25	**9:00 am** 6:00 am	✶☿	♎ 25	**4:20 pm** 1:20 pm
27	**4:22 am** 1:22 am	✶♃	♏ 27	**4:29 pm** 1:29 pm
29	**1:34 pm** 10:34 am	☌☿	♐ 29	**5:58 pm** 2:58 pm
31	**10:30 am** 7:30 am	☌♃	♑ 31	**10:38 pm** 7:38 pm

☽ Phases & Eclipses phase	day	ET / hr:mn / PT
2nd Quarter	5	**12:47 pm** 9:47 am
Full Moon	13	**5:08 pm** 2:08 pm
4th Quarter	21	**8:39 am** 5:39 am
New Moon	27	**11:39 pm** 8:39 pm

Planet Ingress	day	ET / hr:mn / PT
☿ ♏	3	**4:14 am** 1:14 am
♂ ♎	3	9:22 pm
♂ ♎	4	**12:22 am**
♀ ♏	8	**1:06 pm** 10:06 am
☉ ♏	23	**1:20 pm** 10:20 am

Planetary Motion	day	ET / hr:mn / PT
♇ D	2	11:39 pm
♇ D	3	**2:39 am**
☿ ℞	31	**11:41 am** 8:41 am

1 TUESDAY
♀□♇ **12:18 am**
☽✶♄ **4:43 am** 1:43 am
☽△♆ **9:12 am** 6:12 am
☽⚺♃ **11:46 am** 8:46 am
☽✶♇ **3:45 pm** 12:45 pm
☽⚺♀ **5:14 pm** 2:14 pm

2 WEDNESDAY
☽⚺☿ **5:23 am** 2:23 am
☽✶♂ **5:46 am** 2:46 am
☿⚺♂ **11:45 am** 8:45 am
☽⚻♅ **5:30 pm** 2:30 pm
☽✶☉ 9:42 pm

3 THURSDAY
☽✶☉ **12:42 am**
☽⚺♄ **8:34 am** 5:34 am
☽□♆ **1:14 pm** 10:14 am
☽☌♃ **4:40 pm** 1:40 pm
☽⚺♇ **8:24 pm** 5:24 pm

4 FRIDAY
☽✶♀ **3:34 am** 12:34 am
☽□♂ **2:26 pm** 11:26 am
☽✶☿ **5:52 pm** 2:52 pm
☽△♅ 9:08 pm

5 SATURDAY
☽△♅ **12:08 am**
☽□☉ **12:47 pm** 9:47 am
☽☌♄ **4:40 pm** 1:40 pm
☽✶♆ **9:26 pm** 6:26 pm
☽⚺♃ 10:55 pm

6 SUNDAY
☽⚺♃ **1:55 am**
☽☌♇ **5:15 am** 2:15 am
☽□♀ **7:25 pm** 4:25 pm
☿☍♅ 11:17 pm

7 MONDAY
☿☍♅ **2:17 am**
☽△♂ **3:43 am** 12:43 am
☽□♅ **10:32 am** 7:32 am
☽□☿ **11:36 am** 8:36 am
☉□♄ **3:07 pm** 12:07 pm

8 TUESDAY
☽⚺♄ **4:12 am** 1:12 am
☽△☉ **5:20 am** 2:20 am
☽⚺♆ **8:54 am** 5:54 am
☽✶♃ **2:27 pm** 11:27 am
☽⚺♇ **5:08 pm** 2:08 pm

9 WEDNESDAY
☽△♀ **2:47 pm** 11:47 am
☽⚻♂ **7:40 pm** 4:40 pm
☽✶♅ **10:55 pm** 7:55 pm
☉⚻♆ **11:24 pm** 8:24 pm

10 THURSDAY
☽△☿ **7:49 am** 4:49 am
☽✶♄ **5:08 pm** 2:08 pm
☽☌♆ **9:34 pm** 6:34 pm
☽⚻☉ **11:37 pm** 8:37 pm

11 FRIDAY
☽□♃ **4:02 am** 1:02 am
☽✶♇ **5:55 am** 2:55 am

12 SATURDAY
♂⚻♅ **4:00 am** 1:00 am
☽⚻♀ **10:28 am** 7:28 am
☽⚺♅ **11:17 am** 8:17 am
☽☍♂ **11:43 am** 8:43 am
♀☍♅ **6:07 pm** 3:07 pm

13 SUNDAY
☽⚻☿ **3:18 am** 12:18 am
☽□♄ **5:36 am** 2:36 am
☽⚺♆ **9:39 am** 6:39 am
♀⚺♂ **10:17 am** 7:17 am
☉✶♃ **2:02 pm** 11:02 am
☽△♃ **4:55 pm** 1:55 pm
☽☍☉ **5:08 pm** 2:08 pm
☽□♇ **5:59 pm** 2:59 pm
☿✶♄ 11:56 pm

14 MONDAY
☿✶♄ **2:56 am**
☉□♇ **3:38 am** 12:38 am
☽☌♅ **10:29 pm** 7:29 pm
☽⚻♂ 11:24 pm

15 TUESDAY
☽⚻♂ **2:24 am**
☽☍♀ **4:33 am** 1:33 am
☽△♄ **4:44 pm** 1:44 pm
☿△♆ **6:45 pm** 3:45 pm
☽✶♆ **8:23 pm** 5:23 pm
☽☍☿ **8:33 pm** 5:33 pm

16 WEDNESDAY
☽⚻♃ **4:21 am** 1:21 am
☽△♇ **4:37 am** 1:37 am
☽⚻☉ **8:49 am** 5:49 am
♃⚺♇ 10:45 pm

17 THURSDAY
♃⚺♇ **1:45 am**
☽⚺♅ **8:07 am** 5:07 am
☽△♂ **3:11 pm** 12:11 pm
☽⚻♀ **8:25 pm** 5:25 pm
☽⚻♄ 11:12 pm

18 FRIDAY
☽⚻♄ **2:12 am**
☽□♆ **5:25 am** 2:25 am
☽⚻☿ **11:02 am** 8:02 am
☽⚻♇ **1:30 pm** 10:30 am
☽☍♃ **1:58 pm** 10:58 am
☽△☉ **10:14 pm** 7:14 pm

19 SATURDAY
☽✶♅ **3:47 pm** 12:47 pm
☿✶♇ **6:21 pm** 3:21 pm
☽□♂ 10:35 pm

20 SUNDAY
☽□♂ **1:35 am**
☿⚺♃ **7:23 am** 4:23 am
☽△♀ **9:26 am** 6:26 am
☽☍♄ **9:29 am** 6:29 am
♀✶♄ **9:58 am** 6:58 am
☽△♆ **12:17 pm** 9:17 am
☽☍♇ **8:07 pm** 5:07 pm
☽⚻♃ **9:14 pm** 6:14 pm
☽△☿ **10:06 pm** 7:06 pm

21 MONDAY
☽□☉ **8:39 am** 5:39 am
♀△♆ **3:40 pm** 12:40 pm
☽□♅ **8:56 pm** 5:56 pm

22 TUESDAY
☽✶♂ **8:58 am** 5:58 am
☽⚻♄ **2:05 pm** 11:05 am
☽⚻♆ **4:28 pm** 1:28 pm
☽□♀ **6:54 pm** 3:54 pm
☽⚻♇ 9:01 pm
☽△♃ 10:41 pm

23 WEDNESDAY
☽⚻♇ **12:01 am**
☽△♃ **1:41 am**
☽□☿ **5:14 am** 2:14 am
☽✶☉ **3:39 pm** 12:39 pm
☽△♅ **11:24 pm** 8:24 pm

24 THURSDAY
☽⚺♂ **1:18 pm** 10:18 am
☽△♄ **4:05 pm** 1:05 pm
☽☍♆ **6:07 pm** 3:07 pm
☽✶♀ 10:02 pm
☽△♇ 10:26 pm

25 FRIDAY
☽✶♀ **1:02 am**
☽△♇ **1:26 am**
☽□♃ **3:37 am** 12:37 am
♀✶♇ **5:52 am** 2:52 am
☽✶☿ **9:00 am** 6:00 am
☽⚺☉ **7:58 pm** 4:58 pm
☽⚻♅ **11:52 pm** 8:52 pm

26 SATURDAY
♀⚺♃ **12:47 pm** 9:47 am
☽☌♂ **3:48 pm** 12:48 pm
☽□♄ **4:32 pm** 1:32 pm
☽⚻♆ **6:18 pm** 3:18 pm
☽□♇ 10:38 pm

27 SUNDAY
☽□♇ **1:38 am**
☽✶♃ **4:22 am** 1:22 am
☽⚺♀ **5:34 am** 2:34 am
♂□♄ **10:31 am** 7:31 am
☽⚺☿ **11:03 am** 8:03 am
☽☌☉ **11:39 pm** 8:39 pm
☽☍♅ **11:58 pm** 8:58 pm

28 MONDAY
☉☍♅ **4:15 am** 1:15 am
☽✶♄ **5:19 pm** 2:19 pm
☽⚺♂ **6:37 pm** 3:37 pm
☽△♆ **6:52 pm** 3:52 pm
♂⚻♆ **11:57 pm** 8:57 pm
☽✶♇ 11:32 pm

29 TUESDAY
☽✶♇ **2:32 am**
☽⚺♃ **5:58 am** 2:58 am
☽☌♀ **11:14 am** 8:14 am
☽☌☿ **1:34 pm** 10:34 am
☽⚻♅ 10:41 pm

30 WEDNESDAY
☽⚻♅ **1:41 am**
☽⚺☉ **5:19 am** 2:19 am
☿☌♀ **6:05 pm** 3:05 pm
☽⚺♄ **8:28 pm** 5:28 pm
☽□♆ **9:49 pm** 6:49 pm
☽✶♂ 9:10 pm

31 THURSDAY
☽✶♂ **12:10 am**
☽⚺♇ **6:07 am** 3:07 am
☽☌♃ **10:30 am** 7:30 am
☽⚺☿ **6:20 pm** 3:20 pm
☽⚺♀ **8:47 pm** 5:47 pm

Eastern time in bold type
Pacific time in medium type

OCTOBER 2019

DATE	SID.TIME	SUN	MOON	NODE	MERCURY	VENUS	MARS	JUPITER	SATURN	URANUS	NEPTUNE	PLUTO	CERES	PALLAS	JUNO	VESTA	CHIRON
1 T	0 37 45	7 ♎ 31 37	8 ♏ 47	13 ♋ 30 ℞	26 ♎ 37	20 ♎ 25	27 ♍ 57	18 ♐ 11	14 ♑ 02	5 ♉ 40 ℞	16 ♓ 45 ℞	20 ♑ 38 ℞	14 ♐ 00	13 ♏ 50	16 ♍ 32	27 ♉ 29 ℞	3 ♈ 29 ℞
2 W	0 41 42	8 30 37	23 09	13 22	28 04	21 39	28 36	18 19	14 04	5 38	16 44	20 38	14 19	14 14	16 57	27 25	3 26
3 Th	0 45 38	9 29 38	7 ♐ 02	13 16	29 31	22 54	29 14	18 28	14 05	5 36	16 42	20 38D	14 37	14 39	17 22	27 22	3 23
4 F	0 49 35	10 28 42	20 25	13 13	0 ♏ 56	24 09	29 53	18 36	14 07	5 34	16 41	20 38	14 56	15 04	17 47	27 18	3 20
5 Sa	0 53 31	11 27 47	3 ♑ 21	13 12	2 20	25 23	0 ♎ 32	18 45	14 08	5 32	16 39	20 38	15 15	15 28	18 11	27 13	3 18
6 Su	0 57 28	12 26 55	15 53	13 12	3 43	26 38	1 10	18 54	14 10	5 30	16 38	20 38	15 34	15 53	18 36	27 08	3 15
7 M	1 1 24	13 26 04	28 08	13 12	5 06	27 52	1 49	19 03	14 12	5 27	16 36	20 38	15 53	16 18	19 01	27 02	3 12
8 T	1 5 21	14 25 14	10 ♒ 10	13 10	6 27	29 07	2 28	19 12	14 14	5 25	16 35	20 38	16 12	16 43	19 25	26 56	3 10
9 W	1 9 17	15 24 27	22 04	13 06	7 46	0 ♏ 21	3 06	19 21	14 16	5 23	16 34	20 39	16 32	17 08	19 50	26 50	3 07
10 Th	1 13 14	16 23 41	3 ♓ 54	12 59	9 05	1 36	3 45	19 30	14 18	5 21	16 32	20 39	16 51	17 33	20 14	26 43	3 05
11 F	1 17 11	17 22 57	15 45	12 49	10 23	2 51	4 24	19 40	14 20	5 18	16 31	20 39	17 11	17 57	20 39	26 36	3 02
12 Sa	1 21 7	18 22 15	27 38	12 37	11 39	4 05	5 02	19 49	14 22	5 16	16 30	20 39	17 30	18 22	21 03	26 28	2 59
13 Su	1 25 4	19 21 35	9 ♈ 36	12 23	12 54	5 20	5 41	19 59	14 24	5 14	16 28	20 39	17 50	18 47	21 27	26 20	2 57
14 M	1 29 0	20 20 57	21 41	12 09	14 07	6 34	6 20	20 09	14 27	5 11	16 27	20 40	18 10	19 13	21 51	26 11	2 54
15 T	1 32 57	21 20 21	3 ♉ 53	11 55	15 18	7 49	6 59	20 18	14 29	5 09	16 26	20 40	18 30	19 38	22 15	26 02	2 52
16 W	1 36 53	22 19 47	16 13	11 44	16 28	9 03	7 37	20 28	14 32	5 07	16 24	20 40	18 50	20 03	22 39	25 53	2 49
17 Th	1 40 50	23 19 15	28 41	11 35	17 36	10 18	8 16	20 38	14 35	5 04	16 23	20 41	19 10	20 28	23 03	25 43	2 47
18 F	1 44 46	24 18 45	11 ♊ 20	11 28	18 42	11 33	8 55	20 49	14 37	5 02	16 22	20 41	19 30	20 53	23 27	25 33	2 44
19 Sa	1 48 43	25 18 18	24 11	11 25	19 45	12 47	9 34	20 59	14 40	4 59	16 21	20 42	19 51	21 18	23 51	25 23	2 42
20 Su	1 52 39	26 17 53	7 ♋ 17	11 24 D	20 46	14 02	10 13	21 09	14 43	4 57	16 19	20 42	20 11	21 44	24 14	25 12	2 39
21 M	1 56 36	27 17 31	20 39	11 24 ℞	21 45	15 16	10 52	21 20	14 46	4 55	16 18	20 43	20 32	22 09	24 38	25 00	2 37
22 T	2 0 33	28 17 10	4 ♌ 20	11 24	22 40	16 31	11 31	21 30	14 50	4 52	16 17	20 43	20 53	22 34	25 01	24 49	2 34
23 W	2 4 29	29 16 52	18 21	11 23	23 32	17 45	12 09	21 41	14 53	4 50	16 16	20 44	21 13	23 00	25 25	24 37	2 32
24 Th	2 8 26	0 ♏ 16 37	2 ♍ 43	11 19	24 20	19 00	12 48	21 52	14 56	4 47	16 15	20 44	21 34	23 25	25 48	24 24	2 30
25 F	2 12 22	1 16 23	17 24	11 13	25 04	20 15	13 27	22 03	15 00	4 45	16 14	20 45	21 55	23 51	26 11	24 12	2 27
26 Sa	2 16 19	2 16 12	2 ♎ 17	11 05	25 44	21 29	14 06	22 14	15 03	4 42	16 13	20 46	22 16	24 16	26 34	23 59	2 25
27 Su	2 20 15	3 16 02	17 16	10 54	26 19	22 44	14 45	22 25	15 07	4 40	16 12	20 46	22 37	24 41	26 57	23 45	2 23
28 M	2 24 12	4 15 55	2 ♏ 10	10 44	26 48	23 58	15 24	22 36	15 10	4 37	16 11	20 47	22 59	25 07	27 20	23 32	2 21
29 T	2 28 8	5 15 50	16 51	10 34	27 11	25 13	16 03	22 47	15 14	4 35	16 10	20 48	23 20	25 33	27 43	23 18	2 19
30 W	2 32 5	6 15 47	1 ♐ 12	10 26	27 27	26 27	16 42	22 58	15 18	4 32	16 09	20 49	23 41	25 58	28 06	23 04	2 16
31 Th	2 36 2	7 15 45	15 06	10 21	27 37 ℞	27 42	17 22	23 10	15 22	4 30	16 08	20 49	24 03	26 24	28 28	22 49	2 14

EPHEMERIS CALCULATED FOR 12 MIDNIGHT GREENWICH MEAN TIME. ALL OTHER DATA AND FACING ASPECTARIAN PAGE IN **EASTERN TIME (BOLD)** AND PACIFIC TIME (REGULAR).

NOVEMBER 2019

☽ Last Aspect day	ET	PT	asp	☽ Ingress sign	day	ET	PT
2		10:46 pm	⚹ ☿	♒	3	**6:19 am**	3:19 am
3	**1:46 am**		⚹ ☿	♒	3	**6:19 am**	3:19 am
5	**9:37 am**	6:37 am	□ ☿	♓	5	**6:08 pm**	3:08 pm
7	**8:13 pm**	5:13 pm	□ ♃	♈	8	**6:49 am**	3:49 am
10	**9:00 am**	6:00 am	△ ♃	♉	10	**6:18 pm**	3:18 pm
12	**10:48 am**	7:48 am	△ ♇	♊	13	**3:46 am**	12:46 am
15	**6:40 am**	3:40 am	△ ♂	♋	15	**11:15 am**	8:15 am
17	**3:14 pm**	12:14 pm	□ ♂	♌	17	**4:57 pm**	1:57 pm
19	**4:11 pm**	1:11 pm	□ ☉	♍	19	**8:54 pm**	5:54 pm
21	**10:31 pm**	7:31 pm	⚹ ☉	♎	21	**11:20 pm**	8:20 pm
23	**9:49 pm**	6:49 pm	⚹ ♃	♏	23		9:58 pm
23	**9:49 pm**	6:49 pm	⚹ ♃	♏	24	**12:58 am**	
25	**12:30 pm**	9:30 am	⚹ ♇	♐	26	**3:11 am**	12:11 am
28	**5:50 am**	2:50 am	☌ ♃	♑	28	**7:33 am**	4:33 am
29	**10:57 pm**	7:57 pm	☌ ♇	♒	30	**3:13 pm**	12:13 pm

☽ Phases & Eclipses phase	day	ET	PT
2nd Quarter	4	**5:23 am**	2:23 am
Full Moon	12	**8:34 am**	5:34 am
4th Quarter	19	**4:11 pm**	1:11 pm
New Moon	26	**10:06 am**	7:06 am

Planet Ingress		day	ET	PT
♀	♐	1	**4:25 pm**	1:25 pm
⚵	♎	3	**9:28 pm**	6:28 pm
⚴	♐	8	**5:18 am**	2:18 am
⚳	♑	15	**11:36 pm**	8:36 pm
♂	♏	18		11:40 pm
♂	♏	19	**2:40 am**	
☉	♐	22	**9:59 am**	6:59 am
♀	♑	25	**7:28 pm**	4:28 pm

Planetary Motion		day	ET	PT
☿	D	20	**2:12 pm**	11:12 am
♆	D	27	**7:32 am**	4:32 am

1 FRIDAY
☽ △ ♅ **6:47 am** 3:47 am
☽ ⚹ ☉ **3:21 pm** 12:21 pm

2 SATURDAY
☽ ☌ ♄ **3:29 am** 12:29 am
☽ ⚹ ♆ **4:35 am** 1:35 am
☽ □ ♂ **10:11 am** 7:11 am
☽ ☌ ♇ **1:39 pm** 10:39 am
☽ ⚺ ♃ **7:10 pm** 4:10 pm
☽ ⚹ ☿ 10:46 pm

3 SUNDAY
☽ ⚹ ☿ **1:46 am**
☽ ⚹ ♀ **10:42 am** 7:42 am
☽ □ ♅ **2:50 pm** 11:50 am

4 MONDAY
☽ □ ☉ **5:23 am** 2:23 am
☽ ⚺ ♄ **1:21 pm** 10:21 am
☽ ⚺ ♆ **2:06 pm** 11:06 am
☽ △ ♂ **11:28 pm** 8:28 pm
☽ ⚺ ♇ **11:47 pm** 8:47 pm
♀ ⚻ ♅ 11:09 pm

5 TUESDAY
♀ ⚻ ♅ **2:09 am**
♂ □ ♇ **5:28 am** 2:28 am
☽ ⚹ ♃ **6:29 am** 3:29 am
☽ □ ☿ **9:37 am** 6:37 am
☽ ⚹ ♅ 11:43 pm

6 WEDNESDAY
☽ ⚹ ♅ **2:43 am**
☽ □ ♀ **5:41 am** 2:41 am
☿ ⚺ ♃ **7:48 pm** 4:48 pm
☽ △ ☉ **11:25 pm** 8:25 pm
☽ ⚹ ♄ 11:18 pm
☽ ☌ ♆ 11:37 pm

7 THURSDAY
☽ ⚹ ♄ **2:18 am**
☽ ☌ ♆ **2:37 am**
☽ ⚹ ♇ **12:33 pm** 9:33 am
☽ ⚻ ♂ **3:40 pm** 12:40 pm
☽ △ ☿ **5:52 pm** 2:52 pm
☽ □ ♃ **8:13 pm** 5:13 pm

8 FRIDAY
☿ ⚺ ♂ **7:38 am** 4:38 am
☉ ⚹ ♄ **12:06 pm** 9:06 am
☉ △ ♆ **12:56 pm** 9:56 am
☽ ⚺ ♅ **3:07 pm** 12:07 pm
♄ ⚹ ♆ **9:45 pm** 6:45 pm
☽ △ ♀ 10:15 pm

9 SATURDAY
☽ △ ♀ **1:15 am**
☽ ⚺ ♆ **2:48 pm** 11:48 am
☽ □ ♄ **2:55 pm** 11:55 am
☽ ⚻ ☉ **5:09 pm** 2:09 pm
☿ ⚹ ♇ **9:09 pm** 6:09 pm
☽ ⚻ ☿ 9:17 pm
☽ □ ♇ 9:37 pm

10 SUNDAY
☽ ⚻ ☿ **12:17 am**
☽ □ ♇ **12:37 am**
☽ ☍ ♂ **6:58 am** 3:58 am
☽ △ ♃ **9:00 am** 6:00 am
☽ ☌ ♅ 11:10 pm

11 MONDAY
☽ ☌ ♅ **2:10 am**
☉ ☌ ☿ **10:22 am** 7:22 am
☽ ⚻ ♀ **6:40 pm** 3:40 pm
☽ ⚹ ♆ 10:11 pm
☽ △ ♄ 10:44 pm

12 TUESDAY
☽ ⚹ ♆ **1:11 am**
☽ △ ♄ **1:44 am**
☽ ☍ ☿ **4:51 am** 1:51 am
☽ ☍ ☉ **8:34 am** 5:34 am
☽ △ ♇ **10:48 am** 7:48 am
♂ ⚹ ♃ **1:21 pm** 10:21 am
☽ ⚻ ♃ **7:45 pm** 4:45 pm
☽ ⚻ ♂ **7:59 pm** 4:59 pm

13 WEDNESDAY
☿ ⚹ ♄ **9:35 am** 6:35 am
☽ ⚺ ♅ **11:11 am** 8:11 am
☉ ⚹ ♇ **1:00 pm** 10:00 am
☿ △ ♆ **5:34 pm** 2:34 pm

14 THURSDAY
☿ ⚺ ♀ **3:09 am** 12:09 am
☽ ⚻ ☿ **8:14 am** 5:14 am
☽ ☍ ♀ **9:16 am** 6:16 am
☽ □ ♆ **9:32 am** 6:32 am
☽ ⚻ ♄ **10:27 am** 7:27 am
♀ □ ♆ **12:06 pm** 9:06 am
☽ ⚻ ♇ **6:56 pm** 3:56 pm
☽ ⚻ ☉ **9:23 pm** 6:23 pm
♀ ⚺ ♄ **10:32 pm** 7:32 pm

15 FRIDAY
☽ ☍ ♃ **4:24 am** 1:24 am
☽ △ ♂ **6:40 am** 3:40 am
☽ ⚹ ♅ **6:16 pm** 3:16 pm

16 SATURDAY
☽ △ ☿ **11:08 am** 8:08 am
☽ △ ♆ **4:02 pm** 1:02 pm
☽ ☍ ♄ **5:18 pm** 2:18 pm
☽ ⚻ ♀ **9:21 pm** 6:21 pm
☽ ☍ ♇ 10:15 pm

17 SUNDAY
☽ ☍ ♇ **1:15 am**
☽ △ ☉ **7:53 am** 4:53 am
☽ ⚻ ♃ **11:10 am** 8:10 am
☽ □ ♂ **3:14 pm** 12:14 pm
☽ □ ♅ **11:35 pm** 8:35 pm

18 MONDAY
☽ □ ☿ **1:53 pm** 10:53 am
♀ ⚺ ♇ **4:25 pm** 1:25 pm
☽ ⚻ ♆ **8:47 pm** 5:47 pm
☽ ⚻ ♄ **10:21 pm** 7:21 pm

19 TUESDAY
☽ ⚻ ♇ **5:48 am** 2:48 am
☽ △ ♀ **7:04 am** 4:04 am
☉ ⚺ ♃ **2:54 pm** 11:54 am
☽ △ ♃ **4:06 pm** 1:06 pm
☽ □ ☉ **4:11 pm** 1:11 pm
☽ ⚹ ♂ **9:48 pm** 6:48 pm

20 WEDNESDAY
☽ △ ♅ **3:12 am** 12:12 am
☽ ⚹ ☿ **4:32 pm** 1:32 pm
☽ ☍ ♆ **11:51 pm** 8:51 pm
☽ △ ♄ 10:43 pm

21 THURSDAY
☽ △ ♄ **1:43 am**
☽ △ ♇ **8:42 am** 5:42 am
☽ □ ♀ **2:39 pm** 11:39 am
☽ □ ♃ **7:25 pm** 4:25 pm
☽ ⚹ ☉ **10:31 pm** 7:31 pm
☽ ⚺ ♂ 11:36 pm

22 FRIDAY
☽ ⚺ ♂ **2:36 am**
☽ ⚻ ♅ **5:21 am** 2:21 am
☽ ⚺ ☿ **7:14 pm** 4:14 pm
☽ ⚻ ♆ 10:43 pm

23 SATURDAY
☽ ⚻ ♆ **1:43 am**
☽ □ ♄ **3:53 am** 12:53 am
☽ □ ♇ **10:32 am** 7:32 am
☽ ⚹ ♀ **9:00 pm** 6:00 pm
☽ ⚹ ♃ **9:49 pm** 6:49 pm

24 SUNDAY
☽ ⚺ ☉ **3:54 am** 12:54 am
☽ ☌ ♂ **6:36 am** 3:36 am
☽ ☍ ♅ **6:51 am** 3:51 am
♀ ☌ ♃ **8:33 am** 5:33 am
♂ ☍ ♅ **11:51 am** 8:51 am
☽ ☌ ☿ **10:50 pm** 7:50 pm

25 MONDAY
☽ △ ♆ **3:27 am** 12:27 am
☽ ⚹ ♄ **5:59 am** 2:59 am
☽ ⚹ ♇ **12:30 pm** 9:30 am
☉ ⚻ ♅ **9:00 pm** 6:00 pm
☽ ⚺ ♃ 9:44 pm

26 TUESDAY
☽ ⚺ ♃ **12:44 am**
☽ ⚺ ♀ **3:56 am** 12:56 am
☽ ⚻ ♅ **9:07 am** 6:07 am
☽ ☌ ☉ **10:06 am** 7:06 am
☽ ⚺ ♂ **11:28 am** 8:28 am

27 WEDNESDAY
☽ ⚺ ☿ **4:57 am** 1:57 am
☽ □ ♆ **6:37 am** 3:37 am
☽ ⚺ ♄ **9:38 am** 6:38 am
☽ ⚺ ♇ **4:11 pm** 1:11 pm

28 THURSDAY
☿ △ ♆ **4:51 am** 1:51 am
☽ ☌ ♃ **5:50 am** 2:50 am
♀ △ ♅ **1:27 pm** 10:27 am
☽ △ ♅ **1:41 pm** 10:41 am
☽ ☌ ♀ **1:43 pm** 10:43 am
☉ ⚺ ♂ **2:21 pm** 11:21 am
☽ ⚹ ♂ **7:06 pm** 4:06 pm
☽ ⚺ ☉ **7:14 pm** 4:14 pm

29 FRIDAY
☽ ⚹ ♆ **12:39 pm** 9:39 am
☽ ⚹ ☿ **3:30 pm** 12:30 pm
☽ ☌ ♄ **4:17 pm** 1:17 pm
☽ ☌ ♇ **10:57 pm** 7:57 pm
☿ ⚹ ♄ 10:13 pm

30 SATURDAY
☿ ⚹ ♄ **1:13 am**
☽ ⚺ ♃ **2:23 pm** 11:23 am
☽ □ ♅ **9:38 pm** 6:38 pm

Eastern time in bold type
Pacific time in medium type

NOVEMBER 2019

DATE	SID.TIME	SUN	MOON	NODE	MERCURY	VENUS	MARS	JUPITER	SATURN	URANUS	NEPTUNE	PLUTO	CERES	PALLAS	JUNO	VESTA	CHIRON
1 F	2 39 58	8 ♏ 15 46	28 ♐ 33	10 ♋ 19 D	27 ♏ 38 ℞	28 ♏ 57	18 ♎ 01	23 ♐ 21	15 ♑ 26	4 ♉ 28 ℞	16 ♓ 07 ℞	20 ♑ 50	24 ♐ 24	26 ♏ 49	28 ♍ 51	22 ♉ 35 ℞	2 ♈ 12 ℞
2 Sa	2 43 55	9 15 48	11 ♑ 33	10 18	27 31	0 ♐ 11	18 40	23 33	15 30	4 25	16 06	20 51	24 46	27 15	29 13	22 20	2 10
3 Su	2 47 51	10 15 51	24 10	10 18	27 14	1 26	19 19	23 44	15 34	4 23	16 06	20 52	25 08	27 41	29 36	22 05	2 08
4 M	2 51 48	11 15 56	6 ♒ 27	10 19 ℞	26 49	2 40	19 58	23 56	15 38	4 20	16 05	20 53	25 29	28 06	29 58	21 50	2 06
5 T	2 55 44	12 16 03	18 31	10 19	26 13	3 55	20 37	24 08	15 43	4 18	16 04	20 54	25 51	28 32	0 ♎ 20	21 35	2 04
6 W	2 59 41	13 16 11	0 ♓ 26	10 17	25 28	5 09	21 16	24 20	15 47	4 15	16 03	20 55	26 13	28 58	0 42	21 20	2 02
7 Th	3 3 37	14 16 21	12 17	10 13	24 34	6 24	21 56	24 32	15 52	4 13	16 03	20 56	26 35	29 23	1 04	21 04	2 01
8 F	3 7 34	15 16 32	24 08	10 07	23 31	7 38	22 35	24 44	15 56	4 10	16 02	20 57	26 57	29 49	1 26	20 48	1 59
9 Sa	3 11 31	16 16 45	6 ♈ 05	9 58	22 21	8 53	23 14	24 56	16 01	4 08	16 01	20 58	27 19	0 ♐ 15	1 47	20 33	1 57
10 Su	3 15 27	17 17 00	18 08	9 49	21 06	10 07	23 53	25 08	16 05	4 06	16 01	20 59	27 41	0 40	2 09	20 17	1 55
11 M	3 19 24	18 17 16	0 ♉ 22	9 39	19 47	11 22	24 32	25 20	16 10	4 03	16 00	21 00	28 04	1 06	2 30	20 01	1 54
12 T	3 23 20	19 17 34	12 46	9 29	18 27	12 36	25 12	25 32	16 15	4 01	16 00	21 01	28 26	1 32	2 51	19 46	1 52
13 W	3 27 17	20 17 53	25 21	9 20	17 09	13 51	25 51	25 45	16 20	3 59	15 59	21 02	28 48	1 58	3 13	19 30	1 50
14 Th	3 31 13	21 18 14	8 ♊ 08	9 14	15 54	15 05	26 30	25 57	16 25	3 56	15 59	21 03	29 11	2 23	3 34	19 14	1 49
15 F	3 35 10	22 18 37	21 07	9 10	14 47	16 20	27 10	26 10	16 30	3 54	15 58	21 05	29 33	2 49	3 55	18 59	1 47
16 Sa	3 39 6	23 19 02	4 ♋ 16	9 09 D	13 47	17 34	27 49	26 22	16 35	3 52	15 58	21 06	29 56	3 15	4 16	18 43	1 46
17 Su	3 43 3	24 19 29	17 37	9 09	12 58	18 49	28 29	26 35	16 40	3 49	15 57	21 07	0 ♑ 18	3 41	4 36	18 28	1 45
18 M	3 47 0	25 19 58	1 ♌ 10	9 10	12 20	20 03	29 08	26 47	16 45	3 47	15 57	21 08	0 41	4 07	4 57	18 12	1 43
19 T	3 50 56	26 20 28	14 55	9 11 ℞	11 54	21 18	29 47	27 00	16 51	3 45	15 57	21 10	1 04	4 32	5 17	17 57	1 42
20 W	3 54 53	27 21 00	28 53	9 12	11 39 D	22 32	0 ♏ 27	27 13	16 56	3 43	15 57	21 11	1 26	4 58	5 38	17 42	1 41
21 Th	3 58 49	28 21 34	13 ♍ 03	9 11	11 35	23 46	1 06	27 26	17 02	3 41	15 56	21 12	1 49	5 24	5 58	17 27	1 39
22 F	4 2 46	29 22 10	27 24	9 08	11 43	25 01	1 46	27 39	17 07	3 38	15 56	21 14	2 12	5 50	6 18	17 12	1 38
23 Sa	4 6 42	0 ♐ 22 47	11 ♎ 52	9 04	12 01	26 15	2 25	27 51	17 13	3 36	15 56	21 15	2 35	6 16	6 38	16 58	1 37
24 Su	4 10 39	1 23 26	26 23	8 58	12 28	27 30	3 05	28 04	17 18	3 34	15 56	21 17	2 58	6 41	6 58	16 43	1 36
25 M	4 14 35	2 24 07	10 ♏ 52	8 52	13 03	28 44	3 44	28 17	17 24	3 32	15 56	21 18	3 21	7 07	7 17	16 29	1 35
26 T	4 18 32	3 24 49	25 10	8 46	13 46	29 59	4 24	28 30	17 30	3 30	15 56	21 19	3 44	7 33	7 37	16 15	1 34
27 W	4 22 29	4 25 33	9 ♐ 14	8 42	14 36	1 ♑ 13	5 04	28 44	17 35	3 28	15 56 D	21 21	4 07	7 59	7 56	16 02	1 33
28 Th	4 26 25	5 26 18	22 58	8 39	15 31	2 27	5 43	28 57	17 41	3 26	15 56	21 22	4 30	8 25	8 15	15 48	1 32
29 F	4 30 22	6 27 05	6 ♑ 20	8 38 D	16 32	3 42	6 23	29 10	17 47	3 24	15 56	21 24	4 53	8 51	8 35	15 35	1 32
30 Sa	4 34 18	7 27 52	19 20	8 39	17 37	4 56	7 03	29 23	17 53	3 22	15 56	21 26	5 16	9 16	8 53	15 22	1 31

EPHEMERIS CALCULATED FOR 12 MIDNIGHT GREENWICH MEAN TIME. ALL OTHER DATA AND FACING ASPECTARIAN PAGE IN **EASTERN TIME (BOLD)** AND PACIFIC TIME (REGULAR).

DECEMBER 2019

☽ Last Aspect day	ET / hr:mn / PT	asp	☽ Ingress sign	day	ET / hr:mn / PT
2	**7:27 am** 4:27 am	□☿	♓	2	11:11 pm
2	**7:27 am** 4:27 am	□☿	♓	3	**2:11 am**
5	**3:15 am** 12:15 am	△☿	♈	5	**2:44 pm** 11:44 am
7	**10:01 am** 7:01 am	□♇	♉	7	11:29 pm
7	**10:01 am** 7:01 am	□♇	♉	8	**2:29 am**
9	**8:13 pm** 5:13 pm	△♇	♊	10	**11:47 am** 8:47 am
11	9:12 pm	☍☉	♋	12	**6:23 pm** 3:23 pm
12	**12:12 am**	☍☉	♋	12	**6:23 pm** 3:23 pm
14	**10:57 am** 7:57 am	☍♀	♌	14	**10:56 pm** 7:56 pm
16	**5:10 pm** 2:10 pm	△☉	♍	16	11:16 pm
16	**5:10 pm** 2:10 pm	△☉	♍	17	**2:16 am**
19	**3:07 am** 12:07 am	△♀	♎	19	**5:04 am** 2:04 am
21	**6:45 am** 3:45 am	⚹☉	♏	21	**7:57 am** 4:57 am
22	**10:27 pm** 7:27 pm	☌♂	♐	23	**11:34 am** 8:34 am
25	**6:18 am** 3:18 am	☌☿	♑	25	**4:45 pm** 1:45 pm
27	**4:03 pm** 1:03 pm	⚹♂	♒	27	9:21 pm
27	**4:03 pm** 1:03 pm	⚹♂	♒	28	**12:21 am**
30	**5:24 am** 2:24 am	□♂	♓	30	**10:41 am** 7:41 am

☽ Phases & Eclipses phase	day	ET / hr:mn / PT
2nd Quarter	3	10:58 pm
2nd Quarter	4	**1:58 am**
Full Moon	11	9:12 pm
Full Moon	12	**12:12 am**
4th Quarter	18	**11:57 pm** 8:57 pm
New Moon	25	9:13 pm
New Moon	26	**12:13 am**
●	25/26	4° ♑ 07'

Planet Ingress		day	ET / hr:mn / PT
♃	♑	2	**1:20 pm** 10:20 am
☿	♐	9	**4:42 am** 1:42 am
♀	♒	19	10:42 pm
♀	♒	20	**1:42 am**
☉	♑	21	**11:19 pm** 8:19 pm
☿	♑	28	**11:55 pm** 8:55 pm

Planetary Motion		day	ET / hr:mn / PT
⚷	D	12	**10:48 pm** 7:48 pm
⚶	D	29	**5:40 pm** 2:40 pm

1 SUNDAY
☽ ⚺ ♀ **4:01 am** 1:01 am
☽ □ ♂ **6:43 am** 3:43 am
☽ ⚹ ☉ **8:43 am** 5:43 am
☽ ⚺ ♆ **10:12 pm** 7:12 pm
☽ ⚺ ♄ 11:30 pm

2 MONDAY
☽ ⚺ ♄ **2:30 am**
☽ □ ☿ **7:27 am** 4:27 am
☽ ⚺ ♇ **9:12 am** 6:12 am
☿ ⚹ ♇ 9:23 pm
☽ ⚹ ♃ 11:25 pm

3 TUESDAY
☿ ⚹ ♇ **12:23 am**
☽ ⚹ ♃ **2:25 am**
☽ ⚹ ♅ **8:43 am** 5:43 am
♀ ⚹ ♂ **10:47 am** 7:47 am
☽ △ ♂ **9:51 pm** 6:51 pm
☽ ⚹ ♀ **10:26 pm** 7:26 pm
☽ □ ☉ 10:58 pm

4 WEDNESDAY
☽ □ ☉ **1:58 am**
☽ ☌ ♆ **10:19 am** 7:19 am
☽ ⚹ ♄ **3:14 pm** 12:14 pm
☽ ⚹ ♇ **9:41 pm** 6:41 pm

5 THURSDAY
☽ △ ☿ **3:15 am** 12:15 am
☽ □ ♃ **4:09 pm** 1:09 pm
☽ ⚺ ♅ **9:10 pm** 6:10 pm

6 FRIDAY
☽ ⚻ ♂ **1:57 pm** 10:57 am
☽ □ ♀ **5:57 pm** 2:57 pm
☽ △ ☉ **8:04 pm** 5:04 pm
☽ ⚺ ♆ **10:45 pm** 7:45 pm

7 SATURDAY
☽ □ ♄ **4:05 am** 1:05 am
☽ □ ♇ **10:01 am** 7:01 am
☽ ⚻ ☿ **11:02 pm** 8:02 pm

8 SUNDAY
☉ □ ♆ **4:00 am** 1:00 am
☽ △ ♃ **4:58 am** 1:58 am
☽ ☌ ♅ **8:34 am** 5:34 am
♀ ⚹ ♆ **4:48 pm** 1:48 pm

9 MONDAY
☽ ☍ ♂ **4:10 am** 1:10 am
☽ ⚹ ♆ **9:20 am** 6:20 am
☽ △ ♀ **11:07 am** 8:07 am
☽ ⚻ ☉ **11:53 am** 8:53 am
☽ △ ♄ **2:54 pm** 11:54 am
☽ △ ♇ **8:13 pm** 5:13 pm

10 TUESDAY
☿ ⚺ ♃ **9:58 am** 6:58 am
☽ ⚻ ♃ **3:10 pm** 12:10 pm
☽ ☍ ☿ **3:43 pm** 12:43 pm
☽ ⚺ ♅ **5:28 pm** 2:28 pm

11 WEDNESDAY
☉ ⚺ ♀ **3:26 am** 12:26 am
♀ ☌ ♄ **5:05 am** 2:05 am
☉ ⚺ ♄ **5:29 am** 2:29 am
☿ ⚻ ♅ **6:55 am** 3:55 am
☽ ⚻ ♂ **3:12 pm** 12:12 pm
☽ □ ♆ **5:11 pm** 2:11 pm
☽ ⚻ ♄ **10:55 pm** 7:55 pm
☽ ☍ ☉ 9:12 pm
☽ ⚻ ♀ 9:35 pm

12 THURSDAY
☽ ☍ ☉ **12:12 am**
☽ ⚻ ♀ **12:35 am**
☽ ⚻ ♇ **3:38 am** 12:38 am
☽ ☍ ♃ **10:33 pm** 7:33 pm
☽ ⚹ ♅ **11:43 pm** 8:43 pm

13 FRIDAY
☽ ⚻ ☿ **4:48 am** 1:48 am
♂ △ ♆ **6:55 am** 3:55 am
♀ ☌ ♇ **10:16 am** 7:16 am
☉ ⚺ ♇ **10:27 am** 7:27 am
☽ △ ♆ **10:37 am** 7:37 am
☽ △ ♂ **11:25 pm** 8:25 pm

14 SATURDAY
☽ ☍ ♄ **4:32 am** 1:32 am
☽ ☍ ♇ **8:47 am** 5:47 am
☽ ⚻ ☉ **9:35 am** 6:35 am
☽ ☍ ♀ **10:57 am** 7:57 am

15 SUNDAY
☽ ⚻ ♃ **3:51 am** 12:51 am
☽ □ ♅ **4:02 am** 1:02 am
♃ △ ♅ **2:01 pm** 11:01 am
☽ △ ☿ **3:18 pm** 12:18 pm
☽ ⚻ ♆ 11:28 pm

16 MONDAY
☽ ⚻ ♆ **2:28 am**
☽ □ ♂ **5:47 am** 2:47 am
☽ ⚻ ♄ **8:37 am** 5:37 am
☽ ⚻ ♇ **12:29 pm** 9:29 am
☽ △ ☉ **5:10 pm** 2:10 pm
☽ ⚻ ♀ **7:26 pm** 4:26 pm

17 TUESDAY
☽ △ ♅ **7:12 am** 4:12 am
☽ △ ♃ **7:56 am** 4:56 am
☽ □ ☿ 9:29 pm

18 WEDNESDAY
☽ □ ☿ **12:29 am**
☽ ☍ ♆ **5:29 am** 2:29 am
☽ ⚹ ♂ **11:14 am** 8:14 am
☽ △ ♄ **11:56 am** 8:56 am
☽ △ ♇ **3:29 pm** 12:29 pm
☽ □ ☉ **11:57 pm** 8:57 pm

19 THURSDAY
☽ △ ♀ **3:07 am** 12:07 am
♂ ⚹ ♄ **5:00 am** 2:00 am
☽ ⚻ ♅ **9:55 am** 6:55 am
☽ □ ♃ **11:34 am** 8:34 am
☿ □ ♆ **11:19 pm** 8:19 pm

20 FRIDAY
☽ ⚻ ♆ **8:18 am** 5:18 am
☽ ⚹ ☿ **9:22 am** 6:22 am
☽ □ ♄ **3:08 pm** 12:08 pm
☽ ⚺ ♂ **4:33 pm** 1:33 pm
☽ □ ♇ **6:24 pm** 3:24 pm

21 SATURDAY
☽ ⚹ ☉ **6:45 am** 3:45 am
☽ □ ♀ **10:51 am** 7:51 am
☽ ☍ ♅ **12:47 pm** 9:47 am
☽ ⚹ ♃ **3:21 pm** 12:21 pm

22 SUNDAY
♀ □ ♅ **8:30 am** 5:30 am
♂ ⚹ ♇ **9:32 am** 6:32 am
☽ △ ♆ **11:32 am** 8:32 am
☿ ⚺ ♄ **6:24 pm** 3:24 pm
☽ ⚹ ♄ **6:51 pm** 3:51 pm
☽ ⚺ ☿ **6:54 pm** 3:54 pm
☽ ⚹ ♇ **9:52 pm** 6:52 pm
☽ ☌ ♂ **10:27 pm** 7:27 pm

23 MONDAY
☽ ⚺ ☉ **2:28 pm** 11:28 am
☽ ⚻ ♅ **4:26 pm** 1:26 pm
☽ ⚹ ♀ **7:38 pm** 4:38 pm
☽ ⚺ ♃ **8:01 pm** 5:01 pm
☿ ⚺ ♇ **10:08 pm** 7:08 pm
♀ ⚺ ♃ 9:51 pm

24 TUESDAY
♀ ⚺ ♃ **12:51 am**
☽ □ ♆ **3:56 pm** 12:56 pm
☉ △ ♅ **4:44 pm** 1:44 pm
☽ ⚺ ♄ **11:53 pm** 8:53 pm
☿ ⚺ ♂ 9:53 pm
☽ ⚺ ♇ 11:40 pm

25 WEDNESDAY
☿ ⚺ ♂ **12:53 am**
☽ ⚺ ♇ **2:40 am**
☽ ⚺ ♂ **5:56 am** 2:56 am
☽ ☌ ☿ **6:18 am** 3:18 am
☽ △ ♅ **9:45 pm** 6:45 pm
☽ ☌ ☉ 9:13 pm
☽ ☌ ♃ 11:29 pm

26 THURSDAY
☽ ☌ ☉ **12:13 am**
☽ ☌ ♃ **2:29 am**
☽ ⚺ ♀ **6:39 am** 3:39 am
☽ ⚹ ♆ **10:23 pm** 7:23 pm

27 FRIDAY
☽ ☌ ♄ **7:08 am** 4:08 am
☽ ☌ ♇ **9:42 am** 6:42 am
☉ ☌ ♃ **1:25 pm** 10:25 am
☽ ⚹ ♂ **4:03 pm** 1:03 pm
☽ ⚺ ☿ **9:02 pm** 6:02 pm

28 SATURDAY
☽ □ ♅ **5:33 am** 2:33 am
☽ ⚺ ♃ **11:37 am** 8:37 am
☽ ⚺ ☉ **1:09 pm** 10:09 am
☽ ☌ ♀ **9:07 pm** 6:07 pm

29 SUNDAY
☽ ⚺ ♆ **7:34 am** 4:34 am
☽ ⚺ ♄ **5:13 pm** 2:13 pm
☽ ⚺ ♇ **7:31 pm** 4:31 pm

30 MONDAY
☽ □ ♂ **5:24 am** 2:24 am
☽ ⚹ ☿ **3:52 pm** 12:52 pm
☽ ⚹ ♅ **4:04 pm** 1:04 pm
☿ △ ♅ **5:22 pm** 2:22 pm
☽ ⚹ ♃ **11:37 pm** 8:37 pm

31 TUESDAY
☽ ⚹ ☉ **5:32 am** 2:32 am
☽ ⚺ ♀ **3:07 pm** 12:07 pm
☽ ☌ ♆ **7:15 pm** 4:15 pm

Eastern time in bold type
Pacific time in medium type

DECEMBER 2019

DATE	SID.TIME	SUN	MOON	NODE	MERCURY	VENUS	MARS	JUPITER	SATURN	URANUS	NEPTUNE	PLUTO	CERES	PALLAS	JUNO	VESTA	CHIRON
1 Su	4 38 15	8 ♐ 28 41	1 ♒ 58	8 ♋ 40	18 ♏ 46	6 ♑ 10	7 ♏ 42	29 ♐ 36	17 ♑ 59	3 ♉ 20 ℞	15 ♓ 56	21 ♑ 27	5 ♑ 40	9 ♐ 42	9 ♎ 12	15 ♉ 10 ℞	1 ♈ 30 ℞
2 M	4 42 11	9 29 30	14 19	8 42	19 58	7 25	8 22	29 50	18 05	3 18	15 56	21 29	6 03	10 08	9 31	14 58	1 29
3 T	4 46 8	10 30 21	26 25	8 43	21 13	8 39	9 02	0 ♑ 03	18 11	3 17	15 56	21 30	6 26	10 34	9 49	14 46	1 29
4 W	4 50 5	11 31 12	8 ♓ 22	8 44 ℞	22 31	9 53	9 42	0 17	18 17	3 15	15 56	21 32	6 50	10 59	10 07	14 35	1 28
5 Th	4 54 1	12 32 04	20 14	8 44	23 51	11 08	10 21	0 30	18 23	3 13	15 57	21 34	7 13	11 25	10 26	14 24	1 28
6 F	4 57 58	13 32 57	2 ♈ 07	8 42	25 12	12 22	11 01	0 43	18 30	3 11	15 57	21 35	7 37	11 51	10 44	14 13	1 27
7 Sa	5 1 54	14 33 51	14 04	8 40	26 35	13 36	11 41	0 57	18 36	3 10	15 57	21 37	8 00	12 17	11 01	14 03	1 27
8 Su	5 5 51	15 34 45	26 11	8 37	28 00	14 50	12 21	1 10	18 42	3 08	15 57	21 39	8 23	12 42	11 19	13 53	1 27
9 M	5 9 47	16 35 40	8 ♉ 30	8 33	29 25	16 05	13 01	1 24	18 49	3 06	15 58	21 40	8 47	13 08	11 36	13 43	1 27
10 T	5 13 44	17 36 37	21 04	8 29	0 ♐ 52	17 19	13 40	1 38	18 55	3 05	15 58	21 42	9 11	13 34	11 53	13 34	1 26
11 W	5 17 40	18 37 34	3 ♊ 53	8 26	2 19	18 33	14 20	1 51	19 01	3 03	15 59	21 44	9 34	13 59	12 11	13 26	1 26
12 Th	5 21 37	19 38 31	16 59	8 24	3 47	19 47	15 00	2 05	19 08	3 02	15 59	21 45	9 58	14 25	12 27	13 18	1 26
13 F	5 25 34	20 39 30	0 ♋ 21	8 23 D	5 16	21 01	15 40	2 18	19 14	3 00	16 00	21 47	10 21	14 50	12 44	13 10	1 26 D
14 Sa	5 29 30	21 40 30	13 56	8 23	6 45	22 15	16 20	2 32	19 21	2 59	16 00	21 49	10 45	15 16	13 01	13 03	1 26
15 Su	5 33 27	22 41 30	27 43	8 24	8 14	23 29	17 00	2 46	19 27	2 58	16 01	21 51	11 09	15 41	13 17	12 56	1 26
16 M	5 37 23	23 42 32	11 ♌ 40	8 25	9 44	24 43	17 40	2 59	19 34	2 56	16 01	21 53	11 32	16 07	13 33	12 49	1 26
17 T	5 41 20	24 43 34	25 44	8 26	11 15	25 57	18 20	3 13	19 41	2 55	16 02	21 54	11 56	16 33	13 49	12 43	1 26
18 W	5 45 16	25 44 37	9 ♍ 52	8 27	12 46	27 11	19 00	3 27	19 47	2 54	16 03	21 56	12 20	16 58	14 05	12 38	1 27
19 Th	5 49 13	26 45 42	24 03	8 27 ℞	14 17	28 25	19 40	3 41	19 54	2 53	16 04	21 58	12 44	17 23	14 20	12 32	1 27
20 F	5 53 9	27 46 47	8 ♎ 14	8 27	15 48	29 39	20 20	3 54	20 01	2 51	16 04	22 00	13 08	17 49	14 35	12 28	1 27
21 Sa	5 57 6	28 47 53	22 23	8 26	17 20	0 ♒ 53	21 00	4 08	20 08	2 50	16 05	22 02	13 31	18 14	14 51	12 23	1 28
22 Su	6 1 3	29 48 59	6 ♏ 28	8 25	18 51	2 07	21 41	4 22	20 14	2 49	16 06	22 04	13 55	18 40	15 05	12 20	1 28
23 M	6 4 59	0 ♑ 50 07	20 27	8 24	20 23	3 21	22 21	4 36	20 21	2 48	16 07	22 06	14 19	19 05	15 20	12 16	1 29
24 T	6 8 56	1 51 15	4 ♐ 15	8 24	21 56	4 35	23 01	4 50	20 28	2 47	16 08	22 08	14 43	19 30	15 35	12 13	1 29
25 W	6 12 52	2 52 24	17 52	8 23	23 28	5 49	23 41	5 03	20 35	2 47	16 09	22 09	15 07	19 56	15 49	12 11	1 30
26 Th	6 16 49	3 53 34	1 ♑ 14	8 23 D	25 01	7 03	24 21	5 17	20 42	2 46	16 09	22 11	15 31	20 21	16 03	12 09	1 31
27 F	6 20 45	4 54 44	14 21	8 23	26 34	8 16	25 02	5 31	20 49	2 45	16 10	22 13	15 55	20 46	16 17	12 07	1 31
28 Sa	6 24 42	5 55 54	27 11	8 23	28 07	9 30	25 42	5 45	20 56	2 44	16 11	22 15	16 19	21 11	16 30	12 06	1 32
29 Su	6 28 38	6 57 04	9 ♒ 45	8 23	29 41	10 44	26 22	5 59	21 03	2 43	16 13	22 17	16 42	21 36	16 43	12 06 D	1 33
30 M	6 32 35	7 58 14	22 04	8 23 ℞	1 ♑ 15	11 57	27 02	6 13	21 10	2 43	16 14	22 19	17 06	22 01	16 56	12 05	1 34
31 T	6 36 32	8 59 24	4 ♓ 10	8 23	2 49	13 11	27 43	6 26	21 17	2 42	16 15	22 21	17 30	22 27	17 09	12 06	1 35

EPHEMERIS CALCULATED FOR 12 MIDNIGHT GREENWICH MEAN TIME. ALL OTHER DATA AND FACING ASPECTARIAN PAGE IN **EASTERN TIME (BOLD)** AND PACIFIC TIME (REGULAR).

JANUARY 2020

☽ Last Aspect day	ET / hr:mn / PT		asp	☽ Ingress sign	day	ET / hr:mn / PT	
1	9:14 pm	6:14 pm	△♂	♈	1	11:00 pm	8:00 pm
3	8:18 pm	5:18 pm	□♇	♉	4	11:15 am	8:15 am
6	7:08 am	4:08 am	△♇	♊	6	9:11 pm	6:11 pm
8	5:16 pm	2:16 pm	△♀	♋	9	3:43 am	12:43 am
10	6:58 pm	3:58 pm	☍♇	♌	11	7:16 am	4:16 am
13	8:42 am	5:42 am	☍♀	♍	13	9:06 am	6:06 am
15	7:12 am	4:12 am	△☿	♎	15	10:43 am	7:43 am
17	7:58 am	4:58 am	□☉	♏	17	1:20 pm	10:20 am
19	4:22 pm	1:22 pm	✶☉	♐	19	5:41 pm	2:41 pm
20	11:46 pm	8:46 pm	□♆	♑	21		9:00 pm

☽ Last Aspect day	ET / hr:mn / PT		asp	☽ Ingress sign	day	ET / hr:mn / PT	
20	11:46 pm	8:46 pm	□♆	♑	22	12:00 am	
23	9:08 pm	6:08 pm	☌♄	♒	24	8:20 am	5:20 am
25	2:06 pm	11:06 am	☌☿	♓	26	6:44 pm	3:44 pm
28	8:08 pm	5:08 pm	✶♄	♈	29	6:51 am	3:51 am
31	10:10 am	7:10 am	✶☿	♉	31	7:28 pm	4:28 pm

☽ Phases & Eclipses phase	day	ET / hr:mn / PT	
2nd Quarter	2	11:45 pm	8:45 pm
Full Moon	10	2:21 pm	11:21 am
(eclipse)	10	20° ♋ 00'	
4th Quarter	17	7:58 am	4:58 am
New Moon	24	4:42 pm	1:42 pm

Planet Ingress	day	ET / hr:mn / PT	
♂ ♐	3	4:37 am	1:37 am
♀ ♓	13	1:39 pm	10:39 am
☿ ♒	16	1:31 pm	10:31 am
⚴ ♑	18	5:33 am	2:33 am
☉ ♒	20	9:55 am	6:55 am
⚳ ♒	31	3:01 am	12:01 am

Planetary Motion	day	ET / hr:mn / PT	
♅ D	10	8:49 pm	5:49 pm

1 WEDNESDAY
☽ ✶ ♄ **5:43 am** 2:43 am
☽ ✶ ♇ **7:39 am** 4:39 am
☽ △ ♂ **9:14 pm** 6:14 pm

2 THURSDAY
☽ ⚺ ♅ **4:26 am** 1:26 am
♀ ⚺ ♆ **7:56 am** 4:56 am
☿ ☌ ♃ **11:42 am** 8:42 am
☽ □ ♃ **1:19 pm** 10:19 am
☽ □ ☿ **1:32 pm** 10:32 am
☽ □ ☉ **11:45 pm** 8:45 pm

3 FRIDAY
☽ ⚺ ♆ **7:56 am** 4:56 am
☽ ✶ ♀ **10:38 am** 7:38 am
☽ □ ♄ **6:50 pm** 3:50 pm
☽ □ ♇ **8:18 pm** 5:18 pm

4 SATURDAY
☽ ⚻ ♂ **1:03 pm** 10:03 am
☽ ☌ ♅ **4:31 pm** 1:31 pm
☽ △ ♃ 11:20 pm

5 SUNDAY
☽ △ ♃ **2:20 am**
☽ △ ☿ **10:18 am** 7:18 am
☽ △ ☉ **4:37 pm** 1:37 pm
☽ ✶ ♆ **7:15 pm** 4:15 pm

6 MONDAY
☽ □ ♀ **4:08 am** 1:08 am
☽ △ ♄ **6:07 am** 3:07 am
☽ △ ♇ **7:08 am** 4:08 am
☉ ✶ ♆ 10:21 pm
☽ ☍ ♂ 11:05 pm
☽ ⚺ ♅ 11:09 pm
♀ ⚺ ♄ 11:39 pm

7 TUESDAY
☉ ✶ ♆ **1:21 am**
☽ ☍ ♂ **2:05 am**
☽ ⚺ ♅ **2:09 am**
♀ ⚺ ♄ **2:39 am**
♂ ⚻ ♅ **3:13 am** 12:13 am
♀ ⚺ ♇ **11:53 am** 8:53 am
☽ ⚻ ♃ **12:28 pm** 9:28 am
☽ ⚻ ☿ 11:49 pm

8 WEDNESDAY
☽ ⚻ ☿ **2:49 am**
☽ □ ♆ **3:27 am** 12:27 am
☽ ⚻ ☉ **5:35 am** 2:35 am
☿ ✶ ♆ **8:03 am** 5:03 am
☽ ⚻ ♄ **2:04 pm** 11:04 am
☽ ⚻ ♇ **2:40 pm** 11:40 am
☽ △ ♀ **5:16 pm** 2:16 pm

9 THURSDAY
☽ ✶ ♅ **8:23 am** 5:23 am
☽ ⚻ ♂ **11:09 am** 8:09 am
☽ ☍ ♃ **7:00 pm** 4:00 pm

10 FRIDAY
☽ △ ♆ **8:19 am** 5:19 am
☉ ☌ ☿ **10:19 am** 7:19 am
☽ ☍ ☉ **2:21 pm** 11:21 am
☽ ☍ ☿ **2:33 pm** 11:33 am
☽ ☍ ♄ **6:43 pm** 3:43 pm
☽ ☍ ♇ **6:58 pm** 3:58 pm
☽ ⚻ ♀ 11:12 pm

11 SATURDAY
☽ ⚻ ♀ **2:12 am**
☽ □ ♅ **11:43 am** 8:43 am
☽ △ ♂ **4:54 pm** 1:54 pm
☽ ⚻ ♃ **10:43 pm** 7:43 pm

12 SUNDAY
☿ ☌ ♄ **4:51 am** 1:51 am
☿ ☌ ♇ **5:14 am** 2:14 am
☽ ⚻ ♆ **10:50 am** 7:50 am
♄ ☌ ♇ **11:59 am** 8:59 am
☽ ⚻ ☉ **8:23 pm** 5:23 pm
☽ ⚻ ♇ **9:12 pm** 6:12 pm
☽ ⚻ ♄ **9:15 pm** 6:15 pm
☽ ⚻ ☿ **11:13 pm** 8:13 pm

13 MONDAY
☉ ☌ ♇ **8:21 am** 5:21 am
☽ ☍ ♀ **8:42 am** 5:42 am
☉ ☌ ♄ **10:15 am** 7:15 am
☽ △ ♅ **1:29 pm** 10:29 am
☽ □ ♂ **9:00 pm** 6:00 pm
☽ △ ♃ 10:07 pm

14 TUESDAY
☽ △ ♃ **1:07 am**
☽ ☍ ♆ **12:27 pm** 9:27 am
☽ △ ♇ **10:51 pm** 7:51 pm
☽ △ ♄ **11:12 pm** 8:12 pm
☽ △ ☉ 10:41 pm

15 WEDNESDAY
☽ △ ☉ **1:41 am**
☽ △ ☿ **7:12 am** 4:12 am
☽ ⚻ ♀ **2:52 pm** 11:52 am
☽ ⚻ ♅ **3:09 pm** 12:09 pm
♀ ✶ ♅ **6:18 pm** 3:18 pm
☽ ✶ ♂ 10:14 pm

16 THURSDAY
☽ ✶ ♂ **1:14 am**
☽ □ ♃ **3:45 am** 12:45 am
☽ ⚻ ♆ **2:36 pm** 11:36 am
☽ □ ♇ 10:16 pm
☽ □ ♄ 10:56 pm

17 FRIDAY
☽ □ ♇ **1:16 am**
☽ □ ♄ **1:56 am**
☽ □ ☉ **7:58 am** 4:58 am
☽ □ ☿ **4:36 pm** 1:36 pm
☽ ☍ ♅ **5:55 pm** 2:55 pm
☽ △ ♀ **10:26 pm** 7:26 pm

18 SATURDAY
☿ □ ♅ **3:32 am** 12:32 am
☽ ⚺ ♂ **6:56 am** 3:56 am
☽ ✶ ♃ **7:45 am** 4:45 am
☽ △ ♆ **6:13 pm** 3:13 pm

19 SUNDAY
☽ ✶ ♇ **5:18 am** 2:18 am
☽ ✶ ♄ **6:19 am** 3:19 am
♂ ⚺ ♃ **7:46 am** 4:46 am
☽ ✶ ☉ **4:22 pm** 1:22 pm
☽ ⚻ ♅ **10:28 pm** 7:28 pm

20 MONDAY
☽ ✶ ☿ **4:40 am** 1:40 am
☽ □ ♀ **8:20 am** 5:20 am
☽ ⚺ ♃ **1:42 pm** 10:42 am
☽ ☌ ♂ **2:47 pm** 11:47 am
☽ □ ♆ **11:46 pm** 8:46 pm

21 TUESDAY
☽ ⚺ ♇ **11:17 am** 8:17 am
☽ ⚺ ♄ **12:41 pm** 9:41 am

22 WEDNESDAY
☽ ⚺ ☉ **3:14 am** 12:14 am
☽ △ ♅ **5:00 am** 2:00 am
☽ ⚺ ☿ **7:47 pm** 4:47 pm
☽ ✶ ♀ **8:52 pm** 5:52 pm
☽ ☌ ♃ **9:45 pm** 6:45 pm
☽ ⚺ ♂ 9:58 pm
☉ □ ♅ 10:54 pm

23 THURSDAY
☽ ⚺ ♂ **12:58 am**
☉ □ ♅ **1:54 am**
☽ ✶ ♆ **7:20 am** 4:20 am
♀ ✶ ♃ **8:07 am** 5:07 am
☿ ⚺ ♃ **12:17 pm** 9:17 am
☽ ☌ ♇ **7:18 pm** 4:18 pm
☿ ⚺ ♀ **8:07 pm** 5:07 pm
☽ ☌ ♄ **9:08 pm** 6:08 pm

24 FRIDAY
☽ □ ♅ **1:34 pm** 10:34 am
☽ ☌ ☉ **4:42 pm** 1:42 pm

25 SATURDAY
☽ ⚺ ♃ **7:56 am** 4:56 am
☿ ✶ ♂ **8:09 am** 5:09 am
☽ ⚺ ♀ **12:08 pm** 9:08 am
☽ ✶ ♂ **1:34 pm** 10:34 am
☽ ☌ ☿ **2:06 pm** 11:06 am
☽ ⚺ ♆ **4:58 pm** 1:58 pm

26 SUNDAY
☽ ⚺ ♇ **5:23 am** 2:23 am
☽ ⚺ ♄ **7:42 am** 4:42 am
☿ ⚺ ♆ **10:50 am** 7:50 am
♀ □ ♂ **8:37 pm** 5:37 pm
☽ ✶ ♅ 9:12 pm

27 MONDAY
☽ ✶ ♅ **12:12 am**
☽ ⚺ ☉ **8:47 am** 5:47 am
♀ ☌ ♆ **3:00 pm** 12:00 pm
☽ ✶ ♃ **8:13 pm** 5:13 pm

28 TUESDAY
☽ □ ♂ **4:30 am** 1:30 am
☽ ☌ ♆ **4:34 am** 1:34 am
♂ □ ♆ **5:34 am** 2:34 am
☽ ☌ ♀ **6:02 am** 3:02 am
☽ ⚺ ☿ **11:27 am** 8:27 am
☽ ✶ ♇ **5:21 pm** 2:21 pm
☽ ✶ ♄ **8:08 pm** 5:08 pm

29 WEDNESDAY
☽ ⚺ ♅ **12:31 pm** 9:31 am
☽ ✶ ☉ 11:50 pm

30 THURSDAY
☽ ✶ ☉ **2:50 am**
☿ ⚺ ♇ **5:26 am** 2:26 am
☽ □ ♃ **9:54 am** 6:54 am
☽ ⚺ ♆ **5:21 pm** 2:21 pm
☽ △ ♂ **8:49 pm** 5:49 pm
☽ ⚺ ♀ 10:26 pm

31 FRIDAY
☽ ⚺ ♀ **1:26 am**
☿ ⚺ ♄ **4:26 am** 1:26 am
☽ □ ♇ **6:11 am** 3:11 am
☽ □ ♄ **9:24 am** 6:24 am
☽ ✶ ☿ **10:10 am** 7:10 am
☽ ☌ ♅ 10:10 pm

Eastern time in bold type
Pacific time in medium type

JANUARY 2020

DATE	SID.TIME	SUN	MOON	NODE	MERCURY	VENUS	MARS	JUPITER	SATURN	URANUS	NEPTUNE	PLUTO	CERES	PALLAS	JUNO	VESTA	CHIRON
1 W	6 40 28	10♑00 34	16♓08	8♋23℞	4♑23	14♒25	28♏23	6♑40	21♑24	2♉42℞	16♓16	22♑23	17♑54	22♐52	17♎22	12♉06	1♈36
2 Th	6 44 25	11 01 44	28 01	8 23	5 58	15 38	29 03	6 54	21 31	2 41	16 17	22 25	18 18	23 17	17 34	12 08	1 37
3 F	6 48 21	12 02 54	9♈53	8 23D	7 33	16 52	29 44	7 08	21 38	2 41	16 18	22 27	18 42	23 41	17 46	12 09	1 38
4 Sa	6 52 18	13 04 04	21 50	8 23	9 08	18 05	0♐24	7 22	21 45	2 40	16 19	22 29	19 06	24 06	17 58	12 11	1 39
5 Su	6 56 14	14 05 13	3♉55	8 23	10 44	19 18	1 05	7 35	21 52	2 40	16 21	22 31	19 30	24 31	18 09	12 13	1 40
6 M	7 0 11	15 06 22	16 14	8 24	12 20	20 32	1 45	7 49	21 59	2 40	16 22	22 33	19 54	24 56	18 21	12 16	1 42
7 T	7 4 7	16 07 31	28 50	8 24	13 56	21 45	2 25	8 03	22 06	2 39	16 23	22 35	20 18	25 21	18 32	12 20	1 43
8 W	7 8 4	17 08 39	11♊47	8 25	15 33	22 58	3 06	8 17	22 13	2 39	16 25	22 37	20 42	25 45	18 42	12 23	1 44
9 Th	7 12 1	18 09 48	25 05	8 26	17 10	24 11	3 46	8 31	22 20	2 39	16 26	22 39	21 06	26 10	18 53	12 27	1 46
10 F	7 15 57	19 10 56	8♋44	8 26℞	18 47	25 24	4 27	8 44	22 27	2 39	16 27	22 41	21 30	26 35	19 03	12 32	1 47
11 Sa	7 19 54	20 12 03	22 44	8 26	20 25	26 37	5 08	8 58	22 34	2 39D	16 29	22 43	21 54	26 59	19 13	12 37	1 49
12 Su	7 23 50	21 13 11	7♌00	8 25	22 04	27 50	5 48	9 12	22 42	2 39	16 30	22 45	22 18	27 24	19 22	12 42	1 50
13 M	7 27 47	22 14 18	21 27	8 23	23 43	29 03	6 29	9 25	22 49	2 39	16 32	22 47	22 42	27 48	19 32	12 47	1 52
14 T	7 31 43	23 15 25	6♍00	8 21	25 22	0♓16	7 09	9 39	22 56	2 39	16 33	22 49	23 06	28 12	19 41	12 53	1 54
15 W	7 35 40	24 16 31	20 32	8 19	27 02	1 29	7 50	9 53	23 03	2 39	16 35	22 51	23 30	28 37	19 50	13 00	1 55
16 Th	7 39 36	25 17 38	4♎58	8 18	28 42	2 42	8 31	10 06	23 10	2 40	16 36	22 53	23 54	29 01	19 58	13 06	1 57
17 F	7 43 33	26 18 44	19 14	8 17D	0♒23	3 54	9 11	10 20	23 17	2 40	16 38	22 55	24 18	29 25	20 06	13 14	1 59
18 Sa	7 47 30	27 19 51	3♏18	8 17	2 04	5 07	9 52	10 34	23 24	2 40	16 40	22 57	24 42	29 49	20 14	13 21	2 01
19 Su	7 51 26	28 20 57	17 08	8 18	3 46	6 20	10 33	10 47	23 31	2 41	16 41	22 59	25 06	0♑13	20 21	13 29	2 03
20 M	7 55 23	29 22 03	0♐44	8 19	5 28	7 32	11 13	11 01	23 38	2 41	16 43	23 01	25 30	0 38	20 28	13 37	2 05
21 T	7 59 19	0♒23 08	14 07	8 21	7 10	8 44	11 54	11 14	23 45	2 42	16 45	23 03	25 54	1 01	20 35	13 45	2 07
22 W	8 3 16	1 24 13	27 17	8 22℞	8 53	9 57	12 35	11 28	23 53	2 42	16 46	23 05	26 18	1 25	20 42	13 54	2 09
23 Th	8 7 12	2 25 18	10♑14	8 22	10 36	11 09	13 16	11 41	24 00	2 43	16 48	23 07	26 41	1 49	20 48	14 04	2 11
24 F	8 11 9	3 26 22	23 00	8 21	12 20	12 21	13 57	11 54	24 07	2 43	16 50	23 09	27 05	2 13	20 54	14 13	2 13
25 Sa	8 15 6	4 27 26	5♒33	8 19	14 03	13 33	14 37	12 08	24 14	2 44	16 52	23 11	27 29	2 37	20 59	14 23	2 15
26 Su	8 19 2	5 28 28	17 56	8 16	15 46	14 45	15 18	12 21	24 21	2 45	16 53	23 13	27 53	3 00	21 04	14 33	2 17
27 M	8 22 59	6 29 30	0♓08	8 11	17 30	15 57	15 59	12 34	24 28	2 46	16 55	23 15	28 17	3 24	21 09	14 44	2 19
28 T	8 26 55	7 30 30	12 12	8 05	19 13	17 09	16 40	12 48	24 35	2 46	16 57	23 17	28 41	3 47	21 14	14 54	2 22
29 W	8 30 52	8 31 30	24 08	8 00	20 56	18 20	17 21	13 01	24 42	2 47	16 59	23 19	29 05	4 11	21 18	15 06	2 24
30 Th	8 34 48	9 32 28	6♈00	7 55	22 38	19 32	18 02	13 14	24 49	2 48	17 01	23 21	29 28	4 34	21 22	15 17	2 26
31 F	8 38 45	10 33 26	17 52	7 51	24 19	20 44	18 43	13 27	24 56	2 49	17 03	23 23	29 52	4 57	21 25	15 29	2 29

EPHEMERIS CALCULATED FOR 12 MIDNIGHT GREENWICH MEAN TIME. ALL OTHER DATA AND FACING ASPECTARIAN PAGE IN **EASTERN TIME (BOLD)** AND PACIFIC TIME (REGULAR).

FEBRUARY 2020

☽ Last Aspect day	ET / hr:mn / PT	asp	☽ Ingress sign	day	ET / hr:mn / PT
3	**6:28 am** 3:28 am	□☿	♊	3	**6:29 am** 3:29 am
5	**9:20 am** 6:20 am	□♀	♋	5	**2:03 pm** 11:03 am
7	**10:43 am** 7:43 am	☍♄	♌	7	**5:45 pm** 2:45 pm
9	**11:08 am** 8:08 am	△♂	♍	9	**6:39 pm** 3:39 pm
11	**1:26 pm** 10:26 am	□♂	♎	11	**6:37 pm** 3:37 pm
13	**4:40 pm** 1:40 pm	⚹♂	♏	13	**7:37 pm** 4:37 pm
15	**5:20 pm** 2:20 pm	⚹♄	♐	15	**11:07 pm** 8:07 pm
18	**4:03 am** 1:03 am	⚹☉	♑	18	**5:37 am** 2:37 am
20	**9:18 am** 6:18 am	☌♄	♒	20	**2:42 pm** 11:42 am
21	**11:08 pm** 8:08 pm	⚹♀	♓	22	10:37 pm

☽ Last Aspect day	ET / hr:mn / PT	asp	☽ Ingress sign	day	ET / hr:mn / PT
21	**11:08 pm** 8:08 pm	⚹♀	♓	23	**1:37 am**
25	**9:12 am** 6:12 am	⚹♄	♈	25	**1:47 pm** 10:47 am
27	**10:25 pm** 7:25 pm	□♄	♉	27	11:30 pm
27	**10:25 pm** 7:25 pm	□♄	♉	28	**2:30 am**

☽ Phases & Eclipses phase	day	ET / hr:mn / PT
2nd Quarter	1	**8:42 pm** 5:42 pm
Full Moon	8	11:33 pm
Full Moon	9	**2:33 am**
4th Quarter	15	**5:17 pm** 2:17 pm
New Moon	23	**10:32 am** 7:32 am

Planet Ingress	day	ET / hr:mn / PT
☿ ♓	3	**6:37 am** 3:37 am
♀ ♈	7	**3:02 pm** 12:02 pm
♂ ♑	16	**6:33 am** 3:33 am
☉ ♓	18	**11:57 pm** 8:57 pm

Planetary Motion	day	ET / hr:mn / PT
⚵ ℞	8	**12:59 pm** 9:59 am
☿ ℞	16	**7:54 pm** 4:54 pm

1 SATURDAY
- ☽☌♅ **1:10 am**
- ☽□☉ **8:42 pm** 5:42 pm
- ☽△♃ **11:12 pm** 8:12 pm
- ♀⚹♇ 11:07 pm

2 SUNDAY
- ♀⚹♇ **2:07 am**
- ☽⚹♆ **5:30 am** 2:30 am
- ☽⚻♂ **12:14 pm** 9:14 am
- ☽△♇ **5:54 pm** 2:54 pm
- ☽⚹♀ **7:32 pm** 4:32 pm
- ☽△♄ **9:24 pm** 6:24 pm

3 MONDAY
- ☽□☿ **6:28 am** 3:28 am
- ☉⚺♃ **10:00 am** 7:00 am
- ☽⚺♅ **12:01 pm** 9:01 am
- ♀⚹♄ **5:01 pm** 2:01 pm

4 TUESDAY
- ☽⚻♃ **9:45 am** 6:45 am
- ☽△☉ **11:20 am** 8:20 am
- ☽□♆ **2:50 pm** 11:50 am
- ☽☍♂ 9:07 pm
- ☽⚻♇ 11:27 pm

5 WEDNESDAY
- ☽☍♂ **12:07 am**
- ☽⚻♇ **2:27 am**
- ☿⚹♅ **4:43 am** 1:43 am
- ☽⚻♄ **6:04 am** 3:04 am
- ☽□♀ **9:20 am** 6:20 am
- ☽⚹♅ **7:17 pm** 4:17 pm
- ☽△☿ **9:00 pm** 6:00 pm

6 THURSDAY
- ☉⚺♆ **9:39 am** 6:39 am
- ☽☍♃ **4:14 pm** 1:14 pm
- ☽△♆ **8:15 pm** 5:15 pm
- ☽⚻☉ **9:03 pm** 6:03 pm
- ♂⚺♇ **11:03 pm** 8:03 pm

7 FRIDAY
- ☽☍♇ **7:02 am** 4:02 am
- ☽⚻♂ **7:26 am** 4:26 am
- ☽☍♄ **10:43 am** 7:43 am
- ☽△♀ **5:59 pm** 2:59 pm
- ☽□♅ **10:43 pm** 7:43 pm

8 SATURDAY
- ☽⚻☿ **5:26 am** 2:26 am
- ☽⚻♃ **7:04 pm** 4:04 pm
- ☽⚻♆ **10:15 pm** 7:15 pm
- ☽☍☉ 11:33 pm

9 SUNDAY
- ☽☍☉ **2:33 am**
- ☽⚻♇ **8:30 am** 5:30 am
- ☽△♂ **11:08 am** 8:08 am
- ☽⚻♄ **12:17 pm** 9:17 am
- ☽⚻♀ **11:02 pm** 8:02 pm
- ☽△♅ **11:31 pm** 8:31 pm

10 MONDAY
- ♀⚺♅ **5:23 am** 2:23 am
- ☽☍☿ **9:51 am** 6:51 am
- ♂⚺♄ **4:30 pm** 1:30 pm
- ☽△♃ **7:55 pm** 4:55 pm
- ☽☍♆ **10:29 pm** 7:29 pm

11 TUESDAY
- ☽⚻☉ **6:05 am** 3:05 am
- ☽△♇ **8:36 am** 5:36 am
- ☽△♄ **12:37 pm** 9:37 am
- ☽□♂ **1:26 pm** 10:26 am
- ☽⚻♅ **11:36 pm** 8:36 pm

12 WEDNESDAY
- ☽☍♀ **3:06 am** 12:06 am
- ☽⚻☿ **12:55 pm** 9:55 am
- ☉⚺♇ **8:25 pm** 5:25 pm
- ☽□♃ **8:54 pm** 5:54 pm
- ☽⚻♆ **10:57 pm** 7:57 pm

13 THURSDAY
- ☽□♇ **9:20 am** 6:20 am
- ☽△☉ **10:17 am** 7:17 am
- ☽□♄ **1:46 pm** 10:46 am
- ☽⚹♂ **4:40 pm** 1:40 pm
- ☽☍♅ 9:54 pm

14 FRIDAY
- ☽☍♅ **12:54 am**
- ☽⚻♀ **8:52 am** 5:52 am
- ☽△☿ **4:43 pm** 1:43 pm
- ☽⚹♃ **11:52 pm** 8:52 pm
- ☽△♆ 10:25 pm

15 SATURDAY
- ☽△♆ **1:25 am**
- ☽⚹♇ **12:21 pm** 9:21 am
- ☽□☉ **5:17 pm** 2:17 pm
- ☽⚹♄ **5:20 pm** 2:20 pm
- ☉⚺♄ **5:57 pm** 2:57 pm
- ☽⚺♂ **10:43 pm** 7:43 pm

16 SUNDAY
- ☽⚻♅ **4:49 am** 1:49 am
- ☽△♀ **6:06 pm** 3:06 pm
- ☽□☿ **10:10 pm** 7:10 pm

17 MONDAY
- ☽⚺♃ **5:52 am** 2:52 am
- ☽□♆ **6:49 am** 3:49 am
- ☽⚺♇ **6:22 pm** 3:22 pm
- ☽⚺♄ **11:58 pm** 8:58 pm

18 TUESDAY
- ☽⚹☉ **4:03 am** 1:03 am
- ☽☌♂ **8:16 am** 5:16 am
- ☽△♅ **11:45 am** 8:45 am
- ☿⚺♀ **12:02 pm** 9:02 am

19 WEDNESDAY
- ☽⚹☿ **4:56 am** 1:56 am
- ☽□♀ **7:08 am** 4:08 am
- ☽☌♃ **2:50 pm** 11:50 am
- ☽⚹♆ **3:05 pm** 12:05 pm

20 THURSDAY
- ☽☌♇ **3:07 am** 12:07 am
- ☽☌♄ **9:18 am** 6:18 am
- ♃⚹♆ **10:56 am** 7:56 am
- ☽⚺☉ **6:08 pm** 3:08 pm
- ☽⚺♂ **8:50 pm** 5:50 pm
- ☽□♅ **9:13 pm** 6:13 pm

21 FRIDAY
- ♂△♅ **4:10 am** 1:10 am
- ☽⚺☿ **12:15 pm** 9:15 am
- ☽⚹♀ **11:08 pm** 8:08 pm
- ☽⚺♆ 10:31 pm
- ☽⚺♃ 11:02 pm

22 SATURDAY
- ☽⚺♆ **1:31 am**
- ☽⚺♃ **2:02 am**
- ☉⚹♅ **9:13 am** 6:13 am
- ☽⚺♇ **1:51 pm** 10:51 am
- ☽⚺♄ **8:36 pm** 5:36 pm
- ♀⚺♆ 10:27 pm

23 SUNDAY
- ♀⚺♆ **1:27 am**
- ☽⚹♅ **8:29 am** 5:29 am
- ☽☌☉ **10:32 am** 7:32 am
- ☽⚹♂ **11:30 am** 8:30 am
- ♀□♃ **11:59 am** 8:59 am
- ☽☌☿ **7:39 pm** 4:39 pm

24 MONDAY
- ☽☌♆ **1:26 pm** 10:26 am
- ☽⚹♃ **2:45 pm** 11:45 am
- ☽⚺♀ **5:05 pm** 2:05 pm
- ☉⚹♂ **9:06 pm** 6:06 pm
- ☽⚹♇ 10:57 pm

25 TUESDAY
- ☽⚹♇ **1:57 am**
- ☽⚹♄ **9:12 am** 6:12 am
- ☉☌☿ **8:45 pm** 5:45 pm
- ☽⚺♅ **8:56 pm** 5:56 pm
- ☿⚹♂ 9:59 pm

26 WEDNESDAY
- ☿⚹♂ **12:59 am**
- ☽⚺☿ **3:11 am** 12:11 am
- ☽□♂ **3:32 am** 12:32 am
- ☽⚺☉ **4:26 am** 1:26 am
- ☽⚺♆ 11:14 pm

27 THURSDAY
- ☽⚺♆ **2:14 am**
- ☽□♃ **4:22 am** 1:22 am
- ☽☌♀ **12:05 pm** 9:05 am
- ☽□♇ **2:47 pm** 11:47 am
- ☽□♄ **10:25 pm** 7:25 pm

28 FRIDAY
- ☽☌♅ **9:50 am** 6:50 am
- ☽⚹☿ **10:51 am** 7:51 am
- ♀□♇ **5:08 pm** 2:08 pm
- ☽△♂ **7:56 pm** 4:56 pm
- ☿⚹♅ **10:13 pm** 7:13 pm
- ☽⚹☉ **10:40 pm** 7:40 pm

29 SATURDAY
- ☽⚹♆ **2:50 pm** 11:50 am
- ☽△♃ **5:41 pm** 2:41 pm

Eastern time in bold type
Pacific time in medium type

FEBRUARY 2020

DATE	SID.TIME	SUN	MOON	NODE	MERCURY	VENUS	MARS	JUPITER	SATURN	URANUS	NEPTUNE	PLUTO	CERES	PALLAS	JUNO	VESTA	CHIRON
1 Sa	8 42 41	11♒34 22	29♈46	7♋49℞	25♒59	21♓55	19♐24	13♑40	25♑03	2♉50	17♓05	23♑25	0♒16	5♑20	21♎28	15♉41	2♈31
2 Su	8 46 38	12 35 17	11♉48	7 48D	27 37	23 06	20 05	13 53	25 10	2 51	17 07	23 27	0 40	5 43	21 31	15 53	2 34
3 M	8 50 34	13 36 10	24 03	7 48	29 14	24 17	20 46	14 06	25 16	2 53	17 09	23 29	1 03	6 06	21 33	16 05	2 36
4 T	8 54 31	14 37 02	6♊35	7 50	0♓48	25 29	21 27	14 19	25 23	2 54	17 11	23 31	1 27	6 29	21 35	16 18	2 39
5 W	8 58 28	15 37 53	19 28	7 51	2 20	26 40	22 08	14 32	25 30	2 55	17 13	23 33	1 50	6 52	21 37	16 31	2 42
6 Th	9 2 24	16 38 43	2♋47	7 53℞	3 48	27 50	22 49	14 45	25 37	2 56	17 15	23 34	2 14	7 15	21 38	16 45	2 44
7 F	9 6 21	17 39 31	16 33	7 52	5 11	29 01	23 30	14 58	25 44	2 58	17 17	23 36	2 38	7 37	21 39	16 58	2 47
8 Sa	9 10 17	18 40 18	0♌45	7 50	6 31	0♈12	24 11	15 10	25 50	2 59	17 19	23 38	3 01	8 00	21 39℞	17 12	2 50
9 Su	9 14 14	19 41 03	15 21	7 46	7 44	1 22	24 52	15 23	25 57	3 01	17 21	23 40	3 25	8 22	21 39	17 26	2 52
10 M	9 18 10	20 41 47	0♍13	7 40	8 52	2 32	25 33	15 35	26 04	3 02	17 23	23 42	3 48	8 44	21 39	17 41	2 55
11 T	9 22 7	21 42 30	15 14	7 34	9 53	3 43	26 14	15 48	26 11	3 04	17 25	23 44	4 12	9 07	21 38	17 56	2 58
12 W	9 26 4	22 43 11	0♎14	7 27	10 46	4 53	26 55	16 00	26 17	3 05	17 27	23 46	4 35	9 29	21 37	18 10	3 01
13 Th	9 30 0	23 43 52	15 04	7 20	11 30	6 03	27 36	16 13	26 24	3 07	17 29	23 47	4 59	9 51	21 36	18 25	3 04
14 F	9 33 57	24 44 31	29 38	7 16	12 06	7 12	28 18	16 25	26 30	3 09	17 31	23 49	5 22	10 13	21 34	18 41	3 07
15 Sa	9 37 53	25 45 09	13♏50	7 13D	12 32	8 22	28 59	16 37	26 37	3 10	17 33	23 51	5 45	10 35	21 32	18 56	3 10
16 Su	9 41 50	26 45 46	27 40	7 12	12 48	9 31	29 40	16 50	26 43	3 12	17 36	23 53	6 08	10 56	21 29	19 12	3 12
17 M	9 45 46	27 46 22	11♐08	7 13	12 53℞	10 41	0♑21	17 02	26 50	3 14	17 38	23 54	6 32	11 18	21 26	19 28	3 15
18 T	9 49 43	28 46 57	24 17	7 14	12 49	11 50	1 03	17 14	26 56	3 16	17 40	23 56	6 55	11 39	21 23	19 44	3 18
19 W	9 53 39	29 47 31	7♑09	7 15℞	12 33	12 59	1 44	17 26	27 03	3 18	17 42	23 58	7 18	12 01	21 19	20 01	3 22
20 Th	9 57 36	0♓48 03	19 47	7 14	12 08	14 08	2 25	17 38	27 09	3 20	17 44	24 00	7 41	12 22	21 15	20 17	3 25
21 F	10 1 33	1 48 34	2♒13	7 11	11 34	15 16	3 07	17 50	27 15	3 22	17 46	24 01	8 04	12 43	21 11	20 34	3 28
22 Sa	10 5 29	2 49 03	14 30	7 05	10 51	16 25	3 48	18 01	27 22	3 24	17 49	24 03	8 27	13 04	21 06	20 51	3 31
23 Su	10 9 26	3 49 31	26 40	6 57	10 01	17 33	4 29	18 13	27 28	3 26	17 51	24 05	8 50	13 25	21 00	21 08	3 34
24 M	10 13 22	4 49 57	8♓43	6 46	9 04	18 41	5 11	18 25	27 34	3 28	17 53	24 06	9 13	13 46	20 55	21 26	3 37
25 T	10 17 19	5 50 22	20 41	6 34	8 04	19 49	5 52	18 36	27 40	3 30	17 55	24 08	9 36	14 07	20 49	21 43	3 40
26 W	10 21 15	6 50 44	2♈35	6 22	7 00	20 57	6 33	18 48	27 46	3 32	17 58	24 09	9 59	14 27	20 42	22 01	3 44
27 Th	10 25 12	7 51 05	14 26	6 11	5 55	22 05	7 15	18 59	27 52	3 34	18 00	24 11	10 22	14 48	20 35	22 19	3 47
28 F	10 29 8	8 51 24	26 17	6 01	4 50	23 12	7 56	19 10	27 58	3 37	18 02	24 12	10 45	15 08	20 28	22 37	3 50
29 Sa	10 33 5	9 51 42	8♉11	5 54	3 48	24 19	8 38	19 22	28 04	3 39	18 04	24 14	11 08	15 28	20 21	22 56	3 53

EPHEMERIS CALCULATED FOR 12 MIDNIGHT GREENWICH MEAN TIME. ALL OTHER DATA AND FACING ASPECTARIAN PAGE IN **EASTERN TIME (BOLD)** AND PACIFIC TIME (REGULAR).

MARCH 2020

☽ Last Aspect day	ET / hr:mn	PT	asp	☽ Ingress sign day	ET / hr:mn	PT
1	**10:52 am**	7:52 am	△♄	♊ 1	**2:21 pm**	11:21 am
3	**9:20 pm**	6:20 pm	⚹♀	♋ 3	**11:25 pm**	8:25 pm
5		11:11 pm	☍♄	♌ 6	**4:27 am**	1:27 am
6	**2:11 am**		☍♄	♌ 6	**4:27 am**	1:27 am
8	**4:12 am**	12:12 am	☍☿	♍ 8	**6:47 am**	3:47 am
10	**4:32 am**	1:32 am	△♄	♎ 10	**6:03 am**	3:03 am
12	**4:12 am**	1:12 am	□♄	♏ 12	**5:28 am**	2:28 am
14	**6:06 am**	3:06 am	⚹♄	♐ 14	**7:09 am**	4:09 am
16	**5:34 am**	2:34 am	□☉	♑ 16	**12:25 pm**	9:25 am
18	**8:48 pm**	5:48 pm	☌♄	♒ 18	**9:16 pm**	6:16 pm
20	**5:00 am**	2:00 am	□♀	♓ 21	**8:33 am**	5:33 am
23	**10:51 am**	7:51 am	⚹♂	♈ 23	**8:58 pm**	5:58 pm
26	**3:16 am**	12:16 am	□♂	♉ 26	**9:37 am**	6:37 am
28	**7:05 pm**	4:05 pm	△♂	♊ 28	**9:38 pm**	6:38 pm
30	**11:10 am**	8:10 am	□♆	♋ 31	**7:43 am**	4:43 am

☽ Phases & Eclipses phase	day	ET / hr:mn	PT
2nd Quarter	2	**2:57 pm**	11:57 am
Full Moon	9	**1:48 pm**	10:48 am
4th Quarter	16	**5:34 am**	2:34 am
New Moon	24	**5:28 am**	2:28 am

Planet Ingress	day	ET / hr:mn	PT
☿ ♒	4	**6:08 am**	3:08 am
♀ ♉	4	**10:07 pm**	7:07 pm
☿ ♓	16	**3:42 am**	12:42 am
☉ ♈	19	**11:50 pm**	8:50 pm
⚶ ♊	20		10:10 pm
⚶ ♊	21	**1:10 am**	
♄ ♒	21	**11:58 pm**	8:58 pm
♂ ♒	30	**3:43 pm**	12:43 pm

Planetary Motion	day	ET / hr:mn	PT
☿ D	9	**11:49 pm**	8:49 pm

1 SUNDAY
☽ △ ♇ **3:04 am** 12:04 am
☽ ⚺ ♀ **6:25 am** 3:25 am
☽ △ ♄ **10:52 am** 7:52 am
☽ □ ☿ **6:05 pm** 3:05 pm
☽ ⚺ ♅ **9:38 pm** 6:38 pm

2 MONDAY
☽ ⚻ ♂ **10:39 am** 7:39 am
☽ □ ☉ **2:57 pm** 11:57 am
☽ □ ♆ 10:24 pm

3 TUESDAY
☽ □ ♆ **1:24 am**
☽ ⚻ ♃ **4:47 am** 1:47 am
♀ □ ♄ **11:44 am** 8:44 am
☽ ⚻ ♇ **12:55 pm** 9:55 am
☽ ⚻ ♄ **8:35 pm** 5:35 pm
☽ ⚹ ♀ **9:20 pm** 6:20 pm
☽ △ ☿ **11:44 pm** 8:44 pm

4 WEDNESDAY
☽ ⚹ ♅ **6:26 am** 3:26 am
☿ ⚹ ♀ **4:24 pm** 1:24 pm
☽ ☍ ♂ **9:25 pm** 6:25 pm
☽ △ ☉ 11:49 pm

5 THURSDAY
☽ △ ☉ **2:49 am**
☽ △ ♆ **8:14 am** 5:14 am
☽ ☍ ♃ **11:56 am** 8:56 am
☽ ☍ ♇ **6:50 pm** 3:50 pm

Eastern time in bold type
Pacific time in medium type

☽ ☍ ♄ 11:11 pm
☽ ⚻ ☿ 11:47 pm

6 FRIDAY
☽ ☍ ♄ **2:11 am**
☽ ⚻ ☿ **2:47 am**
☽ □ ♀ **7:00 am** 4:00 am
☽ □ ♅ **11:06 am** 8:06 am
☿ ⚺ ♄ **8:08 pm** 5:08 pm

7 SATURDAY
☽ ⚻ ♂ **3:23 am** 12:23 am
☽ ⚻ ☉ **9:35 am** 6:35 am
☽ ⚻ ♆ **11:00 am** 8:00 am
☽ ⚻ ♃ **2:55 pm** 11:55 am
☽ ⚻ ♇ **8:50 pm** 5:50 pm

8 SUNDAY
☽ ☍ ☿ **4:12 am** 12:12 am
☽ ⚻ ♄ **4:57 am** 12:57 am
☉ ☌ ♆ **8:23 am** 5:23 am
☽ △ ♀ **1:00 pm** 10:00 am
☽ △ ♅ **1:11 pm** 10:11 am
♀ ☌ ♅ **3:38 pm** 12:38 pm

9 MONDAY
☽ △ ♂ **6:48 am** 3:48 am
☽ ☍ ♆ **11:57 am** 8:57 am
☽ ☍ ☉ **1:48 pm** 10:48 am
☽ △ ♃ **4:08 pm** 1:08 pm
☽ △ ♇ **9:24 pm** 6:24 pm

10 TUESDAY
☽ ⚻ ☿ **3:15 am** 12:15 am
☽ △ ♄ **4:32 am** 1:32 am
☽ ⚻ ♅ **12:28 pm** 9:28 am
☽ ⚻ ♀ **3:43 pm** 12:43 pm

11 WEDNESDAY
☽ □ ♂ **8:06 am** 5:06 am
☉ ⚹ ♃ **8:27 am** 5:27 am
☽ ⚻ ♆ **11:09 am** 8:09 am
☽ □ ♃ **3:48 pm** 12:48 pm
☽ ⚻ ☉ **4:14 pm** 1:14 pm
☽ □ ♇ **8:41 pm** 5:41 pm
☽ △ ☿ 11:58 pm

12 THURSDAY
☽ △ ☿ **2:58 am**
☽ □ ♄ **4:12 am** 1:12 am
☽ ☍ ♅ **12:14 pm** 9:14 am
☽ ☍ ♀ **7:10 pm** 4:10 pm

13 FRIDAY
☽ ⚹ ♂ **11:00 am** 8:00 am
☽ △ ♆ **11:53 am** 8:53 am
☽ ⚹ ♃ **5:14 pm** 2:14 pm
☽ △ ☉ **8:47 pm** 5:47 pm
☽ ⚹ ♇ **9:53 pm** 6:53 pm

14 SATURDAY
☽ □ ☿ **5:36 am** 2:36 am
☽ ⚹ ♄ **6:06 am** 3:06 am
♂ ⚹ ♆ **6:32 am** 3:32 am
☉ ⚹ ♇ **12:47 pm** 9:47 am
☽ ⚻ ♅ **2:32 pm** 11:32 am

☿ ⚺ ♄ 10:50 pm
☽ ⚻ ♀ 11:00 pm

15 SUNDAY
☿ ⚺ ♄ **1:50 am**
☽ ⚻ ♀ **2:00 am**
☽ □ ♆ **3:51 pm** 12:51 pm
☽ ⚺ ♂ **5:35 pm** 2:35 pm
☽ ⚺ ♃ **10:05 pm** 7:05 pm
☽ ⚺ ♇ 11:33 pm

16 MONDAY
☽ ⚺ ♇ **2:33 am**
☽ □ ☉ **5:34 am** 2:34 am
☽ ⚺ ♄ **11:38 am** 8:38 am
☽ ⚹ ☿ **12:49 pm** 9:49 am
☽ △ ♅ **8:33 pm** 5:33 pm

17 TUESDAY
☽ △ ♀ **1:31 pm** 10:31 am
☽ ⚹ ♆ **11:36 pm** 8:36 pm

18 WEDNESDAY
☽ ☌ ♂ **4:32 am** 1:32 am
☽ ☌ ♃ **6:47 am** 3:47 am
☽ ☌ ♇ **10:53 am** 7:53 am
☽ ⚹ ☉ **6:57 pm** 3:57 pm
☽ ☌ ♄ **8:48 pm** 5:48 pm
☽ ⚺ ☿ 9:54 pm

19 THURSDAY
☽ ⚺ ☿ **12:54 am**
☽ □ ♅ **6:04 am** 3:04 am
☉ ⚹ ♄ **7:50 pm** 4:50 pm

20 FRIDAY
☽ □ ♀ **5:00 am** 2:00 am
♂ ☌ ♃ **7:35 am** 4:35 am
☽ ⚺ ♆ **10:20 am** 7:20 am
☽ ⚺ ♃ **6:21 pm** 3:21 pm
☽ ⚺ ♂ **6:52 pm** 3:52 pm
☽ ⚺ ♇ **9:56 pm** 6:56 pm

21 SATURDAY
☽ ⚺ ♄ **8:27 am** 5:27 am
☽ ⚺ ☉ **11:31 am** 8:31 am
☽ ☌ ☿ **4:39 pm** 1:39 pm
☽ ⚹ ♅ **5:51 pm** 2:51 pm

22 SUNDAY
☿ ⚹ ♅ **9:19 am** 6:19 am
☽ ⚹ ♀ **10:36 pm** 7:36 pm
☽ ☌ ♆ **10:38 pm** 7:38 pm
♀ ⚹ ♆ **11:08 pm** 8:08 pm
♂ ☌ ♇ 10:21 pm

23 MONDAY
♂ ☌ ♇ **1:21 am**
☽ ⚹ ♃ **7:20 am** 4:20 am
☽ ⚹ ♇ **10:18 am** 7:18 am
☽ ⚹ ♂ **10:51 am** 7:51 am
☽ ⚹ ♄ **9:15 pm** 6:15 pm

24 TUESDAY
☽ ☌ ☉ **5:28 am** 2:28 am
☽ ⚺ ♅ **6:36 am** 3:36 am
☽ ⚺ ☿ **10:27 am** 7:27 am
☉ ⚺ ♅ **7:44 pm** 4:44 pm

25 WEDNESDAY
☽ ⚺ ♆ **11:28 am** 8:28 am
☽ ⚺ ♀ **4:46 pm** 1:46 pm
☽ □ ♃ **8:43 pm** 5:43 pm
☽ □ ♇ **11:03 pm** 8:03 pm

26 THURSDAY
☽ □ ♂ **3:16 am** 12:16 am
☽ □ ♄ **10:15 am** 7:15 am
☽ ☌ ♅ **7:29 pm** 4:29 pm
☽ ⚺ ☉ **11:35 pm** 8:35 pm

27 FRIDAY
☽ ⚹ ☿ **5:03 am** 2:03 am
☽ ⚹ ♆ 9:02 pm
♀ △ ♃ 9:24 pm

28 SATURDAY
☽ ⚹ ♆ **12:02 am**
♀ △ ♃ **12:24 am**
☽ △ ♃ **9:39 am** 6:39 am
☽ ☌ ♀ **10:20 am** 7:20 am
☽ △ ♇ **11:20 am** 8:20 am
☽ △ ♂ **7:05 pm** 4:05 pm
☽ △ ♄ **10:36 pm** 7:36 pm
♀ △ ♇ **10:57 pm** 7:57 pm

29 SUNDAY
☽ ⚺ ♅ **7:33 am** 4:33 am
☽ ⚹ ☉ **4:32 pm** 1:32 pm
☽ □ ☿ **10:58 pm** 7:58 pm

30 MONDAY
☽ □ ♆ **11:10 am** 8:10 am
☽ ⚻ ♃ **8:52 pm** 5:52 pm
☽ ⚻ ♇ **9:55 pm** 6:55 pm
☽ ⚺ ♀ 10:40 pm

31 TUESDAY
☽ ⚺ ♀ **1:40 am**
☽ ⚻ ♂ **8:39 am** 5:39 am
☽ ⚻ ♄ **8:56 am** 5:56 am
♂ ☌ ♄ **2:31 pm** 11:31 am
☽ ⚹ ♅ **5:24 pm** 2:24 pm

MARCH 2020

DATE	SID.TIME	SUN	MOON	NODE	MERCURY	VENUS	MARS	JUPITER	SATURN	URANUS	NEPTUNE	PLUTO	CERES	PALLAS	JUNO	VESTA	CHIRON
1 Su	10 37 1	10♓51 57	20♉12	5♋49℞	2♓48℞	25♈26	9♑19	19♑33	28♑10	3♉41	18♓07	24♑16	11♒30	15♑48	20♎13℞	23♉14	3♈57
2 M	10 40 58	11 52 10	2♊23	5 47D	1 53	26 33	10 01	19 44	28 16	3 44	18 09	24 17	11 53	16 08	20 05	23 33	4 00
3 T	10 44 55	12 52 21	14 49	5 47	1 03	27 39	10 42	19 55	28 21	3 46	18 11	24 18	12 15	16 28	19 56	23 52	4 03
4 W	10 48 51	13 52 30	27 36	5 47℞	0 18	28 45	11 23	20 05	28 27	3 49	18 13	24 20	12 38	16 47	19 47	24 11	4 07
5 Th	10 52 48	14 52 37	10♋48	5 47	29♒41	29 51	12 05	20 16	28 33	3 51	18 16	24 21	13 00	17 07	19 38	24 30	4 10
6 F	10 56 44	15 52 42	24 28	5 46	29 09	0♉57	12 46	20 27	28 38	3 54	18 18	24 23	13 23	17 26	19 29	24 49	4 13
7 Sa	11 0 41	16 52 45	8♌39	5 42	28 45	2 03	13 28	20 37	28 44	3 56	18 20	24 24	13 45	17 45	19 19	25 09	4 17
8 Su	11 4 37	17 52 45	23 17	5 36	28 28	3 08	14 09	20 48	28 49	3 59	18 23	24 25	14 07	18 04	19 09	25 28	4 20
9 M	11 8 34	18 52 44	8♍19	5 27	28 17	4 13	14 51	20 58	28 55	4 02	18 25	24 27	14 30	18 23	18 58	25 48	4 24
10 T	11 12 30	19 52 40	23 35	5 16	28 13D	5 17	15 33	21 08	29 00	4 04	18 27	24 28	14 52	18 42	18 47	26 08	4 27
11 W	11 16 27	20 52 35	8♎54	5 05	28 15	6 22	16 14	21 18	29 05	4 07	18 29	24 29	15 14	19 00	18 36	26 28	4 31
12 Th	11 20 24	21 52 28	24 05	4 55	28 23	7 26	16 56	21 28	29 11	4 10	18 32	24 31	15 36	19 19	18 25	26 48	4 34
13 F	11 24 20	22 52 19	8♏58	4 47	28 37	8 30	17 37	21 38	29 16	4 12	18 34	24 32	15 58	19 37	18 14	27 08	4 37
14 Sa	11 28 17	23 52 08	23 26	4 42	28 56	9 33	18 19	21 48	29 21	4 15	18 36	24 33	16 20	19 55	18 02	27 29	4 41
15 Su	11 32 13	24 51 56	7♐26	4 39	29 21	10 36	19 01	21 58	29 26	4 18	18 38	24 34	16 42	20 13	17 50	27 49	4 44
16 M	11 36 10	25 51 42	20 59	4 38D	29 50	11 39	19 42	22 07	29 31	4 21	18 41	24 35	17 03	20 31	17 37	28 10	4 48
17 T	11 40 6	26 51 27	4♑06	4 38℞	0♓23	12 42	20 24	22 17	29 36	4 24	18 43	24 37	17 25	20 48	17 25	28 31	4 51
18 W	11 44 3	27 51 09	16 52	4 38	1 01	13 44	21 05	22 26	29 41	4 27	18 45	24 38	17 47	21 06	17 12	28 52	4 55
19 Th	11 47 59	28 50 50	29 21	4 36	1 43	14 46	21 47	22 35	29 45	4 30	18 47	24 39	18 08	21 23	16 59	29 13	4 58
20 F	11 51 56	29 50 29	11♒37	4 31	2 29	15 47	22 29	22 45	29 50	4 32	18 50	24 40	18 30	21 40	16 46	29 34	5 02
21 Sa	11 55 53	0♈50 07	23 43	4 24	3 18	16 48	23 10	22 54	29 55	4 35	18 52	24 41	18 51	21 57	16 33	29 55	5 06
22 Su	11 59 49	1 49 42	5♓43	4 14	4 10	17 49	23 52	23 02	29 59	4 38	18 54	24 42	19 12	22 13	16 19	0♊17	5 09
23 M	12 3 46	2 49 16	17 38	4 01	5 05	18 49	24 34	23 11	0♒04	4 42	18 56	24 43	19 34	22 30	16 06	0 38	5 13
24 T	12 7 42	3 48 47	29 31	3 46	6 03	19 49	25 16	23 20	0 08	4 45	18 59	24 44	19 55	22 46	15 52	1 00	5 16
25 W	12 11 39	4 48 17	11♈23	3 32	7 04	20 48	25 57	23 28	0 12	4 48	19 01	24 45	20 16	23 02	15 38	1 22	5 20
26 Th	12 15 35	5 47 44	23 15	3 17	8 08	21 47	26 39	23 37	0 17	4 51	19 03	24 46	20 37	23 18	15 24	1 44	5 23
27 F	12 19 32	6 47 09	5♉09	3 05	9 14	22 46	27 21	23 45	0 21	4 54	19 05	24 47	20 58	23 34	15 10	2 06	5 27
28 Sa	12 23 28	7 46 33	17 07	2 56	10 22	23 44	28 02	23 53	0 25	4 57	19 07	24 47	21 19	23 49	14 56	2 28	5 30
29 Su	12 27 25	8 45 54	29 10	2 49	11 33	24 41	28 44	24 01	0 29	5 00	19 10	24 48	21 39	24 04	14 41	2 50	5 34
30 M	12 31 21	9 45 12	11♊23	2 45	12 46	25 38	29 26	24 09	0 33	5 03	19 12	24 49	22 00	24 19	14 27	3 12	5 37
31 T	12 35 18	10 44 29	23 49	2 44D	14 00	26 35	0♒07	24 16	0 37	5 07	19 14	24 50	22 21	24 34	14 13	3 34	5 41

EPHEMERIS CALCULATED FOR 12 MIDNIGHT GREENWICH MEAN TIME. ALL OTHER DATA AND FACING ASPECTARIAN PAGE IN **EASTERN TIME (BOLD)** AND PACIFIC TIME (REGULAR).

APRIL 2020

☽ Last Aspect day	ET / hr:mn / PT	asp	☽ Ingress sign	day	ET / hr:mn / PT
2	**12:49 pm** 9:49 am	⚹ ♀	♌	2	**2:26 pm** 11:26 am
3	**3:29 pm** 12:29 pm	△ ☉	♍	4	**5:18 pm** 2:18 pm
6	**9:29 am** 6:29 am	△ ♃	♎	6	**5:16 pm** 2:16 pm
8	**8:50 am** 5:50 am	□ ♃	♏	8	**4:17 pm** 1:17 pm
10	**3:35 pm** 12:35 pm	△ ☿	♐	10	**4:35 pm** 1:35 pm
12	**7:46 am** 4:46 am	△ ☉	♑	12	**8:05 pm** 5:05 pm
14	**7:47 pm** 4:47 pm	☌ ♃	♒	15	**3:37 am** 12:37 am
17	**10:34 am** 7:34 am	⚹ ☉	♓	17	**2:29 pm** 11:29 am
19	**7:31 pm** 4:31 pm	⚹ ♃	♈	20	**3:00 am** 12:00 am
22	**8:32 am** 5:32 am	□ ♃	♉	22	**3:36 pm** 12:36 pm
24	**8:43 pm** 5:43 pm	△ ♃	♊	25	**3:20 am** 12:20 am
27	**1:00 pm** 10:00 am	⚹ ☿	♋	27	**1:28 pm** 10:28 am
29	**3:29 pm** 12:29 pm	☍ ♃	♌	29	**9:06 pm** 6:06 pm

☽ Phases & Eclipses phase	day	ET / hr:mn / PT
2nd Quarter	1	**6:21 am** 3:21 am
Full Moon	7	**10:35 pm** 7:35 pm
4th Quarter	14	**6:56 pm** 3:56 pm
New Moon	22	**10:26 pm** 7:26 pm
2nd Quarter	30	**4:38 pm** 1:38 pm

Planet Ingress		day	ET / hr:mn / PT
♀	♊	3	**1:11 pm** 10:11 am
☿	♈	10	9:48 pm
☿	♈	11	**12:48 am**
☉	♉	19	**10:45 am** 7:45 am
⚳	♓	23	**4:20 pm** 1:20 pm
☿	♉	27	**3:53 pm** 12:53 pm
♀	♒	29	**8:29 pm** 5:29 pm

Planetary Motion		day	ET / hr:mn / PT
♇	R̸	25	**2:54 pm** 11:54 am

1 WEDNESDAY
☽ □ ☉ **6:21 am** 3:21 am
☽ △ ☿ **1:51 pm** 10:51 am
☽ △ ♆ **7:23 pm** 4:23 pm

2 THURSDAY
☽ ☍ ♃ **4:49 am** 1:49 am
☽ ☍ ♇ **5:20 am** 2:20 am
☽ ⚹ ♀ **12:49 pm** 9:49 am
☽ ☍ ♄ **3:49 pm** 12:49 pm
☽ ☍ ♂ **6:13 pm** 3:13 pm
☽ □ ♅ **11:40 pm** 8:40 pm

3 FRIDAY
☽ △ ☉ **3:29 pm** 12:29 pm
☿ ☌ ♆ **9:15 pm** 6:15 pm
☽ ⚻ ♆ **11:42 pm** 8:42 pm
☽ ⚻ ☿ **11:58 pm** 8:58 pm

4 SATURDAY
☽ ⚻ ♃ **8:46 am** 5:46 am
☽ ⚻ ♇ **8:52 am** 5:52 am
♀ △ ♄ **1:09 pm** 10:09 am
☽ ⚻ ♄ **6:48 pm** 3:48 pm
☽ □ ♀ **7:08 pm** 4:08 pm
♃ ☌ ♇ **10:45 pm** 7:45 pm
☽ ⚻ ♂ **11:20 pm** 8:20 pm
☽ △ ♅ 11:06 pm

5 SUNDAY
☽ △ ♅ **2:06 am**
☽ ⚻ ☉ **8:12 pm** 5:12 pm
☽ ☍ ♆ 9:38 pm

Eastern time in bold type
Pacific time in medium type

6 MONDAY
☽ ☍ ♆ **12:38 am**
☽ ☍ ☿ **5:49 am** 2:49 am
☽ △ ♇ **9:15 am** 6:15 am
☽ △ ♃ **9:29 am** 6:29 am
☽ △ ♄ **6:52 pm** 3:52 pm
☽ △ ♀ **9:56 pm** 6:56 pm
☽ △ ♂ 10:20 pm
☽ ⚻ ♅ 10:54 pm

7 TUESDAY
☽ △ ♂ **1:20 am**
☽ ⚻ ♅ **1:54 am**
♂ □ ♅ **2:50 pm** 11:50 am
☿ ⚹ ♇ **5:28 pm** 2:28 pm
☿ ⚹ ♃ **10:20 pm** 7:20 pm
☽ ☍ ☉ **10:35 pm** 7:35 pm
☽ ⚻ ♆ **11:49 pm** 8:49 pm

8 WEDNESDAY
☽ □ ♇ **8:17 am** 5:17 am
☽ □ ♃ **8:50 am** 5:50 am
☽ ⚻ ☿ **9:54 am** 6:54 am
☽ □ ♄ **6:03 pm** 3:03 pm
☉ ⚺ ♆ **6:34 pm** 3:34 pm
☽ ⚻ ♀ **11:46 pm** 8:46 pm
☽ ☍ ♅ 10:09 pm
☽ □ ♂ 11:41 pm

9 THURSDAY
☽ ☍ ♅ **1:09 am**
☽ □ ♂ **2:41 am**

☽ △ ♆ **11:32 pm** 8:32 pm
☽ ⚻ ☉ 10:32 pm
♀ ⚺ ♅ 11:40 pm

10 FRIDAY
☽ ⚻ ☉ **1:32 am**
♀ ⚺ ♅ **2:40 am**
☽ ⚹ ♇ **8:15 am** 5:15 am
☽ ⚹ ♃ **9:08 am** 6:08 am
☽ △ ☿ **3:35 pm** 12:35 pm
☽ ⚹ ♄ **6:37 pm** 3:37 pm
☽ ⚻ ♅ 11:08 pm

11 SATURDAY
☽ ⚻ ♅ **2:08 am**
☽ ☍ ♀ **3:28 am** 12:28 am
☽ ⚹ ♂ **6:03 am** 3:03 am
☿ ⚹ ♄ **7:58 pm** 4:58 pm
☽ □ ♆ 10:53 pm

12 SUNDAY
☽ □ ♆ **1:53 am**
☽ △ ☉ **7:46 am** 4:46 am
☽ ⚺ ♇ **11:09 am** 8:09 am
☽ ⚺ ♃ **12:26 pm** 9:26 am
☽ ⚺ ♄ **10:27 pm** 7:27 pm
☽ □ ☿ 11:00 pm

13 MONDAY
☽ □ ☿ **2:00 am**
☽ △ ♅ **6:36 am** 3:36 am
☽ ⚻ ♀ **11:10 am** 8:10 am
☽ ⚺ ♂ **1:33 pm** 10:33 am

14 TUESDAY
☉ □ ♇ **7:07 am** 4:07 am
☽ ⚹ ♆ **8:10 am** 5:10 am
☿ ⚺ ♅ **4:06 pm** 1:06 pm
☽ ☌ ♇ **6:02 pm** 3:02 pm
☽ □ ☉ **6:56 pm** 3:56 pm
☽ ☌ ♃ **7:47 pm** 4:47 pm

15 WEDNESDAY
☽ ☌ ♄ **6:21 am** 3:21 am
☉ □ ♃ **6:59 am** 3:59 am
☽ □ ♅ **3:09 pm** 12:09 pm
☽ ⚹ ☿ **6:41 pm** 3:41 pm
☽ △ ♀ **11:29 pm** 8:29 pm
☽ ☌ ♂ 10:42 pm

16 THURSDAY
☽ ☌ ♂ **1:42 am**
☽ ⚺ ♆ **6:13 pm** 3:13 pm

17 FRIDAY
☽ ⚺ ♇ **4:28 am** 1:28 am
☽ ⚺ ♃ **6:43 am** 3:43 am
☽ ⚹ ☉ **10:34 am** 7:34 am
☽ ⚺ ♄ **5:32 pm** 2:32 pm
☿ ⚹ ♀ 10:36 pm
☽ ⚹ ♅ 11:47 pm

18 SATURDAY
☿ ⚹ ♀ **1:36 am**
☽ ⚹ ♅ **2:47 am**
☽ □ ♀ **2:57 pm** 11:57 am
☽ ⚺ ☿ **4:22 pm** 1:22 pm
☽ ⚺ ♂ **5:07 pm** 2:07 pm
☿ ⚹ ♂ **11:55 pm** 8:55 pm

19 SUNDAY
☽ ☌ ♆ **6:32 am** 3:32 am
☽ ⚹ ♇ **4:51 pm** 1:51 pm
☽ ⚹ ♃ **7:31 pm** 4:31 pm

20 MONDAY
☽ ⚺ ☉ **4:28 am** 1:28 am
☽ ⚹ ♄ **6:16 am** 3:16 am
☽ ⚺ ♅ **3:43 pm** 12:43 pm

21 TUESDAY
☉ □ ♄ **3:00 am** 12:00 am
☽ ⚹ ♀ **7:17 am** 4:17 am
☽ ⚹ ♂ **9:35 am** 6:35 am
☽ ☌ ☿ **4:06 pm** 1:06 pm
☽ ⚺ ♆ **7:23 pm** 4:23 pm

22 WEDNESDAY
☽ □ ♇ **5:31 am** 2:31 am
☽ □ ♃ **8:32 am** 5:32 am
☿ ⚺ ♆ **1:11 pm** 10:11 am
☽ □ ♄ **6:59 pm** 3:59 pm
☽ ☌ ☉ **10:26 pm** 7:26 pm

23 THURSDAY
☽ ☌ ♅ **4:29 am** 1:29 am
☽ ⚺ ♀ **10:50 pm** 7:50 pm
☽ □ ♂ 10:30 pm

24 FRIDAY
☽ □ ♂ **1:30 am**
☽ ⚹ ♆ **7:38 am** 4:38 am
☽ ⚺ ☿ **3:30 pm** 12:30 pm
☽ △ ♇ **5:27 pm** 2:27 pm
☽ △ ♃ **8:43 pm** 5:43 pm

25 SATURDAY
☿ □ ♇ **3:36 am** 12:36 am
☽ △ ♄ **6:47 am** 3:47 am
☽ ⚺ ☉ **3:10 pm** 12:10 pm
☽ ⚺ ♅ **4:13 pm** 1:13 pm
☿ □ ♃ 9:31 pm

26 SUNDAY
☿ □ ♃ **12:31 am**
☉ ☌ ♅ **5:01 am** 2:01 am
☽ ☌ ♀ **12:39 pm** 9:39 am
☽ △ ♂ **3:55 pm** 12:55 pm
☽ □ ♆ **6:31 pm** 3:31 pm

27 MONDAY
☽ ⚻ ♇ **3:54 am** 12:54 am
☽ ⚻ ♃ **7:20 am** 4:20 am
☽ ⚹ ☿ **1:00 pm** 10:00 am
☽ ⚻ ♄ **4:54 pm** 1:54 pm
☽ ⚹ ♅ 11:08 pm

28 TUESDAY
☽ ⚹ ♅ **2:08 am**
☽ ⚹ ☉ **5:38 am** 2:38 am
☿ □ ♄ **1:28 pm** 10:28 am
♂ ⚺ ♆ **4:48 pm** 1:48 pm
☽ ⚺ ♀ **11:45 pm** 8:45 pm

29 WEDNESDAY
☽ △ ♆ **3:12 am** 12:12 am
☽ ⚻ ♂ **3:46 am** 12:46 am
☽ ☍ ♇ **12:01 pm** 9:01 am
☽ ☍ ♃ **3:29 pm** 12:29 pm
☽ ☍ ♄ 9:27 pm

30 THURSDAY
☽ ☍ ♄ **12:27 am**
☽ □ ☿ **6:46 am** 3:46 am
☽ □ ♅ **9:21 am** 6:21 am
☽ □ ☉ **4:38 pm** 1:38 pm
☿ ☌ ♅ **11:41 pm** 8:41 pm

APRIL 2020

DATE	SID.TIME	SUN	MOON	NODE	MERCURY	VENUS	MARS	JUPITER	SATURN	URANUS	NEPTUNE	PLUTO	CERES	PALLAS	JUNO	VESTA	CHIRON
1 W	12 39 15	11♈43 43	6♋33	2♋44℞	15♓17	27♉31	0♒49	24♑24	0♒40	5♉10	19♓16	24♑51	22♒41	24♑49	13♎59℞	3♊57	5♈44
2 Th	12 43 11	12 42 55	19 39	2 44	16 36	28 26	1 31	24 31	0 44	5 13	19 18	24 51	23 01	25 03	13 44	4 19	5 48
3 F	12 47 8	13 42 05	3♌11	2 42	17 56	29 21	2 13	24 38	0 48	5 16	19 20	24 52	23 22	25 17	13 30	4 42	5 51
4 Sa	12 51 4	14 41 12	17 10	2 39	19 18	0♊15	2 54	24 46	0 51	5 20	19 23	24 53	23 42	25 31	13 16	5 05	5 55
5 Su	12 55 1	15 40 17	1♍39	2 33	20 42	1 09	3 36	24 52	0 55	5 23	19 25	24 53	24 02	25 45	13 01	5 28	5 58
6 M	12 58 57	16 39 19	16 32	2 25	22 08	2 02	4 18	24 59	0 58	5 26	19 27	24 54	24 22	25 58	12 47	5 50	6 02
7 T	13 2 54	17 38 19	1♎44	2 15	23 35	2 54	4 59	25 06	1 01	5 29	19 29	24 54	24 42	26 12	12 33	6 13	6 05
8 W	13 6 50	18 37 18	17 05	2 04	25 04	3 46	5 41	25 12	1 04	5 33	19 31	24 55	25 02	26 24	12 19	6 36	6 09
9 Th	13 10 47	19 36 14	2♏21	1 54	26 35	4 37	6 23	25 19	1 08	5 36	19 33	24 55	25 21	26 37	12 05	7 00	6 12
10 F	13 14 44	20 35 08	17 24	1 46	28 07	5 27	7 04	25 25	1 11	5 40	19 35	24 56	25 41	26 50	11 51	7 23	6 16
11 Sa	13 18 40	21 34 00	2♐03	1 41	29 41	6 16	7 46	25 31	1 13	5 43	19 37	24 56	26 00	27 02	11 37	7 46	6 19
12 Su	13 22 37	22 32 51	16 15	1 38	1♈16	7 05	8 28	25 37	1 16	5 46	19 39	24 57	26 20	27 14	11 24	8 09	6 23
13 M	13 26 33	23 31 40	29 57	1 37D	2 53	7 52	9 10	25 43	1 19	5 50	19 41	24 57	26 39	27 25	11 10	8 33	6 26
14 T	13 30 30	24 30 27	13♑11	1 37℞	4 32	8 39	9 51	25 48	1 22	5 53	19 43	24 58	26 58	27 37	10 57	8 56	6 29
15 W	13 34 26	25 29 13	26 00	1 38	6 12	9 25	10 33	25 54	1 24	5 56	19 45	24 58	27 17	27 48	10 44	9 20	6 33
16 Th	13 38 23	26 27 56	8♒29	1 37	7 54	10 10	11 15	25 59	1 27	6 00	19 47	24 58	27 36	27 59	10 31	9 44	6 36
17 F	13 42 19	27 26 39	20 43	1 34	9 37	10 54	11 56	26 04	1 29	6 03	19 49	24 58	27 55	28 10	10 18	10 07	6 39
18 Sa	13 46 16	28 25 19	2♓45	1 29	11 22	11 37	12 38	26 09	1 31	6 07	19 50	24 59	28 13	28 20	10 06	10 31	6 43
19 Su	13 50 13	29 23 57	14 41	1 21	13 09	12 19	13 20	26 14	1 34	6 10	19 52	24 59	28 32	28 30	9 53	10 55	6 46
20 M	13 54 9	0♉22 34	26 32	1 12	14 57	13 00	14 01	26 18	1 36	6 14	19 54	24 59	28 50	28 40	9 41	11 19	6 49
21 T	13 58 6	1 21 09	8♈24	1 01	16 47	13 40	14 43	26 23	1 38	6 17	19 56	24 59	29 09	28 49	9 29	11 43	6 53
22 W	14 2 2	2 19 42	20 16	0 49	18 38	14 19	15 25	26 27	1 40	6 20	19 58	24 59	29 27	28 58	9 18	12 07	6 56
23 Th	14 5 59	3 18 13	2♉11	0 38	20 31	14 56	16 06	26 31	1 41	6 24	20 00	24 59	29 45	29 07	9 06	12 31	6 59
24 F	14 9 55	4 16 43	14 11	0 29	22 26	15 33	16 48	26 35	1 43	6 27	20 01	24 59	0♓03	29 15	8 55	12 55	7 02
25 Sa	14 13 52	5 15 11	26 17	0 21	24 22	16 08	17 29	26 39	1 45	6 31	20 03	25 00℞	0 20	29 24	8 44	13 20	7 06
26 Su	14 17 48	6 13 36	8♊30	0 16	26 20	16 41	18 11	26 42	1 46	6 34	20 05	25 00	0 38	29 32	8 34	13 44	7 09
27 M	14 21 45	7 12 00	20 52	0 14D	28 20	17 13	18 52	26 45	1 48	6 38	20 07	25 00	0 56	29 39	8 24	14 08	7 12
28 T	14 25 42	8 10 22	3♋27	0 14	0♉21	17 44	19 34	26 49	1 49	6 41	20 08	24 59	1 13	29 46	8 14	14 33	7 15
29 W	14 29 38	9 08 41	16 16	0 14	2 23	18 13	20 15	26 52	1 50	6 45	20 10	24 59	1 30	29 53	8 04	14 57	7 18
30 Th	14 33 35	10 06 59	29 23	0 16℞	4 27	18 41	20 57	26 54	1 51	6 48	20 12	24 59	1 47	0♒00	7 55	15 22	7 21

EPHEMERIS CALCULATED FOR 12 MIDNIGHT GREENWICH MEAN TIME. ALL OTHER DATA AND FACING ASPECTARIAN PAGE IN **EASTERN TIME (BOLD)** AND PACIFIC TIME (REGULAR).

MAY 2020

☽ Last Aspect day	ET / hr:mn / PT	asp	☽ Ingress sign day	ET / hr:mn / PT
1	**12:04 pm** 9:04 am	☍♂	♍ 1	10:35 pm
1	**12:04 pm** 9:04 am	☍♂	♍ 2	**1:35 am**
3	**10:25 pm** 7:25 pm	△♃	♎ 4	**3:09 am** 12:09 am
5	**10:31 pm** 7:31 pm	□♃	♏ 6	**3:05 am** 12:05 am
7	**10:39 pm** 7:39 pm	⚹♃	♐ 8	**3:15 am** 12:15 am
9	11:11 pm	⚹♂	♑ 10	**5:39 am** 2:39 am
10	**2:11 am**	⚹♂	♑ 10	**5:39 am** 2:39 am
12	**6:30 am** 3:30 am	☌♃	♒ 12	**11:39 am** 8:39 am
14	**10:03 am** 7:03 am	□☉	♓ 14	**9:24 pm** 6:24 pm
17	**3:59 am** 12:59 am	⚹♃	♈ 17	**9:36 am** 6:36 am
19	**4:33 pm** 1:33 pm	□♃	♉ 19	**10:10 pm** 7:10 pm
22	**4:01 am** 1:01 am	△♃	♊ 22	**9:36 am** 6:36 am
24	**7:09 am** 4:09 am	☌☿	♋ 24	**7:09 pm** 4:09 pm
26	**9:06 pm** 6:06 pm	☍♃	♌ 26	11:33 pm
26	**9:06 pm** 6:06 pm	☍♃	♌ 27	**2:33 am**
28	**9:30 am** 6:30 am	⚹♀	♍ 29	**7:40 am** 4:40 am
31	**5:17 am** 2:17 am	△♃	♎ 31	**10:38 am** 7:38 am

☽ Phases & Eclipses phase	day	ET / hr:mn / PT
Full Moon	7	**6:45 am** 3:45 am
4th Quarter	14	**10:03 am** 7:03 am
New Moon	22	**1:39 pm** 10:39 am
2nd Quarter	29	**11:30 pm** 8:30 pm

Planet Ingress	day	ET / hr:mn / PT
☿ ♊	11	**5:58 pm** 2:58 pm
♂ ♓	12	9:17 pm
♂ ♓	13	**12:17 am**
☉ ♊	20	**9:49 am** 6:49 am
☿ ♋	28	**2:09 pm** 11:09 am

Planetary Motion	day	ET / hr:mn / PT
♄ ℞	10	9:09 pm
♄ ℞	11	**12:09 am**
♀ ℞	12	11:45 pm
♀ ℞	13	**2:45 am**
♃ ℞	14	**10:32 am** 7:32 am
⚴ ℞	17	**4:29 am** 1:29 am
⚵ D	26	**10:51 pm** 7:51 pm

1 FRIDAY
☽ ⚹ ♀ **7:16 am** 4:16 am
☽ ⚻ ♆ **8:51 am** 5:51 am
☽ ☍ ♂ **12:04 pm** 9:04 am
☽ ⚻ ♇ **5:02 pm** 2:02 pm
☽ ⚻ ♃ **8:28 pm** 5:28 pm

2 SATURDAY
☽ ⚻ ♄ **4:48 am** 1:48 am
☽ △ ♅ **1:19 pm** 10:19 am
☽ △ ☿ **7:38 pm** 4:38 pm
☽ △ ☉ **11:40 pm** 8:40 pm

3 SUNDAY
☽ □ ♀ **11:06 am** 8:06 am
☽ ☍ ♆ **11:22 am** 8:22 am
☽ ⚻ ♂ **4:47 pm** 1:47 pm
☽ △ ♇ **7:01 pm** 4:01 pm
☽ △ ♃ **10:25 pm** 7:25 pm
♀ □ ♆ **11:52 pm** 8:52 pm

4 MONDAY
☽ △ ♄ **6:15 am** 3:15 am
☽ ⚻ ♅ **2:32 pm** 11:32 am
☉ ☌ ☿ **5:41 pm** 2:41 pm

5 TUESDAY
☽ ⚻ ☉ **3:39 am** 12:39 am
☽ ⚻ ☿ **4:34 am** 1:34 am
☽ ⚻ ♆ **11:43 am** 8:43 am
☽ △ ♀ **12:23 pm** 9:23 am
♂ ⚺ ♇ **4:11 pm** 1:11 pm
☽ □ ♇ **7:05 pm** 4:05 pm
☽ △ ♂ **7:13 pm** 4:13 pm
☽ □ ♃ **10:31 pm** 7:31 pm

6 WEDNESDAY
☽ □ ♄ **6:10 am** 3:10 am
☽ ☍ ♅ **2:31 pm** 11:31 am

7 THURSDAY
☿ ⚹ ♆ **6:42 am** 3:42 am
☽ ☍ ☉ **6:45 am** 3:45 am
☽ △ ♆ **11:40 am** 8:40 am
☽ ☍ ☿ **12:30 pm** 9:30 am
☽ ⚻ ♀ **1:04 pm** 10:04 am
☿ ⚺ ♀ **4:39 pm** 1:39 pm
☽ ⚹ ♇ **7:03 pm** 4:03 pm
☽ □ ♂ **9:33 pm** 6:33 pm
☽ ⚹ ♃ **10:39 pm** 7:39 pm

8 FRIDAY
☽ ⚹ ♄ **6:27 am** 3:27 am
☽ ⚻ ♅ **3:15 pm** 12:15 pm
♂ ⚺ ♃ **9:53 pm** 6:53 pm

9 SATURDAY
☿ △ ♇ **9:17 am** 6:17 am
☽ ⚻ ☉ **11:35 am** 8:35 am
☽ □ ♆ **1:14 pm** 10:14 am
☽ ☍ ♀ **3:13 pm** 12:13 pm
☽ ⚺ ♇ **8:55 pm** 5:55 pm
☽ ⚻ ☿ **11:03 pm** 8:03 pm
☽ ⚺ ♃ 9:49 pm
☽ ⚹ ♂ 11:11 pm

10 SUNDAY
☽ ⚺ ♃ **12:49 am**
☽ ⚹ ♂ **2:11 am**
☽ ⚺ ♄ **9:03 am** 6:03 am
☿ △ ♃ **10:36 am** 7:36 am
☉ ⚹ ♆ **12:16 pm** 9:16 am
☽ △ ♅ **6:38 pm** 3:38 pm

11 MONDAY
☿ □ ♂ **3:33 am** 12:33 am
☽ ⚹ ♆ **6:05 pm** 3:05 pm
☽ △ ☉ **8:24 pm** 5:24 pm
☽ ⚻ ♀ **8:30 pm** 5:30 pm
☉ ⚺ ♀ **9:57 pm** 6:57 pm
☽ ☌ ♇ 11:14 pm

12 TUESDAY
☽ ☌ ♇ **2:14 am**
☽ ☌ ♃ **6:30 am** 3:30 am
☽ ⚺ ♂ **10:56 am** 7:56 am
☽ △ ☿ **3:07 pm** 12:07 pm
☽ ☌ ♄ **3:18 pm** 12:18 pm
☿ △ ♄ **4:14 pm** 1:14 pm
☽ □ ♅ 10:52 pm

13 WEDNESDAY
☽ □ ♅ **1:52 am**
☽ ⚺ ♆ 11:50 pm

14 THURSDAY
☽ ⚺ ♆ **2:50 am**
☽ △ ♀ **5:20 am** 2:20 am
☽ □ ☉ **10:03 am** 7:03 am
☽ ⚺ ♇ **11:23 am** 8:23 am
☽ ⚺ ♃ **3:58 pm** 12:58 pm
☽ ☌ ♂ 9:06 pm
☽ ⚺ ♄ 10:15 pm
☉ △ ♇ 11:49 pm

15 FRIDAY
☽ ☌ ♂ **12:06 am**
☽ ⚺ ♄ **1:15 am**
☉ △ ♇ **2:49 am**
☿ ⚺ ♅ **11:17 am** 8:17 am
☽ ⚹ ♅ **12:41 pm** 9:41 am
☽ □ ☿ **12:57 pm** 9:57 am
♂ ⚺ ♄ **8:25 pm** 5:25 pm

16 SATURDAY
☽ ☌ ♆ **2:34 pm** 11:34 am
☽ □ ♀ **4:35 pm** 1:35 pm
☽ ⚹ ♇ **11:15 pm** 8:15 pm

17 SUNDAY
☽ ⚹ ☉ **3:13 am** 12:13 am
☽ ⚹ ♃ **3:59 am** 12:59 am
☉ △ ♃ **12:40 pm** 9:40 am
☽ ⚹ ♄ **1:29 pm** 10:29 am
☽ ⚺ ♂ **4:01 pm** 1:01 pm
☽ ⚺ ♅ 10:27 pm

18 MONDAY
☽ ⚺ ♅ **1:27 am**
☽ ⚹ ☿ **1:17 pm** 10:17 am

19 TUESDAY
☽ ⚺ ♆ **3:20 am** 12:20 am
☽ ⚹ ♀ **4:17 am** 1:17 am
☽ □ ♇ **11:51 am** 8:51 am
☽ □ ♃ **4:33 pm** 1:33 pm
☽ ⚺ ☉ **9:09 pm** 6:09 pm
☽ □ ♄ 10:58 pm

20 WEDNESDAY
☽ □ ♄ **1:58 am**
☽ ⚹ ♂ **8:10 am** 5:10 am
☽ ☌ ♅ **2:07 pm** 11:07 am
♀ □ ♆ **7:03 pm** 4:03 pm

21 THURSDAY
☽ ⚺ ☿ **12:01 pm** 9:01 am
☽ ⚺ ♀ **2:46 pm** 11:46 am
☽ ⚹ ♆ **3:19 pm** 12:19 pm
☽ △ ♇ **11:29 pm** 8:29 pm

22 FRIDAY
☽ △ ♃ **4:01 am** 1:01 am
☿ ☌ ♀ **4:41 am** 1:41 am
☉ △ ♄ **8:02 am** 5:02 am
☿ □ ♆ **11:43 am** 8:43 am
☽ △ ♄ **1:12 pm** 10:12 am
☽ ☌ ☉ **1:39 pm** 10:39 am
☽ □ ♂ **10:43 pm** 7:43 pm
☽ ⚺ ♅ 10:20 pm

23 SATURDAY
☽ ⚺ ♅ **1:20 am**
☽ ☌ ♀ **11:15 pm** 8:15 pm
☽ □ ♆ 10:34 pm

24 SUNDAY
☽ □ ♆ **1:34 am**
☽ ☌ ☿ **7:09 am** 4:09 am
☽ ⚻ ♇ **9:19 am** 6:19 am
☽ ⚻ ♃ **1:38 pm** 10:38 am
☽ ⚻ ♄ **10:32 pm** 7:32 pm
☿ ⚻ ♇ 9:26 pm
♂ ⚹ ♅ 11:48 pm

25 MONDAY
☿ ⚻ ♇ **12:26 am**
♂ ⚹ ♅ **2:48 am**
☽ ⚺ ☉ **3:43 am** 12:43 am
☽ ⚹ ♅ **10:34 am** 7:34 am
☽ △ ♂ **10:58 am** 7:58 am

26 TUESDAY
☽ ⚺ ♀ **5:31 am** 2:31 am
☽ △ ♆ **9:43 am** 6:43 am
☿ ⚻ ♃ **11:35 am** 8:35 am
☽ ☍ ♇ **5:03 pm** 2:03 pm
☽ ☍ ♃ **9:06 pm** 6:06 pm
☽ ⚺ ☿ **10:19 pm** 7:19 pm

27 WEDNESDAY
☽ ☍ ♄ **5:42 am** 2:42 am
☽ ⚹ ☉ **3:02 pm** 12:02 pm
☽ □ ♅ **5:34 pm** 2:34 pm
☽ ⚻ ♂ **8:36 pm** 5:36 pm

28 THURSDAY
☽ ⚹ ♀ **9:30 am** 6:30 am
☽ ⚻ ♆ **3:36 pm** 12:36 pm
☽ ⚻ ♇ **10:31 pm** 7:31 pm
☽ ⚻ ♃ 11:17 pm

29 FRIDAY
☽ ⚻ ♃ **2:17 am**
☉ ⚺ ♅ **4:13 am** 1:13 am
☽ ⚹ ☿ **9:32 am** 6:32 am
☽ ⚻ ♄ **10:35 am** 7:35 am
☿ ⚻ ♄ **8:25 pm** 5:25 pm
☽ △ ♅ **10:15 pm** 7:15 pm
☽ □ ☉ **11:30 pm** 8:30 pm

30 SATURDAY
☽ ☍ ♂ **3:34 am** 12:34 am
☽ □ ♀ **11:18 am** 8:18 am
☽ ☍ ♆ **7:14 pm** 4:14 pm
☽ △ ♇ 10:46 pm

31 SUNDAY
☽ △ ♇ **1:46 am**
☽ △ ♃ **5:17 am** 2:17 am
☽ △ ♄ **1:20 pm** 10:20 am
☽ □ ☿ **5:16 pm** 2:16 pm
☽ ⚻ ♅ 9:52 pm

Eastern time in bold type
Pacific time in medium type

MAY 2020

DATE	SID.TIME	SUN	MOON	NODE	MERCURY	VENUS	MARS	JUPITER	SATURN	URANUS	NEPTUNE	PLUTO	CERES	PALLAS	JUNO	VESTA	CHIRON
1 F	14 37 31	11♉05 14	12♌52	0♋16℞	6♉33	19♊07	21♒38	26♑57	1♒52	6♉52	20♓13	24♑59℞	2♓04	0♒06	7♎45℞	15♊46	7♈24
2 Sa	14 41 28	12 03 28	26 43	0 15	8 39	19 31	22 19	26 59	1 53	6 55	20 15	24 59	2 21	0 12	7 37	16 11	7 28
3 Su	14 45 24	13 01 39	10♍58	0 12	10 47	19 54	23 01	27 02	1 54	6 58	20 16	24 59	2 37	0 18	7 28	16 35	7 31
4 M	14 49 21	13 59 48	25 35	0 07	12 55	20 15	23 42	27 04	1 55	7 02	20 18	24 59	2 54	0 23	7 20	17 00	7 34
5 T	14 53 17	14 57 56	10♎29	0 01	15 05	20 34	24 23	27 06	1 56	7 05	20 19	24 58	3 10	0 28	7 12	17 25	7 36
6 W	14 57 14	15 56 01	25 33	29♊55	17 15	20 51	25 05	27 07	1 56	7 09	20 21	24 58	3 26	0 32	7 05	17 50	7 39
7 Th	15 1 11	16 54 05	10♏37	29 48	19 25	21 06	25 46	27 09	1 57	7 12	20 22	24 58	3 42	0 36	6 58	18 14	7 42
8 F	15 5 7	17 52 07	25 33	29 43	21 35	21 19	26 27	27 10	1 57	7 16	20 24	24 57	3 58	0 40	6 51	18 39	7 45
9 Sa	15 9 4	18 50 07	10♐10	29 40	23 45	21 29	27 08	27 11	1 57	7 19	20 25	24 57	4 14	0 43	6 45	19 04	7 48
10 Su	15 13 0	19 48 06	24 24	29 39D	25 55	21 38	27 49	27 12	1 57	7 22	20 26	24 57	4 29	0 47	6 39	19 29	7 51
11 M	15 16 57	20 46 04	8♑12	29 39	28 03	21 44	28 31	27 13	1 57℞	7 26	20 28	24 56	4 44	0 49	6 33	19 54	7 54
12 T	15 20 53	21 44 00	21 32	29 40	0♊11	21 48	29 12	27 14	1 57	7 29	20 29	24 56	4 59	0 51	6 28	20 19	7 56
13 W	15 24 50	22 41 55	4♒27	29 41	2 17	21 50℞	29 53	27 14	1 57	7 32	20 30	24 55	5 14	0 53	6 23	20 44	7 59
14 Th	15 28 46	23 39 49	17 01	29 43℞	4 22	21 50	0♓34	27 14℞	1 57	7 36	20 32	24 55	5 29	0 55	6 18	21 10	8 02
15 F	15 32 43	24 37 41	29 17	29 43	6 24	21 47	1 15	27 14	1 57	7 39	20 33	24 54	5 44	0 56	6 14	21 35	8 05
16 Sa	15 36 40	25 35 32	11♓21	29 41	8 25	21 42	1 56	27 14	1 56	7 42	20 34	24 54	5 58	0 57	6 10	22 00	8 07
17 Su	15 40 36	26 33 22	23 17	29 39	10 23	21 34	2 36	27 14	1 56	7 46	20 35	24 53	6 12	0 57℞	6 06	22 25	8 10
18 M	15 44 33	27 31 11	5♈08	29 35	12 19	21 24	3 17	27 13	1 55	7 49	20 37	24 53	6 26	0 57	6 03	22 51	8 12
19 T	15 48 29	28 28 58	17 00	29 30	14 12	21 11	3 58	27 13	1 54	7 52	20 38	24 52	6 40	0 57	6 00	23 16	8 15
20 W	15 52 26	29 26 44	28 55	29 24	16 02	20 56	4 39	27 12	1 54	7 56	20 39	24 51	6 54	0 56	5 57	23 41	8 17
21 Th	15 56 22	0♊24 29	10♉55	29 19	17 50	20 39	5 19	27 11	1 53	7 59	20 40	24 51	7 07	0 54	5 55	24 07	8 20
22 F	16 0 19	1 22 13	23 04	29 15	19 35	20 19	6 00	27 09	1 52	8 02	20 41	24 50	7 20	0 53	5 53	24 32	8 22
23 Sa	16 4 15	2 19 56	5♊21	29 12	21 16	19 58	6 40	27 08	1 51	8 05	20 42	24 49	7 33	0 51	5 51	24 58	8 25
24 Su	16 8 12	3 17 37	17 48	29 10D	22 55	19 34	7 21	27 06	1 49	8 09	20 43	24 48	7 46	0 48	5 50	25 23	8 27
25 M	16 12 9	4 15 17	0♋27	29 09	24 30	19 07	8 01	27 04	1 48	8 12	20 44	24 48	7 59	0 45	5 49	25 49	8 29
26 T	16 16 5	5 12 56	13 18	29 10	26 02	18 39	8 42	27 02	1 47	8 15	20 45	24 47	8 11	0 42	5 49	26 14	8 31
27 W	16 20 2	6 10 33	26 23	29 11	27 31	18 09	9 22	27 00	1 45	8 18	20 46	24 46	8 23	0 38	5 48D	26 40	8 34
28 Th	16 23 58	7 08 09	9♌43	29 13	28 57	17 38	10 02	26 57	1 44	8 21	20 46	24 45	8 35	0 34	5 48	27 05	8 36
29 F	16 27 55	8 05 44	23 18	29 14	0♋20	17 05	10 42	26 55	1 42	8 24	20 47	24 44	8 47	0 29	5 49	27 31	8 38
30 Sa	16 31 51	9 03 17	7♍09	29 14℞	1 39	16 30	11 22	26 52	1 40	8 27	20 48	24 43	8 58	0 24	5 50	27 57	8 40
31 Su	16 35 48	10 00 48	21 16	29 14	2 55	15 55	12 02	26 49	1 39	8 31	20 49	24 42	9 09	0 19	5 51	28 22	8 42

EPHEMERIS CALCULATED FOR 12 MIDNIGHT GREENWICH MEAN TIME. ALL OTHER DATA AND FACING ASPECTARIAN PAGE IN **EASTERN TIME (BOLD)** AND PACIFIC TIME (REGULAR).

JUNE 2020

☽ Last Aspect			☽ Ingress		
day	ET / hr:mn / PT	asp	sign day	ET / hr:mn / PT	
2	**6:40 am** 3:40 am	□♃	♏ 2	**12:06 pm** 9:06 am	
4	**7:36 am** 4:36 am	⚹♃	♐ 4	**1:17 pm** 10:17 am	
5	9:10 pm	□♆	♑ 6	**3:44 pm** 12:44 pm	
6	**12:10 am**	□♆	♑ 6	**3:44 pm** 12:44 pm	
8	**2:06 pm** 11:06 am	☌♃	♒ 8	**8:54 pm** 5:54 pm	
10	**10:35 am** 7:35 am	△☉	♓ 11	**5:32 am** 2:32 am	
13	**8:45 am** 5:45 am	⚹♃	♈ 13	**5:03 pm** 2:03 pm	
15	**8:49 pm** 5:49 pm	□♃	♉ 16	**5:35 am** 2:35 am	
18	**8:02 am** 5:02 am	△♃	♊ 18	**5:00 pm** 2:00 pm	
20	**5:48 pm** 2:48 pm	□♂	♋ 20	11:02 pm	

☽ Last Aspect			☽ Ingress	
day	ET / hr:mn / PT	asp	sign day	ET / hr:mn / PT
20	**5:48 pm** 2:48 pm	□♂	♋ 21	**2:02 am**
23	**3:20 am** 12:20 am	△♂	♌ 23	**8:33 am** 5:33 am
23	10:34 pm	□♅	♍ 25	**1:05 pm** 10:05 am
24	**1:34 am**	□♅	♍ 25	**1:05 pm** 10:05 am
27	**4:02 pm** 1:02 pm	☍♂	♎ 27	**4:16 pm** 1:16 pm
29	**9:02 am** 6:02 am	□♃	♏ 29	**6:48 pm** 3:48 pm

☽ Phases & Eclipses		
phase	day	ET / hr:mn / PT
Full Moon	5	**3:12 pm** 12:12 pm
●	5	15° ♐ 34'
4th Quarter	12	11:24 pm
4th Quarter	13	**2:24 am**
New Moon	20	11:41 pm
New Moon	21	**2:41 am**
●	20/21	0° ♋ 21'
2nd Quarter	28	**4:16 am** 1:16 am

Planet Ingress		
	day	ET / hr:mn / PT
♀ ♑	2	**8:55 pm** 5:55 pm
⚵ ♋	3	**2:55 pm** 11:55 am
☉ ♋	20	**5:44 pm** 2:44 pm
♂ ♈	27	**9:45 pm** 6:45 pm

Planetary Motion		
	day	ET / hr:mn / PT
☿ ℞	17	9:59 pm
☿ ℞	18	**12:59 am**
♆ ℞	22	9:32 pm
♆ ℞	23	**12:32 am**
♀ D	24	11:48 pm
♀ D	25	**2:48 am**

1 MONDAY
☽ ⚻ ♅ **12:52 am**
☽ △ ☉ **5:28 am** 2:28 am
☽ ⚻ ♂ **8:15 am** 5:15 am
☽ △ ♀ **11:20 am** 8:20 am
☽ ⚻ ♆ **9:05 pm** 6:05 pm

2 TUESDAY
☽ □ ♇ **3:22 am** 12:22 am
☽ □ ♃ **6:40 am** 3:40 am
☽ □ ♄ **2:38 pm** 11:38 am
♀ □ ♂ **8:41 pm** 5:41 pm
☽ △ ☿ **10:41 pm** 7:41 pm
☽ ☍ ♅ 11:17 pm

3 WEDNESDAY
☽ ☍ ♅ **2:17 am**
☽ ⚻ ☉ **10:05 am** 7:05 am
☽ ⚻ ♀ **10:28 am** 7:28 am
☽ △ ♂ **11:44 am** 8:44 am
☉ ☌ ♀ **1:44 pm** 10:44 am
☽ △ ♆ **10:14 pm** 7:14 pm

4 THURSDAY
☽ ⚹ ♇ **4:27 am** 1:27 am
☽ ⚹ ♃ **7:36 am** 4:36 am
☽ ⚹ ♄ **3:43 pm** 12:43 pm

5 FRIDAY
☽ ⚻ ☿ **3:38 am** 12:38 am
☽ ⚻ ♅ **3:50 am** 12:50 am
☿ ⚹ ♅ **7:05 am** 4:05 am
☽ ☍ ♀ **9:57 am** 6:57 am
☽ ☍ ☉ **3:12 pm** 12:12 pm
☽ □ ♂ **3:44 pm** 12:44 pm
☽ □ ♆ 9:10 pm

6 SATURDAY
☽ □ ♆ **12:10 am**
☽ ⚺ ♇ **6:30 am** 3:30 am
☽ ⚺ ♃ **9:36 am** 6:36 am
☉ □ ♂ **3:11 pm** 12:11 pm
☽ ⚺ ♄ **6:08 pm** 3:08 pm

7 SUNDAY
☽ △ ♅ **7:08 am** 4:08 am
☽ ☍ ☿ **10:06 am** 7:06 am
☽ ⚻ ♀ **11:11 am** 8:11 am
☿ ⚺ ♀ **9:29 pm** 6:29 pm
☽ ⚹ ♂ **10:07 pm** 7:07 pm
☽ ⚻ ☉ **10:51 pm** 7:51 pm

8 MONDAY
☽ ⚹ ♆ **4:25 am** 1:25 am
☽ ☌ ♇ **11:01 am** 8:01 am
☽ ☌ ♃ **2:06 pm** 11:06 am
☽ ☌ ♄ **11:17 pm** 8:17 pm

9 TUESDAY
☽ □ ♅ **1:30 pm** 10:30 am
☽ △ ♀ **3:15 pm** 12:15 pm
☽ ⚻ ☿ **7:33 pm** 4:33 pm

10 WEDNESDAY
☽ ⚺ ♂ **8:15 am** 5:15 am
☽ △ ☉ **10:35 am** 7:35 am
☽ ⚺ ♆ **12:01 pm** 9:01 am
☽ ⚺ ♇ **6:56 pm** 3:56 pm
☽ ⚺ ♃ **9:56 pm** 6:56 pm

11 THURSDAY
☉ □ ♆ **5:37 am** 2:37 am
♀ ⚺ ♅ **5:50 am** 2:50 am
☽ ⚺ ♄ **7:51 am** 4:51 am
☽ □ ♀ **10:35 pm** 7:35 pm
☽ ⚹ ♅ **11:20 pm** 8:20 pm

12 FRIDAY
☽ △ ☿ **8:07 am** 5:07 am
☽ ☌ ♂ **10:13 pm** 7:13 pm
☽ ☌ ♆ **10:51 pm** 7:51 pm
☽ □ ☉ 11:24 pm

13 SATURDAY
☽ □ ☉ **2:24 am**
☽ ⚹ ♇ **5:56 am** 2:56 am
☽ ⚹ ♃ **8:45 am** 5:45 am
♂ ☌ ♆ **10:13 am** 7:13 am
☽ ⚹ ♄ **7:12 pm** 4:12 pm

14 SUNDAY
☽ ⚹ ♀ **8:24 am** 5:24 am
☽ ⚺ ♅ **11:38 am** 8:38 am
☉ ⚻ ♇ **9:58 pm** 6:58 pm
☽ □ ☿ **10:07 pm** 7:07 pm

15 MONDAY
☽ ⚺ ♆ **11:21 am** 8:21 am
☽ ⚺ ♂ **2:08 pm** 11:08 am
☽ □ ♇ **6:22 pm** 3:22 pm
☽ ⚹ ☉ **8:11 pm** 5:11 pm
☽ □ ♃ **8:49 pm** 5:49 pm

16 TUESDAY
☉ ⚻ ♃ **3:33 am** 12:33 am
☽ □ ♄ **7:29 am** 4:29 am
☽ ⚺ ♀ **7:01 pm** 4:01 pm
☽ ☌ ♅ 9:15 pm

17 WEDNESDAY
☽ ☌ ♅ **12:15 am**
☽ ⚹ ☿ **11:03 am** 8:03 am
☽ ⚹ ♆ **11:18 pm** 8:18 pm

18 THURSDAY
☽ ⚹ ♂ **5:16 am** 2:16 am
☽ △ ♇ **6:01 am** 3:01 am
☽ △ ♃ **8:02 am** 5:02 am
☽ ⚺ ☉ **12:54 pm** 9:54 am
☽ △ ♄ **6:34 pm** 3:34 pm
♂ ⚹ ♇ **7:08 pm** 4:08 pm

19 FRIDAY
☽ ☌ ♀ **4:40 am** 1:40 am
☽ ⚺ ♅ **11:12 am** 8:12 am
☽ ⚺ ☿ **9:09 pm** 6:09 pm

20 SATURDAY
♂ ⚹ ♃ **3:56 am** 12:56 am
☽ □ ♆ **9:07 am** 6:07 am
☽ ⚻ ♇ **3:26 pm** 12:26 pm
☽ ⚻ ♃ **5:01 pm** 2:01 pm
☽ □ ♂ **5:48 pm** 2:48 pm
☽ ☌ ☉ 11:41 pm

21 SUNDAY
☽ ☌ ☉ **2:41 am**
☽ ⚻ ♄ **3:17 am** 12:17 am
☉ ⚻ ♄ **10:14 am** 7:14 am
☽ ⚺ ♀ **12:22 pm** 9:22 am
☽ ⚹ ♅ **7:35 pm** 4:35 pm

22 MONDAY
☽ ☌ ☿ **4:01 am** 1:01 am
☽ △ ♆ **4:22 pm** 1:22 pm
☽ ☍ ♇ **10:19 pm** 7:19 pm
☽ ☍ ♃ **11:29 pm** 8:29 pm

23 TUESDAY
☽ △ ♂ **3:20 am** 12:20 am
☽ ☍ ♄ **9:31 am** 6:31 am
☽ ⚺ ☉ **1:20 pm** 10:20 am
☽ ⚹ ♀ **6:05 pm** 3:05 pm
☽ □ ♅ 10:34 pm

24 WEDNESDAY
☽ □ ♅ **1:34 am**
☽ ⚺ ☿ **8:09 am** 5:09 am
☽ ⚻ ♆ **9:25 pm** 6:25 pm

25 THURSDAY
☽ ⚻ ♇ **3:05 am** 12:05 am
☽ ⚻ ♃ **3:53 am** 12:53 am
☽ ⚻ ♂ **10:29 am** 7:29 am
☽ ⚻ ♄ **1:47 pm** 10:47 am
☽ ⚹ ☉ **9:33 pm** 6:33 pm
☽ □ ♀ **10:17 pm** 7:17 pm

26 FRIDAY
☽ △ ♅ **5:44 am** 2:44 am
☉ ⚺ ♀ **8:41 am** 5:41 am
☽ ⚹ ☿ **10:18 am** 7:18 am
☽ ☍ ♆ 9:56 pm

27 SATURDAY
☽ ☍ ♆ **12:56 am**
☽ △ ♇ **6:24 am** 3:24 am
☽ △ ♃ **6:51 am** 3:51 am
☽ ☍ ♂ **4:02 pm** 1:02 pm
☽ △ ♄ **4:44 pm** 1:44 pm
☽ △ ♀ 10:34 pm

28 SUNDAY
☽ △ ♀ **1:34 am**
☽ □ ☉ **4:16 am** 1:16 am
♂ ⚹ ♄ **6:59 am** 3:59 am
☽ ⚻ ♅ **8:47 am** 5:47 am
☽ □ ☿ **11:14 am** 8:14 am

29 MONDAY
☽ ⚻ ♆ **3:35 am** 12:35 am
☽ □ ♇ **8:55 am** 5:55 am
☽ □ ♃ **9:02 am** 6:02 am
☽ □ ♄ **7:01 pm** 4:01 pm
☽ ⚻ ♂ **8:47 pm** 5:47 pm
♃ ☌ ♇ 10:46 pm

30 TUESDAY
♃ ☌ ♇ **1:46 am**
☽ ⚻ ♀ **4:34 am** 1:34 am
☽ △ ☉ **10:20 am** 7:20 am
☽ ☍ ♅ **11:21 am** 8:21 am
☽ △ ☿ **11:39 am** 8:39 am
☿ ⚹ ♅ **6:12 pm** 3:12 pm
☉ ☌ ☿ **10:53 pm** 7:53 pm
☉ ⚹ ♅ 11:07 pm

Eastern time in bold type
Pacific time in medium type

JUNE 2020

DATE	SID.TIME	SUN	MOON	NODE	MERCURY	VENUS	MARS	JUPITER	SATURN	URANUS	NEPTUNE	PLUTO	CERES	PALLAS	JUNO	VESTA	CHIRON
1 M	16 39 44	10♊58 18	5♎38	29♊13℞	4♋07	15♊18℞	12♓42	26♑46℞	1♒37℞	8♉34	20♓50	24♑42℞	9♓20	0♒13℞	5♎52	28♊48	8♈44
2 T	16 43 41	11 55 47	20 11	29 11	5 16	14 41	13 22	26 43	1 35	8 37	20 50	24 41	9 31	0 07	5 54	29 14	8 46
3 W	16 47 38	12 53 14	4♏50	29 09	6 21	14 04	14 01	26 39	1 33	8 40	20 51	24 40	9 42	0 00	5 56	29 40	8 48
4 Th	16 51 34	13 50 41	19 30	29 07	7 23	13 26	14 41	26 35	1 30	8 43	20 52	24 39	9 52	29♑53	5 59	0♋05	8 50
5 F	16 55 31	14 48 06	4♐04	29 06	8 21	12 48	15 20	26 32	1 28	8 46	20 52	24 38	10 02	29 46	6 01	0 31	8 52
6 Sa	16 59 27	15 45 31	18 25	29 05D	9 16	12 11	16 00	26 28	1 26	8 48	20 53	24 37	10 12	29 38	6 04	0 57	8 54
7 Su	17 3 24	16 42 54	2♑28	29 05	10 06	11 34	16 39	26 23	1 23	8 51	20 53	24 36	10 21	29 30	6 08	1 23	8 55
8 M	17 7 20	17 40 17	16 11	29 05	10 53	10 58	17 19	26 19	1 21	8 54	20 54	24 34	10 30	29 21	6 11	1 49	8 57
9 T	17 11 17	18 37 39	29 30	29 06	11 35	10 23	17 58	26 15	1 18	8 57	20 54	24 33	10 39	29 12	6 15	2 15	8 59
10 W	17 15 13	19 35 00	12♒28	29 07	12 14	9 49	18 37	26 10	1 16	9 00	20 55	24 32	10 48	29 02	6 19	2 41	9 00
11 Th	17 19 10	20 32 21	25 05	29 08	12 48	9 17	19 16	26 05	1 13	9 03	20 55	24 31	10 56	28 53	6 24	3 07	9 02
12 F	17 23 7	21 29 41	7♓24	29 08	13 19	8 46	19 55	26 00	1 10	9 05	20 56	24 30	11 05	28 42	6 28	3 33	9 03
13 Sa	17 27 3	22 27 01	19 30	29 09℞	13 44	8 17	20 33	25 55	1 07	9 08	20 56	24 29	11 13	28 32	6 33	3 59	9 05
14 Su	17 31 0	23 24 20	1♈28	29 09	14 06	7 50	21 12	25 50	1 04	9 11	20 56	24 28	11 20	28 21	6 39	4 25	9 06
15 M	17 34 56	24 21 39	13 21	29 08	14 22	7 25	21 50	25 44	1 01	9 14	20 57	24 26	11 27	28 10	6 44	4 51	9 08
16 T	17 38 53	25 18 58	25 14	29 08	14 35	7 02	22 29	25 39	0 58	9 16	20 57	24 25	11 34	27 58	6 50	5 17	9 09
17 W	17 42 49	26 16 16	7♉11	29 07	14 43	6 41	23 07	25 33	0 55	9 19	20 57	24 24	11 41	27 46	6 56	5 43	9 10
18 Th	17 46 46	27 13 34	19 17	29 07	14 46℞	6 23	23 45	25 27	0 52	9 21	20 57	24 23	11 48	27 34	7 03	6 09	9 12
19 F	17 50 42	28 10 51	1♊33	29 07D	14 44	6 07	24 23	25 21	0 48	9 24	20 57	24 21	11 54	27 21	7 10	6 35	9 13
20 Sa	17 54 39	29 08 09	14 02	29 07	14 39	5 53	25 01	25 15	0 45	9 26	20 57	24 20	12 00	27 08	7 16	7 01	9 14
21 Su	17 58 36	0♋05 25	26 46	29 07℞	14 29	5 42	25 38	25 09	0 41	9 29	20 58	24 19	12 05	26 55	7 24	7 27	9 15
22 M	18 2 32	1 02 42	9♋45	29 07	14 14	5 33	26 16	25 03	0 38	9 31	20 58	24 18	12 10	26 41	7 31	7 53	9 16
23 T	18 6 29	1 59 58	22 59	29 07	13 56	5 26	26 53	24 56	0 34	9 34	20 58℞	24 16	12 15	26 27	7 39	8 20	9 17
24 W	18 10 25	2 57 13	6♌27	29 06	13 34	5 22	27 30	24 50	0 31	9 36	20 58	24 15	12 20	26 13	7 47	8 46	9 18
25 Th	18 14 22	3 54 28	20 08	29 06	13 08	5 20D	28 07	24 43	0 27	9 39	20 58	24 14	12 24	25 59	7 55	9 12	9 19
26 F	18 18 18	4 51 42	4♍01	29 05	12 40	5 21	28 44	24 36	0 23	9 41	20 57	24 12	12 28	25 44	8 03	9 38	9 20
27 Sa	18 22 15	5 48 56	18 03	29 05	12 09	5 24	29 21	24 29	0 20	9 43	20 57	24 11	12 32	25 29	8 12	10 04	9 20
28 Su	18 26 12	6 46 09	2♎12	29 05D	11 36	5 29	29 57	24 22	0 16	9 45	20 57	24 10	12 35	25 14	8 21	10 31	9 21
29 M	18 30 8	7 43 22	16 26	29 05	11 01	5 36	0♈34	24 15	0 12	9 48	20 57	24 08	12 38	24 59	8 30	10 57	9 22
30 T	18 34 5	8 40 34	0♏43	29 05	10 25	5 45	1 10	24 08	0 08	9 50	20 57	24 07	12 41	24 43	8 39	11 23	9 23

EPHEMERIS CALCULATED FOR 12 MIDNIGHT GREENWICH MEAN TIME. ALL OTHER DATA AND FACING ASPECTARIAN PAGE IN **EASTERN TIME (BOLD)** AND PACIFIC TIME (REGULAR).

JULY 2020

☽ Last Aspect day	ET / hr:mn / PT	asp	☽ Ingress sign	day	ET / hr:mn / PT	☽ Last Aspect day	ET / hr:mn / PT	asp	☽ Ingress sign	day	ET / hr:mn / PT
1	**9:20 pm** 6:20 pm	✶ ♄	♐	1	**9:21 pm** 6:21 pm	15	**11:21 pm** 8:21 pm	△ ♄	♊	16	**1:19 am**
3	**9:06 am** 6:06 am	□ ♆	♑	3	9:48 pm	17	**5:14 pm** 2:14 pm	□ ♆	♋	18	**10:24 am** 7:24 am
3	**9:06 am** 6:06 am	□ ♆	♑	4	**12:48 am**	20	**1:55 pm** 10:55 am	☍ ♄	♌	20	**4:16 pm** 1:16 pm
6	**5:35 am** 2:35 am	☌ ♄	♒	6	**6:08 am** 3:08 am	21	**8:27 pm** 5:27 pm	✶ ♀	♍	22	**7:40 pm** 4:40 pm
6	9:37 pm	□ ♅	♓	8	**2:13 pm** 11:13 am	24	**7:08 pm** 4:08 pm	△ ♄	♎	24	**9:54 pm** 6:54 pm
7	**12:37 am**	□ ♅	♓	8	**2:13 pm** 11:13 am	26	**9:09 pm** 6:09 pm	□ ♄	♏	26	9:12 pm
10	**11:49 pm** 8:49 pm	✶ ♄	♈	10	10:06 pm	26	**9:09 pm** 6:09 pm	□ ♄	♏	27	**12:12 am**
10	**11:49 pm** 8:49 pm	✶ ♄	♈	11	**1:06 am**	28	9:01 pm	✶ ♄	♐	29	**3:25 am** 12:25 am
13	**11:54 am** 8:54 am	□ ♄	♉	13	**1:34 pm** 10:34 am	29	**12:01 am**	✶ ♄	♐	29	**3:25 am** 12:25 am
15	**11:21 pm** 8:21 pm	△ ♄	♊	15	10:19 pm	30	**8:08 pm** 5:08 pm	☍ ♀	♑	31	**7:58 am** 4:58 am

☽ Phases & Eclipses phase	day	ET / hr:mn / PT
Full Moon	4	9:44 pm
Full Moon	5	**12:44 am**
☍ (eclipse)	4/5	13° ♑ 38'
4th Quarter	12	**7:29 pm** 4:29 pm
New Moon	20	**1:33 pm** 10:33 am
2nd Quarter	27	**8:33 am** 5:33 am

Planet Ingress	day	ET / hr:mn / PT
♄ ♑	1	**7:39 pm** 4:39 pm
☉ ♌	22	**4:37 am** 1:37 am

Planetary Motion	day	ET / hr:mn / PT
⚳ R	6	9:01 pm
⚳ R	7	**12:01 am**
⚷ R	11	**5:09 pm** 2:09 pm

1 WEDNESDAY
☉ ✶ ♅ **2:07 am**
☽ △ ♆ **6:02 am** 3:02 am
☽ ✶ ♃ **11:06 am** 8:06 am
☽ ✶ ♇ **11:20 am** 8:20 am
☽ ✶ ♄ **9:20 pm** 6:20 pm
☽ △ ♂ 10:35 pm

2 THURSDAY
☽ △ ♂ **1:35 am**
☽ ☍ ♀ **8:02 am** 5:02 am
☽ ⚻ ☿ **12:20 pm** 9:20 am
☽ ⚻ ♅ **2:13 pm** 11:13 am
☽ ⚻ ☉ **4:45 pm** 1:45 pm

3 FRIDAY
☽ □ ♆ **9:06 am** 6:06 am
☽ ⚺ ♃ **1:51 pm** 10:51 am
☽ ⚺ ♇ **2:26 pm** 11:26 am
☽ ⚺ ♄ 9:32 pm

4 SATURDAY
☽ ⚺ ♄ **12:32 am**
☽ □ ♂ **7:28 am** 4:28 am
☽ ⚻ ♀ **12:55 pm** 9:55 am
☽ ☍ ☿ **2:13 pm** 11:13 am
☽ △ ♅ **6:19 pm** 3:19 pm
☽ ☍ ☉ 9:44 pm

5 SUNDAY
☽ ☍ ☉ **12:44 am**
☿ ⚺ ♀ **10:45 am** 7:45 am
☽ ✶ ♆ **1:44 pm** 10:44 am
☽ ☌ ♃ **6:13 pm** 3:13 pm
☽ ☌ ♇ **7:14 pm** 4:14 pm

6 MONDAY
☽ ☌ ♄ **5:35 am** 2:35 am
☽ ✶ ♂ **3:37 pm** 12:37 pm
☽ ⚻ ☿ **6:20 pm** 3:20 pm
☽ △ ♀ **8:22 pm** 5:22 pm
☽ □ ♅ 9:37 pm

7 TUESDAY
☽ □ ♅ **12:37 am**
☽ ⚻ ☉ **11:37 am** 8:37 am
☽ ⚺ ♆ **8:53 pm** 5:53 pm
☽ ⚺ ♃ 10:05 pm
☽ ⚺ ♇ 11:36 pm

8 WEDNESDAY
☽ ⚺ ♃ **1:05 am**
☽ ⚺ ♇ **2:36 am**
☿ □ ♂ **6:42 am** 3:42 am
☽ ⚺ ♄ **1:19 pm** 10:19 am
☽ △ ☿ 10:35 pm
☽ ⚺ ♂ 11:56 pm

9 THURSDAY
☽ △ ☿ **1:35 am**
☽ ⚺ ♂ **2:56 am**
☽ □ ♀ **7:15 am** 4:15 am
☽ ✶ ♅ **9:50 am** 6:50 am
☽ △ ☉ 11:09 pm

10 FRIDAY
☽ △ ☉ **2:09 am**
☽ ☌ ♆ **6:57 am** 3:57 am
☽ ✶ ♃ **10:47 am** 7:47 am
☽ ✶ ♇ **12:52 pm** 9:52 am
☽ ✶ ♄ **11:49 pm** 8:49 pm

11 SATURDAY
☽ □ ☿ **12:09 pm** 9:09 am
☽ ☌ ♂ **5:16 pm** 2:16 pm
☽ ✶ ♀ **9:21 pm** 6:21 pm
☽ ⚺ ♅ **9:36 pm** 6:36 pm

12 SUNDAY
♀ ⚺ ♅ **3:12 am** 12:12 am
☉ △ ♆ **2:43 pm** 11:43 am
☽ ⚺ ♆ **7:06 pm** 4:06 pm
☽ □ ☉ **7:29 pm** 4:29 pm
☽ □ ♃ **10:25 pm** 7:25 pm
☽ □ ♇ 10:03 pm

13 MONDAY
☽ □ ♇ **1:03 am**
☽ □ ♄ **11:54 am** 8:54 am
☽ ✶ ☿ 9:56 pm

14 TUESDAY
☽ ✶ ☿ **12:56 am**
☉ ☍ ♃ **3:58 am** 12:58 am
☽ ⚺ ♂ **8:43 am** 5:43 am
☽ ☌ ♅ **10:14 am** 7:14 am
☽ ⚺ ♀ **12:47 pm** 9:47 am

15 WEDNESDAY
☽ ✶ ♆ **7:16 am** 4:16 am
☽ △ ♃ **9:56 am** 6:56 am
☽ ✶ ☉ **12:50 pm** 9:50 am
☽ △ ♇ **1:01 pm** 10:01 am
☉ ☍ ♇ **3:13 pm** 12:13 pm
♂ ⚺ ♅ **7:55 pm** 4:55 pm
☽ △ ♄ **11:21 pm** 8:21 pm

16 THURSDAY
☽ ⚺ ☿ **1:40 pm** 10:40 am
☽ ⚺ ♅ **9:21 pm** 6:21 pm
☽ ✶ ♂ **10:26 pm** 7:26 pm
☽ ☌ ♀ 11:40 pm

17 FRIDAY
☽ ☌ ♀ **2:40 am**
☽ □ ♆ **5:14 pm** 2:14 pm
☽ ⚻ ♃ **7:15 pm** 4:15 pm
☽ ⚻ ♇ **10:39 pm** 7:39 pm

18 SATURDAY
☽ ⚺ ☉ **3:13 am** 12:13 am
☽ ⚻ ♄ **8:13 am** 5:13 am
☽ ☌ ☿ 9:19 pm

19 SUNDAY
☽ ☌ ☿ **12:19 am**
☽ ✶ ♅ **5:24 am** 2:24 am
☽ □ ♂ **8:38 am** 5:38 am
☽ ⚺ ♀ **1:12 pm** 10:12 am
☽ △ ♆ 9:01 pm
☽ ☍ ♃ 10:27 pm

20 MONDAY
☽ △ ♆ **12:01 am**
☽ ☍ ♃ **1:27 am**
☽ ☍ ♇ **5:04 am** 2:04 am
☽ ☌ ☉ **1:33 pm** 10:33 am
☽ ☍ ♄ **1:55 pm** 10:55 am
☉ ☍ ♄ **6:28 pm** 3:28 pm

21 TUESDAY
☽ ⚺ ☿ **8:22 am** 5:22 am
☽ □ ♅ **10:22 am** 7:22 am
☽ △ ♂ **3:23 pm** 12:23 pm
☽ ✶ ♀ **8:27 pm** 5:27 pm

22 WEDNESDAY
☽ ⚻ ♆ **3:59 am** 12:59 am
☽ ⚻ ♃ **4:57 am** 1:57 am
☽ ⚻ ♇ **8:48 am** 5:48 am
☿ ✶ ♅ **4:25 pm** 1:25 pm
☽ ⚻ ♄ **5:08 pm** 2:08 pm
☽ ⚺ ☉ **8:45 pm** 5:45 pm

23 THURSDAY
☽ △ ♅ **1:16 pm** 10:16 am
☽ ✶ ☿ **2:47 pm** 11:47 am
☽ ⚻ ♂ **7:55 pm** 4:55 pm
☽ □ ♀ 10:46 pm

24 FRIDAY
☽ □ ♀ **1:46 am**
☽ ☍ ♆ **6:23 am** 3:23 am
☽ △ ♃ **6:57 am** 3:57 am
☽ △ ♇ **11:05 am** 8:05 am
☽ △ ♄ **7:08 pm** 4:08 pm
☽ ✶ ☉ 11:33 pm

25 SATURDAY
☽ ✶ ☉ **2:33 am**
☽ ⚻ ♅ **3:28 pm** 12:28 pm
☽ □ ☿ **9:11 pm** 6:11 pm
☽ ☍ ♂ **11:50 pm** 8:50 pm

26 SUNDAY
☽ △ ♀ **6:45 am** 3:45 am
☽ ⚻ ♆ **8:29 am** 5:29 am
☽ □ ♃ **8:41 am** 5:41 am
☽ □ ♇ **1:12 pm** 10:12 am
☽ □ ♄ **9:09 pm** 6:09 pm

27 MONDAY
☽ □ ☉ **8:33 am** 5:33 am
♃ ✶ ♆ **12:07 pm** 9:07 am
♀ ⚻ ♃ **1:36 pm** 10:36 am
♀ □ ♆ **1:48 pm** 10:48 am
☿ □ ♂ **5:46 pm** 2:46 pm
☽ ☍ ♅ **6:04 pm** 3:04 pm

28 TUESDAY
☽ ⚻ ♂ **4:18 am** 1:18 am
☽ △ ☿ **5:04 am** 2:04 am
☽ ✶ ♃ **11:08 am** 8:08 am
☽ △ ♆ **11:18 am** 8:18 am
☽ ⚻ ♀ **12:38 pm** 9:38 am
☽ ✶ ♇ **4:05 pm** 1:05 pm
☽ ✶ ♄ 9:01 pm

29 WEDNESDAY
☽ ✶ ♄ **12:01 am**
☽ △ ☉ **3:47 pm** 12:47 pm
☽ ⚻ ♅ **9:47 pm** 6:47 pm

30 THURSDAY
☽ △ ♂ **10:02 am** 7:02 am
☿ ☍ ♃ **10:17 am** 7:17 am
☿ △ ♆ **2:45 pm** 11:45 am
☽ ⚺ ♃ **2:47 pm** 11:47 am
☽ □ ♆ **3:20 pm** 12:20 pm
☽ ⚻ ☿ **3:25 pm** 12:25 pm
☽ ☍ ♀ **8:08 pm** 5:08 pm
☽ ⚺ ♇ **8:14 pm** 5:14 pm
♀ ⚻ ♇ **9:51 pm** 6:51 pm

31 FRIDAY
☽ ⚺ ♄ **4:12 am** 1:12 am
☽ ⚻ ☉ 9:46 pm
☽ △ ♅ 11:56 pm

Eastern time in bold type
Pacific time in medium type

JULY 2020

DATE	SID.TIME	SUN	MOON	NODE	MERCURY	VENUS	MARS	JUPITER	SATURN	URANUS	NEPTUNE	PLUTO	CERES	PALLAS	JUNO	VESTA	CHIRON
1 W	18 38 1	9♋37 46	14♏59	29♊06	9♋49℞	5♊56	1♈46	24♑01℞	0♒04℞	9♉52	20♓57℞	24♑05℞	12♓43	24♑27℞	8♎49	11♋49	9♈23
2 Th	18 41 58	10 34 57	29 12	29 07	9 13	6 10	2 21	23 54	0 00	9 54	20 56	24 04	12 45	24 11	8 59	12 16	9 24
3 F	18 45 54	11 32 08	13♐18	29 08	8 38	6 25	2 57	23 46	29♑56	9 56	20 56	24 03	12 46	23 55	9 09	12 42	9 24
4 Sa	18 49 51	12 29 19	27 14	29 08℞	8 04	6 43	3 32	23 39	29 52	9 58	20 56	24 01	12 48	23 39	9 19	13 08	9 25
5 Su	18 53 47	13 26 30	10♑57	29 08	7 33	7 02	4 08	23 32	29 48	10 00	20 55	24 00	12 49	23 23	9 29	13 34	9 25
6 M	18 57 44	14 23 41	24 24	29 07	7 04	7 23	4 42	23 24	29 43	10 02	20 55	23 58	12 49	23 07	9 40	14 01	9 25
7 T	19 1 41	15 20 52	7♒34	29 05	6 38	7 46	5 17	23 17	29 39	10 04	20 55	23 57	12 49℞	22 50	9 51	14 27	9 26
8 W	19 5 37	16 18 03	20 26	29 03	6 16	8 10	5 52	23 09	29 35	10 06	20 54	23 56	12 49	22 34	10 02	14 53	9 26
9 Th	19 9 34	17 15 15	3♓01	29 00	5 57	8 36	6 26	23 01	29 31	10 07	20 54	23 54	12 49	22 17	10 13	15 20	9 26
10 F	19 13 30	18 12 26	15 20	28 58	5 43	9 04	7 00	22 54	29 27	10 09	20 53	23 53	12 48	22 01	10 24	15 46	9 26
11 Sa	19 17 27	19 09 38	27 27	28 55	5 34	9 33	7 34	22 46	29 22	10 11	20 53	23 51	12 47	21 44	10 36	16 12	9 26℞
12 Su	19 21 23	20 06 51	9♈25	28 54	5 30 D	10 03	8 07	22 38	29 18	10 12	20 52	23 50	12 45	21 27	10 48	16 38	9 26
13 M	19 25 20	21 04 03	21 18	28 54 D	5 31	10 35	8 41	22 31	29 13	10 14	20 51	23 48	12 43	21 11	11 00	17 05	9 26
14 T	19 29 16	22 01 17	3♉12	28 54	5 37	11 09	9 14	22 23	29 09	10 16	20 51	23 47	12 41	20 54	11 12	17 31	9 26
15 W	19 33 13	22 58 31	15 10	28 55	5 48	11 43	9 46	22 15	29 05	10 17	20 50	23 45	12 38	20 38	11 24	17 57	9 26
16 Th	19 37 10	23 55 46	27 17	28 57	6 05	12 19	10 19	22 07	29 00	10 19	20 49	23 44	12 36	20 21	11 36	18 24	9 26
17 F	19 41 6	24 53 01	9♊38	28 58	6 27	12 56	10 51	22 00	28 56	10 20	20 49	23 43	12 32	20 05	11 49	18 50	9 26
18 Sa	19 45 3	25 50 17	22 16	28 59℞	6 55	13 35	11 23	21 52	28 51	10 22	20 48	23 41	12 28	19 49	12 02	19 17	9 25
19 Su	19 48 59	26 47 33	5♋13	29 00	7 28	14 14	11 54	21 44	28 47	10 23	20 47	23 40	12 24	19 32	12 15	19 43	9 25
20 M	19 52 56	27 44 50	18 31	28 58	8 07	14 54	12 26	21 37	28 43	10 24	20 46	23 38	12 20	19 16	12 28	20 09	9 25
21 T	19 56 52	28 42 08	2♌08	28 56	8 52	15 36	12 57	21 29	28 38	10 25	20 45	23 37	12 15	19 00	12 41	20 36	9 24
22 W	20 0 49	29 39 26	16 03	28 52	9 41	16 18	13 27	21 21	28 34	10 27	20 45	23 35	12 10	18 45	12 55	21 02	9 24
23 Th	20 4 45	0♌36 44	0♍12	28 47	10 36	17 02	13 57	21 14	28 29	10 28	20 44	23 34	12 05	18 29	13 08	21 28	9 23
24 F	20 8 42	1 34 03	14 30	28 43	11 36	17 46	14 27	21 06	28 25	10 29	20 43	23 32	11 59	18 14	13 22	21 55	9 22
25 Sa	20 12 39	2 31 22	28 52	28 38	12 42	18 31	14 57	20 59	28 20	10 30	20 42	23 31	11 53	17 58	13 36	22 21	9 22
26 Su	20 16 35	3 28 42	13♎13	28 35	13 52	19 17	15 26	20 51	28 16	10 31	20 41	23 30	11 46	17 43	13 50	22 47	9 21
27 M	20 20 32	4 26 02	27 31	28 34 D	15 08	20 04	15 55	20 44	28 12	10 32	20 40	23 28	11 39	17 29	14 04	23 14	9 20
28 T	20 24 28	5 23 22	11♏41	28 34	16 28	20 51	16 23	20 37	28 07	10 33	20 39	23 27	11 32	17 14	14 19	23 40	9 20
29 W	20 28 25	6 20 43	25 42	28 35	17 53	21 40	16 51	20 30	28 03	10 34	20 38	23 25	11 25	17 00	14 33	24 06	9 19
30 Th	20 32 21	7 18 05	9♐34	28 36	19 23	22 29	17 19	20 22	27 58	10 35	20 37	23 24	11 17	16 46	14 48	24 33	9 18
31 F	20 36 18	8 15 26	23 15	28 37℞	20 57	23 19	17 46	20 15	27 54	10 36	20 36	23 23	11 09	16 32	15 03	24 59	9 17

EPHEMERIS CALCULATED FOR 12 MIDNIGHT GREENWICH MEAN TIME. ALL OTHER DATA AND FACING ASPECTARIAN PAGE IN **EASTERN TIME (BOLD)** AND PACIFIC TIME (REGULAR).

AUGUST 2020

☽ Last Aspect day	ET	PT	asp	☽ Ingress sign	day	ET	PT
2	**9:59 am**	6:59 am	☌ ♄	♒	2	**2:11 pm**	11:11 am
4	**5:45 pm**	2:45 pm	△ ♀	♓	4	**10:28 pm**	7:28 pm
7	**8:53 am**	5:53 am	□ ♀	♈	7	**9:05 am**	6:05 am
9	**3:50 pm**	12:50 pm	□ ♄	♉	9	**9:28 pm**	6:28 pm
12	**3:55 am**	12:55 am	△ ♄	♊	12	**9:46 am**	6:46 am
14	**7:19 am**	4:19 am	⚹ ♂	♋	14	**7:35 pm**	4:35 pm
16	**7:59 pm**	4:59 pm	☍ ♄	♌	16		10:38 pm
16	**7:59 pm**	4:59 pm	☍ ♄	♌	17	**1:38 am**	
18		10:38 pm	☌ ☿	♍	19	**4:20 am**	1:20 am
19	**1:38 am**		☌ ☿	♍	19	**4:20 am**	1:20 am
20	**11:37 pm**	8:37 pm	△ ♄	♎	21	**5:16 am**	2:16 am
22		9:20 pm	□ ♄	♏	23	**6:16 am**	3:16 am
23	**12:20 am**		□ ♄	♏	23	**6:16 am**	3:16 am
24		11:27 pm	⚹ ♄	♐	25	**8:49 am**	5:49 am
25	**2:27 am**		⚹ ♄	♐	25	**8:49 am**	5:49 am
27	**8:00 am**	5:00 am	△ ♂	♑	27	**1:37 pm**	10:37 am
29	**3:31 pm**	12:31 pm	□ ♂	♒	29	**8:37 pm**	5:37 pm
31		9:56 pm	⚹ ♂	♓	9/1	**5:34 am**	2:34 am

☽ Phases & Eclipses phase	day	ET	PT
Full Moon	3	**11:59 am**	8:59 am
4th Quarter	11	**12:45 pm**	9:45 am
New Moon	18	**10:42 pm**	7:42 pm
2nd Quarter	25	**1:58 pm**	10:58 am

Planet Ingress	day	ET	PT
☿ ♌	4	**11:32 pm**	8:32 pm
♀ ♋	7	**11:21 am**	8:21 am
⚶ ♌	11	**7:17 am**	4:17 am
☿ ♍	19	**9:30 pm**	6:30 pm
☉ ♍	22	**11:45 am**	8:45 am

Planetary Motion	day	ET	PT
♅ ℞	15	**10:25 am**	7:25 am

1 SATURDAY
☽ ⚻ ☉ **12:46 am**
☽ △ ♅ **2:56 am**
☿ ☍ ♇ **6:52 am** 3:52 am
☽ □ ♂ **5:23 pm** 2:23 pm
☽ ☌ ♃ **7:57 pm** 4:57 pm
☽ ⚹ ♆ **8:55 pm** 5:55 pm
☽ ☌ ♇ 10:57 pm

2 SUNDAY
☽ ☌ ♇ **1:57 am**
☽ ☍ ☿ **4:53 am** 1:53 am
☽ ⚻ ♀ **5:39 am** 2:39 am
☉ □ ♅ **7:19 am** 4:19 am
☽ ☌ ♄ **9:59 am** 6:59 am
☿ ⚺ ♀ **3:26 pm** 12:26 pm

3 MONDAY
☽ □ ♅ **9:52 am** 6:52 am
☽ ☍ ☉ **11:59 am** 8:59 am
☿ ☍ ♄ **5:00 pm** 2:00 pm
☽ ⚹ ♂ 11:45 pm

4 TUESDAY
☽ ⚹ ♂ **2:45 am**
☽ ⚺ ♃ **3:01 am** 12:01 am
☽ ⚺ ♆ **4:24 am** 1:24 am
♂ □ ♃ **9:07 am** 6:07 am
☽ ⚺ ♇ **9:38 am** 6:38 am
☽ △ ♀ **5:45 pm** 2:45 pm
☽ ⚺ ♄ **5:47 pm** 2:47 pm
♀ ⚻ ♄ **6:07 pm** 3:07 pm
☽ ⚻ ☿ **10:16 pm** 7:16 pm

5 WEDNESDAY
☽ ⚹ ♅ **7:01 pm** 4:01 pm
☽ ⚻ ☉ 11:00 pm

6 THURSDAY
☽ ⚻ ☉ **2:00 am**
♂ ⚺ ♆ **3:30 am** 12:30 am
☽ ⚹ ♃ **12:20 pm** 9:20 am
☽ ☌ ♆ **2:12 pm** 11:12 am
☽ ⚺ ♂ **2:35 pm** 11:35 am
☽ ⚹ ♇ **7:38 pm** 4:38 pm

7 FRIDAY
☽ ⚹ ♄ **3:53 am** 12:53 am
☽ □ ♀ **8:53 am** 5:53 am
☽ △ ☿ **8:12 pm** 5:12 pm

8 SATURDAY
☽ ⚺ ♅ **6:25 am** 3:25 am
☽ △ ☉ **6:49 pm** 3:49 pm
☽ □ ♃ **11:44 pm** 8:44 pm
☽ ⚺ ♆ 11:03 pm

9 SUNDAY
☽ ⚺ ♆ **2:03 am**
☽ ☌ ♂ **4:35 am** 1:35 am
☽ □ ♇ **7:38 am** 4:38 am
☽ □ ♄ **3:50 pm** 12:50 pm
☽ ⚹ ♀ 11:23 pm

10 MONDAY
☽ ⚹ ♀ **2:23 am**
☿ □ ♅ **8:52 am** 5:52 am
☽ ☌ ♅ **7:05 pm** 4:05 pm
☽ □ ☿ **9:12 pm** 6:12 pm
☉ ⚻ ♃ 11:35 pm

11 TUESDAY
☉ ⚻ ♃ **2:35 am**
☽ △ ♃ **11:51 am** 8:51 am
☽ □ ☉ **12:45 pm** 9:45 am
☽ ⚹ ♆ **2:32 pm** 11:32 am
☽ ⚺ ♂ **7:04 pm** 4:04 pm
☽ △ ♇ **8:03 pm** 5:03 pm

12 WEDNESDAY
☽ △ ♄ **3:55 am** 12:55 am
☉ ⚻ ♆ **10:32 am** 7:32 am
☽ ⚺ ♀ **7:37 pm** 4:37 pm

13 THURSDAY
♂ □ ♇ **3:14 am** 12:14 am
☽ ⚺ ♅ **6:45 am** 3:45 am
☽ ⚹ ☿ **8:33 pm** 5:33 pm
☽ ⚻ ♃ **10:24 pm** 7:24 pm
☽ □ ♆ 10:16 pm

14 FRIDAY
☽ □ ♆ **1:16 am**
☽ ⚹ ☉ **4:32 am** 1:32 am
☽ ⚻ ♇ **6:32 am** 3:32 am
☽ ⚹ ♂ **7:19 am** 4:19 am
☿ ⚻ ♃ **7:28 am** 4:28 am
☽ ⚻ ♄ **1:47 pm** 10:47 am
☿ ⚻ ♆ 10:13 pm

15 SATURDAY
☿ ⚻ ♆ **1:13 am**
☉ ⚻ ♇ **6:13 am** 3:13 am
☽ ☌ ♀ **9:26 am** 6:26 am
☽ ⚹ ♅ **3:18 pm** 12:18 pm

16 SUNDAY
☽ ☍ ♃ **5:33 am** 2:33 am
☽ △ ♆ **8:28 am** 5:28 am
☿ ⚻ ♇ **9:38 am** 6:38 am
☉ △ ♂ **10:02 am** 7:02 am
☽ ☍ ♇ **1:24 pm** 10:24 am
☽ ⚺ ☿ **2:03 pm** 11:03 am
☽ □ ♂ **3:32 pm** 12:32 pm
☽ ⚺ ☉ **3:49 pm** 12:49 pm
☽ ☍ ♄ **7:59 pm** 4:59 pm
☿ △ ♂ 10:29 pm

17 MONDAY
☿ △ ♂ **1:29 am**
☉ ☌ ☿ **11:07 am** 8:07 am
☽ ⚺ ♀ **6:33 pm** 3:33 pm
☽ □ ♅ **8:01 pm** 5:01 pm

18 TUESDAY
☿ ⚻ ♄ **5:17 am** 2:17 am
☽ ⚻ ♃ **9:05 am** 6:05 am
☽ ⚻ ♆ **12:02 pm** 9:02 am
♀ ⚹ ♅ **3:28 pm** 12:28 pm
☽ ⚻ ♇ **4:41 pm** 1:41 pm
☽ △ ♂ **7:51 pm** 4:51 pm
☽ ☌ ☉ **10:42 pm** 7:42 pm
☽ ⚻ ♄ **10:46 pm** 7:46 pm
☉ ⚻ ♄ **11:48 pm** 8:48 pm
☽ ☌ ☿ 10:38 pm

19 WEDNESDAY
☽ ☌ ☿ **1:38 am**
☽ △ ♅ **9:52 pm** 6:52 pm
☽ ⚹ ♀ 9:05 pm

20 THURSDAY
☽ ⚹ ♀ **12:05 am**
☽ △ ♃ **10:13 am** 7:13 am
☽ ☍ ♆ **1:15 pm** 10:15 am
☽ △ ♇ **5:48 pm** 2:48 pm
☽ ⚻ ♂ **9:52 pm** 6:52 pm
☽ △ ♄ **11:37 pm** 8:37 pm

21 FRIDAY
☽ ⚺ ☉ **3:08 am** 12:08 am
☽ ⚺ ☿ **10:06 am** 7:06 am
☽ ⚻ ♅ **10:36 pm** 7:36 pm

22 SATURDAY
☽ □ ♀ **4:25 am** 1:25 am
☽ □ ♃ **10:45 am** 7:45 am
☽ ⚻ ♆ **1:58 pm** 10:58 am
☽ □ ♇ **6:34 pm** 3:34 pm
☽ ☍ ♂ **11:35 pm** 8:35 pm
☽ □ ♄ 9:20 pm

23 SUNDAY
☽ □ ♄ **12:20 am**
☽ ⚹ ☉ **7:35 am** 4:35 am
☽ ⚹ ☿ **6:42 pm** 3:42 pm
☽ ☍ ♅ 9:00 pm

24 MONDAY
☽ ☍ ♅ **12:00 am**
☽ △ ♀ **9:51 am** 6:51 am
☽ ⚹ ♃ **12:21 pm** 9:21 am
♂ □ ♄ **2:19 pm** 11:19 am
☽ △ ♆ **3:47 pm** 12:47 pm
☽ ⚹ ♇ **8:36 pm** 5:36 pm
☽ ⚹ ♄ 11:27 pm
☽ ⚻ ♂ 11:41 pm

25 TUESDAY
☽ ⚹ ♄ **2:27 am**
☽ ⚻ ♂ **2:41 am**
☿ △ ♅ **11:18 am** 8:18 am
☽ □ ☉ **1:58 pm** 10:58 am
♀ ☍ ♃ **6:26 pm** 3:26 pm

26 WEDNESDAY
☽ ⚻ ♅ **3:17 am** 12:17 am
☽ □ ☿ **5:47 am** 2:47 am
☽ ⚺ ♃ **4:00 pm** 1:00 pm
☽ ⚻ ♀ **5:53 pm** 2:53 pm
☽ □ ♆ **7:43 pm** 4:43 pm
☽ ⚺ ♇ 9:46 pm

27 THURSDAY
☽ ⚺ ♇ **12:46 am**
☽ ⚺ ♄ **6:46 am** 3:46 am
☽ △ ♂ **8:00 am** 5:00 am
♀ △ ♆ **5:13 pm** 2:13 pm
☽ △ ☉ **11:09 pm** 8:09 pm

28 FRIDAY
☽ △ ♅ **8:51 am** 5:51 am
☽ △ ☿ **8:04 pm** 5:04 pm
☽ ☌ ♃ **9:56 pm** 6:56 pm
☽ ⚹ ♆ 10:54 pm

29 SATURDAY
☽ ⚹ ♆ **1:54 am**
☽ ☍ ♀ **4:51 am** 1:51 am
☽ ☌ ♇ **7:12 am** 4:12 am
☿ △ ♃ **9:28 am** 6:28 am
☽ ☌ ♄ **1:18 pm** 10:18 am
☽ □ ♂ **3:31 pm** 12:31 pm

30 SUNDAY
♀ ☍ ♇ **9:31 am** 6:31 am
☽ ⚻ ☉ **11:03 am** 8:03 am
☿ ☍ ♆ **2:44 pm** 11:44 am
☽ □ ♅ **4:31 pm** 1:31 pm

31 MONDAY
☽ ⚺ ♃ **5:55 am** 2:55 am
☽ ⚺ ♆ **10:06 am** 7:06 am
☽ ⚻ ☿ **1:14 pm** 10:14 am
☽ ⚺ ♇ **3:38 pm** 12:38 pm
☽ ⚻ ♀ **6:28 pm** 3:28 pm
☽ ⚺ ♄ **9:49 pm** 6:49 pm
☽ ⚹ ♂ 9:56 pm

Eastern time in bold type
Pacific time in medium type

AUGUST 2020

DATE	SID.TIME	SUN	MOON	NODE	MERCURY	VENUS	MARS	JUPITER	SATURN	URANUS	NEPTUNE	PLUTO	CERES	PALLAS	JUNO	VESTA	CHIRON
1 Sa	20 40 14	9♌12 49	6♑45	28♊37R	22♋35	24♊09	18♈13	20♑08R	27♑50R	10♉36	20♓34R	23♑21R	11♓00R	16♑19R	15♎18	25♋25	9♈16R
2 Su	20 44 11	10 10 12	20 03	28 35	24 17	25 00	18 39	20 02	27 46	10 37	20 33	23 20	10 52	16 06	15 33	25 51	9 15
3 M	20 48 8	11 07 36	3♒09	28 31	26 02	25 52	19 05	19 55	27 41	10 38	20 32	23 18	10 42	15 53	15 48	26 18	9 14
4 T	20 52 4	12 05 01	16 03	28 26	27 51	26 44	19 31	19 48	27 37	10 38	20 31	23 17	10 33	15 40	16 03	26 44	9 13
5 W	20 56 1	13 02 27	28 43	28 18	29 43	27 37	19 56	19 42	27 33	10 39	20 30	23 16	10 23	15 28	16 19	27 10	9 11
6 Th	20 59 57	13 59 54	11♓10	28 10	1♌38	28 31	20 21	19 35	27 29	10 39	20 29	23 14	10 14	15 16	16 34	27 37	9 10
7 F	21 3 54	14 57 22	23 24	28 02	3 35	29 25	20 45	19 29	27 25	10 40	20 27	23 13	10 03	15 05	16 50	28 03	9 09
8 Sa	21 7 50	15 54 51	5♈28	27 55	5 34	0♋20	21 08	19 23	27 20	10 40	20 26	23 12	9 53	14 53	17 05	28 29	9 08
9 Su	21 11 47	16 52 21	17 25	27 49	7 34	1 15	21 31	19 17	27 16	10 40	20 25	23 10	9 42	14 43	17 21	28 55	9 06
10 M	21 15 43	17 49 52	29 17	27 45	9 35	2 11	21 54	19 11	27 12	10 41	20 23	23 09	9 31	14 32	17 37	29 21	9 05
11 T	21 19 40	18 47 25	11♉08	27 43D	11 38	3 07	22 16	19 05	27 08	10 41	20 22	23 08	9 20	14 22	17 53	29 48	9 03
12 W	21 23 37	19 45 00	23 05	27 43	13 41	4 04	22 38	18 59	27 04	10 41	20 21	23 07	9 09	14 12	18 10	0♌14	9 02
13 Th	21 27 33	20 42 36	5♊11	27 44	15 44	5 01	22 59	18 54	27 01	10 41	20 19	23 05	8 57	14 03	18 26	0 40	9 00
14 F	21 31 30	21 40 13	17 32	27 45R	17 47	5 58	23 19	18 48	26 57	10 41	20 18	23 04	8 45	13 54	18 42	1 06	8 59
15 Sa	21 35 26	22 37 52	0♋13	27 45	19 50	6 56	23 39	18 43	26 53	10 42R	20 17	23 03	8 33	13 45	18 59	1 32	8 57
16 Su	21 39 23	23 35 32	13 17	27 44	21 52	7 55	23 58	18 38	26 49	10 42	20 15	23 02	8 21	13 37	19 16	1 59	8 55
17 M	21 43 19	24 33 14	26 46	27 40	23 53	8 54	24 17	18 33	26 46	10 41	20 14	23 01	8 09	13 29	19 32	2 25	8 54
18 T	21 47 16	25 30 57	10♌41	27 35	25 54	9 53	24 35	18 28	26 42	10 41	20 12	22 59	7 56	13 21	19 49	2 51	8 52
19 W	21 51 12	26 28 42	24 58	27 27	27 54	10 53	24 52	18 23	26 38	10 41	20 11	22 58	7 44	13 14	20 06	3 17	8 50
20 Th	21 55 9	27 26 28	9♍32	27 18	29 53	11 53	25 09	18 19	26 35	10 41	20 09	22 57	7 31	13 07	20 23	3 43	8 48
21 F	21 59 6	28 24 15	24 17	27 09	1♍50	12 53	25 25	18 14	26 31	10 41	20 08	22 56	7 18	13 01	20 40	4 09	8 46
22 Sa	22 3 2	29 22 03	9♎05	27 00	3 47	13 54	25 40	18 10	26 28	10 40	20 06	22 55	7 05	12 55	20 58	4 35	8 44
23 Su	22 6 59	0♍19 53	23 46	26 54	5 42	14 55	25 55	18 06	26 25	10 40	20 05	22 54	6 52	12 50	21 15	5 01	8 42
24 M	22 10 55	1 17 44	8♏16	26 50	7 35	15 56	26 09	18 02	26 22	10 40	20 03	22 53	6 38	12 44	21 32	5 27	8 40
25 T	22 14 52	2 15 36	22 31	26 48D	9 28	16 58	26 22	17 59	26 18	10 39	20 02	22 52	6 25	12 40	21 50	5 53	8 38
26 W	22 18 48	3 13 29	6♐28	26 47	11 19	18 00	26 35	17 55	26 15	10 39	20 00	22 51	6 12	12 35	22 07	6 19	8 36
27 Th	22 22 45	4 11 24	20 08	26 48R	13 09	19 02	26 47	17 52	26 12	10 38	19 59	22 50	5 59	12 31	22 25	6 45	8 34
28 F	22 26 41	5 09 19	3♑33	26 48	14 58	20 04	26 58	17 49	26 09	10 38	19 57	22 49	5 45	12 28	22 43	7 11	8 32
29 Sa	22 30 38	6 07 17	16 43	26 46	16 45	21 07	27 08	17 46	26 06	10 37	19 55	22 48	5 32	12 24	23 01	7 37	8 30
30 Su	22 34 35	7 05 15	29 40	26 42	18 31	22 10	27 17	17 43	26 04	10 36	19 54	22 47	5 19	12 22	23 19	8 03	8 28
31 M	22 38 31	8 03 15	12♒26	26 35	20 15	23 14	27 26	17 41	26 01	10 36	19 52	22 46	5 05	12 19	23 37	8 29	8 26

EPHEMERIS CALCULATED FOR 12 MIDNIGHT GREENWICH MEAN TIME. ALL OTHER DATA AND FACING ASPECTARIAN PAGE IN **EASTERN TIME (BOLD)** AND PACIFIC TIME (REGULAR).

SEPTEMBER 2020

☽ Last Aspect / ☽ Ingress

day	ET / hr:mn / PT		asp	sign	day	ET / hr:mn / PT	
1	**12:56 am**		⚹♂	♓	1	**5:34 am**	2:34 am
3	**10:34 am**	7:34 am	△♀	♈	3	**4:22 pm**	1:22 pm
5		9:45 pm	☌♂	♉	6	**4:43 am**	1:43 am
6	**12:45 am**		☌♂	♉	6	**4:43 am**	1:43 am
8	**8:47 am**	5:47 am	△♄	♊	8	**5:28 pm**	2:28 pm
10		9:48 pm	⚹♂	♋	11	**4:23 am**	1:23 am
11	**12:48 am**		⚹♂	♋	11	**4:23 am**	1:23 am
13	**8:05 am**	5:05 am	□♂	♌	13	**11:32 am**	8:32 am
15	**11:09 am**	8:09 am	△♂	♍	15	**2:37 pm**	11:37 am
17	**7:42 am**	4:42 am	△♄	♎	17	**2:56 pm**	11:56 am

☽ Last Aspect / ☽ Ingress

day	ET / hr:mn / PT		asp	sign	day	ET / hr:mn / PT	
19	**10:29 am**	7:29 am	☍♂	♏	19	**2:33 pm**	11:33 am
21	**2:13 pm**	11:13 am	⚹☉	♐	21	**3:32 pm**	12:32 pm
23	**1:31 pm**	10:31 am	△♂	♑	23	**7:16 pm**	4:16 pm
25	**11:36 pm**	8:36 pm	□☿	♒	25		11:08 pm
25	**11:36 pm**	8:36 pm	□☿	♒	26	**2:08 am**	
28	**3:18 am**	12:18 am	⚹♂	♓	28	**11:34 am**	8:34 am
30	**1:30 pm**	10:30 am	⚹♄	♈	30	**10:47 pm**	7:47 pm

☽ Phases & Eclipses

phase	day	ET / hr:mn / PT	
Full Moon	1		10:22 pm
Full Moon	2	**1:22 am**	
4th Quarter	10	**5:26 am**	2:26 am
New Moon	17	**7:00 am**	4:00 am
2nd Quarter	23	**9:55 pm**	6:55 pm

Planet Ingress

		day	ET / hr:mn / PT	
☿	♎	5	**3:46 pm**	12:46 pm
♀	♌	6	**3:22 am**	12:22 am
⚵	♏	20	**7:19 am**	4:19 am
☉	♎	22	**9:31 am**	6:31 am
⚳	♒	27	**3:08 am**	12:08 am
☿	♏	27	**3:41 am**	12:41 am

Planetary Motion

		day	ET / hr:mn / PT	
♀	D	5	**9:06 pm**	6:06 pm
♂	℞	9	**6:22 pm**	3:22 pm
♃	D	12	**8:41 pm**	5:41 pm
♄	D	28		10:11 pm
♄	D	29	**1:11 am**	

1 TUESDAY
☽ ⚹ ♂ **12:56 am**
☿ △ ♇ **6:42 am** 3:42 am
☽ ☍ ☉ 10:22 pm
☽ ⚹ ♅ 11:04 pm

2 WEDNESDAY
☽ ☍ ☉ **1:22 am**
☽ ⚹ ♅ **2:04 am**
♀ ☍ ♄ **8:18 am** 5:18 am
☉ △ ♅ **10:09 am** 7:09 am
☽ ⚹ ♃ **3:48 pm** 12:48 pm
☽ ☌ ♆ **8:09 pm** 5:09 pm
☽ ⚹ ♇ 10:55 pm

3 THURSDAY
☽ ⚹ ♇ **1:55 am**
☿ △ ♄ **3:23 am** 12:23 am
☽ ⚹ ♄ **8:10 am** 5:10 am
☽ ☍ ☿ **8:56 am** 5:56 am
☽ △ ♀ **10:34 am** 7:34 am
☽ ⚺ ♂ **12:07 pm** 9:07 am

4 FRIDAY
♀ □ ♂ **5:12 am** 2:12 am
☿ ⚻ ♂ **9:15 am** 6:15 am
☽ ⚺ ♅ **1:24 pm** 10:24 am
☿ ⚹ ♀ **4:32 pm** 1:32 pm
☽ ⚻ ☉ **6:00 pm** 3:00 pm

5 SATURDAY
☽ □ ♃ **3:26 am** 12:26 am
☽ ⚺ ♆ **7:55 am** 4:55 am
☽ □ ♇ **1:54 pm** 10:54 am
☽ □ ♄ **8:09 pm** 5:09 pm
☽ ☌ ♂ 9:45 pm

6 SUNDAY
☽ ☌ ♂ **12:45 am**
☽ □ ♀ **4:52 am** 1:52 am
☽ ⚻ ☿ **6:46 am** 3:46 am
☽ ☌ ♅ 11:00 pm

7 MONDAY
☽ ☌ ♅ **2:00 am**
☽ △ ☉ **12:09 pm** 9:09 am
☽ △ ♃ **4:08 pm** 1:08 pm
☽ ⚹ ♆ **8:35 pm** 5:35 pm
☽ △ ♇ 11:39 pm

8 TUESDAY
☽ △ ♇ **2:39 am**
☽ △ ♄ **8:47 am** 5:47 am
☽ ⚺ ♂ **1:42 pm** 10:42 am
☽ ⚹ ♀ **11:41 pm** 8:41 pm

9 WEDNESDAY
☽ △ ☿ **4:38 am** 1:38 am
☉ △ ♃ **12:04 pm** 9:04 am
☽ ⚺ ♅ **2:17 pm** 11:17 am

10 THURSDAY
☽ ⚻ ♃ **4:02 am** 1:02 am
☽ □ ☉ **5:26 am** 2:26 am
☽ □ ♆ **8:16 am** 5:16 am
☽ ⚻ ♇ **2:11 pm** 11:11 am
☽ ⚻ ♄ **7:57 pm** 4:57 pm
☽ ⚹ ♂ 9:48 pm

11 FRIDAY
☽ ⚹ ♂ **12:48 am**
☽ ⚺ ♀ **3:51 pm** 12:51 pm
☉ ☍ ♆ **4:26 pm** 1:26 pm
☽ □ ☿ **10:49 pm** 7:49 pm
☽ ⚹ ♅ **11:57 pm** 8:57 pm

12 SATURDAY
☿ ⚻ ♅ **8:35 am** 5:35 am
☽ ☍ ♃ **12:54 pm** 9:54 am
☽ △ ♆ **4:45 pm** 1:45 pm
☽ ⚹ ☉ **6:44 pm** 3:44 pm
☽ ☍ ♇ **10:19 pm** 7:19 pm

13 SUNDAY
☽ ☍ ♄ **3:37 am** 12:37 am
☽ □ ♂ **8:05 am** 5:05 am
☽ ☌ ♀ 11:53 pm

14 MONDAY
☽ ☌ ♀ **2:53 am**
☽ □ ♅ **5:33 am** 2:33 am
☽ ⚹ ☿ **10:53 am** 7:53 am
☽ ⚻ ♃ **5:38 pm** 2:38 pm
☉ △ ♇ **7:09 pm** 4:09 pm
☽ ⚻ ♆ **9:05 pm** 6:05 pm
☽ ⚻ ♇ 11:18 pm
☽ ⚺ ☉ 11:50 pm

15 TUESDAY
☽ ⚻ ♇ **2:18 am**
☽ ⚺ ☉ **2:50 am**
☽ ⚻ ♄ **7:10 am** 4:10 am
☽ △ ♂ **11:09 am** 8:09 am
♀ □ ♅ **11:29 am** 8:29 am

16 WEDNESDAY
☽ △ ♅ **7:24 am** 4:24 am
☽ ⚺ ♀ **9:04 am** 6:04 am
☽ ⚺ ☿ **5:43 pm** 2:43 pm
☽ △ ♃ **6:54 pm** 3:54 pm
☽ ☍ ♆ **10:03 pm** 7:03 pm

17 THURSDAY
☽ △ ♇ **3:06 am** 12:06 am
☿ □ ♃ **6:34 am** 3:34 am
☽ ☌ ☉ **7:00 am** 4:00 am
☽ △ ♄ **7:42 am** 4:42 am
☽ ⚻ ♂ **11:17 am** 8:17 am
☉ △ ♄ **5:36 pm** 2:36 pm

18 FRIDAY
☽ ⚻ ♅ **7:09 am** 4:09 am
☽ ⚹ ♀ **12:41 pm** 9:41 am
☿ ⚻ ♆ **4:05 pm** 1:05 pm
☽ □ ♃ **6:36 pm** 3:36 pm
☽ ⚻ ♆ **9:35 pm** 6:35 pm
☽ ☌ ☿ **10:08 pm** 7:08 pm
☽ □ ♇ 11:39 pm

19 SATURDAY
☽ □ ♇ **2:39 am**
☽ □ ♄ **7:14 am** 4:14 am
☽ ⚺ ☉ **9:53 am** 6:53 am
☽ ☍ ♂ **10:29 am** 7:29 am
☉ ⚻ ♂ **5:55 pm** 2:55 pm

20 SUNDAY
☽ ☍ ♅ **6:56 am** 3:56 am
☽ □ ♀ **4:42 pm** 1:42 pm
☽ ⚹ ♃ **6:51 pm** 3:51 pm
☽ △ ♆ **9:47 pm** 6:47 pm
☿ □ ♇ 10:21 pm

21 MONDAY
☿ □ ♇ **1:21 am**
☽ ⚹ ♇ **3:07 am** 12:07 am
☽ ⚺ ☿ **3:17 am** 12:17 am
☽ ⚹ ♄ **7:50 am** 4:50 am
☽ ⚻ ♂ **10:45 am** 7:45 am
☽ ⚹ ☉ **2:13 pm** 11:13 am
♀ ⚻ ♃ **9:12 pm** 6:12 pm

22 TUESDAY
☽ ⚻ ♅ **8:38 am** 5:38 am
☽ ⚺ ♃ **9:27 pm** 6:27 pm
☽ △ ♀ **11:34 pm** 8:34 pm
☽ □ ♆ 9:20 pm

23 WEDNESDAY
☽ □ ♆ **12:20 am**
☽ ⚺ ♇ **6:04 am** 3:04 am
☿ □ ♄ **6:38 am** 3:38 am
♀ ⚻ ♆ **8:45 am** 5:45 am
☽ ⚺ ♄ **11:04 am** 8:04 am
☽ ⚹ ☿ **11:31 am** 8:31 am
☽ △ ♂ **1:31 pm** 10:31 am
☽ □ ☉ **9:55 pm** 6:55 pm

24 THURSDAY
☿ ☍ ♂ **6:53 am** 3:53 am
☽ △ ♅ **1:20 pm** 10:20 am

25 FRIDAY
☽ ☌ ♃ **3:11 am** 12:11 am
☽ ⚹ ♆ **6:00 am** 3:00 am
☽ ⚻ ♀ **10:29 am** 7:29 am
☽ ☌ ♇ **12:09 pm** 9:09 am
☽ ☌ ♄ **5:26 pm** 2:26 pm
☽ □ ♂ **7:12 pm** 4:12 pm
☽ □ ☿ **11:36 pm** 8:36 pm

26 SATURDAY
♀ ⚻ ♇ **5:22 am** 2:22 am
☽ △ ☉ **9:30 am** 6:30 am
☽ □ ♅ **9:01 pm** 6:01 pm

27 SUNDAY
☽ ⚺ ♃ **11:51 am** 8:51 am
☽ ⚺ ♆ **2:29 pm** 11:29 am
☽ ⚺ ♇ **9:00 pm** 6:00 pm
☽ ☍ ♀ 10:04 pm
☽ ⚺ ♄ 11:30 pm

28 MONDAY
☽ ☍ ♀ **1:04 am**
☽ ⚺ ♄ **2:30 am**
☽ ⚹ ♂ **3:18 am** 12:18 am
☽ △ ☿ **2:44 pm** 11:44 am
♀ ⚻ ♄ **4:23 pm** 1:23 pm
♀ △ ♂ **9:01 pm** 6:01 pm
☽ ⚻ ☉ 9:14 pm

29 TUESDAY
☽ ⚻ ☉ **12:14 am**
☽ ⚹ ♅ **6:58 am** 3:58 am
♂ □ ♄ **5:50 pm** 2:50 pm
☽ ⚹ ♃ **10:40 pm** 7:40 pm
☽ ☌ ♆ 10:00 pm

30 WEDNESDAY
☽ ☌ ♆ **1:00 am**
☽ ⚹ ♇ **7:50 am** 4:50 am
☽ ⚺ ♂ **1:04 pm** 10:04 am
☽ ⚹ ♄ **1:30 pm** 10:30 am
☽ ⚻ ♀ **6:17 pm** 3:17 pm

Eastern time in bold type
Pacific time in medium type

SEPTEMBER 2020

DATE	SID.TIME	SUN	MOON	NODE	MERCURY	VENUS	MARS	JUPITER	SATURN	URANUS	NEPTUNE	PLUTO	CERES	PALLAS	JUNO	VESTA	CHIRON
1 T	22 42 28	9♍01 16	25♒02	26♊26℞	21♍59	24♋18	27♈34	17♑38℞	25♑58℞	10♉35℞	19♓51℞	22♑45℞	4♓52℞	12♑17℞	23♎55	8♌54	8♈23℞
2 W	22 46 24	9 59 19	7♓27	26 14	23 41	25 22	27 41	17 36	25 56	10 34	19 49	22 44	4 39	12 15	24 13	9 20	8 21
3 Th	22 50 21	10 57 23	19 43	26 01	25 22	26 26	27 48	17 34	25 53	10 33	19 47	22 43	4 26	12 14	24 31	9 46	8 19
4 F	22 54 17	11 55 29	1♈50	25 48	27 01	27 30	27 53	17 32	25 51	10 32	19 46	22 42	4 13	12 13	24 49	10 12	8 16
5 Sa	22 58 14	12 53 37	13 49	25 36	28 40	28 35	27 58	17 31	25 49	10 31	19 44	22 41	4 00	12 13	25 08	10 37	8 14
6 Su	23 2 10	13 51 47	25 42	25 26	0♎17	29 40	28 02	17 29	25 46	10 30	19 42	22 41	3 47	12 12D	25 26	11 03	8 12
7 M	23 6 7	14 49 58	7♉32	25 18	1 53	0♌45	28 05	17 28	25 44	10 29	19 41	22 40	3 34	12 13	25 45	11 29	8 09
8 T	23 10 4	15 48 12	19 22	25 13	3 28	1 51	28 07	17 27	25 42	10 28	19 39	22 39	3 21	12 13	26 03	11 54	8 07
9 W	23 14 0	16 46 28	1♊16	25 10	5 02	2 56	28 08℞	17 26	25 40	10 27	19 37	22 38	3 09	12 14	26 22	12 20	8 04
10 Th	23 17 57	17 44 45	13 20	25 10	6 34	4 02	28 09	17 25	25 38	10 26	19 36	22 38	2 57	12 15	26 41	12 45	8 02
11 F	23 21 53	18 43 05	25 38	25 10	8 06	5 08	28 08	17 25	25 36	10 25	19 34	22 37	2 44	12 17	26 59	13 11	7 59
12 Sa	23 25 50	19 41 27	8♋16	25 09	9 36	6 15	28 07	17 24	25 35	10 23	19 33	22 36	2 32	12 19	27 18	13 36	7 57
13 Su	23 29 46	20 39 51	21 19	25 07	11 05	7 21	28 04	17 24D	25 33	10 22	19 31	22 36	2 21	12 21	27 37	14 02	7 54
14 M	23 33 43	21 38 18	4♌49	25 03	12 33	8 28	28 01	17 24	25 32	10 21	19 29	22 35	2 09	12 24	27 56	14 27	7 52
15 T	23 37 39	22 36 46	18 49	24 56	14 00	9 35	27 57	17 25	25 30	10 19	19 28	22 35	1 58	12 27	28 15	14 53	7 49
16 W	23 41 36	23 35 16	3♍17	24 47	15 25	10 42	27 52	17 25	25 29	10 18	19 26	22 34	1 47	12 30	28 34	15 18	7 47
17 Th	23 45 33	24 33 48	18 07	24 36	16 49	11 50	27 46	17 26	25 28	10 16	19 24	22 34	1 36	12 34	28 53	15 43	7 44
18 F	23 49 29	25 32 22	3♎12	24 25	18 13	12 57	27 40	17 27	25 26	10 15	19 23	22 33	1 25	12 37	29 12	16 08	7 41
19 Sa	23 53 26	26 30 58	18 21	24 14	19 34	14 05	27 32	17 28	25 25	10 13	19 21	22 33	1 15	12 42	29 32	16 34	7 39
20 Su	23 57 22	27 29 36	3♏24	24 06	20 55	15 13	27 24	17 29	25 24	10 12	19 19	22 32	1 05	12 46	29 51	16 59	7 36
21 M	0 1 19	28 28 16	18 12	24 00	22 14	16 21	27 15	17 31	25 24	10 10	19 18	22 32	0 55	12 51	0♏10	17 24	7 33
22 T	0 5 15	29 26 57	2♐40	23 57	23 32	17 29	27 05	17 32	25 23	10 08	19 16	22 31	0 45	12 56	0 30	17 49	7 31
23 W	0 9 12	0♎25 40	16 44	23 56D	24 49	18 37	26 54	17 34	25 22	10 07	19 14	22 31	0 36	13 02	0 49	18 14	7 28
24 Th	0 13 8	1 24 25	0♑25	23 55℞	26 03	19 46	26 42	17 36	25 22	10 05	19 13	22 31	0 27	13 08	1 09	18 39	7 25
25 F	0 17 5	2 23 11	13 43	23 55	27 17	20 54	26 30	17 38	25 21	10 03	19 11	22 31	0 19	13 14	1 28	19 04	7 23
26 Sa	0 21 1	3 21 59	26 43	23 53	28 28	22 03	26 17	17 41	25 21	10 01	19 10	22 30	0 10	13 20	1 48	19 29	7 20
27 Su	0 24 58	4 20 49	9♒27	23 49	29 38	23 12	26 03	17 43	25 20	10 00	19 08	22 30	0 02	13 27	2 07	19 54	7 17
28 M	0 28 55	5 19 41	21 59	23 42	0♏46	24 21	25 49	17 46	25 20	9 58	19 06	22 30	29♒55	13 34	2 27	20 18	7 15
29 T	0 32 51	6 18 34	4♓19	23 32	1 52	25 31	25 34	17 49	25 20D	9 56	19 05	22 30	29 47	13 41	2 47	20 43	7 12
30 W	0 36 48	7 17 29	16 31	23 20	2 56	26 40	25 19	17 52	25 20	9 54	19 03	22 30	29 40	13 49	3 06	21 08	7 09

EPHEMERIS CALCULATED FOR 12 MIDNIGHT GREENWICH MEAN TIME. ALL OTHER DATA AND FACING ASPECTARIAN PAGE IN **EASTERN TIME (BOLD)** AND PACIFIC TIME (REGULAR).

OCTOBER 2020

☽ Last Aspect day	ET / hr:mn / PT		asp	☽ Ingress sign	day	ET / hr:mn / PT	
2		10:47 pm	□♄	♉	3	**11:12 am**	8:12 am
3	**1:47 am**		□♄	♉	3	**11:12 am**	8:12 am
5	**2:41 pm**	11:41 am	△♄	♊	5		9:03 pm
5	**2:41 pm**	11:41 am	△♄	♊	6	**12:03 am**	
7	**9:57 pm**	6:57 pm	⚹♂	♋	8	**11:45 am**	8:45 am
10	**12:04 pm**	9:04 am	☍♄	♌	10	**8:24 pm**	5:24 pm
12	**10:29 am**	7:29 am	△♂	♍	12		9:56 pm
12	**10:29 am**	7:29 am	△♂	♍	13	**12:56 am**	
14	**6:47 pm**	3:47 pm	△♄	♎	14		10:54 pm
14	**6:47 pm**	3:47 pm	△♄	♎	15	**1:54 am**	
16	**6:11 pm**	3:11 pm	□♄	♏	16		10:05 pm
16	**6:11 pm**	3:11 pm	□♄	♏	17	**1:05 am**	
18	**5:43 pm**	2:43 pm	⚹♄	♐	18		9:43 pm
18	**5:43 pm**	2:43 pm	⚹♄	♐	19	**12:43 am**	
20	**11:38 pm**	8:38 pm	⚹☉	♑	20		11:44 pm
20	**11:38 pm**	8:38 pm	⚹☉	♑	21	**2:44 am**	
22		9:35 pm	☌♄	♒	23	**8:17 am**	5:17 am
23	**12:35 am**		☌♄	♒	23	**8:17 am**	5:17 am
24	**5:54 pm**	2:54 pm	⚹♂	♓	25	**5:18 pm**	2:18 pm
27	**8:46 pm**	5:46 pm	⚹♄	♈	28	**4:45 am**	1:45 am
30	**12:12 pm**	9:12 am	☍☿	♉	30	**5:19 pm**	2:19 pm

☽ Phases & Eclipses phase	day	ET / hr:mn / PT	
Full Moon	1	**5:05 pm**	2:05 pm
4th Quarter	9	**8:40 pm**	5:40 pm
New Moon	16	**3:31 pm**	12:31 pm
2nd Quarter	23	**9:23 am**	6:23 am
Full Moon	31	**10:49 am**	7:49 am

Planet Ingress		day	ET / hr:mn / PT	
♀	♍	2	**4:48 pm**	1:48 pm
⚵	♍	22	**3:38 am**	12:38 am
☉	♏	22	**7:00 pm**	4:00 pm
☿	♎	27	**9:33 pm**	6:33 pm
♀	♎	27	**9:41 pm**	6:41 pm

Planetary Motion		day	ET / hr:mn / PT	
♇	D	4	**9:32 am**	6:32 am
☿	℞	13	**9:05 pm**	6:05 pm
⚷	D	18	**12:59 pm**	9:59 pm

1 THURSDAY
☽⚻☿ **7:39 am** 4:39 am
☽☍☉ **5:05 pm** 2:05 pm
☽⚺♅ **6:29 pm** 3:29 pm

2 FRIDAY
☉⚻♅ **9:31 am** 6:31 am
☽□♃ **10:58 am** 7:58 am
☽⚺♆ **12:55 pm** 9:55 am
☽□♇ **8:00 pm** 5:00 pm
☽☌♂ **11:57 pm** 8:57 pm
☽□♄ 10:47 pm

3 SATURDAY
☽□♄ **1:47 am**
☽△♀ **1:13 pm** 10:13 am
☽☍☿ 10:17 pm

4 SUNDAY
☽☍☿ **1:17 am**
☽☌♅ **6:59 am** 3:59 am
☽⚻☉ **11:15 am** 8:15 am
☽△♃ 9:07 pm
☽⚹♆ 10:37 pm

5 MONDAY
☽△♃ **12:07 am**
☽⚹♆ **1:37 am**
☽△♇ **8:50 am** 5:50 am
☽⚺♂ **11:19 am** 8:19 am
☽△♄ **2:41 pm** 11:41 am

6 TUESDAY
☽□♀ **8:41 am** 5:41 am
☽⚻☿ **6:11 pm** 3:11 pm
☽⚺♅ **7:29 pm** 4:29 pm

7 WEDNESDAY
☽△☉ **5:18 am** 2:18 am
☽⚻♃ **12:53 pm** 9:53 am
☽□♆ **1:51 pm** 10:51 am
☿☍♅ **4:55 pm** 1:55 pm
☽⚻♇ **9:01 pm** 6:01 pm
☽⚹♂ **9:57 pm** 6:57 pm
☽⚻♄ 11:46 pm

8 THURSDAY
☽⚻♄ **2:46 am**
☽⚹♀ 11:16 pm

9 FRIDAY
☽⚹♀ **2:16 am**
☽⚹♅ **6:14 am** 3:14 am
☽△☿ **8:03 am** 5:03 am
♂□♇ **9:09 am** 6:09 am
☽□☉ **8:40 pm** 5:40 pm
☽☍♃ **11:17 pm** 8:17 pm
☽△♆ **11:44 pm** 8:44 pm

10 SATURDAY
☽□♂ **6:05 am** 3:05 am
☽☍♇ **6:36 am** 3:36 am
☽☍♄ **12:04 pm** 9:04 am
♀△♅ **7:08 pm** 4:08 pm

11 SUNDAY
☉□♃ **9:34 am** 6:34 am
☉⚻♆ **11:31 am** 8:31 am
☽□♅ **1:27 pm** 10:27 am
☽⚺♀ **3:16 pm** 12:16 pm
☽□☿ **4:50 pm** 1:50 pm

12 MONDAY
♃⚹♆ **3:06 am** 12:06 am
☽⚻♆ **5:43 am** 2:43 am
☽⚻♃ **5:44 am** 2:44 am
☽⚹☉ **7:09 am** 4:09 am
☽△♂ **10:29 am** 7:29 am
☽⚻♇ **12:11 pm** 9:11 am
☿⚹♀ **12:39 pm** 9:39 am
☽⚻♄ **5:18 pm** 2:18 pm

13 TUESDAY
☽△♅ **4:35 pm** 1:35 pm
☉☍♂ **7:26 pm** 4:26 pm
☽⚹☿ **8:19 pm** 5:19 pm
☽☌♀ **10:55 pm** 7:55 pm

14 WEDNESDAY
☽☍♆ **7:47 am** 4:47 am
☽△♃ **8:12 am** 5:12 am
☽⚻♂ **11:16 am** 8:16 am
☽⚺☉ **12:46 pm** 9:46 am
☽△♇ **1:55 pm** 10:55 am
☽△♄ **6:47 pm** 3:47 pm

15 THURSDAY
☉□♇ **6:15 am** 3:15 am
☽⚻♅ **4:39 pm** 1:39 pm

☽⚺☿ **7:57 pm** 4:57 pm
☽⚺♀ 11:53 pm

16 FRIDAY
☽⚺♀ **2:53 am**
☽⚻♆ **7:20 am** 4:20 am
☽□♃ **8:06 am** 5:06 am
☽☍♂ **9:49 am** 6:49 am
☽□♇ **1:22 pm** 10:22 am
☽☌☉ **3:31 pm** 12:31 pm
☽□♄ **6:11 pm** 3:11 pm

17 SATURDAY
☽☍♅ **3:37 pm** 12:37 pm
☽☌☿ **5:52 pm** 2:52 pm

18 SUNDAY
☽⚹♀ **6:05 am** 3:05 am
☽△♆ **6:28 am** 3:28 am
☽⚹♃ **7:39 am** 4:39 am
☽⚻♂ **8:08 am** 5:08 am
☉□♄ **9:58 am** 6:58 am
♀☍♆ **10:49 am** 7:49 am
☽⚹♇ **12:43 pm** 9:43 am
☽⚹♄ **5:43 pm** 2:43 pm
☽⚺☉ **6:15 pm** 3:15 pm
♂□♃ 10:38 pm

19 MONDAY
♂□♃ **1:38 am**
♀⚻♂ **3:03 am** 12:03 am
♀△♃ **3:35 am** 12:35 am
☽⚻♅ **3:40 pm** 12:40 pm
☽⚺☿ **4:02 pm** 1:02 pm
☿☍♅ **10:53 pm** 7:53 pm

20 TUESDAY
☽□♆ **7:19 am** 4:19 am
☽△♂ **8:08 am** 5:08 am
☽⚺♃ **9:01 am** 6:01 am
☽□♀ **11:28 am** 8:28 am
☽⚺♇ **2:00 pm** 11:00 am
☽⚺♄ **7:24 pm** 4:24 pm
☽⚹☉ **11:38 pm** 8:38 pm

21 WEDNESDAY
☽⚹☿ **3:49 pm** 12:49 pm
♀△♇ **5:42 pm** 2:42 pm
☽△♅ **6:33 pm** 3:33 pm

22 THURSDAY
♂⚺♆ **5:10 am** 2:10 am
☽□♂ **11:16 am** 8:16 am
☽⚹♆ **11:23 am** 8:23 am
☽☌♃ **1:44 pm** 10:44 am
☽☌♇ **6:40 pm** 3:40 pm
☽△♀ **9:09 pm** 6:09 pm
☽☌♄ 9:35 pm

23 FRIDAY
☽☌♄ **12:35 am**
☽□☉ **9:23 am** 6:23 am
☽□☿ **5:49 pm** 2:49 pm
☽□♅ 10:02 pm

24 SATURDAY
☽□♅ **1:02 am**
♀△♄ **11:41 am** 8:41 am
☽⚹♂ **5:54 pm** 2:54 pm
☽⚺♆ **7:05 pm** 4:05 pm

☽⚺♃ **10:13 pm** 7:13 pm
☽⚺♇ 11:57 pm

25 SUNDAY
☽⚺♇ **2:57 am**
☽⚺♄ **9:21 am** 6:21 am
☽⚻♀ **11:37 am** 8:37 am
☉☌☿ **2:23 pm** 11:23 am
☽△☿ **9:59 pm** 6:59 pm
☽△☉ **11:31 pm** 8:31 pm

26 MONDAY
☽⚹♅ **10:44 am** 7:44 am

27 TUESDAY
☽⚺♂ **3:23 am** 12:23 am
☽☌♆ **5:40 am** 2:40 am
☽⚹♃ **9:38 am** 6:38 am
☽⚹♇ **1:58 pm** 10:58 am
☽⚹♄ **8:46 pm** 5:46 pm
☿⚺♀ **9:37 pm** 6:37 pm

28 WEDNESDAY
☽⚻☿ **4:08 am** 1:08 am
☽☍♀ **5:32 am** 2:32 am
☽⚻☉ **4:34 pm** 1:34 pm
☽⚺♅ **10:25 pm** 7:25 pm

29 THURSDAY
☽☌♂ **2:33 pm** 11:33 am
☽⚺♆ **5:51 pm** 2:51 pm
☽□♃ **10:39 pm** 7:39 pm
☽□♇ 11:26 pm

30 FRIDAY
☽□♇ **2:26 am**
☽□♄ **9:30 am** 6:30 am
☽☍☿ **12:12 pm** 9:12 am
☽⚻♀ 10:02 pm

31 SATURDAY
☽⚻♀ **1:02 am**
☽☍☉ **10:49 am** 7:49 am
☽☌♅ **10:55 am** 7:55 am
☉☍♅ **11:53 am** 8:53 am
☽⚺♂ 11:22 pm

Eastern time in bold type
Pacific time in medium type

OCTOBER 2020

DATE	SID.TIME	SUN	MOON	NODE	MERCURY	VENUS	MARS	JUPITER	SATURN	URANUS	NEPTUNE	PLUTO	CERES	PALLAS	JUNO	VESTA	CHIRON
1 Th	0 40 44	8 ♎ 16 26	28 ♓ 36	23 ♊ 07 ℞	3 ♏ 57	27 ♌ 50	25 ♈ 03 ℞	17 ♑ 55	25 ♑ 20	9 ♉ 52 ℞	19 ♓ 02 ℞	22 ♑ 29 ℞	29 ♒ 34 ℞	13 ♑ 57	3 ♏ 26	21 ♌ 32	7 ♈ 06 ℞
2 F	0 44 41	9 15 25	10 ♈ 35	22 53	4 56	28 59	24 46	17 59	25 21	9 50	19 00	22 29	29 27	14 05	3 46	21 57	7 04
3 Sa	0 48 37	10 14 26	22 29	22 41	5 52	0 ♍ 09	24 29	18 03	25 21	9 48	18 59	22 29	29 22	14 13	4 06	22 21	7 01
4 Su	0 52 34	11 13 29	4 ♉ 20	22 30	6 45	1 19	24 12	18 06	25 21	9 46	18 57	22 29D	29 16	14 21	4 26	22 46	6 58
5 M	0 56 30	12 12 34	16 09	22 22	7 35	2 29	23 54	18 11	25 22	9 44	18 56	22 29	29 11	14 30	4 46	23 10	6 56
6 T	1 0 27	13 11 42	28 00	22 17	8 21	3 40	23 36	18 15	25 23	9 41	18 54	22 29	29 06	14 39	5 06	23 34	6 53
7 W	1 4 24	14 10 52	9 ♊ 55	22 14	9 04	4 50	23 18	18 19	25 23	9 39	18 53	22 29	29 01	14 49	5 26	23 58	6 50
8 Th	1 8 20	15 10 04	21 58	22 13D	9 42	6 01	22 59	18 24	25 24	9 37	18 51	22 29	28 57	14 58	5 46	24 23	6 48
9 F	1 12 17	16 09 18	4 ♋ 15	22 13	10 16	7 11	22 40	18 28	25 25	9 35	18 50	22 29	28 54	15 08	6 06	24 47	6 45
10 Sa	1 16 13	17 08 35	16 49	22 14 ℞	10 45	8 22	22 21	18 33	25 26	9 33	18 49	22 30	28 50	15 18	6 26	25 11	6 42
11 Su	1 20 10	18 07 54	29 47	22 13	11 08	9 33	22 02	18 39	25 27	9 31	18 47	22 30	28 47	15 28	6 46	25 35	6 40
12 M	1 24 6	19 07 16	13 ♌ 11	22 11	11 25	10 44	21 43	18 44	25 28	9 28	18 46	22 30	28 44	15 39	7 06	25 59	6 37
13 T	1 28 3	20 06 39	27 05	22 06	11 36	11 55	21 23	18 49	25 30	9 26	18 44	22 30	28 42	15 50	7 26	26 22	6 34
14 W	1 31 59	21 06 05	11 ♍ 28	21 59	11 40 ℞	13 07	21 04	18 55	25 31	9 24	18 43	22 31	28 40	16 00	7 46	26 46	6 32
15 Th	1 35 56	22 05 33	26 18	21 50	11 37	14 18	20 45	19 01	25 33	9 21	18 42	22 31	28 39	16 12	8 07	27 10	6 29
16 F	1 39 53	23 05 03	11 ♎ 27	21 41	11 25	15 30	20 26	19 07	25 34	9 19	18 40	22 31	28 37	16 23	8 27	27 33	6 27
17 Sa	1 43 49	24 04 36	26 45	21 32	11 06	16 41	20 08	19 13	25 36	9 17	18 39	22 31	28 37	16 35	8 47	27 57	6 24
18 Su	1 47 46	25 04 10	12 ♏ 01	21 25	10 38	17 53	19 49	19 19	25 38	9 14	18 38	22 32	28 36D	16 46	9 07	28 20	6 21
19 M	1 51 42	26 03 47	27 05	21 20	10 01	19 05	19 31	19 25	25 40	9 12	18 37	22 32	28 36	16 58	9 28	28 43	6 19
20 T	1 55 39	27 03 25	11 ♐ 48	21 18D	9 15	20 17	19 13	19 32	25 42	9 10	18 35	22 33	28 36	17 10	9 48	29 07	6 16
21 W	1 59 35	28 03 05	26 05	21 18	8 22	21 29	18 56	19 39	25 44	9 07	18 34	22 33	28 37	17 23	10 08	29 30	6 14
22 Th	2 3 32	29 02 47	9 ♑ 55	21 19	7 21	22 41	18 39	19 45	25 46	9 05	18 33	22 34	28 38	17 35	10 29	29 53	6 11
23 F	2 7 28	0 ♏ 02 31	23 18	21 20 ℞	6 13	23 53	18 23	19 53	25 48	9 02	18 32	22 34	28 39	17 48	10 49	0 ♍ 16	6 09
24 Sa	2 11 25	1 02 16	6 ♒ 18	21 20	5 01	25 05	18 07	20 00	25 51	9 00	18 31	22 35	28 41	18 01	11 10	0 38	6 07
25 Su	2 15 22	2 02 03	18 59	21 18	3 46	26 17	17 51	20 07	25 53	8 57	18 30	22 35	28 43	18 14	11 30	1 01	6 04
26 M	2 19 18	3 01 51	1 ♓ 23	21 14	2 30	27 30	17 37	20 15	25 56	8 55	18 29	22 36	28 46	18 28	11 50	1 24	6 02
27 T	2 23 15	4 01 41	13 35	21 09	1 15	28 42	17 22	20 22	25 58	8 53	18 28	22 37	28 49	18 41	12 11	1 46	6 00
28 W	2 27 11	5 01 33	25 38	21 01	0 04	29 55	17 09	20 30	26 01	8 50	18 27	22 37	28 52	18 55	12 31	2 09	5 57
29 Th	2 31 8	6 01 27	7 ♈ 35	20 52	28 ♎ 59	1 ♎ 08	16 56	20 38	26 04	8 48	18 26	22 38	28 55	19 09	12 52	2 31	5 55
30 F	2 35 4	7 01 22	19 28	20 44	28 02	2 20	16 44	20 46	26 07	8 45	18 25	22 39	28 59	19 23	13 12	2 53	5 53
31 Sa	2 39 1	8 01 20	1 ♉ 20	20 35	27 14	3 33	16 33	20 54	26 10	8 43	18 24	22 40	29 03	19 37	13 33	3 15	5 51

EPHEMERIS CALCULATED FOR 12 MIDNIGHT GREENWICH MEAN TIME. ALL OTHER DATA AND FACING ASPECTARIAN PAGE IN **EASTERN TIME (BOLD)** AND PACIFIC TIME (REGULAR).

NOVEMBER 2020

☽ Last Aspect				☽ Ingress			
day	ET / hr:mn / PT		asp	sign	day	ET / hr:mn / PT	
1	**9:29 pm**	6:29 pm	△♄	♊	2	**5:00 am**	2:00 am
4	**8:49 am**	5:49 am	△☿	♋	4	**4:45 pm**	1:45 pm
6	**8:27 pm**	5:27 pm	□☿	♌	6		11:18 pm
6	**8:27 pm**	5:27 pm	□☿	♌	7	**2:18 am**	
9	**6:05 am**	3:05 am	✶☿	♍	9	**8:30 am**	5:30 am
11	**5:58 am**	2:58 am	△♄	♎	11	**11:09 am**	8:09 am
13	**6:32 am**	3:32 am	□♄	♏	13	**11:19 am**	8:19 am
15	**6:13 am**	3:13 am	✶♄	♐	15	**10:47 am**	7:47 am
16		11:55 pm	✶♀	♑	17	**11:35 am**	8:35 am
17	**2:55 am**		✶♀	♑	17	**11:35 am**	8:35 am
19	**11:30 am**	8:30 am	✶☉	♒	19	**3:25 pm**	12:25 pm
20	**7:49 pm**	4:49 pm	✶♂	♓	21	**11:06 pm**	8:06 pm
24	**5:44 am**	2:44 am	✶♄	♈	24	**10:05 am**	7:05 am
26	**6:46 pm**	3:46 pm	□♄	♉	26	**10:43 pm**	7:43 pm
29	**7:48 am**	4:48 am	△♄	♊	29	**11:16 am**	8:16 am
30	**11:22 pm**	8:22 pm	□♆	♋	12/1	**10:33 pm**	7:33 pm

☽ Phases & Eclipses			
phase	day	ET / hr:mn / PT	
4th Quarter	8	**8:46 am**	5:46 am
New Moon	14		9:07 pm
New Moon	15	**12:07 am**	
2nd Quarter	21	**11:45 pm**	8:45 pm
Full Moon	30	**4:30 am**	1:30 am
☊	30	8° ♊ 38′	

Planet Ingress				
		day	ET / hr:mn / PT	
⚳	♓	9	**9:48 am**	6:48 am
☿	♏	10	**4:55 pm**	1:55 pm
♀	♏	21	**8:22 am**	5:22 am
☉	♐	21	**3:40 pm**	12:40 pm

Planetary Motion				
		day	ET / hr:mn / PT	
☿	D	3	**12:50 pm**	9:50 am
♂	D	13	**7:36 pm**	4:36 pm
♆	D	28	**7:36 pm**	4:36 pm

1 SUNDAY
- ☽ ⊻ ♂ **1:22 am**
- ☽ ✶ ♆ **5:31 am** 2:31 am
- ☽ △ ♃ **11:07 am** 8:07 am
- ☿ □ ♄ **2:06 pm** 11:06 am
- ☽ △ ♇ **2:14 pm** 11:14 am
- ☽ ⊼ ☿ **9:15 pm** 6:15 pm
- ☽ △ ♄ **9:29 pm** 6:29 pm

2 MONDAY
- ☽ △ ♀ **7:31 pm** 4:31 pm
- ☽ ⊻ ♅ **10:14 pm** 7:14 pm

3 TUESDAY
- ☽ ⊼ ☉ **3:52 am** 12:52 am
- ☽ ✶ ♂ **12:57 pm** 9:57 am
- ☽ □ ♆ **5:43 pm** 2:43 pm
- ♀ ⊼ ♅ **9:22 pm** 6:22 pm
- ☽ ⊼ ♃ 9:00 pm
- ☽ ⊼ ♇ 11:24 pm

4 WEDNESDAY
- ☽ ⊼ ♃ **12:00 am**
- ☽ ⊼ ♇ **2:24 am**
- ☽ △ ☿ **8:49 am** 5:49 am
- ☽ ⊼ ♄ **9:43 am** 6:43 am

5 THURSDAY
- ☽ ✶ ♅ **9:19 am** 6:19 am
- ☽ □ ♀ **1:22 pm** 10:22 am
- ☽ △ ☉ **8:07 pm** 5:07 pm
- ☽ □ ♂ **11:08 pm** 8:08 pm

Eastern time in bold type
Pacific time in medium type

6 FRIDAY
- ☿ □ ♄ **4:12 am** 1:12 am
- ☽ △ ♆ **4:13 am** 1:13 am
- ☽ ☍ ♃ **11:01 am** 8:01 am
- ☽ ☍ ♇ **12:41 pm** 9:41 am
- ☽ ☍ ♄ **7:52 pm** 4:52 pm
- ☽ □ ☿ **8:27 pm** 5:27 pm

7 SATURDAY
- ☉ ⊼ ♂ **6:41 am** 3:41 am
- ☽ □ ♅ **5:49 pm** 2:49 pm

8 SUNDAY
- ☽ ✶ ♀ **3:36 am** 12:36 am
- ☽ △ ♂ **6:39 am** 3:39 am
- ☽ □ ☉ **8:46 am** 5:46 am
- ☽ ⊼ ♆ **11:46 am** 8:46 am
- ☽ ⊼ ♃ **6:49 pm** 3:49 pm
- ☽ ⊼ ♇ **7:49 pm** 4:49 pm
- ☽ ⊼ ♄ 11:44 pm

9 MONDAY
- ☽ ⊼ ♄ **2:44 am**
- ☽ ✶ ☿ **6:05 am** 3:05 am
- ♀ ☍ ♂ **11:08 am** 8:08 am
- ☽ △ ♅ **10:50 pm** 7:50 pm
- ☉ △ ♆ 9:11 pm

10 TUESDAY
- ☉ △ ♆ **12:11 am**
- ☽ ⊼ ♂ **10:45 am** 7:45 am
- ☽ ⊻ ♀ **1:04 pm** 10:04 am
- ☽ ☍ ♆ **3:42 pm** 12:42 pm
- ☽ ✶ ☉ **4:53 pm** 1:53 pm
- ☽ △ ♃ **10:55 pm** 7:55 pm
- ☽ △ ♇ **11:20 pm** 8:20 pm

11 WEDNESDAY
- ☽ △ ♄ **5:58 am** 2:58 am
- ☽ ⊻ ☿ **12:35 pm** 9:35 am
- ♀ ⊼ ♆ **7:31 pm** 4:31 pm
- ☽ ⊼ ♅ 9:31 pm

12 THURSDAY
- ☽ ⊼ ♅ **12:31 am**
- ☽ ☍ ♂ **11:50 am** 8:50 am
- ☽ ⊼ ♆ **4:37 pm** 1:37 pm
- ♃ ☌ ♇ **4:39 pm** 1:39 pm
- ☽ ☌ ♀ **6:31 pm** 3:31 pm
- ☽ ⊻ ☉ **9:17 pm** 6:17 pm
- ☽ □ ♇ 9:00 pm
- ☽ □ ♃ 9:05 pm

13 FRIDAY
- ☽ □ ♇ **12:00 am**
- ☽ □ ♃ **12:05 am**
- ☽ □ ♄ **6:32 am** 3:32 am
- ☽ ☌ ☿ **4:44 pm** 1:44 pm
- ☽ ☍ ♅ 9:10 pm

14 SATURDAY
- ☽ ☍ ♅ **12:10 am**
- ☽ ⊼ ♂ **11:23 am** 8:23 am
- ☉ ✶ ♇ **2:48 pm** 11:48 am
- ☽ △ ♆ **4:05 pm** 1:05 pm
- ☽ ⊻ ♀ **10:11 pm** 7:11 pm
- ☉ ✶ ♃ **10:57 pm** 7:57 pm
- ☽ ✶ ♇ **11:31 pm** 8:31 pm
- ☽ ✶ ♃ 9:03 pm
- ☽ ☌ ☉ 9:07 pm

15 SUNDAY
- ☽ ✶ ♃ **12:03 am**
- ☽ ☌ ☉ **12:07 am**
- ☽ ✶ ♄ **6:13 am** 3:13 am
- ♀ □ ♇ **2:43 pm** 11:43 am
- ☽ ⊻ ☿ **8:48 pm** 5:48 pm
- ☽ ⊼ ♅ **11:40 pm** 8:40 pm
- ♀ □ ♃ 9:33 pm

16 MONDAY
- ♀ □ ♃ **12:33 am**
- ☽ △ ♂ **11:21 am** 8:21 am
- ☽ □ ♆ **4:07 pm** 1:07 pm
- ☽ ⊻ ♇ **11:53 pm** 8:53 pm
- ☽ ⊻ ♃ 9:58 pm
- ☽ ✶ ♀ 11:55 pm

17 TUESDAY
- ☽ ⊻ ♃ **12:58 am**
- ☽ ✶ ♀ **2:55 am**
- ☿ ☍ ♅ **3:07 am** 12:07 am
- ☽ ⊻ ☉ **4:03 am** 1:03 am
- ☽ ⊻ ♄ **7:03 am** 4:03 am
- ☽ △ ♅ 10:00 pm

18 WEDNESDAY
- ☽ △ ♅ **1:00 am**
- ☽ ✶ ☿ **3:32 am** 12:32 am
- ☽ □ ♂ **1:42 pm** 10:42 am
- ☽ ✶ ♆ **6:34 pm** 3:34 pm
- ☉ ✶ ♄ 11:18 pm
- ☽ ☌ ♇ 11:58 pm

19 THURSDAY
- ☉ ✶ ♄ **2:18 am**
- ☽ ☌ ♇ **2:58 am**
- ☽ ☌ ♃ **4:43 am** 1:43 am
- ♀ □ ♄ **6:29 am** 3:29 am
- ☽ ☌ ♄ **10:51 am** 7:51 am
- ☽ □ ♀ **11:16 am** 8:16 am
- ☽ ✶ ☉ **11:30 am** 8:30 am
- ☉ ⊻ ♀ **11:45 pm** 8:45 pm

20 FRIDAY
- ☽ □ ♅ **5:41 am** 2:41 am
- ☽ □ ☿ **3:15 pm** 12:15 pm
- ☽ ✶ ♂ **7:49 pm** 4:49 pm
- ☽ ⊻ ♆ 9:42 pm

21 SATURDAY
- ☽ ⊻ ♆ **12:42 am**
- ☽ ⊻ ♇ **9:51 am** 6:51 am
- ☽ ⊻ ♃ **12:25 pm** 9:25 am
- ☽ ⊻ ♄ **6:34 pm** 3:34 pm
- ☽ □ ☉ **11:45 pm** 8:45 pm
- ☽ △ ♀ 9:43 pm

22 SUNDAY
- ☽ △ ♀ **12:43 am**
- ☿ ⊼ ♂ **9:00 am** 6:00 am
- ☽ ✶ ♅ **2:11 pm** 11:11 am

23 MONDAY
- ☽ ⊻ ♂ **5:52 am** 2:52 am
- ☽ △ ☿ **8:37 am** 5:37 am
- ☽ ☌ ♆ **10:31 am** 7:31 am
- ☽ ✶ ♇ **8:18 pm** 5:18 pm
- ☿ △ ♆ **11:40 pm** 8:40 pm
- ☽ ✶ ♃ **11:47 pm** 8:47 pm

24 TUESDAY
- ☽ ✶ ♄ **5:44 am** 2:44 am
- ☽ △ ☉ **4:13 pm** 1:13 pm
- ☽ ⊼ ♀ **6:36 pm** 3:36 pm
- ☽ ⊻ ♅ 10:35 pm

25 WEDNESDAY
- ☽ ⊻ ♅ **1:35 am**
- ☽ ☌ ♂ **6:39 pm** 3:39 pm
- ☽ ⊻ ♆ **10:43 pm** 7:43 pm

26 THURSDAY
- ☽ ⊼ ☿ **5:46 am** 2:46 am
- ☽ □ ♇ **8:50 am** 5:50 am
- ☽ □ ♃ **1:15 pm** 10:15 am
- ☽ □ ♄ **6:46 pm** 3:46 pm

27 FRIDAY
- ☿ ✶ ♇ **5:38 am** 2:38 am
- ☽ ⊼ ☉ **10:35 am** 7:35 am
- ♀ ☍ ♅ **12:11 pm** 9:11 am
- ☽ ☌ ♅ **2:10 pm** 11:10 am
- ☽ ☍ ♀ **2:25 pm** 11:25 am

28 SATURDAY
- ☽ ⊻ ♂ **8:17 am** 5:17 am
- ☽ ✶ ♆ **11:29 am** 8:29 am
- ☽ △ ♇ **9:40 pm** 6:40 pm
- ☿ ✶ ♃ **9:51 pm** 6:51 pm
- ☽ △ ♃ 11:53 pm

29 SUNDAY
- ☽ △ ♃ **2:53 am**
- ☉ ⊼ ♅ **3:20 am** 12:20 am
- ☽ ☍ ☿ **3:33 am** 12:33 am
- ☽ △ ♄ **7:48 am** 4:48 am
- ☽ ⊻ ♅ 11:19 pm

30 MONDAY
- ☽ ⊻ ♅ **2:19 am**
- ☽ ☍ ☉ **4:30 am** 1:30 am
- ☽ ⊼ ♀ **9:38 am** 6:38 am
- ☿ ✶ ♄ **2:01 pm** 11:01 am
- ☽ ✶ ♂ **9:13 pm** 6:13 pm
- ☽ □ ♆ **11:22 pm** 8:22 pm

NOVEMBER 2020

DATE	SID.TIME	SUN	MOON	NODE	MERCURY	VENUS	MARS	JUPITER	SATURN	URANUS	NEPTUNE	PLUTO	CERES	PALLAS	JUNO	VESTA	CHIRON
1 Su	2 42 57	9 ♏ 01 19	13 ♉ 10	20 ♊ 29 ℞	26 ♎ 37 ℞	4 ♎ 46	16 ♈ 22 ℞	21 ♑ 03	26 ♑ 13	8 ♉ 40 ℞	18 ♓ 23 ℞	22 ♑ 40	29 ♒ 08	19 ♑ 51	13 ♏ 53	3 ♍ 37	5 ♈ 48 ℞
2 M	2 46 54	10 01 20	25 03	20 23	26 11	5 59	16 12	21 11	26 16	8 38	18 22	22 41	29 13	20 05	14 14	3 59	5 46
3 T	2 50 50	11 01 23	6 ♊ 58	20 21	25 57 D	7 12	16 03	21 20	26 20	8 35	18 21	22 42	29 18	20 20	14 34	4 21	5 44
4 W	2 54 47	12 01 28	18 59	20 19 D	25 54	8 25	15 54	21 28	26 23	8 33	18 20	22 43	29 23	20 35	14 55	4 42	5 42
5 Th	2 58 44	13 01 35	1 ♋ 09	20 20	26 03	9 39	15 47	21 37	26 26	8 30	18 19	22 44	29 29	20 50	15 15	5 04	5 40
6 F	3 2 40	14 01 44	13 30	20 21	26 21	10 52	15 40	21 46	26 30	8 28	18 19	22 45	29 35	21 05	15 36	5 25	5 38
7 Sa	3 6 37	15 01 56	26 06	20 23	26 50	12 05	15 34	21 55	26 34	8 25	18 18	22 46	29 42	21 20	15 56	5 47	5 36
8 Su	3 10 33	16 02 09	9 ♌ 02	20 24 ℞	27 28	13 19	15 29	22 05	26 37	8 23	18 17	22 47	29 48	21 35	16 17	6 08	5 34
9 M	3 14 30	17 02 24	22 20	20 24	28 13	14 32	15 24	22 14	26 41	8 21	18 17	22 48	29 55	21 51	16 37	6 29	5 32
10 T	3 18 26	18 02 41	6 ♍ 04	20 23	29 06	15 46	15 21	22 24	26 45	8 18	18 16	22 49	0 ♓ 03	22 06	16 58	6 50	5 31
11 W	3 22 23	19 03 01	20 14	20 20	0 ♏ 05	16 59	15 18	22 33	26 49	8 16	18 15	22 50	0 11	22 22	17 18	7 10	5 29
12 Th	3 26 20	20 03 22	4 ♎ 48	20 17	1 10	18 13	15 16	22 43	26 53	8 13	18 15	22 51	0 19	22 38	17 39	7 31	5 27
13 F	3 30 16	21 03 45	19 44	20 12	2 19	19 27	15 14	22 53	26 57	8 11	18 14	22 52	0 27	22 54	17 59	7 51	5 25
14 Sa	3 34 13	22 04 10	4 ♏ 52	20 08	3 33	20 41	15 14 D	23 03	27 01	8 08	18 14	22 53	0 35	23 10	18 20	8 11	5 24
15 Su	3 38 9	23 04 37	20 04	20 05	4 50	21 55	15 14	23 13	27 06	8 06	18 13	22 54	0 44	23 26	18 40	8 32	5 22
16 M	3 42 6	24 05 05	5 ♐ 09	20 03	6 10	23 08	15 16	23 23	27 10	8 04	18 13	22 55	0 53	23 43	19 01	8 51	5 20
17 T	3 46 2	25 05 35	19 58	20 02 D	7 32	24 22	15 18	23 33	27 15	8 01	18 12	22 57	1 03	23 59	19 21	9 11	5 19
18 W	3 49 59	26 06 07	4 ♑ 26	20 03	8 57	25 36	15 20	23 44	27 19	7 59	18 12	22 58	1 13	24 16	19 42	9 31	5 17
19 Th	3 53 55	27 06 40	18 26	20 04	10 23	26 50	15 24	23 54	27 24	7 57	18 11	22 59	1 23	24 33	20 02	9 50	5 16
20 F	3 57 52	28 07 14	2 ♒ 00	20 05	11 51	28 05	15 28	24 05	27 28	7 55	18 11	23 00	1 33	24 49	20 23	10 10	5 15
21 Sa	4 1 49	29 07 49	15 07	20 07	13 20	29 19	15 33	24 16	27 33	7 52	18 11	23 02	1 43	25 06	20 43	10 29	5 13
22 Su	4 5 45	0 ♐ 08 26	27 52	20 07 ℞	14 50	0 ♏ 33	15 39	24 27	27 38	7 50	18 11	23 03	1 54	25 23	21 04	10 48	5 12
23 M	4 9 42	1 09 03	10 ♓ 17	20 07	16 21	1 47	15 46	24 38	27 43	7 48	18 10	23 04	2 05	25 41	21 24	11 06	5 11
24 T	4 13 38	2 09 42	22 27	20 06	17 52	3 01	15 53	24 49	27 48	7 46	18 10	23 06	2 16	25 58	21 45	11 25	5 10
25 W	4 17 35	3 10 22	4 ♈ 27	20 04	19 24	4 16	16 01	25 00	27 53	7 43	18 10	23 07	2 28	26 15	22 05	11 43	5 08
26 Th	4 21 31	4 11 03	16 20	20 02	20 57	5 30	16 10	25 11	27 58	7 41	18 10	23 09	2 40	26 33	22 25	12 01	5 07
27 F	4 25 28	5 11 45	28 10	19 59	22 30	6 44	16 19	25 23	28 03	7 39	18 10	23 10	2 52	26 50	22 46	12 19	5 06
28 Sa	4 29 24	6 12 28	10 ♉ 00	19 57	24 03	7 59	16 29	25 34	28 08	7 37	18 10	23 12	3 04	27 08	23 06	12 37	5 05
29 Su	4 33 21	7 13 13	21 54	19 55	25 36	9 13	16 40	25 45	28 14	7 35	18 10 D	23 13	3 16	27 26	23 26	12 55	5 04
30 M	4 37 18	8 13 59	3 ♊ 52	19 54	27 09	10 28	16 51	25 57	28 19	7 33	18 10	23 15	3 29	27 43	23 46	13 12	5 03

EPHEMERIS CALCULATED FOR 12 MIDNIGHT GREENWICH MEAN TIME. ALL OTHER DATA AND FACING ASPECTARIAN PAGE IN **EASTERN TIME (BOLD)** AND PACIFIC TIME (REGULAR).

DECEMBER 2020

☽ Last Aspect day	ET / hr:mn / PT	asp	☽ Ingress sign	day	ET / hr:mn / PT
11/30	**11:22 pm** 8:22 pm	□♆	♋	1	**10:33 pm** 7:33 pm
4	**5:29 am** 2:29 am	☍♄	♌	4	**7:53 am** 4:53 am
5	**5:28 pm** 2:28 pm	△♂	♍	6	**2:46 pm** 11:46 am
8	**5:35 pm** 2:35 pm	△♄	♎	8	**7:01 pm** 4:01 pm
10	**7:56 pm** 4:56 pm	□♄	♏	10	**8:59 pm** 5:59 pm
12	**8:58 pm** 5:58 pm	✶♄	♐	12	**9:39 pm** 6:39 pm
14	**11:17 am** 8:17 am	☌☉	♑	14	**10:35 pm** 7:35 pm
16	9:34 pm	☌♃	♒	16	10:27 pm
17	**12:34 am**	☌♃	♒	17	**1:27 am**
19	**3:45 am** 12:45 am	✶☉	♓	19	**7:39 am** 4:39 am

☽ Last Aspect day	ET / hr:mn / PT	asp	☽ Ingress sign	day	ET / hr:mn / PT
21	**5:25 am** 2:25 am	✶♇	♈	21	**5:32 pm** 2:32 pm
23	**5:51 pm** 2:51 pm	☌♂	♉	24	**5:55 am** 2:55 am
26	**6:32 am** 3:32 am	△♇	♊	26	**6:33 pm** 3:33 pm
28	**10:01 pm** 7:01 pm	✶♂	♋	29	**5:28 am** 2:28 am
31	**8:45 am** 5:45 am	□♂	♌	31	**1:58 pm** 10:58 am

☽ Phases & Eclipses phase	day	ET / hr:mn / PT
4th Quarter	7	**7:37 pm** 4:37 pm
New Moon	14	**11:17 am** 8:17 am
●	14	23° ♐ 08'
2nd Quarter	21	**6:41 pm** 3:41 pm
Full Moon	29	**10:28 pm** 7:28 pm

Planet Ingress		day	ET / hr:mn / PT
☿	♐	1	**2:51 pm** 11:51 am
♀	♒	7	**7:14 am** 4:14 am
♀	♐	15	**11:21 am** 8:21 am
♄	♒	16	9:04 pm
♄	♒	17	**12:04am**
⚵	♐	18	**12:25 pm** 9:25 am
♃	♒	19	**8:07 am** 5:07 am
☿	♑	20	**6:07 pm** 3:07 pm
☉	♑	21	**5:02 am** 2:02 am

Planetary Motion		day	ET / hr:mn / PT
⚷	D	15	**5:17 pm** 2:17 pm

1 TUESDAY
☽ ⚻ ♇ **9:26 am** 6:26 am
☽ ⚻ ♃ **3:22 pm** 12:22 pm
☽ ⚻ ♄ **7:38 pm** 4:38 pm
☽ ⚻ ☿ **11:40 pm** 8:40 pm

2 WEDNESDAY
☽ ✶ ♅ **1:00 pm** 10:00 am
☽ ⚻ ☉ **8:28 pm** 5:28 pm
☽ △ ♀ 11:43 pm

3 THURSDAY
☽ △ ♀ **2:43 am**
☽ □ ♂ **8:28 am** 5:28 am
☽ △ ♆ **9:32 am** 6:32 am
☽ ☍ ♇ **7:22 pm** 4:22 pm
☽ ☍ ♃ 10:52 pm

4 FRIDAY
☽ ☍ ♃ **1:52 am**
☽ ☍ ♄ **5:29 am** 2:29 am
☽ △ ☿ **4:52 pm** 1:52 pm
☽ □ ♅ **9:38 pm** 6:38 pm

5 SATURDAY
☽ △ ☉ **9:41 am** 6:41 am
♂ ⚺ ♆ **4:44 pm** 1:44 pm
☽ □ ♀ **4:47 pm** 1:47 pm
☽ ⚻ ♆ **5:27 pm** 2:27 pm
☽ △ ♂ **5:28 pm** 2:28 pm
♀ △ ♆ **11:53 pm** 8:53 pm
♀ ⚻ ♂ 10:41 pm
☽ ⚻ ♇ 11:56 pm

Eastern time in bold type
Pacific time in medium type

6 SUNDAY
♀ ⚻ ♂ **1:41 am**
☽ ⚻ ♇ **2:56 am**
☿ ⚻ ♅ **7:43 am** 4:43 am
☽ ⚻ ♃ **9:53 am** 6:53 am
☽ ⚻ ♄ **12:53 pm** 9:53 am

7 MONDAY
☽ △ ♅ **3:45 am** 12:45 am
☽ □ ☿ **6:24 am** 3:24 am
☽ □ ☉ **7:37 pm** 4:37 pm
☽ ☍ ♆ **10:45 pm** 7:45 pm
☽ ⚻ ♂ **11:47 pm** 8:47 pm

8 TUESDAY
☽ ✶ ♀ **3:21 am** 12:21 am
☽ △ ♇ **7:52 am** 4:52 am
☽ △ ♃ **3:09 pm** 12:09 pm
☽ △ ♄ **5:35 pm** 2:35 pm

9 WEDNESDAY
☽ ⚻ ♅ **7:17 am** 4:17 am
☉ □ ♆ **2:41 pm** 11:41 am
☽ ✶ ☿ **4:13 pm** 1:13 pm
☽ ⚻ ♆ 10:33 pm
☽ ✶ ☉ 11:22 pm

10 THURSDAY
☽ ⚻ ♆ **1:33 am**
☽ ✶ ☉ **2:22 am**
☽ ☍ ♂ **3:31 am** 12:31 am
♀ ✶ ♇ **6:52 am** 3:52 am
☽ □ ♇ **10:21 am** 7:21 am
☽ ⚺ ♀ **10:40 am** 7:40 am
☽ □ ♃ **5:58 pm** 2:58 pm

☽ □ ♄ **7:56 pm** 4:56 pm
☉ △ ♂ 10:01 pm

11 FRIDAY
☉ △ ♂ **1:01 am**
☽ ☍ ♅ **8:43 am** 5:43 am
☽ ⚺ ☿ **11:18 pm** 8:18 pm
☽ △ ♆ 11:35 pm

12 SATURDAY
☽ △ ♆ **2:35 am**
☽ ⚻ ♂ **5:30 am** 2:30 am
☽ ⚺ ☉ **6:58 am** 3:58 am
☽ ✶ ♇ **11:17 am** 8:17 am
☽ ☌ ♀ **3:59 pm** 12:59 pm
☽ ✶ ♃ **7:23 pm** 4:23 pm
☽ ✶ ♄ **8:58 pm** 5:58 pm

13 SUNDAY
☿ □ ♆ **6:38 am** 3:38 am
☽ ⚻ ♅ **9:13 am** 6:13 am

14 MONDAY
☽ □ ♆ **3:15 am** 12:15 am
☽ ☌ ☿ **5:42 am** 2:42 am
☽ △ ♂ **7:14 am** 4:14 am
☽ ☌ ☉ **11:17 am** 8:17 am
☽ ⚺ ♇ **12:07 pm** 9:07 am
♀ ✶ ♃ **3:58 pm** 12:58 pm
☽ ⚺ ♃ **8:59 pm** 5:59 pm
☽ ⚺ ♀ **9:23 pm** 6:23 pm
☽ ⚺ ♄ **10:13 pm** 7:13 pm
☿ △ ♂ **11:24 pm** 8:24 pm
☉ ⚺ ♇ **11:39 pm** 8:39 pm

15 TUESDAY
♀ ✶ ♄ **8:00 am** 5:00 am
☽ △ ♅ **10:22 am** 7:22 am

16 WEDNESDAY
☽ ✶ ♆ **5:12 am** 2:12 am
☽ □ ♂ **10:32 am** 7:32 am
☽ ⚺ ☿ **2:03 pm** 11:03 am
☽ ☌ ♇ **2:33 pm** 11:33 am
☽ ⚺ ☉ **5:32 pm** 2:32 pm
☿ ⚺ ♇ **6:35 pm** 3:35 pm
☽ ☌ ♃ 9:34 pm
☽ ☌ ♄ 10:23 pm

17 THURSDAY
☽ ☌ ♃ **12:34 am**
☽ ☌ ♄ **1:28 am**
☽ ✶ ♀ **5:16 am** 2:16 am
☽ □ ♅ **1:50 pm** 10:50 am

18 FRIDAY
☽ ⚺ ♆ **10:01 am** 7:01 am
☽ ✶ ♂ **5:08 pm** 2:08 pm
☽ ⚺ ♇ **8:06 pm** 5:06 pm
☽ ✶ ☿ 11:49 pm

19 SATURDAY
☽ ✶ ☿ **2:49 am**
☽ ✶ ☉ **3:45 am** 12:45 am
☽ ⚺ ♃ **7:38 am** 4:38 am
☽ ⚺ ♄ **8:07 am** 5:07 am
☽ □ ♀ **5:40 pm** 2:40 pm
☽ ✶ ♅ **8:50 pm** 5:50 pm
☉ ☌ ☿ **10:26 pm** 7:26 pm

20 SUNDAY
☽ ☌ ♆ **6:34 pm** 3:34 pm
☿ ⚺ ♃ **11:34 pm** 8:34 pm
☿ ⚺ ♄ 9:37 pm
♀ ⚻ ♅ 10:12 pm

21 MONDAY
☿ ⚺ ♄ **12:37 am**
♀ ⚻ ♅ **1:12 am**
☽ ⚺ ♂ **3:52 am** 12:52 am
☽ ✶ ♇ **5:25 am** 2:25 am
♃ ☌ ♄ **1:21 pm** 10:21 am
☉ ⚺ ♄ **4:52 pm** 1:52 pm
☉ ⚺ ♃ **5:22 pm** 2:22 pm
☽ ✶ ♄ **6:33 pm** 3:33 pm
☽ ✶ ♃ **6:36 pm** 3:36 pm
☽ □ ☉ **6:41 pm** 3:41 pm
☽ □ ☿ **9:04 pm** 6:04 pm

22 TUESDAY
☽ ⚺ ♅ **7:22 am** 4:22 am
☽ △ ♀ **10:56 am** 7:56 am

23 WEDNESDAY
☽ ⚺ ♆ **6:17 am** 3:17 am
♂ □ ♇ **9:53 am** 6:53 am
☽ □ ♇ **5:37 pm** 2:37 pm
☽ ☌ ♂ **5:51 pm** 2:51 pm

24 THURSDAY
☽ □ ♄ **7:31 am** 4:31 am
☽ □ ♃ **8:10 am** 5:10 am
☽ △ ☉ **12:48 pm** 9:48 am
☽ △ ☿ **6:57 pm** 3:57 pm

☽ ☌ ♅ **7:56 pm** 4:56 pm
☿ △ ♅ 11:05 pm

25 FRIDAY
☿ △ ♅ **2:05 am**
☽ ⚻ ♀ **6:49 am** 3:49 am
☽ ✶ ♆ **7:10 pm** 4:10 pm

26 SATURDAY
☽ △ ♇ **6:32 am** 3:32 am
☽ ⚺ ♂ **8:42 am** 5:42 am
☽ △ ♄ **8:41 pm** 5:41 pm
☽ △ ♃ **9:54 pm** 6:54 pm

27 SUNDAY
☽ ⚻ ☉ **6:53 am** 3:53 am
☽ ⚺ ♅ **8:13 am** 5:13 am
☽ ⚻ ☿ **4:33 pm** 1:33 pm
☉ △ ♅ **10:25 pm** 7:25 pm
☽ ☍ ♀ 10:47 pm

28 MONDAY
☽ ☍ ♀ **1:47 am**
☽ □ ♆ **6:59 am** 3:59 am
☽ ⚻ ♇ **6:03 pm** 3:03 pm
☽ ✶ ♂ **10:01 pm** 7:01 pm

29 TUESDAY
☽ ⚻ ♄ **8:04 am** 5:04 am
☽ ⚻ ♃ **9:47 am** 6:47 am
☽ ✶ ♅ **6:32 pm** 3:32 pm
☽ ☍ ☉ **10:28 pm** 7:28 pm

30 WEDNESDAY
♀ □ ♆ **5:19 am** 2:19 am
☽ ☍ ☿ **11:04 am** 8:04 am

☽ △ ♆ **4:31 pm** 1:31 pm
☽ ⚻ ♀ **5:42 pm** 2:42 pm

31 THURSDAY
☽ ☍ ♇ **3:10 am** 12:10 am
☽ □ ♂ **8:45 am** 5:45 am
☽ ☍ ♄ **4:56 pm** 1:56 pm
☽ ☍ ♃ **7:05 pm** 4:05 pm
☽ □ ♅ 11:26 pm

DECEMBER 2020

DATE	SID.TIME	SUN	MOON	NODE	MERCURY	VENUS	MARS	JUPITER	SATURN	URANUS	NEPTUNE	PLUTO	CERES	PALLAS	JUNO	VESTA	CHIRON
1 T	4 41 14	9 ♐ 14 46	15 ♊ 57	19 ♊ 53 D	28 ♏ 43	11 ♏ 42	17 ♈ 03	26 ♑ 09	28 ♑ 24	7 ♉ 31 ℞	18 ♓ 10	23 ♑ 16	3 ♓ 42	28 ♑ 01	24 ♏ 07	13 ♍ 29	5 ♈ 03 ℞
2 W	4 45 11	10 15 34	28 11	19 53	0 ♐ 16	12 57	17 16	26 21	28 30	7 29	18 10	23 18	3 55	28 19	24 27	13 46	5 02
3 Th	4 49 7	11 16 24	10 ♋ 34	19 54	1 50	14 11	17 29	26 32	28 35	7 27	18 10	23 19	4 09	28 37	24 47	14 03	5 01
4 F	4 53 4	12 17 14	23 09	19 55	3 23	15 26	17 43	26 44	28 41	7 25	18 10	23 21	4 22	28 56	25 07	14 19	5 00
5 Sa	4 57 0	13 18 06	5 ♌ 58	19 55	4 57	16 41	17 57	26 56	28 47	7 23	18 10	23 22	4 36	29 14	25 27	14 35	5 00
6 Su	5 0 57	14 19 00	19 02	19 56	6 31	17 55	18 12	27 09	28 52	7 21	18 11	23 24	4 50	29 32	25 47	14 51	4 59
7 M	5 4 53	15 19 54	2 ♍ 22	19 56	8 05	19 10	18 27	27 21	28 58	7 20	18 11	23 26	5 04	29 51	26 07	15 07	4 59
8 T	5 8 50	16 20 50	16 01	19 56 ℞	9 38	20 25	18 43	27 33	29 04	7 18	18 11	23 27	5 19	0 ♒ 09	26 27	15 23	4 58
9 W	5 12 47	17 21 47	29 59	19 56	11 12	21 40	19 00	27 45	29 10	7 16	18 11	23 29	5 34	0 28	26 47	15 38	4 58
10 Th	5 16 43	18 22 45	14 ♎ 15	19 56	12 46	22 55	19 17	27 58	29 16	7 14	18 12	23 31	5 48	0 46	27 07	15 53	4 57
11 F	5 20 40	19 23 45	28 48	19 56 D	14 20	24 09	19 35	28 10	29 22	7 13	18 12	23 32	6 03	1 05	27 27	16 08	4 57
12 Sa	5 24 36	20 24 46	13 ♏ 32	19 56	15 54	25 24	19 53	28 23	29 28	7 11	18 13	23 34	6 19	1 24	27 47	16 22	4 57
13 Su	5 28 33	21 25 47	28 22	19 56	17 28	26 39	20 11	28 36	29 34	7 10	18 13	23 36	6 34	1 43	28 07	16 37	4 57
14 M	5 32 29	22 26 50	13 ♐ 10	19 56 ℞	19 02	27 54	20 30	28 48	29 40	7 08	18 14	23 38	6 50	2 01	28 27	16 51	4 57
15 T	5 36 26	23 27 54	27 50	19 56	20 36	29 09	20 50	29 01	29 46	7 07	18 14	23 39	7 06	2 20	28 47	17 04	4 56 D
16 W	5 40 22	24 28 58	12 ♑ 14	19 56	22 10	0 ♐ 24	21 10	29 14	29 52	7 05	18 15	23 41	7 22	2 39	29 06	17 18	4 56
17 Th	5 44 19	25 30 03	26 17	19 56	23 45	1 39	21 30	29 27	29 59	7 04	18 15	23 43	7 38	2 59	29 26	17 31	4 56
18 F	5 48 16	26 31 08	9 ♒ 57	19 55	25 19	2 54	21 51	29 40	0 ♒ 05	7 02	18 16	23 45	7 54	3 18	29 46	17 44	4 57
19 Sa	5 52 12	27 32 14	23 11	19 54	26 54	4 09	22 12	29 53	0 11	7 01	18 17	23 47	8 11	3 37	0 ♐ 05	17 56	4 57
20 Su	5 56 9	28 33 20	6 ♓ 02	19 53	28 29	5 24	22 34	0 ♒ 06	0 18	7 00	18 17	23 48	8 27	3 56	0 25	18 08	4 57
21 M	6 0 5	29 34 26	18 31	19 52 D	0 ♑ 03	6 39	22 56	0 19	0 24	6 58	18 18	23 50	8 44	4 16	0 44	18 20	4 57
22 T	6 4 2	0 ♑ 35 33	0 ♈ 44	19 52	1 39	7 54	23 18	0 32	0 31	6 57	18 19	23 52	9 01	4 35	1 04	18 32	4 57
23 W	6 7 58	1 36 40	12 44	19 52	3 14	9 09	23 41	0 46	0 37	6 56	18 20	23 54	9 18	4 54	1 23	18 43	4 58
24 Th	6 11 55	2 37 46	24 37	19 53	4 50	10 24	24 04	0 59	0 44	6 55	18 21	23 56	9 36	5 14	1 43	18 54	4 58
25 F	6 15 51	3 38 53	6 ♉ 26	19 54	6 25	11 39	24 28	1 12	0 50	6 54	18 21	23 58	9 53	5 33	2 02	19 04	4 59
26 Sa	6 19 48	4 40 01	18 17	19 56	8 01	12 54	24 51	1 26	0 57	6 53	18 22	24 00	10 11	5 53	2 21	19 15	4 59
27 Su	6 23 45	5 41 08	0 ♊ 14	19 57	9 38	14 09	25 16	1 39	1 04	6 52	18 23	24 02	10 29	6 12	2 40	19 24	5 00
28 M	6 27 41	6 42 16	12 19	19 58 ℞	11 14	15 24	25 40	1 53	1 10	6 51	18 24	24 04	10 46	6 32	2 59	19 34	5 00
29 T	6 31 38	7 43 23	24 35	19 58	12 51	16 39	26 05	2 06	1 17	6 50	18 25	24 05	11 05	6 52	3 18	19 43	5 01
30 W	6 35 34	8 44 31	7 ♋ 04	19 57	14 28	17 54	26 30	2 20	1 24	6 49	18 26	24 07	11 23	7 12	3 37	19 52	5 02
31 Th	6 39 31	9 45 39	19 47	19 55	16 05	19 10	26 56	2 33	1 31	6 49	18 27	24 09	11 41	7 31	3 56	20 00	5 03

EPHEMERIS CALCULATED FOR 12 MIDNIGHT GREENWICH MEAN TIME. ALL OTHER DATA AND FACING ASPECTARIAN PAGE IN **EASTERN TIME (BOLD)** AND PACIFIC TIME (REGULAR).

JANUARY 2021

☽ Last Aspect day	ET / hr:mn / PT		asp	☽ Ingress sign day	ET / hr:mn / PT	
2	**5:00 pm**	2:00 pm	△♂	♍ 2	**8:13 pm**	5:13 pm
4	**4:34 pm**	1:34 pm	☐♀	♎ 4		9:42 pm
4	**4:34 pm**	1:34 pm	☐♀	♎ 5	**12:42 am**	
6		9:55 pm	⚹♀	♏ 7	**3:53 am**	12:53 am
7	**12:55 am**		⚹♀	♏ 7	**3:53 am**	12:53 am
8	**8:59 pm**	5:59 pm	⚹♇	♐ 9	**6:15 am**	3:15 am
10	**1:29 pm**	10:29 am	☐♆	♑ 11	**8:30 am**	5:30 am
12		11:22 pm	☌♇	♒ 13	**11:44 am**	8:44 am
13	**2:22 am**		☌♇	♒ 13	**11:44 am**	8:44 am
14	**4:28 am**	1:28 am	☌☿	♓ 15	**5:17 pm**	2:17 pm
17	**10:44 pm**	7:44 pm	⚹☉	♈ 17		11:07 pm
17	**10:44 pm**	7:44 pm	⚹☉	♈ 18	**2:07 am**	
20	**3:29 am**	12:29 am	☐♇	♉ 20	**1:56 pm**	10:56 am
22	**4:28 pm**	1:28 pm	△♇	♊ 22		11:43 pm
22	**4:28 pm**	1:28 pm	△♇	♊ 23	**2:43 am**	
24		11:17 pm	△☿	♋ 25	**1:52 pm**	10:52 am
25	**2:17 am**		△☿	♋ 25	**1:52 pm**	10:52 am
27	**12:55 pm**	9:55 am	☍♇	♌ 27	**9:54 pm**	6:54 pm
29	**8:53 pm**	5:53 pm	☍☿	♍ 30	**3:02 am**	12:02 am

☽ Phases & Eclipses phase	day	ET / hr:mn / PT	
4th Quarter	6	**4:37 am**	1:37 am
New Moon	12		9:00 pm
New Moon	13	**12:00 am**	
2nd Quarter	20	**4:02 pm**	1:02 pm
Full Moon	28	**2:16 pm**	11:16 am

Planet Ingress	day	ET / hr:mn / PT	
♂ ♉	6	**5:27 pm**	2:27 pm
☿ ♒	8	**7:00 am**	4:00 am
♀ ♑	8	**10:41 am**	7:41 am
☉ ♒	19	**3:40 pm**	12:40 pm

Planetary Motion	day	ET / hr:mn / PT	
♅ D	14	**3:36 am**	12:36 am
⚶ Rx	19	**3:54 am**	12:54 am
☿ Rx	30	**10:52 am**	7:52 am

1 FRIDAY

☽ ☐ ♅	**2:26 am**	
☿ ⚹ ♆	**6:18 am**	3:18 am
☽ ⚻ ☉	**10:55 am**	7:55 am
☽ ⚻ ♆	**11:39 pm**	8:39 pm
☽ ⚻ ☿		11:02 pm

2 SATURDAY

☽ ⚻ ☿	**2:02 am**	
☽ △ ♀	**6:24 am**	3:24 am
☽ ⚻ ♇	**9:57 am**	6:57 am
☽ △ ♂	**5:00 pm**	2:00 pm
☽ ⚻ ♄	**11:32 pm**	8:32 pm
☽ ⚻ ♃		11:05 pm

3 SUNDAY

☽ ⚻ ♃	**2:05 am**	
☽ △ ♅	**8:12 am**	5:12 am
☽ △ ☉	**8:44 pm**	5:44 pm
♀ ⚺ ♇	**9:19 pm**	6:19 pm

4 MONDAY

☽ ☍ ♆	**4:50 am**	1:50 am
☽ △ ☿	**2:11 pm**	11:11 am
☽ △ ♇	**2:52 pm**	11:52 am
☽ ☐ ♀	**4:34 pm**	1:34 pm
☿ ☌ ♇	**7:58 pm**	4:58 pm
☽ ⚻ ♂	**11:19 pm**	8:19 pm

5 TUESDAY

☽ △ ♄	**4:22 am**	1:22 am
☽ △ ♃	**7:17 am**	4:17 am
☽ ⚻ ♅	**12:19 pm**	9:19 am

6 WEDNESDAY

☽ ☐ ☉	**4:37 am**	1:37 am
☽ ⚻ ♆	**8:32 am**	5:32 am
☽ ☐ ♇	**6:23 pm**	3:23 pm
☽ ☐ ☿		9:21 pm
☽ ⚹ ♀		9:55 pm

7 THURSDAY

☽ ☐ ☿	**12:21 am**	
☽ ⚹ ♀	**12:55 am**	
☽ ☍ ♂	**4:14 am**	1:14 am
☽ ☐ ♄	**7:54 am**	4:54 am
☽ ☐ ♃	**11:11 am**	8:11 am
☽ ☍ ♅	**3:16 pm**	12:16 pm
☿ ⚺ ♀	**7:04 pm**	4:04 pm

8 FRIDAY

☽ ⚹ ☉	**11:11 am**	8:11 am
☽ △ ♆	**11:14 am**	8:14 am
☉ ⚹ ♆	**11:53 am**	8:53 am
☽ ⚹ ♇	**8:59 pm**	5:59 pm
☿ ☐ ♂	**9:44 pm**	6:44 pm

9 SATURDAY

☽ ⚺ ♀	**8:07 am**	5:07 am
☽ ⚻ ♂	**8:17 am**	5:17 am
☽ ⚹ ☿	**9:15 am**	6:15 am
☽ ⚹ ♄	**10:38 am**	7:38 am
♀ △ ♂	**10:53 am**	7:53 am
☽ ⚹ ♃	**2:18 pm**	11:18 am
☽ ⚻ ♅	**5:30 pm**	2:30 pm
☿ ☌ ♄	**10:17 pm**	7:17 pm

10 SUNDAY

☽ ☐ ♆	**1:29 pm**	10:29 am
♀ ⚺ ♄	**3:39 pm**	12:39 pm
☽ ⚺ ☉	**5:12 pm**	2:12 pm
☽ ⚺ ♇	**11:17 pm**	8:17 pm

11 MONDAY

☽ △ ♂	**12:16 pm**	9:16 am
☿ ☌ ♃	**12:19 pm**	9:19 am
☽ ⚺ ♄	**1:20 pm**	10:20 am
☽ ☌ ♀	**3:14 pm**	12:14 pm
☽ ⚺ ♃	**5:28 pm**	2:28 pm
☽ ⚺ ☿	**6:02 pm**	3:02 pm
☽ △ ♅	**7:51 pm**	4:51 pm

12 TUESDAY

☿ ☐ ♅	**10:00 am**	7:00 am
☽ ⚹ ♆	**4:17 pm**	1:17 pm
♀ ⚺ ♃	**9:40 pm**	6:40 pm
☽ ☌ ☉		9:00 pm
☽ ☌ ♇		11:22 pm

13 WEDNESDAY

☽ ☌ ☉	**12:00 am**	
☽ ☌ ♇	**2:22 am**	
♂ ☐ ♄	**6:02 am**	3:02 am
☽ ☌ ♄	**5:11 pm**	2:11 pm
☽ ☐ ♂	**5:30 pm**	2:30 pm
♀ △ ♅	**7:22 pm**	4:22 pm
☽ ☌ ♃	**9:55 pm**	6:55 pm
☽ ☐ ♅	**11:29 pm**	8:29 pm
☽ ⚺ ♀	**11:54 pm**	8:54 pm

14 THURSDAY

☽ ☌ ☿	**4:28 am**	1:28 am
☉ ☌ ♇	**9:19 am**	6:19 am
☽ ⚺ ♆	**8:55 pm**	5:55 pm

15 FRIDAY

☽ ⚺ ♇	**7:33 am**	4:33 am
☽ ⚺ ☉	**9:21 am**	6:21 am
☽ ⚺ ♄	**11:33 pm**	8:33 pm
☽ ⚹ ♂		10:29 pm

16 SATURDAY

☽ ⚹ ♂	**1:29 am**	
☽ ⚺ ♃	**5:03 am**	2:03 am
☽ ⚹ ♅	**5:43 am**	2:43 am
☽ ⚹ ♀	**12:02 pm**	9:02 am
☽ ⚺ ☿	**6:33 pm**	3:33 pm

17 SUNDAY

☽ ☌ ♆	**4:35 am**	1:35 am
☽ ⚹ ♇	**3:55 pm**	12:55 pm
♃ ☐ ♅	**5:50 pm**	2:50 pm
☽ ⚹ ☉	**10:44 pm**	7:44 pm

18 MONDAY

☽ ⚹ ♄	**9:20 am**	6:20 am
☽ ⚺ ♂	**1:16 pm**	10:16 am
☽ ⚺ ♅	**3:20 pm**	12:20 pm
☽ ⚹ ♃	**3:45 pm**	12:45 pm

19 TUESDAY

☽ ☐ ♀	**4:43 am**	1:43 am
☽ ⚹ ☿	**12:54 pm**	9:54 am
☽ ⚺ ♆	**3:34 pm**	12:34 pm

20 WEDNESDAY

☽ ☐ ♇	**3:29 am**	12:29 am
☿ ⚺ ♆	**1:04 pm**	10:04 am
♂ ☌ ♅	**3:38 pm**	12:38 pm
☽ ☐ ☉	**4:02 pm**	1:02 pm
☽ ☐ ♄	**10:00 pm**	7:00 pm

21 THURSDAY

☽ ☌ ♅	**3:37 am**	12:37 am
☽ ☌ ♂	**4:08 am**	1:08 am
☽ ☐ ♃	**5:15 am**	2:15 am
☽ △ ♀		9:28 pm

22 FRIDAY

☽ △ ♀	**12:28 am**	
☽ ⚹ ♆	**4:27 am**	1:27 am
☽ ☐ ☿	**8:59 am**	5:59 am
☽ △ ♇	**4:28 pm**	1:28 pm
♂ ☐ ♃		11:49 pm

23 SATURDAY

♂ ☐ ♃	**2:49 am**	
☽ △ ☉	**10:27 am**	7:27 am
☽ △ ♄	**11:19 am**	8:19 am
♀ ⚹ ♆	**2:49 pm**	11:49 am
☽ ⚺ ♅	**4:16 pm**	1:16 pm
☽ △ ♃	**7:04 pm**	4:04 pm
☽ ⚺ ♂	**7:27 pm**	4:27 pm
☉ ☌ ♄	**10:01 pm**	7:01 pm

24 SUNDAY

☽ ☐ ♆	**4:36 pm**	1:36 pm
☽ ⚻ ♀	**7:28 pm**	4:28 pm
☽ △ ☿		11:17 pm

25 MONDAY

☽ △ ☿	**2:17 am**	
☽ ⚻ ♇	**4:12 am**	1:12 am
☽ ⚻ ♄	**10:38 pm**	7:38 pm
☽ ⚻ ☉		11:23 pm
☽ ⚹ ♅		11:49 pm

26 TUESDAY

☽ ⚻ ☉	**2:23 am**	
☽ ⚹ ♅	**2:49 am**	
☽ ⚻ ♃	**6:32 am**	3:32 am
☉ ☐ ♅	**7:48 am**	4:48 am
☽ ⚹ ♂	**8:17 am**	5:17 am
☿ ⚺ ♇	**9:35 am**	6:35 am
☽ △ ♆		10:57 pm

27 WEDNESDAY

☽ △ ♆	**1:57 am**	
☽ ☍ ♀	**10:37 am**	7:37 am
☽ ☍ ♇	**12:55 pm**	9:55 am
☽ ⚻ ☿	**2:09 pm**	11:09 am

28 THURSDAY

☽ ☍ ♄	**6:41 am**	3:41 am
☽ ☐ ♅	**10:11 am**	7:11 am
♀ ☌ ♇	**11:18 am**	8:18 am
☽ ☍ ☉	**2:16 pm**	11:16 am
☽ ☍ ♃	**2:39 pm**	11:39 am
☽ ☐ ♂	**5:32 pm**	2:32 pm
☉ ☌ ♃	**8:40 pm**	5:40 pm

29 FRIDAY

☽ ⚻ ♆	**8:10 am**	5:10 am
☿ ⚺ ♀	**12:19 pm**	9:19 am
☽ ⚻ ♇	**6:36 pm**	3:36 pm
☽ ☍ ☿	**8:53 pm**	5:53 pm
☽ ⚻ ♀	**9:39 pm**	6:39 pm

30 SATURDAY

☽ ⚻ ♄	**11:54 am**	8:54 am
☽ △ ♅	**2:52 pm**	11:52 am
☽ ⚻ ♃	**8:01 pm**	5:01 pm
☽ ⚻ ☉	**10:51 pm**	7:51 pm
☽ △ ♂	**11:57 pm**	8:57 pm

31 SUNDAY

☽ ☍ ♆	**12:09 pm**	9:09 am
☽ △ ♇	**10:17 pm**	7:17 pm
☽ ⚻ ☿		9:05 pm

Eastern time in bold type
Pacific time in medium type

JANUARY 2021

DATE	SID.TIME	SUN	MOON	NODE	MERCURY	VENUS	MARS	JUPITER	SATURN	URANUS	NEPTUNE	PLUTO	CERES	PALLAS	JUNO	VESTA	CHIRON
1 F	6 43 27	10♑46 47	2♌44	19♊53℞	17♑43	20♐25	27♈21	2♒47	1♒37	6♉48℞	18♓28	24♑11	12♓00	7♒51	4♐15	20♍09	5♈04
2 Sa	6 47 24	11 47 56	15 55	19 49	19 21	21 40	27 48	3 01	1 44	6 47	18 30	24 13	12 18	8 11	4 34	20 16	5 04
3 Su	6 51 21	12 49 04	29 19	19 46	20 59	22 55	28 14	3 14	1 51	6 47	18 31	24 15	12 37	8 31	4 52	20 24	5 05
4 M	6 55 17	13 50 13	12♍55	19 43	22 37	24 10	28 40	3 28	1 58	6 46	18 32	24 17	12 56	8 51	5 11	20 30	5 06
5 T	6 59 14	14 51 22	26 42	19 40	24 15	25 25	29 07	3 42	2 05	6 46	18 33	24 19	13 15	9 11	5 30	20 37	5 08
6 W	7 3 10	15 52 31	10♎39	19 39D	25 54	26 40	29 34	3 56	2 12	6 45	18 34	24 21	13 34	9 31	5 48	20 43	5 09
7 Th	7 7 7	16 53 40	24 45	19 39	27 32	27 56	0♉02	4 10	2 19	6 45	18 36	24 23	13 53	9 51	6 07	20 49	5 10
8 F	7 11 3	17 54 50	8♏58	19 40	29 11	29 11	0 29	4 24	2 26	6 44	18 37	24 25	14 13	10 11	6 25	20 54	5 11
9 Sa	7 15 0	18 56 00	23 16	19 42	0♒49	0♑26	0 57	4 38	2 33	6 44	18 38	24 27	14 32	10 31	6 43	20 59	5 12
10 Su	7 18 56	19 57 09	7♐38	19 43℞	2 27	1 41	1 25	4 52	2 40	6 44	18 40	24 29	14 52	10 51	7 01	21 04	5 14
11 M	7 22 53	20 58 19	21 58	19 44	4 05	2 56	1 54	5 06	2 47	6 44	18 41	24 31	15 11	11 11	7 19	21 08	5 15
12 T	7 26 50	21 59 29	6♑13	19 43	5 43	4 12	2 22	5 20	2 54	6 43	18 42	24 33	15 31	11 31	7 37	21 11	5 16
13 W	7 30 46	23 00 39	20 19	19 40	7 20	5 27	2 51	5 34	3 01	6 43	18 44	24 35	15 51	11 51	7 55	21 14	5 18
14 Th	7 34 43	24 01 48	4♒10	19 35	8 56	6 42	3 20	5 48	3 08	6 43D	18 45	24 37	16 11	12 12	8 13	21 17	5 19
15 F	7 38 39	25 02 57	17 43	19 30	10 30	7 57	3 49	6 02	3 15	6 43	18 47	24 39	16 31	12 32	8 31	21 19	5 21
16 Sa	7 42 36	26 04 05	0♓56	19 23	12 04	9 13	4 19	6 16	3 22	6 43	18 48	24 41	16 52	12 52	8 49	21 21	5 23
17 Su	7 46 32	27 05 12	13 48	19 17	13 35	10 28	4 48	6 30	3 30	6 43	18 50	24 43	17 12	13 12	9 06	21 22	5 24
18 M	7 50 29	28 06 19	26 20	19 11	15 05	11 43	5 18	6 44	3 37	6 44	18 52	24 45	17 32	13 33	9 24	21 23	5 26
19 T	7 54 25	29 07 24	8♈35	19 07	16 32	12 58	5 48	6 59	3 44	6 44	18 53	24 47	17 53	13 53	9 41	21 24℞	5 28
20 W	7 58 22	0♒08 29	20 37	19 05D	17 55	14 13	6 18	7 13	3 51	6 44	18 55	24 49	18 14	14 13	9 58	21 24	5 30
21 Th	8 2 19	1 09 34	2♉30	19 04	19 15	15 29	6 49	7 27	3 58	6 44	18 56	24 51	18 34	14 34	10 15	21 23	5 31
22 F	8 6 15	2 10 37	14 19	19 05	20 31	16 44	7 19	7 41	4 05	6 45	18 58	24 53	18 55	14 54	10 32	21 22	5 33
23 Sa	8 10 12	3 11 39	26 10	19 07	21 42	17 59	7 50	7 55	4 12	6 45	19 00	24 55	19 16	15 14	10 49	21 21	5 35
24 Su	8 14 8	4 12 40	8♊08	19 08℞	22 47	19 14	8 21	8 10	4 19	6 46	19 02	24 57	19 37	15 34	11 06	21 19	5 37
25 M	8 18 5	5 13 41	20 17	19 09	23 45	20 30	8 52	8 24	4 27	6 46	19 03	24 59	19 58	15 55	11 23	21 16	5 39
26 T	8 22 1	6 14 40	26♋41	19 07	24 35	21 45	9 23	8 38	4 34	6 47	19 05	25 01	20 19	16 15	11 39	21 13	5 41
27 W	8 25 58	7 15 39	15 23	19 04	25 18	23 00	9 54	8 52	4 41	6 48	19 07	25 03	20 41	16 36	11 56	21 10	5 44
28 Th	8 29 54	8 16 36	28 24	18 59	25 51	24 15	10 26	9 07	4 48	6 48	19 09	25 05	21 02	16 56	12 12	21 06	5 46
29 F	8 33 51	9 17 33	11♌45	18 51	26 14	25 30	10 57	9 21	4 55	6 49	19 10	25 07	21 23	17 16	12 29	21 02	5 48
30 Sa	8 37 48	10 18 28	25 23	18 42	26 27℞	26 45	11 29	9 35	5 02	6 50	19 12	25 09	21 45	17 37	12 45	20 57	5 50
31 Su	8 41 44	11 19 23	9♍15	18 33	26 29	28 01	12 01	9 49	5 09	6 51	19 14	25 11	22 07	17 57	13 01	20 52	5 53

EPHEMERIS CALCULATED FOR 12 MIDNIGHT GREENWICH MEAN TIME. ALL OTHER DATA AND FACING ASPECTARIAN PAGE IN **EASTERN TIME (BOLD)** AND PACIFIC TIME (REGULAR).

FEBRUARY 2021

☽ Last Aspect day	ET / hr:mn / PT	asp	☽ Ingress sign	day	ET / hr:mn / PT
1	6:10 am 3:10 am	△♀	♎	1	6:25 am 3:25 am
2	10:15 pm	△☿	♏	3	9:15 am 6:15 am
3	1:15 am	△☿	♏	3	9:15 am 6:15 am
5	4:20 am 1:20 am	✶♇	♐	5	12:16 pm 9:16 am
6	10:16 pm	✶☿	♑	7	3:52 pm 12:52 pm
7	1:16 am	✶☿	♑	7	3:52 pm 12:52 pm
9	12:22 pm 9:22 am	☌♇	♒	9	8:20 pm 5:20 pm
11	2:06 pm 11:06 am	☌☉	♓	11	11:23 pm
11	2:06 pm 11:06 am	☌☉	♓	12	2:23 am
13	11:29 pm	✶♇	♈	14	10:54 am 7:54 am
14	2:29 am	✶♇	♈	14	10:54 am 7:54 am
16	7:17 pm 4:17 pm	✶☉	♉	16	10:12 pm 7:12 pm
18	11:28 pm	△♇	♊	19	11:04 am 8:04 am
19	2:28 am	△♇	♊	19	11:04 am 8:04 am
21	1:39 pm 10:39 am	△♀	♋	21	10:53 pm 7:53 pm
23	11:54 pm 8:54 pm	☍♇	♌	24	7:23 am 4:23 am
26	6:32 am 3:32 am	□♂	♍	26	12:07 pm 9:07 am
28	10:58 am 7:58 am	△♂	♎	28	2:17 pm 11:17 am

☽ Phases & Eclipses phase	day	ET / hr:mn / PT
4th Quarter	4	12:37 pm 9:37 am
New Moon	11	2:06 pm 11:06 am
2nd Quarter	19	1:47 pm 10:47 am
Full Moon	27	3:17 am 12:17 am

Planet Ingress	day	ET / hr:mn / PT
♀ ♒	1	9:05 am 6:05 am
☉ ♓	18	5:44 am 2:44 am
⚳ ♈	20	9:23 pm
⚳ ♈	21	12:23 am
♀ ♓	25	8:11 am 5:11 am

Planetary Motion	day	ET / hr:mn / PT
☿ D	20	7:52 pm 4:52 pm

1 MONDAY
	ET	PT
☽⚻☿	12:05 am	
☉□♂	5:34 am	2:34 am
☽△♀	6:10 am	3:10 am
☽△♄	3:32 pm	12:32 pm
☽⚻♅	6:05 pm	3:05 pm
☽△♃	11:58 pm	8:58 pm

2 TUESDAY
	ET	PT
☽⚻♂	4:59 am	1:59 am
☽△☉	5:50 am	2:50 am
☽⚻♆	3:10 pm	12:10 pm
☽□♇		10:15 pm
☽△☿		10:15 pm
☿⚺♇		10:22 pm

3 WEDNESDAY
	ET	PT
☽□♇	1:15 am	
☽△☿	1:15 am	
☿⚺♇	1:22 am	
☽□♀	1:55 pm	10:55 am
☽□♄	6:47 pm	3:47 pm
☽☍♅	8:57 pm	5:57 pm

4 THURSDAY
	ET	PT
☽□♃	3:40 am	12:40 am
☽☍♂	9:51 am	6:51 am
☽□☉	12:37 pm	9:37 am
☽△♆	6:11 pm	3:11 pm
☽□☿		10:27 pm

5 FRIDAY
	ET	PT
☽□☿	1:27 am	
☽✶♇	4:20 am	1:20 am
☽✶♀	10:00 pm	7:00 pm
☽✶♄	10:20 pm	7:20 pm
☽⚻♅		9:10 pm
♀☌♄		11:07 pm

6 SATURDAY
	ET	PT
☽⚻♅	12:10 am	
♀☌♄	2:07 am	
☽✶♃	7:45 am	4:45 am
☽⚻♂	3:12 pm	12:12 pm
☽✶☉	7:56 pm	4:56 pm
☽□♆	9:40 pm	6:40 pm
♀□♅	10:33 pm	7:33 pm
☽✶☿		10:16 pm

7 SUNDAY
	ET	PT
☽✶☿	1:16 am	
☽⚺♇	7:56 am	4:56 am
☉⚺♆	8:32 pm	5:32 pm
☽⚺♄		11:31 pm

8 MONDAY
	ET	PT
☽⚺♄	2:31 am	
☽△♅	4:00 am	1:00 am
☽⚺♀	6:53 am	3:53 am
☉☌☿	8:48 am	5:48 am
☽⚺♃	12:32 pm	9:32 am
☿⚺♆	6:35 pm	3:35 pm
☽△♂	9:21 pm	6:21 pm
☽⚺☿		10:18 pm
☽✶♆		10:55 pm

9 TUESDAY
	ET	PT
☽⚺☿	1:18 am	
☽✶♆	1:55 am	
☽⚺☉	4:11 am	1:11 am
☽☌♇	12:22 pm	9:22 am

10 WEDNESDAY
	ET	PT
☿□♂	7:16 am	4:16 am
☽☌♄	7:42 am	4:42 am
☽□♅	8:51 am	5:51 am
☽☌♀	5:11 pm	2:11 pm
☽☌♃	6:29 pm	3:29 pm
☽☌☿		11:22 pm

11 THURSDAY
	ET	PT
☽☌☿	2:22 am	
☽□♂	4:55 am	1:55 am
☽⚺♆	7:27 am	4:27 am
♀☌♃	10:00 am	7:00 am
☽☌☉	2:06 pm	11:06 am
☽⚺♇	6:14 pm	3:14 pm

12 FRIDAY
	ET	PT
☽⚺♄	2:42 pm	11:42 am
☽✶♅	3:30 pm	12:30 pm
☽⚺♃		11:29 pm
☿☌♀		11:48 pm

13 SATURDAY
	ET	PT
☽⚺♃	2:29 am	
☿☌♀	2:48 am	
☽⚺☿	5:32 am	2:32 am
☽⚺♀	6:03 am	3:03 am
☽✶♂	2:55 pm	11:55 am
☽☌♆	3:11 pm	12:11 pm
♂✶♆	9:13 pm	6:13 pm
☉⚺♇	9:34 pm	6:34 pm
☽✶♇		11:29 pm
☽⚺☉		11:54 pm

14 SUNDAY
	ET	PT
☽✶♇	2:29 am	
☽⚺☉	2:54 am	
☿☌♃	4:40 pm	1:40 pm
☽✶♄		9:23 pm
☽⚺♅		9:49 pm

15 MONDAY
	ET	PT
☽✶♄	12:23 am	
☽⚺♅	12:49 am	
☽✶☿	11:50 am	8:50 am
☽✶♃	1:22 pm	10:22 am
☽✶♀	10:40 pm	7:40 pm
☽⚺♆		10:44 pm

16 TUESDAY
	ET	PT
☽⚺♆	1:44 am	
☽⚺♂	4:08 am	1:08 am
☽□♇	1:32 pm	10:32 am
☽✶☉	7:17 pm	4:17 pm

17 WEDNESDAY
	ET	PT
♀⚺♆	5:00 am	2:00 am
☽□♄	12:48 pm	9:48 am
☽☌♅	12:48 pm	9:48 am
♄□♅	2:08 pm	11:08 am
☽□☿	9:32 pm	6:32 pm
☽□♃		11:51 pm

18 THURSDAY
	ET	PT
☽□♃	2:51 am	
☽✶♆	2:30 pm	11:30 am
☽□♀	6:21 pm	3:21 pm
☽☌♂	7:48 pm	4:48 pm
☽△♇		11:28 pm

19 FRIDAY
	ET	PT
☽△♇	2:28 am	
☽□☉	1:47 pm	10:47 am
♀□♂	6:04 pm	3:04 pm
☽⚺♅		10:50 pm
☽△♄		11:15 pm

20 SATURDAY
	ET	PT
☽⚺♅	1:50 am	
☽△♄	2:15 am	
☽△☿	9:20 am	6:20 am
☽△♃	4:46 pm	1:46 pm

21 SUNDAY
	ET	PT
☽□♆	3:10 am	12:10 am
☽⚺♂	11:06 am	8:06 am
☽△♀	1:39 pm	10:39 am
☽⚻♇	2:45 pm	11:45 am
♀⚺♇		9:31 pm

22 MONDAY
	ET	PT
♀⚺♇	12:31 am	
☽△☉	6:47 am	3:47 am
☽✶♅	1:09 pm	10:09 am
☽⚻♄	1:55 pm	10:55 am
☽⚻☿	8:31 pm	5:31 pm

23 TUESDAY
	ET	PT
☽⚻♃	4:14 am	1:14 am
☽△♆	1:06 pm	10:06 am
☽✶♂	10:59 pm	7:59 pm
☽☍♇	11:54 pm	8:54 pm

24 WEDNESDAY
	ET	PT
☽⚻♀	4:47 am	1:47 am
☽⚻☉	7:18 pm	4:18 pm
☽□♅	8:49 pm	5:49 pm
♂△♇	8:52 pm	5:52 pm
☽☍♄	9:52 pm	6:52 pm

25 THURSDAY
	ET	PT
☽☍☿	4:56 am	1:56 am
☽☍♃	11:40 am	8:40 am
☉✶♅	4:13 pm	1:13 pm
☽⚻♆	7:09 pm	4:09 pm

26 FRIDAY
	ET	PT
☽⚻♇	5:12 am	2:12 am
☽□♂	6:32 am	3:32 am
☉⚺♄	9:25 am	6:25 am
☽☍♀	2:50 pm	11:50 am
☽△♅		9:54 pm
☽⚻♄		11:09 pm

27 SATURDAY
	ET	PT
☽△♅	12:54 am	
☽⚻♄	2:09 am	
☽☍☉	3:17 am	12:17 am
☽⚻☿	10:25 am	7:25 am
☽⚻♃	3:40 pm	12:40 pm
☽☍♆	10:06 pm	7:06 pm

28 SUNDAY
	ET	PT
☽△♇	7:42 am	4:42 am
☽△♂	10:58 am	7:58 am
☽⚻♀	9:36 pm	6:36 pm
☽⚻♅		11:49 pm

Eastern time in bold type
Pacific time in medium type

FEBRUARY 2021

DATE	SID.TIME	SUN	MOON	NODE	MERCURY	VENUS	MARS	JUPITER	SATURN	URANUS	NEPTUNE	PLUTO	CERES	PALLAS	JUNO	VESTA	CHIRON
1 M	8 45 41	12♒20 16	23♍17	18♊25℞	26♒19℞	29♑16	12♉33	10♒04	5♒17	6♉51	19♓16	25♑13	22♓28	18♒17	13♐17	20♍46℞	5♈55
2 T	8 49 37	13 21 09	7♎25	18 18	25 59	0♒31	13 05	10 18	5 24	6 52	19 18	25 15	22 50	18 38	13 33	20 40	5 57
3 W	8 53 34	14 22 01	21 36	18 13	25 27	1 46	13 37	10 32	5 31	6 53	19 20	25 16	23 12	18 58	13 48	20 33	6 00
4 Th	8 57 30	15 22 52	5♏45	18 11D	24 45	3 01	14 10	10 46	5 38	6 54	19 22	25 18	23 34	19 19	14 04	20 26	6 02
5 F	9 1 27	16 23 43	19 52	18 10	23 54	4 17	14 42	11 00	5 45	6 56	19 24	25 20	23 56	19 39	14 19	20 18	6 05
6 Sa	9 5 23	17 24 32	3♐56	18 11	22 56	5 32	15 15	11 15	5 52	6 57	19 26	25 22	24 18	19 59	14 34	20 10	6 07
7 Su	9 9 20	18 25 21	17 55	18 12℞	21 51	6 47	15 47	11 29	5 59	6 58	19 28	25 24	24 40	20 20	14 50	20 02	6 10
8 M	9 13 17	19 26 09	1♑49	18 11	20 42	8 02	16 20	11 43	6 06	6 59	19 30	25 26	25 02	20 40	15 05	19 53	6 12
9 T	9 17 13	20 26 56	15 36	18 08	19 31	9 17	16 53	11 57	6 13	7 00	19 32	25 28	25 24	21 00	15 19	19 43	6 15
10 W	9 21 10	21 27 42	29 15	18 02	18 19	10 32	17 26	12 12	6 20	7 02	19 34	25 30	25 46	21 21	15 34	19 33	6 18
11 Th	9 25 6	22 28 26	12♒43	17 53	17 09	11 48	17 59	12 26	6 27	7 03	19 36	25 31	26 09	21 41	15 49	19 23	6 20
12 F	9 29 3	23 29 09	25 58	17 42	16 03	13 03	18 33	12 40	6 34	7 05	19 38	25 33	26 31	22 01	16 03	19 12	6 23
13 Sa	9 32 59	24 29 51	8♓58	17 30	15 01	14 18	19 06	12 54	6 41	7 06	19 40	25 35	26 53	22 22	16 17	19 01	6 26
14 Su	9 36 56	25 30 31	21 43	17 18	14 05	15 33	19 39	13 08	6 48	7 08	19 42	25 37	27 16	22 42	16 31	18 50	6 29
15 M	9 40 52	26 31 10	4♈11	17 06	13 16	16 48	20 13	13 22	6 55	7 09	19 44	25 39	27 38	23 02	16 45	18 38	6 32
16 T	9 44 49	27 31 47	16 24	16 57	12 35	18 03	20 47	13 36	7 02	7 11	19 47	25 40	28 01	23 22	16 59	18 26	6 35
17 W	9 48 46	28 32 22	28 25	16 50	12 01	19 18	21 20	13 50	7 08	7 13	19 49	25 42	28 24	23 43	17 13	18 13	6 37
18 Th	9 52 42	29 32 56	10♉17	16 46	11 35	20 33	21 54	14 04	7 15	7 14	19 51	25 44	28 46	24 03	17 26	18 00	6 40
19 F	9 56 39	0♓33 28	22 06	16 44D	11 16	21 49	22 28	14 18	7 22	7 16	19 53	25 46	29 09	24 23	17 39	17 47	6 43
20 Sa	10 0 35	1 33 58	3♊55	16 44	11 05	23 04	23 02	14 32	7 29	7 18	19 55	25 47	29 32	24 43	17 52	17 34	6 46
21 Su	10 4 32	2 34 26	15 52	16 44℞	11 01D	24 19	23 36	14 46	7 36	7 20	19 57	25 49	29 55	25 03	18 05	17 20	6 49
22 M	10 8 28	3 34 52	28 01	16 44	11 05	25 34	24 10	15 00	7 42	7 22	20 00	25 51	0♈18	25 24	18 18	17 06	6 52
23 T	10 12 25	4 35 17	10♋27	16 41	11 14	26 49	24 44	15 14	7 49	7 23	20 02	25 52	0 41	25 44	18 31	16 52	6 55
24 W	10 16 21	5 35 40	23 15	16 37	11 30	28 04	25 19	15 28	7 55	7 25	20 04	25 54	1 04	26 04	18 43	16 37	6 59
25 Th	10 20 18	6 36 00	6♌27	16 29	11 51	29 19	25 53	15 42	8 02	7 28	20 06	25 55	1 27	26 24	18 55	16 22	7 02
26 F	10 24 15	7 36 19	20 03	16 20	12 18	0♓34	26 27	15 56	8 09	7 30	20 09	25 57	1 50	26 44	19 07	16 07	7 05
27 Sa	10 28 11	8 36 36	4♍03	16 08	12 50	1 49	27 02	16 09	8 15	7 32	20 11	25 59	2 13	27 04	19 19	15 52	7 08
28 Su	10 32 8	9 36 52	18 21	15 56	13 26	3 04	27 36	16 23	8 22	7 34	20 13	26 00	2 36	27 24	19 31	15 37	7 11

EPHEMERIS CALCULATED FOR 12 MIDNIGHT GREENWICH MEAN TIME. ALL OTHER DATA AND FACING ASPECTARIAN PAGE IN **EASTERN TIME (BOLD)** AND PACIFIC TIME (REGULAR).

MARCH 2021

☽ Last Aspect day	ET / hr:mn / PT		asp	☽ Ingress sign	day	ET / hr:mn / PT	
2	**9:09 am**	6:09 am	□♇	♏	2	**3:38 pm**	12:38 pm
4	**11:10 am**	8:10 am	✶♇	♐	4	**5:43 pm**	2:43 pm
6	**4:44 am**	1:44 am	□♆	♑	6	**9:20 pm**	6:20 pm
8	**7:52 pm**	4:52 pm	☌♇	♒	8		11:41 pm
8	**7:52 pm**	4:52 pm	☌♇	♒	9	**2:41 am**	
10	**10:32 pm**	7:32 pm	☌☿	♓	11	**9:44 am**	6:44 am
13	**11:38 am**	8:38 am	✶♇	♈	13	**6:44 pm**	3:44 pm
15	**11:40 pm**	8:40 pm	□♇	♉	16	**6:56 am**	3:56 am
18	**4:40 pm**	1:40 pm	✶☉	♊	18	**7:47 pm**	4:47 pm
21	**8:04 am**	5:04 am	□♀	♋	21	**8:18 am**	5:18 am

☽ Last Aspect day	ET / hr:mn / PT		asp	☽ Ingress sign	day	ET / hr:mn / PT	
23	**11:26 am**	8:26 am	☍♇	♌	23	**5:56 pm**	2:56 pm
25	**9:27 am**	6:27 am	☍♃	♍	25	**11:25 pm**	8:25 pm
27	**7:48 pm**	4:48 pm	△♇	♎	27		10:22 pm
27	**7:48 pm**	4:48 pm	△♇	♎	28	**1:22 am**	
29	**8:08 pm**	5:08 pm	□♇	♏	29		10:33 pm
29	**8:08 pm**	5:08 pm	□♇	♏	30	**1:33 am**	
31	**8:29 pm**	5:29 pm	✶♇	♐	31		10:59 pm
31	**8:29 pm**	5:29 pm	✶♇	♐	4/1	**1:59 am**	

☽ Phases & Eclipses phase	day	ET / hr:mn / PT	
4th Quarter	5	**8:30 pm**	5:30 pm
New Moon	13	**5:21 am**	2:21 am
2nd Quarter	21	**10:40 am**	7:40 am
Full Moon	28	**2:48 pm**	11:48 am

Planet Ingress		day	ET / hr:mn / PT	
♂	♊	3	**10:30 pm**	7:30 pm
♀	♓	7	**4:06 pm**	1:06 pm
☿	♓	15	**6:26 pm**	3:26 pm
☉	♈	20	**5:37 am**	2:37 am
♀	♈	21	**10:16 am**	7:16 am

Planetary Motion	day	ET / hr:mn / PT

1 MONDAY
☽ ⚻ ♅ **2:49 am**
☽ △ ♄ **4:17 am** 1:17 am
☽ ⚻ ☉ **8:42 am** 5:42 am
☽ △ ☿ **2:27 pm** 11:27 am
☽ △ ♃ **5:57 pm** 2:57 pm
☽ ⚻ ♆ **11:40 pm** 8:40 pm

2 TUESDAY
☽ □ ♇ **9:09 am** 6:09 am
☽ ⚻ ♂ **2:22 pm** 11:22 am

3 WEDNESDAY
☽ △ ♀ **3:39 am** 12:39 am
☽ ☍ ♅ **4:22 am** 1:22 am
☽ □ ♄ **6:05 am** 3:05 am
♀ ✶ ♅ **12:09 pm** 9:09 am
☽ △ ☉ **1:52 pm** 10:52 am
☽ □ ☿ **7:01 pm** 4:01 pm
☽ □ ♃ **8:22 pm** 5:22 pm
☽ △ ♆ 10:30 pm

4 THURSDAY
☽ △ ♆ **1:30 am**
♀ ⚺ ♄ **10:14 am** 7:14 am
☽ ✶ ♇ **11:10 am** 8:10 am
☽ ☍ ♂ **6:32 pm** 3:32 pm
☿ ☌ ♃ **10:27 pm** 7:27 pm

5 FRIDAY
☽ ⚻ ♅ **6:55 am** 3:55 am
☽ ✶ ♄ **8:56 am** 5:56 am
☽ □ ♀ **10:58 am** 7:58 am
☽ □ ☉ **8:30 pm** 5:30 pm
☽ ✶ ♃ 9:07 pm
☽ ✶ ☿ 10:36 pm

6 SATURDAY
☽ ✶ ♃ **12:07 am**
☽ ✶ ☿ **1:36 am**
☽ □ ♆ **4:44 am** 1:44 am
☽ ⚺ ♇ **2:39 pm** 11:39 am
☽ ⚻ ♂ 9:29 pm

7 SUNDAY
☽ ⚻ ♂ **12:29 am**
☽ △ ♅ **11:09 am** 8:09 am
☽ ⚺ ♄ **1:28 pm** 10:28 am
☽ ✶ ♀ **8:29 pm** 5:29 pm
☿ ⚺ ♆ **9:12 pm** 6:12 pm

8 MONDAY
☽ ✶ ☉ **5:15 am** 2:15 am
☽ ⚺ ♃ **5:39 am** 2:39 am
☽ ✶ ♆ **9:41 am** 6:41 am
☽ ⚺ ☿ **10:44 am** 7:44 am
☉ ⚺ ♃ **12:04 pm** 9:04 am
☽ ☌ ♇ **7:52 pm** 4:52 pm

9 TUESDAY
☽ △ ♂ **8:23 am** 5:23 am
☽ □ ♅ **5:06 pm** 2:06 pm
☽ ☌ ♄ **7:45 pm** 4:45 pm

10 WEDNESDAY
☽ ⚺ ♀ **8:16 am** 5:16 am
☽ ☌ ♃ **12:58 pm** 9:58 am
☽ ⚺ ☉ **4:08 pm** 1:08 pm
☽ ⚺ ♆ **4:21 pm** 1:21 pm
☉ ☌ ♆ **7:01 pm** 4:01 pm
☽ ☌ ☿ **10:32 pm** 7:32 pm
☽ ⚺ ♇ 11:48 pm

11 THURSDAY
☽ ⚺ ♇ **2:48 am**
☽ □ ♂ **6:16 pm** 3:16 pm
☽ ✶ ♅ 9:50 pm

12 FRIDAY
☽ ✶ ♅ **12:50 am**
☽ ⚺ ♄ **3:49 am** 12:49 am
♀ ⚺ ♃ **6:53 pm** 3:53 pm
☿ ⚺ ♇ **8:41 pm** 5:41 pm
☽ ⚺ ♃ **10:11 pm** 7:11 pm
☽ ☌ ♀ **10:29 pm** 7:29 pm
☽ ☌ ♆ 9:52 pm

13 SATURDAY
☽ ☌ ♆ **12:52 am**
☽ ☌ ☉ **5:21 am** 2:21 am
☽ ✶ ♇ **11:38 am** 8:38 am
☽ ⚺ ☿ **1:17 pm** 10:17 am
♀ ☌ ♆ **11:08 pm** 8:08 pm

14 SUNDAY
☽ ✶ ♂ **7:28 am** 4:28 am
☽ ⚺ ♅ **11:37 am** 8:37 am
☽ ✶ ♄ **2:58 pm** 11:58 am

15 MONDAY
☽ ✶ ♃ **10:40 am** 7:40 am
☽ ⚺ ♆ **12:35 pm** 9:35 am
☽ ⚺ ♀ **4:39 pm** 1:39 pm
☽ ⚺ ☉ **10:22 pm** 7:22 pm
☽ □ ♇ **11:40 pm** 8:40 pm

16 TUESDAY
☽ ✶ ☿ **8:31 am** 5:31 am
☉ ✶ ♇ **2:26 pm** 11:26 am
☽ ⚺ ♂ **10:12 pm** 7:12 pm
☽ ☌ ♅ **11:37 pm** 8:37 pm

17 WEDNESDAY
☽ □ ♄ **3:20 am** 12:20 am
☽ □ ♃ 9:14 pm
☽ ✶ ♆ 10:16 pm

18 THURSDAY
☽ □ ♃ **12:14 am**
☽ ✶ ♆ **1:16 am**
♂ ⚺ ♅ **4:48 am** 1:48 am
☽ ✶ ♀ **12:24 pm** 9:24 am
☽ △ ♇ **12:30 pm** 9:30 am
♀ ✶ ♇ **1:20 pm** 10:20 am
☽ ✶ ☉ **4:40 pm** 1:40 pm

19 FRIDAY
☽ □ ☿ **5:28 am** 2:28 am
☽ ⚺ ♅ **12:52 pm** 9:52 am
☽ ☌ ♂ **2:25 pm** 11:25 am
☽ △ ♄ **4:50 pm** 1:50 pm

20 SATURDAY
☽ △ ♃ **2:14 pm** 11:14 am
☽ □ ♆ **2:20 pm** 11:20 am
♃ ⚺ ♆ **9:51 pm** 6:51 pm
☽ ⚻ ♇ 10:17 pm

21 SUNDAY
☽ ⚻ ♇ **1:17 am**
☽ □ ♀ **8:04 am** 5:04 am
☽ □ ☉ **10:40 am** 7:40 am
☿ ✶ ♅ **7:35 pm** 4:35 pm
♂ △ ♄ **10:35 pm** 7:35 pm
☽ ✶ ♅ 10:02 pm
☽ △ ☿ 10:46 pm

22 MONDAY
☽ ✶ ♅ **1:02 am**
☽ △ ☿ **1:46 am**
☽ ⚻ ♄ **5:02 am** 2:02 am
☽ ⚺ ♂ **5:19 am** 2:19 am
☽ △ ♆ 10:14 pm
☽ ⚻ ♃ 10:56 pm

23 TUESDAY
☽ △ ♆ **1:14 am**
☽ ⚻ ♃ **1:56 am**
☿ ⚺ ♄ **6:12 am** 3:12 am
☽ ☍ ♇ **11:26 am** 8:26 am
☿ □ ♂ **11:26 pm** 8:26 pm
☽ △ ♀ **11:50 pm** 8:50 pm
☽ △ ☉ 9:54 pm

24 WEDNESDAY
☽ △ ☉ **12:54 am**
☽ □ ♅ **9:45 am** 6:45 am
☽ ☍ ♄ **1:38 pm** 10:38 am
☽ ✶ ♂ **4:08 pm** 1:08 pm
☽ ⚻ ☿ **5:28 pm** 2:28 pm

25 THURSDAY
☽ ⚻ ♆ **8:07 am** 5:07 am
☽ ☍ ♃ **9:27 am** 6:27 am
☽ ⚻ ♇ **5:28 pm** 2:28 pm
☉ ☌ ♀ 11:58 pm

26 FRIDAY
☉ ☌ ♀ **2:58 am**
☽ ⚻ ☉ **9:52 am** 6:52 am
☽ ⚻ ♀ **10:00 am** 7:00 am
☽ △ ♅ **2:17 pm** 11:17 am
☽ ⚻ ♄ **6:00 pm** 3:00 pm
☽ □ ♂ **10:16 pm** 7:16 pm

27 SATURDAY
☽ ☍ ☿ **3:37 am** 12:37 am
☽ ☍ ♆ **11:05 am** 8:05 am
☽ ⚻ ♃ **12:55 pm** 9:55 am
☽ △ ♇ **7:48 pm** 4:48 pm

28 SUNDAY
♀ ⚺ ♅ **12:53 pm** 9:53 am
☽ ☍ ☉ **2:48 pm** 11:48 am
☽ ⚻ ♅ **3:40 pm** 12:40 pm
☽ ☍ ♀ **3:55 pm** 12:55 pm
☽ △ ♄ **7:21 pm** 4:21 pm
☽ △ ♂ 10:12 pm

29 MONDAY
☽ △ ♂ **1:12 am**
☉ ⚺ ♅ **4:34 am** 1:34 am
☽ ⚻ ☿ **10:16 am** 7:16 am
☽ ⚻ ♆ **11:42 am** 8:42 am
☽ △ ♃ **2:01 pm** 11:01 am
☽ □ ♇ **8:08 pm** 5:08 pm
☿ ☌ ♆ **11:24 pm** 8:24 pm

30 TUESDAY
♀ ✶ ♄ **11:47 am** 8:47 am
☽ ☍ ♅ **3:54 pm** 12:54 pm
☽ ⚻ ☉ **6:16 pm** 3:16 pm
☽ □ ♄ **7:39 pm** 4:39 pm
☽ ⚻ ♀ **8:20 pm** 5:20 pm
☿ ⚺ ♃ **11:54 pm** 8:54 pm

31 WEDNESDAY
☽ ⚻ ♂ **3:17 am** 12:17 am
☽ △ ♆ **11:59 am** 8:59 am
☽ □ ♃ **2:52 pm** 11:52 am
☽ △ ☿ **4:35 pm** 1:35 pm
☉ ✶ ♄ **5:04 pm** 2:04 pm
☽ ✶ ♇ **8:29 pm** 5:29 pm

Eastern time in bold type
Pacific time in medium type

MARCH 2021

DATE	SID.TIME	SUN	MOON	NODE	MERCURY	VENUS	MARS	JUPITER	SATURN	URANUS	NEPTUNE	PLUTO	CERES	PALLAS	JUNO	VESTA	CHIRON
1 M	10 36 4	10♓37 05	2♎52	15♊44℞	14♒06	4♓19	28♉11	16♒37	8♒28	7♉36	20♓15	26♑02	2♈59	27♒44	19♐42	15♍22℞	7♈14
2 T	10 40 1	11 37 17	17 28	15 34	14 51	5 34	28 46	16 50	8 34	7 38	20 17	26 03	3 22	28 04	19 53	15 06	7 18
3 W	10 43 57	12 37 27	2♏02	15 27	15 39	6 49	29 20	17 04	8 41	7 41	20 20	26 05	3 46	28 23	20 04	14 50	7 21
4 Th	10 47 54	13 37 36	16 29	15 23	16 30	8 04	29 55	17 17	8 47	7 43	20 22	26 06	4 09	28 43	20 15	14 35	7 24
5 F	10 51 50	14 37 44	0♐46	15 22	17 25	9 18	0♊30	17 31	8 53	7 45	20 24	26 08	4 32	29 03	20 26	14 19	7 27
6 Sa	10 55 47	15 37 49	14 49	15 21	18 22	10 33	1 05	17 44	9 00	7 48	20 27	26 09	4 56	29 23	20 36	14 03	7 31
7 Su	10 59 44	16 37 54	28 40	15 21	19 23	11 48	1 40	17 58	9 06	7 50	20 29	26 11	5 19	29 43	20 46	13 48	7 34
8 M	11 3 40	17 37 57	12♑18	15 20	20 25	13 03	2 14	18 11	9 12	7 52	20 31	26 12	5 42	0♓02	20 56	13 32	7 37
9 T	11 7 37	18 37 58	25 44	15 16	21 31	14 18	2 50	18 24	9 18	7 55	20 33	26 13	6 06	0 22	21 06	13 16	7 41
10 W	11 11 33	19 37 57	9♒00	15 09	22 38	15 33	3 25	18 38	9 24	7 57	20 36	26 15	6 29	0 42	21 16	13 00	7 44
11 Th	11 15 30	20 37 55	22 04	14 59	23 48	16 48	4 00	18 51	9 30	8 00	20 38	26 16	6 53	1 01	21 25	12 45	7 48
12 F	11 19 26	21 37 51	4♓57	14 47	25 00	18 03	4 35	19 04	9 36	8 03	20 40	26 17	7 16	1 21	21 34	12 29	7 51
13 Sa	11 23 23	22 37 45	17 39	14 33	26 13	19 17	5 10	19 17	9 42	8 05	20 43	26 19	7 40	1 40	21 43	12 14	7 54
14 Su	11 27 19	23 37 37	0♈08	14 19	27 29	20 32	5 45	19 30	9 48	8 08	20 45	26 20	8 04	2 00	21 51	11 59	7 58
15 M	11 31 16	24 37 27	12 26	14 07	28 46	21 47	6 21	19 43	9 53	8 11	20 47	26 21	8 27	2 19	22 00	11 44	8 01
16 T	11 35 13	25 37 15	24 32	13 56	0♓05	23 02	6 56	19 56	9 59	8 13	20 49	26 22	8 51	2 39	22 08	11 29	8 05
17 W	11 39 9	26 37 01	6♉29	13 47	1 26	24 17	7 31	20 09	10 05	8 16	20 52	26 23	9 14	2 58	22 16	11 14	8 08
18 Th	11 43 6	27 36 44	18 19	13 42	2 48	25 31	8 07	20 22	10 10	8 19	20 54	26 25	9 38	3 17	22 23	11 00	8 12
19 F	11 47 2	28 36 26	0♊06	13 39	4 12	26 46	8 42	20 35	10 16	8 22	20 56	26 26	10 02	3 36	22 30	10 46	8 15
20 Sa	11 50 59	29 36 05	11 55	13 38D	5 37	28 01	9 18	20 47	10 21	8 25	20 58	26 27	10 25	3 56	22 38	10 32	8 19
21 Su	11 54 55	0♈35 42	23 50	13 39℞	7 04	29 16	9 53	21 00	10 27	8 27	21 01	26 28	10 49	4 15	22 44	10 18	8 22
22 M	11 58 52	1 35 17	5♋56	13 39	8 32	0♈30	10 29	21 12	10 32	8 30	21 03	26 29	11 13	4 34	22 51	10 05	8 26
23 T	12 2 48	2 34 50	18 20	13 37	10 01	1 45	11 05	21 25	10 38	8 33	21 05	26 30	11 37	4 53	22 57	9 52	8 29
24 W	12 6 45	3 34 20	1♌07	13 34	11 32	3 00	11 40	21 37	10 43	8 36	21 07	26 31	12 00	5 12	23 03	9 40	8 33
25 Th	12 10 42	4 33 48	14 20	13 29	13 05	4 14	12 16	21 50	10 48	8 39	21 10	26 32	12 24	5 31	23 09	9 27	8 36
26 F	12 14 38	5 33 14	28 01	13 21	14 38	5 29	12 52	22 02	10 53	8 42	21 12	26 33	12 48	5 49	23 14	9 16	8 40
27 Sa	12 18 35	6 32 37	12♍09	13 11	16 13	6 43	13 27	22 14	10 58	8 45	21 14	26 34	13 12	6 08	23 20	9 04	8 43
28 Su	12 22 31	7 31 58	26 42	13 01	17 50	7 58	14 03	22 26	11 03	8 48	21 16	26 35	13 36	6 27	23 24	8 53	8 47
29 M	12 26 28	8 31 17	11♎32	12 51	19 28	9 13	14 39	22 38	11 08	8 51	21 18	26 36	13 59	6 45	23 29	8 42	8 50
30 T	12 30 24	9 30 34	26 32	12 43	21 07	10 27	15 15	22 50	11 13	8 54	21 21	26 36	14 23	7 04	23 33	8 32	8 54
31 W	12 34 21	10 29 50	11♏30	12 37	22 47	11 42	15 51	23 02	11 18	8 58	21 23	26 37	14 47	7 23	23 37	8 22	8 57

EPHEMERIS CALCULATED FOR 12 MIDNIGHT GREENWICH MEAN TIME. ALL OTHER DATA AND FACING ASPECTARIAN PAGE IN **EASTERN TIME (BOLD)** AND PACIFIC TIME (REGULAR).

APRIL 2021

☽ Last Aspect day	ET / hr:mn / PT		asp	☽ Ingress sign	day	ET / hr:mn / PT	
3/31	**8:29 pm**	5:29 pm	⚹♇	♐	1	**1:59 am**	
2		10:24 pm	□☿	♑	3	**4:13 am**	1:13 am
3	**1:24 am**		□☿	♑	3	**4:13 am**	1:13 am
5	**3:05 am**	12:05 am	☌♇	♒	5	**9:04 am**	6:04 am
7	**6:05 am**	3:05 am	☌♃	♓	7	**4:30 pm**	1:30 pm
9	**7:48 pm**	4:48 pm	⚹♇	♈	9		11:11 pm
9	**7:48 pm**	4:48 pm	⚹♇	♈	10	**2:11 am**	
12	**8:06 am**	5:06 am	☌♀	♉	12	**1:44 pm**	10:44 am
14	**8:00 pm**	5:00 pm	△♇	♊	14		11:35 pm
14	**8:00 pm**	5:00 pm	△♇	♊	15	**2:35 am**	

☽ Last Aspect day	ET / hr:mn / PT		asp	☽ Ingress sign	day	ET / hr:mn / PT	
17	**11:03 am**	8:03 am	⚹☉	♋	17	**3:25 pm**	12:25 pm
19	**8:03 pm**	5:03 pm	☍♇	♌	19		11:11 pm
19	**8:03 pm**	5:03 pm	☍♇	♌	20	**2:11 am**	
22	**8:05 am**	5:05 am	⚹♂	♍	22	**9:08 am**	6:08 am
24	**6:50 am**	3:50 am	△♇	♎	24	**12:06 pm**	9:06 am
26	**8:40 am**	5:40 am	△♃	♏	26	**12:18 pm**	9:18 am
28	**8:31 am**	5:31 am	□♃	♐	28	**11:42 am**	8:42 am
30	**9:27 am**	6:27 am	⚹♃	♑	30	**12:16 pm**	9:16 am

☽ Phases & Eclipses phase	day	ET / hr:mn / PT	
4th Quarter	4	**6:02 am**	3:02 am
New Moon	11	**10:31 pm**	7:31 pm
2nd Quarter	19		11:59 pm
2nd Quarter	20	**2:59 pm**	
Full Moon	26	**11:32 pm**	8:32 pm

Planet Ingress		day	ET / hr:mn / PT	
☿	♈	3	**11:41 pm**	8:41 pm
♀	♉	14	**2:22 pm**	11:22 am
☿	♉	19	**6:29 am**	3:29 am
☉	♉	19	**4:33 pm**	1:33 pm
♂	♋	23	**7:49 am**	4:49 am

Planetary Motion		day	ET / hr:mn / PT	
⚵	℞	12	**6:13 am**	3:13 am
⚶	D	20	**3:06 am**	12:06 am
♇	℞	27	**4:04 pm**	1:04 pm

1 THURSDAY
☽ ⚻ ♅ **4:54 pm** 1:54 pm
☽ ⚹ ♄ **8:53 pm** 5:53 pm
☽ △ ☉ **10:46 pm** 7:46 pm
☽ △ ♀ 10:56 pm
☿ ⚹ ♇ 11:04 pm

2 FRIDAY
☽ △ ♀ **1:56 am**
☿ ⚹ ♇ **2:04 am**
☽ ☍ ♂ **6:40 am** 3:40 am
☽ □ ♆ **1:42 pm** 10:42 am
☽ ⚹ ♃ **5:17 pm** 2:17 pm
☽ ⚺ ♇ **10:30 pm** 7:30 pm
☽ □ ☿ 10:24 pm

3 SATURDAY
☽ □ ☿ **1:24 am**
☽ △ ♅ **8:05 pm** 5:05 pm
☽ ⚺ ♄ 9:21 pm

4 SUNDAY
☽ ⚺ ♄ **12:21 am**
☽ □ ☉ **6:02 am** 3:02 am
☽ □ ♀ **10:33 am** 7:33 am
☽ ⚻ ♂ **12:46 pm** 9:46 am
☽ ⚹ ♆ **5:55 pm** 2:55 pm
☽ ⚺ ♃ **10:18 pm** 7:18 pm

5 MONDAY
☽ ☌ ♇ **3:05 am** 12:05 am
☽ ⚹ ☿ **2:19 pm** 11:19 am
☽ □ ♅ 10:58 pm

6 TUESDAY
☽ □ ♅ **1:58 am**
☽ ☌ ♄ **6:32 am** 3:32 am
♀ ⚹ ♂ **7:18 am** 4:18 am
☽ ⚹ ☉ **4:40 pm** 1:40 pm
☽ △ ♂ **9:55 pm** 6:55 pm
☽ ⚹ ♀ **10:44 pm** 7:44 pm
☽ ⚺ ♆ 9:49 pm

7 WEDNESDAY
☽ ⚺ ♆ **12:49 am**
☽ ☌ ♃ **6:05 am** 3:05 am
☽ ⚺ ♇ **10:18 am** 7:18 am
♀ ⚺ ♆ **8:55 pm** 5:55 pm

8 THURSDAY
☽ ⚺ ☿ **7:36 am** 4:36 am
☽ ⚹ ♅ **10:24 am** 7:24 am
☽ ⚺ ♄ **3:13 pm** 12:13 pm
☿ ⚺ ♅ 11:37 pm

9 FRIDAY
☿ ⚺ ♅ **2:37 am**
☽ ⚺ ☉ **6:19 am** 3:19 am
☽ □ ♂ **9:49 am** 6:49 am
☽ ☌ ♆ **10:04 am** 7:04 am
☽ ⚺ ♀ **2:05 pm** 11:05 am
♂ □ ♆ **3:18 pm** 12:18 pm
☽ ⚺ ♃ **4:15 pm** 1:15 pm
☽ ⚹ ♇ **7:48 pm** 4:48 pm

10 SATURDAY
☿ ⚹ ♄ **11:09 am** 8:09 am
♀ ⚹ ♃ **2:53 pm** 11:53 am
☽ ⚺ ♅ **8:58 pm** 5:58 pm
☽ ⚹ ♄ 11:01 pm

11 SUNDAY
☽ ⚹ ♄ **2:01 am**
☽ ☌ ☿ **4:46 am** 1:46 am
☉ ⚺ ♆ **7:10 am** 4:10 am
☽ ⚺ ♆ **9:18 pm** 6:18 pm
☽ ☌ ☉ **10:31 pm** 7:31 pm
♀ □ ♇ **11:20 pm** 8:20 pm
☽ ⚹ ♂ 9:00 pm

12 MONDAY
☽ ⚹ ♂ **12:00 am**
☽ ⚹ ♃ **4:24 am** 1:24 am
☽ □ ♇ **7:12 am** 4:12 am
☽ ☌ ♀ **8:06 am** 5:06 am

13 TUESDAY
☽ ☌ ♅ **9:18 am** 6:18 am
☽ □ ♄ **2:30 pm** 11:30 am
☉ ⚹ ♂ **7:09 pm** 4:09 pm

14 WEDNESDAY
☽ ⚺ ☿ **5:14 am** 2:14 am
☽ ⚹ ♆ **10:03 am** 7:03 am
☽ ⚺ ♂ **3:54 pm** 12:54 pm
☽ ⚺ ☉ **4:37 pm** 1:37 pm
☽ □ ♃ **6:02 pm** 3:02 pm
☽ △ ♇ **8:00 pm** 5:00 pm

15 THURSDAY
☽ ⚺ ♀ **4:01 am** 1:0⁻ am
☿ ⚺ ♆ **9:32 am** 6:32 am
☉ ⚹ ♃ **12:59 pm** 9:59 am
☽ ⚺ ♅ **10:38 pm** 7:38 pm

16 FRIDAY
☽ △ ♄ **3:53 am** 12:53 am
☉ □ ♇ **9:27 am** 6:27 am
☽ □ ♆ **11:15 pm** 8:15 pm
♂ △ ♃ 10:14 pm

17 SATURDAY
♂ △ ♃ **1:14 am**
☽ ⚹ ☿ **7:05 am** 4:05 am
☽ △ ♃ **7:53 am** 4:53 am
☽ ☌ ♂ **8:08 am** 5:08 am
☽ ⚻ ♇ **8:58 am** 5:58 am
☽ ⚹ ☉ **11:03 am** 8:03 am
☿ ⚹ ♃ **12:00 pm** 9:00 am
☿ ⚹ ♂ **3:09 pm** 12:09 pm
☿ □ ♇ **5:49 pm** 2:49 pm
☽ ⚹ ♀ **11:49 pm** 8:49 pm
♂ ⚻ ♇ 9:26 pm

18 SUNDAY
♂ ⚻ ♇ **12:26 am**
☽ ⚹ ♅ **11:19 am** 8:19 am
☽ ⚻ ♄ **4:24 pm** 1:24 pm
☉ ☌ ☿ **9:50 pm** 6:50 pm

19 MONDAY
☽ △ ♆ **10:56 am** 7:56 am
☽ ⚻ ♃ **7:49 pm** 4:49 pm
☽ ☍ ♇ **8:03 pm** 5:03 pm
☽ ⚺ ♂ **10:15 pm** 7:15 pm
☽ □ ☉ 11:59 pm

20 TUESDAY
☽ □ ☉ **2:59 am**
☽ □ ☿ **6:08 am** 3:08 am
♃ ⚺ ♇ **3:09 pm** 12:09 pm
☽ □ ♀ **4:21 pm** 1:21 pm
☽ □ ♅ **9:11 pm** 6:11 pm
☽ ☍ ♄ 10:56 pm

21 WEDNESDAY
☽ ☍ ♄ **1:56 am**
☽ ⚻ ♆ **7:07 pm** 4:07 pm

22 THURSDAY
☽ ⚻ ♇ **3:29 am** 12:29 am
☽ ☍ ♃ **3:54 am** 12:54 am
☽ ⚹ ♂ **8:05 am** 5:05 am
☽ △ ☉ **2:06 pm** 11:06 am
♀ ☌ ♅ **9:01 pm** 6:01 pm
☽ △ ☿ **10:47 pm** 7:47 pm
☽ △ ♅ 11:57 pm

23 FRIDAY
☽ △ ♅ **2:57 am**
☽ △ ♀ **3:30 am** 12:30 am
☽ ⚻ ♄ **7:19 am** 4:19 am
☽ ☍ ♆ **11:10 pm** 8:10 pm
☿ ☌ ♅ 11:42 pm

24 SATURDAY
☿ ☌ ♅ **2:42 am**
☽ △ ♇ **6:50 am** 3:50 am
☽ ⚻ ♃ **7:47 am** 4:47 am
☽ □ ♂ **1:19 pm** 10:19 am
☽ ⚻ ☉ **8:19 pm** 5:19 pm
♀ □ ♄ 9:22 pm

25 SUNDAY
♀ □ ♄ **12:22 am**
☽ ⚻ ♅ **4:58 am** 1:58 am
☿ □ ♄ **7:58 am** 4:58 am
☽ △ ♄ **9:02 am** 6:02 am
☽ ⚻ ☿ **9:13 am** 6:13 am
☽ ⚻ ♀ **9:48 am** 6:48 am
☿ ☌ ♀ **6:19 pm** 3:19 pm
☽ ⚻ ♆ 9:01 pm

26 MONDAY
☽ ⚻ ♆ **12:01 am**
☽ □ ♇ **7:15 am** 4:15 am
☽ △ ♃ **8:40 am** 5:40 am
☽ △ ♂ **3:29 pm** 12:29 pm
☽ ☍ ☉ **11:32 pm** 8:32 pm

27 TUESDAY
☽ ☍ ♅ **4:51 am** 1:51 am
☽ □ ♄ **8:47 am** 5:47 am
☽ ☍ ♀ **1:35 pm** 10:35 am
☽ ☍ ☿ **4:24 pm** 1:24 pm
☽ △ ♆ **11:31 pm** 8:31 pm

28 WEDNESDAY
☽ ⚹ ♇ **6:38 am** 3:38 am
☽ □ ♃ **8:31 am** 5:31 am
☽ ⚻ ♂ **4:54 pm** 1:54 pm
☽ ⚻ ☉ 11:20 pm

29 THURSDAY
☽ ⚻ ☉ **2:20 am**
☽ ⚻ ♅ **4:38 am** 1:38 am
☽ ⚹ ♄ **8:36 am** 5:36 am
☽ ⚻ ♀ **5:44 pm** 2:44 pm
☿ ⚹ ♆ **10:27 pm** 7:27 pm
☽ □ ♆ **11:42 pm** 8:42 pm
☽ ⚻ ☿ **11:54 pm** 8:54 pm

30 FRIDAY
☽ ⚺ ♇ **7:00 am** 4:00 am
☽ ⚹ ♃ **9:27 am** 6:27 am
☉ ☌ ♅ **3:54 pm** 12:54 pm
☽ ☍ ♂ **7:51 pm** 4:51 pm

Eastern time in bold type
Pacific time in medium type

APRIL 2021

DATE	SID.TIME	SUN	MOON	NODE	MERCURY	VENUS	MARS	JUPITER	SATURN	URANUS	NEPTUNE	PLUTO	CERES	PALLAS	JUNO	VESTA	CHIRON
1 Th	12 38 17	11♈29 03	26♏20	12♊33℞	24♓29	12♈56	16♊27	23♒14	11♒22	9♉01	21♓25	26♑38	15♈11	7♓41	23♐41	8♍12℞	9♈01
2 F	12 42 14	12 28 14	10♐55	12 32D	26 13	14 11	17 03	23 25	11 27	9 04	21 27	26 39	15 35	7 59	23 45	8 03	9 04
3 Sa	12 46 10	13 27 24	25 12	12 33	27 57	15 25	17 38	23 37	11 32	9 07	21 29	26 40	15 59	8 18	23 48	7 55	9 08
4 Su	12 50 7	14 26 32	9♑07	12 33℞	29 44	16 40	18 14	23 49	11 36	9 10	21 31	26 40	16 22	8 36	23 51	7 47	9 11
5 M	12 54 4	15 25 39	22 44	12 33	1♈31	17 54	18 50	24 00	11 41	9 13	21 34	26 41	16 46	8 54	23 53	7 39	9 15
6 T	12 58 0	16 24 43	6♒02	12 31	3 20	19 08	19 26	24 11	11 45	9 17	21 36	26 42	17 10	9 12	23 55	7 32	9 18
7 W	13 1 57	17 23 46	19 03	12 27	5 11	20 23	20 02	24 23	11 49	9 20	21 38	26 42	17 34	9 30	23 57	7 25	9 22
8 Th	13 5 53	18 22 47	1♓51	12 21	7 03	21 37	20 39	24 34	11 53	9 23	21 40	26 43	17 58	9 48	23 59	7 19	9 25
9 F	13 9 50	19 21 46	14 26	12 12	8 56	22 52	21 15	24 45	11 57	9 27	21 42	26 43	18 22	10 06	24 00	7 13	9 29
10 Sa	13 13 46	20 20 43	26 50	12 03	10 51	24 06	21 51	24 56	12 01	9 30	21 44	26 44	18 46	10 24	24 01	7 08	9 32
11 Su	13 17 43	21 19 39	9♈04	11 53	12 47	25 20	22 27	25 07	12 05	9 33	21 46	26 44	19 10	10 42	24 02	7 03	9 36
12 M	13 21 39	22 18 32	21 09	11 44	14 45	26 35	23 03	25 17	12 09	9 36	21 48	26 45	19 34	10 59	24 02℞	6 58	9 39
13 T	13 25 36	23 17 23	3♉07	11 36	16 44	27 49	23 39	25 28	12 13	9 40	21 50	26 45	19 57	11 17	24 02	6 55	9 43
14 W	13 29 33	24 16 13	14 58	11 31	18 44	29 03	24 15	25 39	12 17	9 43	21 52	26 46	20 21	11 34	24 02	6 51	9 46
15 Th	13 33 29	25 15 00	26 46	11 27	20 46	0♉17	24 52	25 49	12 20	9 47	21 54	26 46	20 45	11 52	24 01	6 48	9 50
16 F	13 37 26	26 13 45	8♊33	11 26D	22 49	1 32	25 28	26 00	12 24	9 50	21 56	26 46	21 09	12 09	24 00	6 46	9 53
17 Sa	13 41 22	27 12 28	20 22	11 26	24 53	2 46	26 04	26 10	12 27	9 53	21 58	26 47	21 33	12 26	23 59	6 44	9 56
18 Su	13 45 19	28 11 09	2♋17	11 28	26 58	4 00	26 40	26 20	12 31	9 57	22 00	26 47	21 57	12 43	23 57	6 43	10 00
19 M	13 49 15	29 09 48	14 24	11 29	29 05	5 14	27 17	26 30	12 34	10 00	22 02	26 47	22 21	13 00	23 55	6 42	10 03
20 T	13 53 12	0♉08 24	26 46	11 30℞	1♉12	6 28	27 53	26 40	12 37	10 04	22 04	26 48	22 44	13 17	23 53	6 42D	10 07
21 W	13 57 8	1 06 59	9♌29	11 30	3 19	7 43	28 29	26 50	12 40	10 07	22 06	26 48	23 08	13 34	23 50	6 42	10 10
22 Th	14 1 5	2 05 31	22 37	11 28	5 27	8 57	29 06	26 59	12 43	10 10	22 08	26 48	23 32	13 51	23 47	6 42	10 13
23 F	14 5 2	3 04 01	6♍13	11 24	7 35	10 11	29 42	27 09	12 46	10 14	22 09	26 48	23 56	14 07	23 44	6 43	10 16
24 Sa	14 8 58	4 02 28	20 18	11 19	9 43	11 25	0♋18	27 18	12 49	10 17	22 11	26 48	24 20	14 24	23 40	6 45	10 20
25 Su	14 12 55	5 00 54	4♎50	11 14	11 50	12 39	0 55	27 28	12 52	10 21	22 13	26 48	24 43	14 40	23 36	6 47	10 23
26 M	14 16 51	5 59 17	19 44	11 09	13 57	13 53	1 31	27 37	12 55	10 24	22 15	26 48	25 07	14 57	23 32	6 49	10 26
27 T	14 20 48	6 57 39	4♏52	11 04	16 02	15 07	2 08	27 46	12 57	10 28	22 17	26 48℞	25 31	15 13	23 27	6 52	10 30
28 W	14 24 44	7 55 59	20 05	11 02	18 06	16 21	2 44	27 55	13 00	10 31	22 18	26 48	25 55	15 29	23 22	6 56	10 33
29 Th	14 28 41	8 54 17	5♐12	11 00D	20 09	17 35	3 21	28 04	13 02	10 35	22 20	26 48	26 18	15 45	23 17	7 00	10 36
30 F	14 32 37	9 52 34	20 06	11 00	22 10	18 49	3 57	28 13	13 04	10 38	22 22	26 48	26 42	16 01	23 11	7 04	10 39

EPHEMERIS CALCULATED FOR 12 MIDNIGHT GREENWICH MEAN TIME. ALL OTHER DATA AND FACING ASPECTARIAN PAGE IN **EASTERN TIME (BOLD)** AND PACIFIC TIME (REGULAR).

MAY 2021

☽ Last Aspect day	ET / hr:mn / PT	asp	☽ Ingress sign	day	ET / hr:mn / PT
2	**10:38 am** 7:38 am	△☿	♒	2	**3:31 pm** 12:31 pm
4	**8:05 pm** 5:05 pm	☌♃	♓	4	**10:09 pm** 7:09 pm
7	**3:36 am** 12:36 am	⚹♀	♈	7	**7:52 am** 4:52 am
9	**6:50 pm** 3:50 pm	⚹♃	♉	9	**7:46 pm** 4:46 pm
12	**8:23 am** 5:23 am	□♃	♊	12	**8:43 am** 5:43 am
14	**6:51 am** 3:51 am	□♆	♋	14	**9:30 pm** 6:30 pm
16	11:23 pm	☍♇	♌	17	**8:44 am** 5:44 am
17	**2:23 am**	☍♇	♌	17	**8:44 am** 5:44 am
19	**3:13 pm** 12:13 pm	□☉	♍	19	**4:59 pm** 1:59 pm
21	**3:56 pm** 12:56 pm	△♇	♎	21	**9:35 pm** 6:35 pm

☽ Last Aspect day	ET / hr:mn / PT	asp	☽ Ingress sign	day	ET / hr:mn / PT
23	**5:36 pm** 2:36 pm	□♇	♏	23	**11:00 pm** 8:00 pm
25	**5:20 pm** 2:20 pm	⚹♇	♐	25	**10:39 pm** 7:39 pm
27	**1:35 pm** 10:35 am	☍☿	♑	27	**10:23 pm** 7:23 pm
29	**6:15 pm** 3:15 pm	☌♇	♒	29	9:04 pm
29	**6:15 pm** 3:15 pm	☌♇	♒	30	**12:04 am**
31	11:14 pm	△♀	♓	6/1	**5:07 am** 2:07 am
6/1	**2:14 am**	△♀	♓	6/1	**5:07 am** 2:07 am

☽ Phases & Eclipses phase	day	ET / hr:mn / PT
4th Quarter	3	**3:50 pm** 12:50 pm
New Moon	11	**3:00 pm** 12:00 pm
2nd Quarter	19	**3:13 pm** 12:13 pm
Full Moon	26	**7:14 am** 4:14 am
●	26	5° ♐ 26'

Planet Ingress		day	ET / hr:mn / PT
☿	♊	3	**10:49 pm** 7:49 pm
⚳	♉	8	**4:54 am** 1:54 am
♀	♊	8	**10:01 pm** 7:01 pm
♃	♓	13	**6:36 pm** 3:36 pm
☉	♊	20	**3:37 pm** 12:37 pm

Planetary Motion		day	ET / hr:mn / PT
♄	℞	23	**5:21 am** 2:21 am
☿	℞	29	**6:34 pm** 3:34 pm

1 SATURDAY
☽ △ ♅ **6:13 am** 3:13 am
☽ △ ☉ **7:12 am** 4:12 am
☽ ⚺ ♄ **10:18 am** 7:18 am
☽ △ ♀ 9:42 pm
☽ ⚹ ♆ 11:16 pm

2 SUNDAY
☽ △ ♀ **12:42 am**
☽ ⚹ ♆ **2:16 am**
☿ △ ♇ **5:19 am** 2:19 am
☽ ☌ ♇ **9:54 am** 6:54 am
☽ △ ☿ **10:38 am** 7:38 am
☽ ⚺ ♃ **1:02 pm** 10:02 am
♀ ⚹ ♆ **6:38 pm** 3:38 pm
☽ ⚻ ♂ 11:02 pm

3 MONDAY
☽ ⚻ ♂ **2:02 am**
☿ □ ♃ **5:33 am** 2:33 am
☉ □ ♄ **6:02 am** 3:02 am
☽ □ ♅ **10:52 am** 7:52 am
☽ ☌ ♄ **3:08 pm** 12:08 pm
☽ □ ☉ **3:50 pm** 12:50 pm

4 TUESDAY
☽ ⚺ ♆ **8:08 am** 5:08 am
☽ □ ♀ **12:00 pm** 9:00 am
☽ ⚺ ♇ **4:09 pm** 1:09 pm
☽ ☌ ♃ **8:05 pm** 5:05 pm
☽ □ ☿ 10:54 pm

5 WEDNESDAY
☽ □ ☿ **1:54 am**
☽ △ ♂ **12:07 pm** 9:07 am
☽ ⚹ ♅ **6:57 pm** 3:57 pm
☽ ⚺ ♄ **11:21 pm** 8:21 pm

6 THURSDAY
☽ ⚹ ☉ **4:41 am** 1:41 am
♀ △ ♇ **7:25 am** 4:25 am
☽ ☌ ♆ **5:17 pm** 2:17 pm
☽ ⚹ ♇ 10:34 pm

7 FRIDAY
☽ ⚹ ♇ **1:34 am**
☽ ⚹ ♀ **3:36 am** 12:36 am
☽ ⚺ ♃ **6:21 am** 3:21 am
☽ ⚹ ☿ **9:01 pm** 6:01 pm
☽ □ ♂ 10:35 pm

8 SATURDAY
☽ □ ♂ **1:35 am**
☽ ⚺ ♅ **5:53 am** 2:53 am
♀ □ ♃ **9:38 am** 6:38 am
☽ ⚹ ♄ **10:18 am** 7:18 am
☽ ⚺ ☉ **8:54 pm** 5:54 pm

9 SUNDAY
☽ ⚺ ♆ **4:52 am** 1:52 am
☽ □ ♇ **1:16 pm** 10:16 am
☽ ⚹ ♃ **6:50 pm** 3:50 pm
☽ ⚺ ♀ **10:17 pm** 7:17 pm

10 MONDAY
☿ ⚺ ♂ **7:48 am** 4:48 am
☽ ⚹ ♂ **5:12 pm** 2:12 pm
☽ ⚺ ☿ **5:55 pm** 2:55 pm
☽ ☌ ♅ **6:35 pm** 3:35 pm
☽ □ ♄ **10:55 pm** 7:55 pm
☿ ⚺ ♅ **11:48 pm** 8:48 pm

11 TUESDAY
☽ ☌ ☉ **3:00 pm** 12:00 pm
☽ ⚹ ♆ **5:47 pm** 2:47 pm
♂ ⚹ ♅ **10:48 pm** 7:48 pm
☽ △ ♇ 11:07 pm

12 WEDNESDAY
☽ △ ♇ **2:07 am**
☽ □ ♃ **8:23 am** 5:23 am
☿ △ ♄ **2:34 pm** 11:34 am
☽ ☌ ♀ **6:20 pm** 3:20 pm
☉ ⚹ ♆ 10:45 pm

13 THURSDAY
☉ ⚹ ♆ **1:45 am**
☽ ⚺ ♅ **7:55 am** 4:55 am
☽ ⚺ ♂ **9:33 am** 6:33 am
☽ △ ♄ **12:03 pm** 9:03 am
☽ ☌ ☿ **2:32 pm** 11:32 am

14 FRIDAY
☽ □ ♆ **6:51 am** 3:51 am
☽ ⚺ ☉ **9:22 am** 6:22 am
☽ ⚻ ♇ **2:57 pm** 11:57 am
☽ △ ♃ **9:45 pm** 6:45 pm

15 SATURDAY
♂ ⚻ ♄ **10:49 am** 7:49 am
☽ ⚺ ♀ **1:53 pm** 10:53 am
☽ ⚹ ♅ **8:35 pm** 5:35 pm
☽ ⚻ ♄ 9:24 pm
☽ ☌ ♂ 10:06 pm

16 SUNDAY
☽ ⚻ ♄ **12:24 am**
☽ ☌ ♂ **1:06 am**
☽ ⚺ ☿ **8:51 am** 5:51 am
☽ △ ♆ **6:42 pm** 3:42 pm
☽ ⚹ ☉ 11:05 pm
☽ ☍ ♇ 11:23 pm

17 MONDAY
☽ ⚹ ☉ **2:05 am**
☽ ☍ ♇ **2:23 am**
☉ △ ♇ **5:49 am** 2:49 am
☽ ⚻ ♃ **9:29 am** 6:29 am

18 TUESDAY
☽ ⚹ ♀ **6:43 am** 3:43 am
☽ □ ♅ **7:04 am** 4:04 am
☽ ☍ ♄ **10:29 am** 7:29 am
♀ ⚺ ♅ **10:31 am** 7:31 am
☽ ⚺ ♂ **2:01 pm** 11:01 am
☽ ⚹ ☿ **10:55 pm** 7:55 pm

19 WEDNESDAY
☽ ⚻ ♆ **3:51 am** 12:51 am
☽ ⚻ ♇ **10:58 am** 7:58 am
☽ □ ☉ **3:13 pm** 12:13 pm
☽ ☍ ♃ **6:07 pm** 3:07 pm
♀ △ ♄ **9:58 pm** 6:58 pm

20 THURSDAY
☽ △ ♅ **2:09 pm** 11:09 am
☽ ⚻ ♄ **5:08 pm** 2:08 pm
☽ □ ♀ **7:01 pm** 4:01 pm
☽ ⚹ ♂ **10:57 pm** 7:57 pm

21 FRIDAY
☽ □ ☿ **7:47 am** 4:47 am
☽ ☍ ♆ **9:24 am** 6:24 am
☉ □ ♃ **11:03 am** 8:03 am
☽ △ ♇ **3:56 pm** 12:56 pm
☽ ⚻ ♃ **10:59 pm** 7:59 pm
☽ △ ☉ **11:46 pm** 8:46 pm

22 SATURDAY
☽ ⚻ ♅ **5:34 pm** 2:34 pm
☽ △ ♄ **8:11 pm** 5:11 pm
☿ □ ♆ **10:43 pm** 7:43 pm
☽ △ ♀ 11:36 pm

23 SUNDAY
☽ △ ♀ **2:36 am**
☽ □ ♂ **3:51 am** 12:51 am
☽ ⚻ ♆ **11:33 am** 8:33 am
☽ △ ☿ **11:59 am** 8:59 am
☽ □ ♇ **5:36 pm** 2:36 pm
☽ △ ♃ 9:37 pm

24 MONDAY
☽ △ ♃ **12:37 am**
☽ ⚻ ☉ **4:28 am** 1:28 am
♀ ⚺ ♂ **7:15 am** 4:15 am
☽ ☍ ♅ **6:15 pm** 3:15 pm
☽ □ ♄ **8:35 pm** 5:35 pm

25 TUESDAY
☽ △ ♂ **6:01 am** 3:01 am
☽ ⚻ ♀ **7:01 am** 4:01 am
☽ △ ♆ **11:30 am** 8:30 am
☽ ⚻ ☿ **1:13 pm** 10:13 am
☽ ⚹ ♇ **5:20 pm** 2:20 pm
☽ □ ♃ 9:30 pm

26 WEDNESDAY
☽ □ ♃ **12:30 am**
☽ ☍ ☉ **7:14 am** 4:14 am
☽ ⚻ ♅ **5:52 pm** 2:52 pm
☽ ⚹ ♄ **8:01 pm** 5:01 pm

27 THURSDAY
☽ ⚻ ♂ **7:31 am** 4:31 am
☽ ☍ ♀ **10:43 am** 7:43 am
☽ □ ♆ **11:06 am** 8:06 am
☽ ☍ ☿ **1:35 pm** 10:35 am
♀ □ ♆ **3:25 pm** 12:25 pm
☽ ⚺ ♇ **4:55 pm** 1:55 pm
☽ ⚹ ♃ 9:31 pm

28 FRIDAY
☽ ⚹ ♃ **12:31 am**
☽ ⚻ ☉ **10:32 am** 7:32 am
☽ △ ♅ **6:22 pm** 3:22 pm
☽ ⚺ ♄ **8:23 pm** 5:23 pm
☿ ☌ ♀ 10:13 pm

29 SATURDAY
☿ ☌ ♀ **1:13 am**
☽ ☍ ♂ **10:36 am** 7:36 am
☽ ⚹ ♆ **12:13 pm** 9:13 am
☽ ⚻ ☿ **3:07 pm** 12:07 pm
☽ ⚻ ♀ **4:23 pm** 1:23 pm
☽ ☌ ♇ **6:15 pm** 3:15 pm
☽ ⚺ ♃ 11:34 pm

30 SUNDAY
☽ ⚺ ♃ **2:34 am**
♀ ⚻ ♇ **1:47 pm** 10:47 am
☽ △ ☉ **4:43 pm** 1:43 pm
☽ □ ♅ **9:30 pm** 6:30 pm
☽ ☌ ♄ **11:25 pm** 8:25 pm
♂ △ ♆ 10:15 pm

31 MONDAY
♂ △ ♆ **1:15 am**
☽ ⚺ ♆ **4:27 pm** 1:27 pm
☽ ⚻ ♂ **5:11 pm** 2:11 pm
☽ △ ☿ **7:13 pm** 4:13 pm
☽ ⚺ ♇ **10:48 pm** 7:48 pm
☽ △ ♀ 11:14 pm

Eastern time in bold type
Pacific time in medium type

MAY 2021

DATE	SID.TIME	SUN	MOON	NODE	MERCURY	VENUS	MARS	JUPITER	SATURN	URANUS	NEPTUNE	PLUTO	CERES	PALLAS	JUNO	VESTA	CHIRON
1 Sa	14 36 34	10♉50 49	4♑39	11♊01	24♉08	20♉03	4♋33	28♒21	13♒07	10♉41	22♓23	26♑48℞	27♈06	16♓17	23♐05℞	7♍09	10♈42
2 Su	14 40 31	11 49 02	18 48	11 03	26 04	21 17	5 10	28 30	13 09	10 45	22 25	26 48	27 30	16 32	22 59	7 14	10 45
3 M	14 44 27	12 47 14	2♒32	11 04℞	27 57	22 31	5 46	28 38	13 11	10 48	22 27	26 48	27 53	16 48	22 52	7 19	10 49
4 T	14 48 24	13 45 25	15 53	11 04	29 47	23 45	6 23	28 46	13 13	10 52	22 28	26 48	28 17	17 03	22 45	7 25	10 52
5 W	14 52 20	14 43 34	28 51	11 04	1♊34	24 58	6 59	28 54	13 14	10 55	22 30	26 48	28 40	17 19	22 38	7 32	10 55
6 Th	14 56 17	15 41 41	11♓32	11 02	3 18	26 12	7 36	29 02	13 16	10 59	22 31	26 48	29 04	17 34	22 30	7 39	10 58
7 F	15 0 13	16 39 47	23 56	10 59	4 58	27 26	8 13	29 10	13 18	11 02	22 33	26 47	29 28	17 49	22 22	7 46	11 01
8 Sa	15 4 10	17 37 52	6♈09	10 55	6 35	28 40	8 49	29 18	13 19	11 06	22 34	26 47	29 51	18 04	22 14	7 54	11 04
9 Su	15 8 6	18 35 55	18 11	10 51	8 08	29 54	9 26	29 25	13 21	11 09	22 36	26 47	0♉15	18 19	22 06	8 02	11 07
10 M	15 12 3	19 33 57	0♉07	10 48	9 38	1♊08	10 02	29 32	13 22	11 13	22 37	26 46	0 38	18 34	21 57	8 10	11 10
11 T	15 16 0	20 31 57	11 57	10 45	11 03	2 21	10 39	29 40	13 24	11 16	22 39	26 46	1 02	18 48	21 48	8 19	11 12
12 W	15 19 56	21 29 56	23 45	10 43	12 25	3 35	11 15	29 47	13 25	11 19	22 40	26 46	1 25	19 03	21 38	8 29	11 15
13 Th	15 23 53	22 27 53	5♊33	10 42D	13 43	4 49	11 52	29 54	13 26	11 23	22 41	26 45	1 49	19 17	21 29	8 38	11 18
14 F	15 27 49	23 25 49	17 22	10 42	14 57	6 03	12 29	0♓00	13 27	11 26	22 43	26 45	2 12	19 31	21 19	8 49	11 21
15 Sa	15 31 46	24 23 43	29 15	10 43	16 06	7 16	13 05	0 07	13 28	11 30	22 44	26 44	2 36	19 45	21 09	8 59	11 24
16 Su	15 35 42	25 21 35	11♋16	10 44	17 12	8 30	13 42	0 13	13 28	11 33	22 45	26 44	2 59	19 59	20 58	9 10	11 27
17 M	15 39 39	26 19 26	23 27	10 46	18 13	9 44	14 19	0 20	13 29	11 36	22 47	26 43	3 22	20 13	20 48	9 21	11 29
18 T	15 43 35	27 17 15	5♌52	10 47	19 10	10 57	14 55	0 26	13 30	11 40	22 48	26 43	3 46	20 26	20 37	9 33	11 32
19 W	15 47 32	28 15 03	18 35	10 47℞	20 03	12 11	15 32	0 32	13 30	11 43	22 49	26 42	4 09	20 40	20 25	9 44	11 35
20 Th	15 51 29	29 12 48	1♍40	10 48	20 52	13 24	16 09	0 38	13 30	11 46	22 50	26 42	4 32	20 53	20 14	9 57	11 37
21 F	15 55 25	0♊10 32	15 09	10 47	21 36	14 38	16 46	0 43	13 31	11 50	22 51	26 41	4 55	21 06	20 02	10 09	11 40
22 Sa	15 59 22	1 08 15	29 04	10 47	22 15	15 52	17 22	0 49	13 31	11 53	22 53	26 40	5 18	21 19	19 51	10 22	11 42
23 Su	16 3 18	2 05 55	13♎24	10 46	22 50	17 05	17 59	0 54	13 31℞	11 56	22 54	26 40	5 42	21 32	19 39	10 36	11 45
24 M	16 7 15	3 03 35	28 08	10 45	23 20	18 19	18 36	0 59	13 31	12 00	22 55	26 39	6 05	21 44	19 27	10 49	11 47
25 T	16 11 11	4 01 12	13♏09	10 44	23 46	19 32	19 13	1 04	13 31	12 03	22 56	26 38	6 28	21 57	19 14	11 03	11 50
26 W	16 15 8	4 58 49	28 19	10 44D	24 07	20 46	19 49	1 09	13 31	12 06	22 57	26 37	6 51	22 09	19 02	11 17	11 52
27 Th	16 19 4	5 56 24	13♐30	10 43	24 23	21 59	20 26	1 14	13 30	12 09	22 58	26 37	7 14	22 21	18 49	11 32	11 54
28 F	16 23 1	6 53 58	28 31	10 44	24 34	23 12	21 03	1 18	13 30	12 13	22 59	26 36	7 37	22 33	18 36	11 47	11 57
29 Sa	16 26 58	7 51 31	13♑15	10 44	24 41℞	24 26	21 40	1 22	13 30	12 16	23 00	26 35	8 00	22 45	18 23	12 02	11 59
30 Su	16 30 54	8 49 04	27 36	10 44	24 43	25 39	22 17	1 27	13 29	12 19	23 00	26 34	8 23	22 57	18 10	12 17	12 01
31 M	16 34 51	9 46 35	11♒31	10 44	24 40	26 53	22 53	1 31	13 28	12 22	23 01	26 33	8 45	23 08	17 57	12 33	12 04

EPHEMERIS CALCULATED FOR 12 MIDNIGHT GREENWICH MEAN TIME. ALL OTHER DATA AND FACING ASPECTARIAN PAGE IN **EASTERN TIME (BOLD)** AND PACIFIC TIME (REGULAR).

JUNE 2021

☽ Last Aspect day	ET / hr:mn / PT		asp	☽ Ingress sign	day	ET / hr:mn / PT	
1	**2:14 am**		△♀	♓	1	**5:07 am**	2:07 am
3	**7:10 am**	4:10 am	⚹♇	♈	3	**1:59 pm**	10:59 am
5	**6:47 pm**	3:47 pm	□♂	♉	5		10:46 pm
5	**6:47 pm**	3:47 pm	□♂	♉	6	**1:46 am**	
8	**11:07 am**	8:07 am	⚹♂	♊	8	**2:47 pm**	11:47 am
10	**1:38 pm**	10:38 am	□♆	♋	11	**3:23 am**	12:23 am
13	**7:16 am**	4:16 am	☍♇	♌	13	**2:22 pm**	11:22 am
15	**1:27 pm**	10:27 am	⚹☉	♍	15	**11:02 pm**	8:02 pm
17	**11:54 pm**	8:54 pm	□☉	♎	18	**4:54 am**	1:54 am
20	**6:52 am**	3:52 am	△☉	♏	20	**7:58 am**	4:58 am
21		11:43 pm	⚹♇	♐	22	**8:55 am**	5:55 am
22	**2:43 am**		⚹♇	♐	22	**8:55 am**	5:55 am
23	**10:09 pm**	7:09 pm	□♆	♑	24	**9:05 am**	6:05 am
26	**8:49 am**	5:49 am	☍♀	♒	26	**10:09 am**	7:09 am
27	**3:08 pm**	12:08 pm	△☿	♓	28	**1:51 pm**	10:51 am
30	**1:40 pm**	10:40 am	⚹♇	♈	30	**9:21 pm**	6:21 pm

☽ Phases & Eclipses phase	day	ET / hr:mn / PT	
4th Quarter	2	**3:24 am**	12:24 am
New Moon	10	**6:53 am**	3:53 am
●	10	19° ♊ 47'	
2nd Quarter	17	**11:54 pm**	8:54 pm
Full Moon	24	**2:40 pm**	11:40 am

Planet Ingress	day	ET / hr:mn / PT	
♀ ♋	2	**9:19 am**	6:19 am
♂ ♌	11	**9:34 am**	6:34 am
☉ ♋	20	**11:32 pm**	8:32 pm
♀ ♌	26		9:27 pm
♀ ♌	27	**12:27 am**	

Planetary Motion	day	ET / hr:mn / PT	
♃ ℞	20	**11:06 am**	8:06 am
☿ D	22	**6:00 pm**	3:00 pm
♆ ℞	25	**3:21 pm**	12:21 pm

1 TUESDAY
☽△♀ **2:14 am**
☽☌♃ **8:04 am** 5:04 am

2 WEDNESDAY
☿⚺♂ **3:14 am** 12:14 am
☽□☉ **3:24 am** 12:24 am
☽⚹♅ **4:22 am** 1:22 am
☽⚺♄ **6:08 am** 3:08 am
☉⚺♅ **4:43 pm** 1:43 pm
☽☌♆ 9:31 pm
☽□☿ 11:24 pm

3 THURSDAY
☽☌♆ **12:31 am**
☽□☿ **2:24 am**
☽△♂ **4:08 am** 1:08 am
☽⚹♇ **7:10 am** 4:10 am
☉△♄ **3:05 pm** 12:05 pm
☽□♀ **5:09 pm** 2:09 pm
☽⚺♃ **5:23 pm** 2:23 pm
♀△♃ **7:33 pm** 4:33 pm

4 FRIDAY
☽⚺♅ **2:52 pm** 11:52 am
☽⚹♄ **4:24 pm** 1:24 pm
☽⚹☉ **6:38 pm** 3:38 pm

5 SATURDAY
☽⚺♆ **11:49 am** 8:49 am
☽⚹☿ **11:56 am** 8:56 am
☿□♆ **3:05 pm** 12:05 pm
♂☍♇ **3:45 pm** 12:45 pm
☽□♇ **6:37 pm** 3:37 pm
☽□♂ **6:47 pm** 3:47 pm

6 SUNDAY
☽⚹♃ **5:32 am** 2:32 am
☽⚹♀ **11:57 am** 8:57 am

7 MONDAY
☽☌♅ **3:39 am** 12:39 am
☽□♄ **4:51 am** 1:51 am
☽⚺☉ **12:36 pm** 9:36 am
☽⚺☿ **10:27 pm** 7:27 pm
☽⚹♆ 9:47 pm

8 TUESDAY
☽⚹♆ **12:47 am**
☽△♇ **7:30 am** 4:30 am
☽⚹♂ **11:07 am** 8:07 am
☽□♃ **6:47 pm** 3:47 pm

9 WEDNESDAY
☽⚺♀ **8:01 am** 5:01 am
☽⚺♅ **4:55 pm** 1:55 pm
☽△♄ **5:44 pm** 2:44 pm

10 THURSDAY
☽☌☉ **6:53 am** 3:53 am
☽☌☿ **8:37 am** 5:37 am
☽□♆ **1:38 pm** 10:38 am
☽⚻♇ **8:07 pm** 5:07 pm
☉☌☿ **9:13 pm** 6:13 pm

11 FRIDAY
☽⚺♂ **3:02 am** 12:02 am
☽△♃ **7:28 am** 4:28 am
☽☌♀ 11:59 pm

12 SATURDAY
☽☌♀ **2:59 am**
☽⚹♅ **5:11 am** 2:11 am
☽⚻♄ **5:35 am** 2:35 am
☽⚺☿ **5:38 pm** 2:38 pm
☽⚺☉ **11:33 pm** 8:33 pm
☽△♆ 10:06 pm
♀⚹♅ 10:38 pm

13 SUNDAY
☽△♆ **1:06 am**
♀⚹♅ **1:38 am**
♀⚻♄ **4:15 am** 1:15 am
☽☍♇ **7:16 am** 4:16 am
☽☌♂ **5:08 pm** 2:08 pm
☽⚻♃ **6:27 pm** 3:27 pm
☉□♆ **7:40 pm** 4:40 pm

14 MONDAY
☽□♅ **3:27 pm** 12:27 pm
☽☍♄ **3:28 pm** 12:28 pm
♄□♅ **6:01 pm** 3:01 pm
☽⚺♀ **7:19 pm** 4:19 pm
♂⚻♃ **8:39 pm** 5:39 pm
☽⚹☿ 9:58 pm

15 TUESDAY
☽⚹☿ **12:58 am**
☽⚻♆ **10:22 am** 7:22 am
☽⚹☉ **1:27 pm** 10:27 am
☽⚻♇ **4:10 pm** 1:10 pm

16 WEDNESDAY
☽☍♃ **3:00 am** 12:00 am
☽⚺♂ **4:28 am** 1:28 am
☿⚺♀ **4:11 pm** 1:11 pm
☽⚻♄ **10:47 pm** 7:47 pm
☽△♅ **11:07 pm** 8:07 pm
☉⚻♇ 10:24 pm

17 THURSDAY
☉⚻♇ **1:24 am**
☽□☿ **6:16 am** 3:16 am
☽⚹♀ **8:07 am** 5:07 am
☽☍♆ **4:55 pm** 1:55 pm
☽△♇ **10:18 pm** 7:18 pm
☽□☉ **11:54 pm** 8:54 pm

18 FRIDAY
☽⚻♃ **8:41 am** 5:41 am
☽⚹♂ **12:32 pm** 9:32 am

19 SATURDAY
☽△♄ **3:15 am** 12:15 am
☽⚻♅ **3:53 am** 12:53 am
☽△☿ **9:22 am** 6:22 am
☽□♀ **5:07 pm** 2:07 pm
☽⚻♆ **8:36 pm** 5:36 pm
☽□♇ 10:37 pm

20 SUNDAY
☽□♇ **1:37 am**
☽△☉ **6:52 am** 3:52 am
☽△♃ **11:35 am** 8:35 am
☽□♂ **5:29 pm** 2:29 pm

21 MONDAY
☽□♄ **5:09 am** 2:09 am
☽☍♅ **6:02 am** 3:02 am
♀△♆ **9:57 am** 6:57 am
☽⚻☿ **10:35 am** 7:35 am
☽△♆ **9:57 pm** 6:57 pm
☽△♀ **11:01 pm** 8:01 pm
☽⚹♇ 11:43 pm

22 TUESDAY
☽⚹♇ **2:43 am**
☽⚻☉ **11:12 am** 8:12 am
☽□♃ **12:26 pm** 9:26 am
☽△♂ **8:17 pm** 5:17 pm

23 WEDNESDAY
☽⚹♄ **5:25 am** 2:25 am
☉△♃ **6:11 am** 3:11 am
☽⚻♅ **6:35 am** 3:35 am
☽☍☿ **10:50 am** 7:50 am
♀☍♇ **7:39 pm** 4:39 pm
☽□♆ **10:09 pm** 7:09 pm
☽⚺♇ 11:49 pm

24 THURSDAY
☽⚺♇ **2:49 am**
☽⚻♀ **3:28 am** 12:28 am
☽⚹♃ **12:33 pm** 9:33 am
☽☍☉ **2:40 pm** 11:40 am
☽⚻♂ **10:35 pm** 7:35 pm

25 FRIDAY
☽⚺♄ **5:35 am** 2:35 am
☽△♅ **7:04 am** 4:04 am
☽⚻☿ **11:42 am** 8:42 am
☽⚹♆ **10:51 pm** 7:51 pm

26 SATURDAY
☽☌♇ **3:36 am** 12:36 am
☽☍♀ **8:49 am** 5:49 am
☽⚺♃ **1:42 pm** 10:42 am
☽⚻☉ **7:29 pm** 4:29 pm
☽☍♂ 11:30 pm

27 SUNDAY
☽☍♂ **2:30 am**
☽☌♄ **7:23 am** 4:23 am
☽□♅ **9:16 am** 6:16 am
☽△☿ **3:08 pm** 12:08 pm
☽⚺♆ 10:49 pm

28 MONDAY
☽⚺♆ **1:49 am**
☽⚺♇ **6:47 am** 3:47 am
♀⚻♃ **5:31 pm** 2:31 pm
☽☌♃ **5:33 pm** 2:33 pm
☽⚻♀ **5:34 pm** 2:34 pm

29 TUESDAY
☽△☉ **3:54 am** 12:54 am
☽⚻♂ **9:58 am** 6:58 am
☽⚺♄ **12:24 pm** 9:24 am
☽⚹♅ **2:47 pm** 11:47 am
☽□☿ **11:00 pm** 8:00 pm

30 WEDNESDAY
☽☌♆ **8:25 am** 5:25 am
☽⚹♇ **1:40 pm** 10:40 am
☽⚺♃ 10:12 pm

Eastern time in bold type
Pacific time in medium type

JUNE 2021

DATE	SID.TIME	SUN	MOON	NODE	MERCURY	VENUS	MARS	JUPITER	SATURN	URANUS	NEPTUNE	PLUTO	CERES	PALLAS	JUNO	VESTA	CHIRON
1 T	16 38 47	10♊44 05	25♒00	10♊44R	24♊34R	28♊06	23♋30	1♓34	13♒27R	12♉25	23♓02	26♑33R	9♉08	23♓19	17♐44R	12♍49	12♈06
2 W	16 42 44	11 41 35	8♓02	10 44D	24 22	29 19	24 07	1 38	13 27	12 29	23 03	26 32	9 31	23 30	17 30	13 05	12 08
3 Th	16 46 40	12 39 04	20 43	10 44	24 07	0♋33	24 44	1 41	13 26	12 32	23 04	26 31	9 54	23 41	17 17	13 22	12 10
4 F	16 50 37	13 36 32	3♈05	10 44	23 48	1 46	25 21	1 45	13 25	12 35	23 04	26 30	10 16	23 52	17 03	13 38	12 12
5 Sa	16 54 33	14 33 59	15 12	10 45	23 26	2 59	25 58	1 48	13 23	12 38	23 05	26 29	10 39	24 02	16 50	13 55	12 14
6 Su	16 58 30	15 31 26	27 09	10 45	23 00	4 13	26 34	1 51	13 22	12 41	23 06	26 28	11 02	24 13	16 36	14 13	12 16
7 M	17 2 27	16 28 52	8♉59	10 46	22 32	5 26	27 11	1 53	13 21	12 44	23 06	26 27	11 24	24 23	16 23	14 30	12 18
8 T	17 6 23	17 26 17	20 46	10 46	22 02	6 39	27 48	1 56	13 19	12 47	23 07	26 26	11 47	24 33	16 09	14 48	12 20
9 W	17 10 20	18 23 42	2♊34	10 47R	21 30	7 52	28 25	1 58	13 18	12 50	23 07	26 25	12 09	24 42	15 55	15 06	12 22
10 Th	17 14 16	19 21 06	14 24	10 47	20 57	9 05	29 02	2 00	13 16	12 53	23 08	26 24	12 31	24 52	15 42	15 25	12 23
11 F	17 18 13	20 18 29	26 19	10 46	20 23	10 19	29 39	2 02	13 14	12 56	23 08	26 23	12 54	25 01	15 28	15 43	12 25
12 Sa	17 22 9	21 15 51	8♋21	10 46	19 50	11 32	0♌16	2 04	13 13	12 59	23 09	26 21	13 16	25 10	15 15	16 02	12 27
13 Su	17 26 6	22 13 13	20 33	10 44	19 17	12 45	0 53	2 05	13 11	13 01	23 09	26 20	13 38	25 19	15 01	16 21	12 28
14 M	17 30 2	23 10 33	2♌55	10 43	18 45	13 58	1 30	2 07	13 09	13 04	23 10	26 19	14 00	25 27	14 48	16 40	12 30
15 T	17 33 59	24 07 53	15 31	10 41	18 15	15 11	2 07	2 08	13 07	13 07	23 10	26 18	14 22	25 36	14 34	17 00	12 32
16 W	17 37 56	25 05 12	28 21	10 39	17 47	16 24	2 44	2 09	13 05	13 10	23 10	26 17	14 44	25 44	14 21	17 20	12 33
17 Th	17 41 52	26 02 30	11♍29	10 38	17 22	17 37	3 21	2 10	13 02	13 13	23 11	26 16	15 06	25 52	14 08	17 40	12 35
18 F	17 45 49	26 59 47	24 56	10 38D	17 00	18 50	3 58	2 10	13 00	13 15	23 11	26 14	15 28	25 59	13 55	18 00	12 36
19 Sa	17 49 45	27 57 04	8♎43	10 38	16 41	20 03	4 35	2 11	12 58	13 18	23 11	26 13	15 50	26 07	13 42	18 20	12 37
20 Su	17 53 42	28 54 19	22 50	10 39	16 27	21 16	5 12	2 11R	12 55	13 21	23 11	26 12	16 12	26 14	13 29	18 41	12 39
21 M	17 57 38	29 51 34	7♏17	10 40	16 16	22 29	5 49	2 11	12 53	13 23	23 12	26 11	16 34	26 21	13 16	19 01	12 40
22 T	18 1 35	0♋48 48	22 00	10 41	16 10D	23 42	6 26	2 11	12 50	13 26	23 12	26 09	16 55	26 27	13 04	19 22	12 41
23 W	18 5 32	1 46 02	6♐53	10 42R	16 08	24 55	7 03	2 11	12 47	13 29	23 12	26 08	17 17	26 34	12 52	19 44	12 42
24 Th	18 9 28	2 43 15	21 52	10 41	16 10	26 08	7 40	2 10	12 44	13 31	23 12	26 07	17 38	26 40	12 39	20 05	12 44
25 F	18 13 25	3 40 28	6♑46	10 40	16 18	27 21	8 18	2 09	12 41	13 34	23 12R	26 06	18 00	26 46	12 28	20 26	12 45
26 Sa	18 17 21	4 37 40	21 28	10 38	16 30	28 34	8 55	2 08	12 39	13 36	23 12	26 04	18 21	26 52	12 16	20 48	12 46
27 Su	18 21 18	5 34 52	5♒52	10 34	16 47	29 47	9 32	2 07	12 35	13 38	23 12	26 03	18 43	26 57	12 04	21 10	12 47
28 M	18 25 14	6 32 04	19 52	10 31	17 09	0♌59	10 09	2 06	12 32	13 41	23 12	26 02	19 04	27 02	11 53	21 32	12 48
29 T	18 29 11	7 29 16	3♓26	10 27	17 35	2 12	10 46	2 04	12 29	13 43	23 12	26 00	19 25	27 07	11 42	21 54	12 49
30 W	18 33 7	8 26 28	16 34	10 25	18 06	3 25	11 23	2 03	12 26	13 46	23 12	25 59	19 46	27 11	11 31	22 17	12 49

EPHEMERIS CALCULATED FOR 12 MIDNIGHT GREENWICH MEAN TIME. ALL OTHER DATA AND FACING ASPECTARIAN PAGE IN **EASTERN TIME (BOLD)** AND PACIFIC TIME (REGULAR).

JULY 2021

☽ Last Aspect day	ET / hr:mn	PT	asp	☽ Ingress sign	day	ET / hr:mn	PT
2		9:15 pm	□♇	♉	3	**8:28 am**	5:28 am
3	**12:15 am**		□♇	♉	3	**8:28 am**	5:28 am
5	**12:57 pm**	9:57 am	△♇	♊	5	**9:24 pm**	6:24 pm
7		9:20 pm	☌☿	♋	8	**9:51 am**	6:51 am
8	**12:20 am**		☌☿	♋	8	**9:51 am**	6:51 am
10	**12:10 pm**	9:10 am	☍♇	♌	10	**8:21 pm**	5:21 pm
12	**8:29 am**	5:29 am	☌♂	♍	13	**4:30 am**	1:30 am
14		11:46 pm	△♇	♎	15	**10:32 am**	7:32 am
15	**2:46 am**		△♇	♎	15	**10:32 am**	7:32 am
17	**7:03 am**	4:03 am	□♇	♏	17	**2:38 pm**	11:38 am
19	**12:30 pm**	9:30 am	△☉	♐	19	**5:08 pm**	2:08 pm
21	**6:26 pm**	3:26 pm	△♀	♑	21	**6:36 pm**	3:36 pm
23	**12:34 pm**	9:34 am	☌♇	♒	23	**8:12 pm**	5:12 pm
25	**7:14 pm**	4:14 pm	☍♂	♓	25	**11:30 pm**	8:30 pm
27	**9:13 pm**	6:13 pm	⚹♇	♈	28	**5:58 am**	2:58 am
30	**3:38 pm**	12:38 pm	⚹♃	♉	30	**4:08 pm**	1:08 pm

☽ Phases & Eclipses phase	day	ET / hr:mn	PT
4th Quarter	1	**5:11 pm**	2:11 pm
New Moon	9	**9:17 pm**	6:17 pm
2nd Quarter	17	**6:11 am**	3:11 am
Full Moon	23	**10:37 pm**	7:37 pm
4th Quarter	31	**9:16 am**	6:16 am

Planet Ingress	day	ET / hr:mn	PT
☿ ♋	11	**4:35 pm**	1:35 pm
⚵ ♎	18		11:31 pm
⚵ ♎	19	**2:31 am**	
♀ ♍	21	**8:37 pm**	5:37 pm
☉ ♌	22	**10:26 am**	7:26 am
☿ ♌	27	**9:12 pm**	6:12 pm
♃ ♒	28	**8:43 am**	5:43 am
♂ ♍	29	**4:32 pm**	1:32 pm
⚳ ♊	31	**4:13 am**	1:13 am

Planetary Motion	day	ET / hr:mn	PT
⚴ ℞	14	**3:40 am**	12:40 am
⚷ ℞	15	**12:41 pm**	9:41 am

Day	Aspect	ET	PT
1 THURSDAY	☽⚺♃	**1:12 am**	
	☽△♀	**7:22 am**	4:22 am
	♂☍♄	**9:08 am**	6:08 am
	☽□☉	**5:11 pm**	2:11 pm
	☽⚹♄	**9:16 pm**	6:16 pm
	☽△♂	**9:58 pm**	6:58 pm
	☽⚺♅		9:15 pm
2 FRIDAY	☽⚺♅	**12:15 am**	
	☽⚹☿	**12:12 pm**	9:12 am
	☽⚺♆	**6:48 pm**	3:48 pm
	☽□♇		9:15 pm
3 SATURDAY	☽□♇	**12:15 am**	
	☽⚹♃	**12:19 pm**	9:19 am
	☉⚻♄	**6:51 pm**	3:51 pm
	♂□♅	**9:40 pm**	6:40 pm
	☽□♀		10:44 pm
4 SUNDAY	☽□♀	**1:44 am**	
	☽□♄	**9:06 am**	6:06 am
	☽⚹☉	**10:26 am**	7:26 am
	☽☌♅	**12:41 pm**	9:41 am
	☽□♂	**1:28 pm**	10:28 am
5 MONDAY	☽⚺☿	**5:36 am**	2:36 am
	☽⚹♆	**7:30 am**	4:30 am
	☽△♇	**12:57 pm**	9:57 am
	☉⚹♅	**3:14 pm**	12:14 pm
	☽□♃		10:03 pm
6 TUESDAY	☽□♃	**1:03 am**	
	☿□♆	**3:39 am**	12:39 am
	☽⚹♀	**9:41 pm**	6:41 pm
	☽△♄	**9:47 pm**	6:47 pm
	♀☍♄	**10:36 pm**	7:36 pm
	☽⚺♅		10:50 pm
7 WEDNESDAY	☽⚺♅	**1:50 am**	
	☽⚺☉	**4:44 am**	1:44 am
	☽⚹♂	**5:47 am**	2:47 am
	☽□♆	**8:12 pm**	5:12 pm
	☽☌☿		9:20 pm
	☽⚻♇		10:28 pm
8 THURSDAY	☽☌☿	**12:20 am**	
	☽⚻♇	**1:28 am**	
	☿⚻♇	**11:36 am**	8:36 am
	☽△♃	**1:09 pm**	10:09 am
	♀□♅	**3:25 pm**	12:25 pm
	☉⚺♂	**4:29 pm**	1:29 pm
9 FRIDAY	☽⚻♄	**9:15 am**	6:15 am
	☽⚹♅	**1:38 pm**	10:38 am
	☽⚺♀	**3:59 pm**	12:59 pm
	☽⚺♂	**8:28 pm**	5:28 pm
	☽☌☉	**9:17 pm**	6:17 pm
10 SATURDAY	☽△♆	**7:11 am**	4:11 am
	☽☍♇	**12:10 pm**	9:10 am
	☽⚺☿	**5:49 pm**	2:49 pm
	☽⚻♃	**11:14 pm**	8:14 pm
11 SUNDAY	☽☍♄	**6:32 pm**	3:32 pm
	☽□♅	**11:11 pm**	8:11 pm
12 MONDAY	☽☌♀	**7:14 am**	4:14 am
	☽☌♂	**8:29 am**	5:29 am
	☽⚺☉	**10:56 am**	7:56 am
	☿△♃	**3:45 pm**	12:45 pm
	☽⚻♆	**3:50 pm**	12:50 pm
	☽⚻♇	**8:33 pm**	5:33 pm
13 TUESDAY	☽☍♃	**7:00 am**	4:00 am
	☽⚹☿	**9:05 am**	6:05 am
	♀☌♂	**9:33 am**	6:33 am
	☽⚻♄		10:33 pm
14 WEDNESDAY	☽⚻♄	**1:33 am**	
	☽△♅	**6:25 am**	3:25 am
	☽⚺♂	**5:55 pm**	2:55 pm
	☽⚺♀	**7:28 pm**	4:28 pm
	☽⚹☉	**9:46 pm**	6:46 pm
	☽☍♆	**10:17 pm**	7:17 pm
	☽△♇		11:46 pm
15 THURSDAY	☽△♇	**2:46 am**	
	☉△♆	**4:49 am**	1:49 am
	☽⚻♃	**12:38 pm**	9:38 am
	☽□☿	**10:09 pm**	7:09 pm
	♀⚻♆		11:41 pm
16 FRIDAY	♀⚻♆	**2:41 am**	
	☽△♄	**6:33 am**	3:33 am
	☽⚻♅	**11:37 am**	8:37 am
	☽⚹♂		10:34 pm
	☽⚻♆		11:46 pm
17 SATURDAY	☽⚹♂	**1:04 am**	
	☽⚻♆	**2:46 am**	
	☽⚹♀	**5:04 am**	2:04 am
	☽□☉	**6:11 am**	3:11 am
	☽□♇	**7:03 am**	4:03 am
	☽△♃	**4:23 pm**	1:23 pm
	☉☍♇	**6:46 pm**	3:46 pm
18 SUNDAY	♀⚻♇	**3:48 am**	12:48 am
	☽△☿	**9:13 am**	6:13 am
	☽□♄	**9:45 am**	6:45 am
	☿⚻♄	**1:13 pm**	10:13 am
	♂⚻♆	**2:22 pm**	11:22 am
	☽☍♅	**3:00 pm**	12:00 pm
19 MONDAY	☽△♆	**5:33 am**	2:33 am
	☽□♂	**6:15 am**	3:15 am
	☽⚹♇	**9:40 am**	6:40 am
	☽□♀	**12:27 pm**	9:27 am
	☽△☉	**12:30 pm**	9:30 am
	☉⚺♀	**3:17 pm**	12:17 pm
	☽□♃	**6:32 pm**	3:32 pm
20 TUESDAY	☿⚹♅	**5:38 am**	2:38 am
	☽⚹♄	**11:31 am**	8:31 am
	☽⚻♅	**4:59 pm**	1:59 pm
	☽⚻☿	**6:42 pm**	3:42 pm
21 WEDNESDAY	☽□♆	**7:08 am**	4:08 am
	☽△♂	**10:06 am**	7:06 am
	☽⚺♇	**11:10 am**	8:10 am
	☽⚻☉	**5:30 pm**	2:30 pm
	☽△♀	**6:26 pm**	3:26 pm
	☽⚹♃	**7:41 pm**	4:41 pm
22 THURSDAY	♀☍♃	**8:45 am**	5:45 am
	♂⚻♇	**10:09 am**	7:09 am
	☽⚺♄	**12:38 pm**	9:38 am
	☽△♅	**6:25 pm**	3:25 pm
	☉⚻♃		9:10 pm
23 FRIDAY	☉⚻♃	**12:10 am**	
	☽☍☿	**3:53 am**	12:53 am
	☽⚹♆	**8:32 am**	5:32 am
	☽☌♇	**12:34 pm**	9:34 am
	☽⚻♂	**1:49 pm**	10:49 am
	☽⚺♃	**8:59 pm**	5:59 pm
	☽☍☉	**10:37 pm**	7:37 pm
	☽⚻♀		9:34 pm
24 SATURDAY	☽⚻♀	**12:34 am**	
	☿△♆	**12:35 pm**	9:35 am
	☽☌♄	**2:25 pm**	11:25 am
	☽□♅	**8:43 pm**	5:43 pm
25 SUNDAY	☽⚺♆	**11:14 am**	8:14 am
	☽⚻☿	**3:15 pm**	12:15 pm
	☽⚺♇	**3:25 pm**	12:25 pm
	☿☍♇	**4:15 pm**	1:15 pm
	☽☍♂	**7:14 pm**	4:14 pm
	☽☌♃	**11:56 pm**	8:56 pm
26 MONDAY	☽⚻☉	**5:55 am**	2:55 am
	☽☍♀	**9:04 am**	6:04 am
	☽⚺♄	**6:25 pm**	3:25 pm
	☽⚹♅		10:28 pm
	☿⚺♂		11:48 pm
27 TUESDAY	☽⚹♅	**1:28 am**	
	☿⚺♂	**2:48 am**	
	☽☌♆	**4:47 pm**	1:47 pm
	☽⚹♇	**9:13 pm**	6:13 pm
	☿⚻♃	**9:45 pm**	6:45 pm
28 WEDNESDAY	☽⚻♂	**4:11 am**	1:11 am
	☽⚺♃	**5:59 am**	2:59 am
	☽△☿	**7:42 am**	4:42 am
	☽△☉	**5:19 pm**	2:19 pm
	☽⚻♀	**10:00 pm**	7:00 pm
	☽⚹♄		10:53 pm
29 THURSDAY	☽⚹♄	**1:53 am**	
	☽⚺♅	**9:51 am**	6:51 am
	♂☍♃	**11:50 am**	8:50 am
	☽⚺♆		11:03 pm
30 FRIDAY	☽⚺♆	**2:03 am**	
	☽□♇	**6:44 am**	3:44 am
	♀⚻♄	**12:27 pm**	9:27 am
	☽⚹♃	**3:38 pm**	12:38 pm
	☽△♂	**5:26 pm**	2:26 pm
31 SATURDAY	☽□☿	**6:24 am**	3:24 am
	☽□☉	**9:16 am**	6:16 am
	☽□♄	**12:48 pm**	9:48 am
	☽△♀	**3:41 pm**	12:41 pm
	☽☌♅	**9:34 pm**	6:34 pm

Eastern time in bold type
Pacific time in medium type

JULY 2021

DATE	SID.TIME	SUN	MOON	NODE	MERCURY	VENUS	MARS	JUPITER	SATURN	URANUS	NEPTUNE	PLUTO	CERES	PALLAS	JUNO	VESTA	CHIRON
1 Th	18 37 4	9♋23 40	29♓18	10♊23D	18♊42	4♌37	12♌00	2♓01℞	12♒23℞	13♉48	23♓12℞	25♑58℞	20♉07	27♓16	11♐20℞	22♍40	12♈50
2 F	18 41 1	10 20 52	11♈41	10 23	19 23	5 50	12 38	1 59	12 19	13 50	23 11	25 56	20 28	27 20	11 10	23 02	12 51
3 Sa	18 44 57	11 18 05	23 47	10 23	20 08	7 03	13 15	1 56	12 16	13 52	23 11	25 55	20 49	27 23	11 00	23 25	12 52
4 Su	18 48 54	12 15 17	5♉43	10 25	20 58	8 15	13 52	1 54	12 12	13 55	23 11	25 53	21 10	27 27	10 50	23 48	12 52
5 M	18 52 50	13 12 30	17 32	10 26	21 52	9 28	14 29	1 51	12 09	13 57	23 11	25 52	21 30	27 30	10 40	24 12	12 53
6 T	18 56 47	14 09 43	29 19	10 28℞	22 51	10 41	15 07	1 48	12 05	13 59	23 10	25 51	21 51	27 33	10 31	24 35	12 53
7 W	19 0 43	15 06 56	11♊08	10 28	23 54	11 53	15 44	1 45	12 02	14 01	23 10	25 49	22 12	27 35	10 22	24 59	12 54
8 Th	19 4 40	16 04 10	23 04	10 28	25 01	13 06	16 21	1 42	11 58	14 03	23 10	25 48	22 32	27 37	10 13	25 22	12 54
9 F	19 8 36	17 01 23	5♋07	10 25	26 12	14 18	16 58	1 39	11 54	14 05	23 09	25 46	22 52	27 39	10 05	25 46	12 55
10 Sa	19 12 33	17 58 37	17 22	10 21	27 28	15 31	17 36	1 35	11 50	14 07	23 09	25 45	23 13	27 41	9 57	26 10	12 55
11 Su	19 16 30	18 55 52	29 49	10 15	28 48	16 43	18 13	1 32	11 46	14 09	23 08	25 44	23 33	27 42	9 49	26 35	12 55
12 M	19 20 26	19 53 06	12♌29	10 09	0♋12	17 56	18 50	1 28	11 42	14 11	23 08	25 42	23 53	27 43	9 42	26 59	12 55
13 T	19 24 23	20 50 20	25 23	10 02	1 40	19 08	19 28	1 24	11 38	14 12	23 07	25 41	24 13	27 43	9 34	27 23	12 56
14 W	19 28 19	21 47 34	8♍29	9 56	3 12	20 20	20 05	1 19	11 34	14 14	23 07	25 39	24 33	27 44℞	9 28	27 48	12 56
15 Th	19 32 16	22 44 49	21 49	9 50	4 48	21 33	20 43	1 15	11 30	14 16	23 06	25 38	24 53	27 44	9 21	28 13	12 56℞
16 F	19 36 12	23 42 03	5♎23	9 47	6 27	22 45	21 20	1 10	11 26	14 18	23 05	25 36	25 12	27 43	9 15	28 38	12 56
17 Sa	19 40 9	24 39 18	19 09	9 46D	8 10	23 57	21 57	1 06	11 22	14 19	23 05	25 35	25 32	27 43	9 09	29 03	12 56
18 Su	19 44 5	25 36 32	3♏09	9 46	9 56	25 10	22 35	1 01	11 18	14 21	23 04	25 34	25 51	27 41	9 03	29 28	12 56
19 M	19 48 2	26 33 47	17 21	9 47	11 46	26 22	23 12	0 56	11 14	14 22	23 03	25 32	26 11	27 40	8 58	29 53	12 56
20 T	19 51 59	27 31 02	1♐44	9 48℞	13 39	27 34	23 50	0 50	11 09	14 24	23 03	25 31	26 30	27 38	8 53	0♎19	12 55
21 W	19 55 55	28 28 17	16 15	9 48	15 34	28 46	24 27	0 45	11 05	14 25	23 02	25 29	26 49	27 36	8 49	0 44	12 55
22 Th	19 59 52	29 25 33	0♑51	9 46	17 32	29 58	25 05	0 39	11 01	14 27	23 01	25 28	27 08	27 34	8 45	1 10	12 55
23 F	20 3 48	0♌22 49	15 25	9 42	19 32	1♍10	25 42	0 34	10 56	14 28	23 00	25 26	27 27	27 31	8 41	1 35	12 54
24 Sa	20 7 45	1 20 05	29 53	9 36	21 34	2 22	26 20	0 28	10 52	14 30	22 59	25 25	27 46	27 28	8 37	2 01	12 54
25 Su	20 11 41	2 17 22	14♒06	9 29	23 37	3 34	26 57	0 22	10 48	14 31	22 59	25 23	28 04	27 25	8 34	2 27	12 54
26 M	20 15 38	3 14 40	28 00	9 20	25 42	4 46	27 35	0 16	10 43	14 32	22 58	25 22	28 23	27 21	8 31	2 54	12 53
27 T	20 19 34	4 11 58	11♓32	9 11	27 47	5 58	28 13	0 10	10 39	14 33	22 57	25 21	28 41	27 17	8 29	3 20	12 53
28 W	20 23 31	5 09 17	24 40	9 04	29 54	7 10	28 50	0 03	10 34	14 34	22 56	25 19	29 00	27 12	8 26	3 46	12 52
29 Th	20 27 28	6 06 37	7♈25	8 58	2♌00	8 22	29 28	29♒57	10 30	14 36	22 55	25 18	29 18	27 07	8 25	4 13	12 51
30 F	20 31 24	7 03 58	19 49	8 55	4 07	9 33	0♍05	29 50	10 26	14 37	22 54	25 16	29 36	27 02	8 23	4 39	12 51
31 Sa	20 35 21	8 01 21	1♉56	8 53D	6 13	10 45	0 43	29 44	10 21	14 38	22 53	25 15	29 54	26 57	8 22	5 06	12 50

EPHEMERIS CALCULATED FOR 12 MIDNIGHT GREENWICH MEAN TIME. ALL OTHER DATA AND FACING ASPECTARIAN PAGE IN **EASTERN TIME (BOLD)** AND PACIFIC TIME (REGULAR).

AUGUST 2021

☽ Last Aspect day	ET / hr:mn / PT		asp	☽ Ingress sign	day	ET / hr:mn / PT	
2	**3:41 am**	12:41 am	□ ♃	♊	2	**4:46 am**	1:46 am
4	**3:38 pm**	12:38 pm	△ ♃	♋	4	**5:17 pm**	2:17 pm
6	**6:12 pm**	3:12 pm	☍ ♇	♌	7	**3:31 am**	12:31 am
9	**8:23 am**	5:23 am	☍ ♃	♍	9	**10:56 am**	7:56 am
11	**7:22 am**	4:22 am	△ ♇	♎	11	**4:08 pm**	1:08 pm
13	**4:39 pm**	1:39 pm	△ ♃	♏	13	**8:01 pm**	5:01 pm
15	**11:05 pm**	8:05 pm	✶ ♀	♐	15	**11:12 pm**	8:12 pm
17	**9:43 pm**	6:43 pm	✶ ♃	♑	17		10:58 pm
17	**9:43 pm**	6:43 pm	✶ ♃	♑	18	**1:58 am**	
19	**7:59 pm**	4:59 pm	☌ ♇	♒	20	**4:49 am**	1:49 am

☽ Last Aspect day	ET / hr:mn / PT		asp	☽ Ingress sign	day	ET / hr:mn / PT	
22	**8:02 am**	5:02 am	☍ ☉	♓	22	**8:43 am**	5:43 am
24	**5:12 am**	2:12 am	✶ ♇	♈	24	**2:57 pm**	11:57 am
26	**5:14 pm**	2:14 pm	✶ ♃	♉	26		9:27 pm
26	**5:14 pm**	2:14 pm	✶ ♃	♉	27	**12:27 am**	
29	**10:59 am**	7:59 am	△ ☿	♊	29	**12:42 pm**	9:42 am
31	**4:48 pm**	1:48 pm	△ ♃	♋	31		10:26 pm

☽ Phases & Eclipses phase	day	ET / hr:mn / PT	
New Moon	8	**9:50 am**	6:50 am
2nd Quarter	15	**11:20 am**	8:20 am
Full Moon	22	**8:02 am**	5:02 am
4th Quarter	30	**3:13 am**	12:13 am

Planet Ingress		day	ET / hr:mn / PT	
☿	♍	11	**5:57 pm**	2:57 pm
♀	♎	15		9:27 pm
♀	♎	16	**12:27 am**	
☉	♍	22	**5:35 pm**	2:35 pm
☿	♎	29		10:10 pm
☿	♎	30	1:10 am	

Planetary Motion		day	ET / hr:mn / PT	
✱	D	2	**7:43 pm**	4:43 pm
♅	℞	19	**9:40 pm**	6:40 pm

1 SUNDAY
☉ ☌ ☿ **10:08 am** 7:08 am
☽ ✶ ♆ **2:13 pm** 11:13 am
☿ ☍ ♄ **5:50 pm** 2:50 pm
☽ △ ♇ **7:01 pm** 4:01 pm
☉ ☍ ♄ 11:14 pm

2 MONDAY
☉ ☍ ♄ **2:14 am**
☽ □ ♃ **3:41 am** 12:41 am
☽ □ ♂ **9:30 am** 6:30 am
☽ △ ♄ 10:19 pm
♀ △ ♅ 11:53 pm

3 TUESDAY
☽ △ ♄ **1:19 am**
♀ △ ♅ **2:53 am**
☽ ✶ ☉ **3:30 am** 12:30 am
☽ ✶ ☿ **8:12 am** 5:12 am
☽ ⚺ ♅ **10:34 am** 7:34 am
☽ □ ♀ **11:25 am** 8:25 am
☿ □ ♅ **9:57 pm** 6:57 pm
☽ □ ♆ 11:55 pm

4 WEDNESDAY
☽ □ ♆ **2:55 am**
☽ ⚻ ♇ **7:37 am** 4:37 am
☽ △ ♃ **3:38 pm** 12:38 pm
☿ ⚺ ♀ 9:43 pm
☽ ✶ ♂ 10:12 pm

5 THURSDAY
☿ ⚺ ♀ **12:43 am**
☽ ✶ ♂ **1:12 am**
☽ ⚻ ♄ **12:52 pm** 9:52 am
☽ ⚺ ☉ **8:24 pm** 5:24 pm
☽ ✶ ♅ **10:12 pm** 7:12 pm

6 FRIDAY
☽ ✶ ♀ **5:17 am** 2:17 am
☽ ⚺ ☿ **7:31 am** 4:31 am
☽ △ ♆ **1:43 pm** 10:43 am
☽ ☍ ♇ **6:12 pm** 3:12 pm
☉ □ ♅ **7:57 pm** 4:57 pm
☽ ⚻ ♃ 10:23 pm

7 SATURDAY
☽ ⚻ ♃ **1:23 am**
☽ ⚺ ♂ **2:04 pm** 11:04 am
☽ ☍ ♄ **9:50 pm** 6:50 pm
☿ ⚻ ♆ **10:24 pm** 7:24 pm

8 SUNDAY
☽ □ ♅ **7:04 am** 4:04 am
☽ ☌ ☉ **9:50 am** 6:50 am
☽ ⚺ ♀ **7:24 pm** 4:24 pm
☽ ⚻ ♆ **9:42 pm** 6:42 pm
☽ ☌ ☿ 10:45 pm
☽ ⚻ ♇ 10:57 pm

9 MONDAY
☽ ☌ ☿ **1:45 am**
☽ ⚻ ♇ **1:57 am**
☿ ⚻ ♇ **3:03 am** 12:03 am

☽ ☍ ♃ **8:23 am** 5:23 am
♀ ☍ ♆ **8:20 pm** 5:20 pm
☽ ☌ ♂ **11:42 pm** 8:42 pm

10 TUESDAY
☽ ⚻ ♄ **4:07 am** 1:07 am
☽ △ ♅ **1:19 pm** 10:19 am
☽ ⚺ ☉ **8:03 pm** 5:03 pm
☿ ☍ ♃ **9:20 pm** 6:20 pm

11 WEDNESDAY
☽ ☍ ♆ **3:16 am** 12:16 am
☽ ☌ ♀ **6:15 am** 3:15 am
☽ △ ♇ **7:22 am** 4:22 am
☽ ⚻ ♃ **1:10 pm** 10:10 am
☽ ⚺ ☿ **3:51 pm** 12:51 pm
♀ △ ♇ **6:46 pm** 3:46 pm

12 THURSDAY
☽ ⚺ ♂ **7:03 am** 4:03 am
☽ △ ♄ **8:32 am** 5:32 am
☽ ⚻ ♅ **5:48 pm** 2:48 pm

13 FRIDAY
☽ ✶ ☉ **4:13 am** 1:13 am
☽ ⚻ ♆ **7:19 am** 4:19 am
☽ □ ♇ **11:20 am** 8:20 am
♂ ⚻ ♄ **12:27 pm** 9:27 am
☽ ⚺ ♀ **3:10 pm** 12:10 pm
☽ △ ♃ **4:39 pm** 1:39 pm

14 SATURDAY
☽ ✶ ☿ **3:33 am** 12:33 am
♀ ⚻ ♃ **6:58 am** 3:58 am
☽ □ ♄ **11:54 am** 8:54 am

☽ ✶ ♂ **1:08 pm** 10:08 am
☽ ☍ ♅ **9:18 pm** 6:18 pm
☉ ⚻ ♆ 9:14 pm

15 SUNDAY
☉ ⚻ ♆ **12:14 am**
☽ △ ♆ **10:33 am** 7:33 am
☽ □ ☉ **11:20 am** 8:20 am
☽ ✶ ♇ **2:32 pm** 11:32 am
☽ □ ♃ **7:23 pm** 4:23 pm
☽ ✶ ♀ **11:05 pm** 8:05 pm

16 MONDAY
☽ □ ☿ **1:57 pm** 10:57 am
☽ ✶ ♄ **2:40 pm** 11:40 am
☽ □ ♂ **6:31 pm** 3:31 pm
☿ ⚻ ♄ **7:35 pm** 4:35 pm
☽ ⚻ ♅ 9:15 pm

17 TUESDAY
☽ ⚻ ♅ **12:15 am**
☉ ⚻ ♇ **9:31 am** 6:31 am
☽ □ ♆ **1:19 pm** 10:19 am
☽ ⚺ ♇ **5:17 pm** 2:17 pm
☽ △ ☉ **5:51 pm** 2:51 pm
☽ ✶ ♃ **9:43 pm** 6:43 pm

18 WEDNESDAY
☽ □ ♀ **6:27 am** 3:27 am
☽ ⚺ ♄ **5:08 pm** 2:08 pm
☿ ☌ ♂ **11:28 pm** 8:28 pm
☽ △ ♂ **11:37 pm** 8:37 pm
☽ △ ☿ **11:38 pm** 8:38 pm
☽ △ ♅ 11:59 pm

19 THURSDAY
☽ △ ♅ **2:59 am**
☽ ✶ ♆ **3:59 pm** 12:59 pm
☽ ☌ ♇ **7:59 pm** 4:59 pm
☉ ☍ ♃ **8:29 pm** 5:29 pm
☽ ⚺ ♃ 9:03 pm
☽ ⚻ ☉ 9:21 pm

20 FRIDAY
☽ ⚺ ♃ **12:03 am**
☽ ⚻ ☉ **12:21 am**
☿ △ ♅ **4:06 am** 1:06 am
☽ △ ♀ **2:01 pm** 11:01 am
☽ ☌ ♄ **7:55 pm** 4:55 pm

21 SATURDAY
☽ ⚻ ♂ **5:13 am** 2:13 am
☽ □ ♅ **6:12 am** 3:12 am
☽ ⚻ ☿ **9:41 am** 6:41 am
☽ ⚺ ♆ **7:24 pm** 4:24 pm
☽ ⚺ ♇ **11:32 pm** 8:32 pm
♂ △ ♅ 11:38 pm

22 SUNDAY
♂ △ ♅ **2:38 am**
☽ ☌ ♃ **3:19 am** 12:19 am
☽ ☍ ☉ **8:02 am** 5:02 am
☽ ⚻ ♀ **11:14 pm** 8:14 pm
☽ ⚺ ♄ 9:07 pm

23 MONDAY
☽ ⚺ ♄ **12:07 am**
♀ △ ♄ **8:48 am** 5:48 am
☽ ✶ ♅ **11:04 am** 8:04 am
☽ ☍ ♂ **12:43 pm** 9:43 am

☽ ☍ ☿ **10:03 pm** 7:03 pm
☽ ☌ ♆ 9:50 pm

24 TUESDAY
☽ ☌ ♆ **12:50 am**
☽ ✶ ♇ **5:12 am** 2:12 am
☽ ⚺ ♃ **8:43 am** 5:43 am
☽ ⚻ ☉ **6:37 pm** 3:37 pm
☿ ☍ ♆ **9:14 pm** 6:14 pm

25 WEDNESDAY
☽ ✶ ♄ **6:58 am** 3:58 am
☽ ☍ ♀ **11:57 am** 8:57 am
☽ ⚺ ♅ **6:51 pm** 3:51 pm
☽ ⚻ ♂ **11:37 pm** 8:37 pm

26 THURSDAY
☽ ⚺ ♆ **9:22 am** 6:22 am
☿ △ ♇ **10:23 am** 7:23 am
☽ □ ♇ **2:02 pm** 11:02 am
☽ ⚻ ☿ **2:33 pm** 11:33 am
☽ ✶ ♃ **5:14 pm** 2:14 pm

27 FRIDAY
☽ △ ☉ **9:19 am** 6:19 am
☿ ⚻ ♃ **11:05 am** 8:05 am
☽ □ ♄ **5:04 pm** 2:04 pm

28 SATURDAY
☽ ⚻ ♀ **5:00 am** 2:00 am
☽ ☌ ♅ **5:52 am** 2:52 am
♀ ⚻ ♅ **1:43 pm** 10:43 am
☽ △ ♂ **2:14 pm** 11:14 am
☽ ✶ ♆ **8:56 pm** 5:56 pm
☽ △ ♇ 10:50 pm

29 SUNDAY
☽ △ ♇ **1:50 am**
☽ □ ♃ **4:36 am** 1:36 am
☽ △ ☿ **10:59 am** 7:59 am

30 MONDAY
☽ □ ☉ **3:13 am** 12:13 am
☽ △ ♄ **5:26 am** 2:26 am
☽ ⚺ ♅ **6:40 pm** 3:40 pm
☽ △ ♀ 9:30 pm

31 TUESDAY
☽ △ ♀ **12:30 am**
☉ ⚻ ♄ **4:46 am** 1:46 am
☽ □ ♂ **6:36 am** 3:36 am
☽ □ ♆ **9:41 am** 6:41 am
☽ ⚻ ♇ **2:37 pm** 11:37 am
☽ △ ♃ **4:48 pm** 1:48 pm

Eastern time in bold type
Pacific time in medium type

AUGUST 2021

DATE	SID.TIME	SUN	MOON	NODE	MERCURY	VENUS	MARS	JUPITER	SATURN	URANUS	NEPTUNE	PLUTO	CERES	PALLAS	JUNO	VESTA	CHIRON
1 Su	20 39 17	8♌58 44	13♉52	8♊53	8♌19	11♍57	1♍21	29♒37℞	10♒17℞	14♉39	22♓52℞	25♑14℞	0♊12	26♓51℞	8♐21℞	5♎33	12♈49℞
2 M	20 43 14	9 56 08	25 41	8 54	10 24	13 08	1 58	29 30	10 12	14 40	22 51	25 12	0 29	26 44	8 21D	5 59	12 48
3 T	20 47 10	10 53 34	7♊29	8 54℞	12 28	14 20	2 36	29 23	10 08	14 40	22 49	25 11	0 47	26 38	8 20	6 26	12 47
4 W	20 51 7	11 51 01	19 22	8 53	14 31	15 32	3 14	29 16	10 03	14 41	22 48	25 09	1 04	26 31	8 21	6 54	12 46
5 Th	20 55 3	12 48 29	1♋22	8 51	16 33	16 43	3 52	29 09	9 59	14 42	22 47	25 08	1 21	26 24	8 21	7 21	12 45
6 F	20 59 0	13 45 58	13 35	8 46	18 34	17 55	4 29	29 01	9 54	14 43	22 46	25 07	1 39	26 16	8 22	7 48	12 44
7 Sa	21 2 57	14 43 28	26 02	8 39	20 34	19 06	5 07	28 54	9 50	14 43	22 45	25 05	1 55	26 08	8 23	8 15	12 43
8 Su	21 6 53	15 40 59	8♌46	8 29	22 32	20 17	5 45	28 47	9 46	14 44	22 44	25 04	2 12	25 59	8 25	8 43	12 42
9 M	21 10 50	16 38 32	21 47	8 18	24 28	21 29	6 23	28 39	9 41	14 45	22 42	25 03	2 29	25 51	8 26	9 10	12 41
10 T	21 14 46	17 36 05	5♍03	8 07	26 24	22 40	7 01	28 32	9 37	14 45	22 41	25 01	2 45	25 42	8 29	9 38	12 40
11 W	21 18 43	18 33 39	18 32	7 56	28 17	23 51	7 39	28 24	9 32	14 46	22 40	25 00	3 02	25 32	8 31	10 06	12 38
12 Th	21 22 39	19 31 15	2♎13	7 47	0♍10	25 03	8 17	28 16	9 28	14 46	22 39	24 59	3 18	25 23	8 34	10 34	12 37
13 F	21 26 36	20 28 51	16 03	7 41	2 00	26 14	8 55	28 09	9 24	14 46	22 37	24 58	3 34	25 13	8 37	11 02	12 36
14 Sa	21 30 32	21 26 28	29 59	7 37	3 50	27 25	9 33	28 01	9 19	14 47	22 36	24 56	3 49	25 02	8 40	11 30	12 34
15 Su	21 34 29	22 24 06	14♏01	7 36D	5 37	28 36	10 11	27 53	9 15	14 47	22 34	24 55	4 05	24 52	8 44	11 58	12 33
16 M	21 38 26	23 21 45	28 07	7 35℞	7 24	29 47	10 49	27 45	9 11	14 47	22 33	24 54	4 20	24 41	8 48	12 26	12 31
17 T	21 42 22	24 19 25	12♐17	7 35	9 08	0♎58	11 27	27 37	9 06	14 47	22 32	24 53	4 36	24 29	8 52	12 54	12 30
18 W	21 46 19	25 17 07	26 28	7 34	10 52	2 09	12 05	27 30	9 02	14 47	22 30	24 51	4 51	24 18	8 57	13 23	12 28
19 Th	21 50 15	26 14 49	10♑40	7 31	12 34	3 19	12 43	27 22	8 58	14 48	22 29	24 50	5 06	24 06	9 02	13 51	12 26
20 F	21 54 12	27 12 32	24 49	7 25	14 14	4 30	13 21	27 14	8 54	14 48℞	22 27	24 49	5 20	23 54	9 07	14 20	12 25
21 Sa	21 58 8	28 10 17	8♒53	7 17	15 53	5 41	13 59	27 06	8 50	14 48	22 26	24 48	5 35	23 41	9 13	14 48	12 23
22 Su	22 2 5	29 08 02	22 45	7 06	17 31	6 52	14 37	26 58	8 46	14 47	22 25	24 47	5 49	23 29	9 18	15 17	12 21
23 M	22 6 1	0♍05 49	6♓23	6 54	19 07	8 02	15 15	26 50	8 42	14 47	22 23	24 46	6 03	23 16	9 24	15 46	12 19
24 T	22 9 58	1 03 38	19 43	6 42	20 42	9 13	15 53	26 42	8 38	14 47	22 22	24 45	6 17	23 03	9 31	16 15	12 18
25 W	22 13 55	2 01 28	2♈43	6 31	22 15	10 23	16 31	26 35	8 34	14 47	22 20	24 43	6 31	22 49	9 37	16 44	12 16
26 Th	22 17 51	2 59 19	15 23	6 22	23 47	11 33	17 10	26 27	8 30	14 47	22 18	24 42	6 44	22 36	9 44	17 13	12 14
27 F	22 21 48	3 57 13	27 44	6 15	25 18	12 44	17 48	26 19	8 26	14 46	22 17	24 41	6 58	22 22	9 51	17 42	12 12
28 Sa	22 25 44	4 55 08	9♉51	6 11	26 47	13 54	18 26	26 11	8 23	14 46	22 15	24 40	7 11	22 08	9 59	18 11	12 10
29 Su	22 29 41	5 53 05	21 46	6 10	28 15	15 04	19 04	26 04	8 19	14 46	22 14	24 39	7 23	21 53	10 07	18 40	12 08
30 M	22 33 37	6 51 03	3♊36	6 09	29 42	16 14	19 43	25 56	8 15	14 45	22 12	24 38	7 36	21 39	10 15	19 09	12 06
31 T	22 37 34	7 49 04	15 24	6 09	1♎07	17 24	20 21	25 48	8 12	14 45	22 11	24 37	7 48	21 24	10 23	19 38	12 04

EPHEMERIS CALCULATED FOR 12 MIDNIGHT GREENWICH MEAN TIME. ALL OTHER DATA AND FACING ASPECTARIAN PAGE IN **EASTERN TIME (BOLD)** AND PACIFIC TIME (REGULAR).

SEPTEMBER 2021

☽ Last Aspect day	ET / hr:mn / PT	asp	☽ Ingress sign	day	ET / hr:mn / PT
8/31	**4:48 pm** 1:48 pm	△ ♃	♋	1	**1:26 am**
2	10:37 pm	☍ ♇	♌	3	**11:58 am** 8:58 am
3	**1:37 am**	☍ ♇	♌	3	**11:58 am** 8:58 am
5	**10:22 am** 7:22 am	☍ ♃	♍	5	**7:06 pm** 4:06 pm
7	**3:24 pm** 12:24 pm	☌ ♂	♎	7	**11:20 pm** 8:20 pm
9	9:48 pm	☌ ♀	♏	9	11:05 pm
10	**12:48 am**	☌ ♀	♏	10	**2:05 am**
11	10:33 pm	✶ ♂	♐	12	**4:34 am** 1:34 am
12	**1:33 am**	✶ ♂	♐	12	**4:34 am** 1:34 am
14	**6:57 am** 3:57 am	□ ♂	♑	14	**7:34 am** 4:34 am
15	10:40 pm	☌ ♇	♒	16	**11:23 am** 8:23 am
16	**1:40 am**	☌ ♇	♒	16	**11:23 am** 8:23 am
18	**5:14 am** 2:14 am	☌ ♃	♓	18	**4:22 pm** 1:22 pm
20	**7:55 pm** 4:55 pm	☍ ☉	♈	20	**11:13 pm** 8:13 pm
22	**10:05 pm** 7:05 pm	☍ ☿	♉	23	**8:38 am** 5:38 am
25	**9:09 am** 6:09 am	△ ♇	♊	25	**8:36 pm** 5:36 pm
27	9:18 pm	△ ☿	♋	28	**9:34 am** 6:34 am
28	**12:18 pm**	△ ☿	♋	28	**9:34 am** 6:34 am
30	**10:49 am** 7:49 am	□ ☿	♌	30	**8:53 pm** 5:53 pm

☽ Phases & Eclipses phase	day	ET / hr:mn / PT
New Moon	6	**8:52 pm** 5:52 pm
2nd Quarter	13	**4:39 pm** 1:39 pm
Full Moon	20	**7:55 pm** 4:55 pm
4th Quarter	28	**9:57 pm** 6:57 pm

Planet Ingress	day	ET / hr:mn / PT
♀ ♏	10	**4:39 pm** 1:39 pm
♂ ♎	14	**8:14 pm** 5:14 pm
⚶ ♏	20	**12:57 pm** 9:57 am
☉ ♎	22	**3:21 pm** 12:21 pm

Planetary Motion	day	ET / hr:mn / PT
☿ ℞	26	10:10 pm
☿ ℞	27	**1:10 am**

1 WEDNESDAY
- ☽ □ ☿ **7:46 am** 4:46 am
- ☽ ⚻ ♄ **5:30 pm** 2:30 pm
- ☽ ✶ ☉ **8:52 pm** 5:52 pm

2 THURSDAY
- ☽ ✶ ♅ **6:33 am** 3:33 am
- ♂ ☍ ♆ **1:43 pm** 10:43 am
- ☽ □ ♀ **6:24 pm** 3:24 pm
- ☽ △ ♆ **8:52 pm** 5:52 pm
- ☽ ✶ ♂ **9:16 pm** 6:16 pm
- ☽ ☍ ♇ 10:37 pm

3 FRIDAY
- ☽ ☍ ♇ **1:37 am**
- ☽ ⚻ ♃ **3:12 am** 12:12 am
- ♀ ⚻ ♆ **8:13 pm** 5:13 pm
- ☽ ✶ ☿ 9:45 pm
- ☽ ☍ ♄ 11:55 pm

4 SATURDAY
- ☽ ✶ ☿ **12:45 am**
- ☽ ☍ ♄ **2:55 am**
- ☽ ⚺ ☉ **10:58 am** 7:58 am
- ☽ □ ♅ **3:23 pm** 12:23 pm
- ☿ △ ♄ **9:30 pm** 6:30 pm

5 SUNDAY
- ☽ ⚻ ♆ **4:47 am** 1:47 am
- ☽ ✶ ♀ **7:58 am** 4:58 am
- ☽ ⚺ ♂ **8:07 am** 5:07 am
- ☽ ⚻ ♇ **9:18 am** 6:18 am
- ☽ ☍ ♃ **10:22 am** 7:22 am

Eastern time in bold type
Pacific time in medium type

- ♀ ⚺ ♂ **11:26 am** 8:26 am
- ♀ □ ♇ **11:07 pm** 8:07 pm

6 MONDAY
- ♂ △ ♇ **8:20 am** 5:20 am
- ☽ ⚻ ♄ **8:57 am** 5:57 am
- ♀ △ ♃ **9:05 am** 6:05 am
- ☽ ⚺ ☿ **12:41 pm** 9:41 am
- ☽ ☌ ☉ **8:52 pm** 5:52 pm
- ☽ △ ♅ **8:54 pm** 5:54 pm
- ☉ △ ♅ **9:29 pm** 6:29 pm
- ♂ ⚻ ♃ **11:50 pm** 8:50 pm

7 TUESDAY
- ☽ ☍ ♆ **9:34 am** 6:34 am
- ☽ △ ♇ **1:56 pm** 10:56 am
- ☽ ⚻ ♃ **2:33 pm** 11:33 am
- ☽ ☌ ♂ **3:24 pm** 12:24 pm
- ☽ ⚺ ♀ **5:29 pm** 2:29 pm

8 WEDNESDAY
- ☽ △ ♄ **12:29 pm** 9:29 am
- ☽ ☌ ☿ **9:01 pm** 6:01 pm
- ☽ ⚻ ♅ 9:11 pm

9 THURSDAY
- ☽ ⚻ ♅ **12:11 am**
- ☽ ⚺ ☉ **3:58 am** 12:58 am
- ☽ ⚻ ♆ **12:28 pm** 9:28 am
- ☽ □ ♇ **4:48 pm** 1:48 pm
- ☽ △ ♃ **5:03 pm** 2:03 pm
- ☽ ⚺ ♂ **8:40 pm** 5:40 pm
- ☽ ☌ ♀ 9:48 pm

10 FRIDAY
- ☽ ☌ ♀ **12:48 am**
- ☿ ⚻ ♅ **12:17 pm** 9:17 am
- ☽ □ ♄ **2:53 pm** 11:53 am
- ☽ ☍ ♅ 11:37 pm

11 SATURDAY
- ☽ ☍ ♅ **2:37 am**
- ☽ ⚺ ☿ **3:49 am** 12:49 am
- ♃ ⚺ ♇ **6:06 am** 3:06 am
- ☽ ✶ ☉ **10:08 am** 7:08 am
- ☽ △ ♆ **2:50 pm** 11:50 am
- ☽ □ ♃ **7:08 pm** 4:08 pm
- ☽ ✶ ♇ **7:13 pm** 4:13 pm
- ☽ ✶ ♂ 10:33 pm

12 SUNDAY
- ☽ ✶ ♂ **1:33 am**
- ☽ ⚺ ♀ **7:45 am** 4:45 am
- ☽ ✶ ♄ **5:18 pm** 2:18 pm

13 MONDAY
- ☽ ⚻ ♅ **5:13 am** 2:13 am
- ☽ ✶ ☿ **10:31 am** 7:31 am
- ☽ □ ☉ **4:39 pm** 1:39 pm
- ☽ □ ♆ **5:33 pm** 2:33 pm
- ☽ ✶ ♃ **9:38 pm** 6:38 pm
- ☽ ⚺ ♇ **10:03 pm** 7:03 pm

14 TUESDAY
- ☉ ☍ ♆ **5:21 am** 2:21 am
- ☽ □ ♂ **6:57 am** 3:57 am
- ☽ ✶ ♀ **3:21 pm** 12:21 pm
- ☽ ⚺ ♄ **8:19 pm** 5:19 pm

15 WEDNESDAY
- ☽ △ ♅ **8:31 am** 5:31 am
- ☽ □ ☿ **5:41 pm** 2:41 pm
- ☽ ✶ ♆ **9:01 pm** 6:01 pm
- ☽ △ ☉ 9:07 pm
- ☽ ⚺ ♃ 9:54 pm
- ☽ ☌ ♇ 10:40 pm

16 THURSDAY
- ☽ △ ☉ **12:07 am**
- ☽ ⚺ ♃ **12:54 am**
- ☽ ☌ ♇ **1:40 am**
- ☉ ⚻ ♃ **10:18 am** 7:18 am
- ☽ △ ♂ **1:19 pm** 10:19 am
- ☉ △ ♇ **9:53 pm** 6:53 pm
- ☽ □ ♀ 9:03 pm
- ☽ ☌ ♄ 9:14 pm
- ♀ □ ♄ 11:15 pm

17 FRIDAY
- ☽ □ ♀ **12:03 am**
- ☽ ☌ ♄ **12:14 am**
- ♀ □ ♄ **2:15 am**
- ☽ □ ♅ **12:45 pm** 9:45 am
- ☿ ⚻ ♆ 9:18 pm
- ☽ ⚺ ♆ 10:32 pm
- ☽ △ ☿ 10:36 pm

18 SATURDAY
- ☿ ⚻ ♆ **12:18 am**
- ☽ ⚺ ♆ **1:32 am**
- ☽ △ ☿ **1:36 am**
- ☽ ☌ ♃ **5:14 am** 2:14 am
- ☽ ⚺ ♇ **6:21 am** 3:21 am

- ☽ ⚻ ☉ **8:55 am** 5:55 am
- ☽ ⚻ ♂ **9:04 pm** 6:04 pm

19 SUNDAY
- ☽ ⚺ ♄ **5:27 am** 2:27 am
- ☽ △ ♀ **10:26 am** 7:26 am
- ☽ ✶ ♅ **6:26 pm** 3:26 pm

20 MONDAY
- ☽ ☌ ♆ **7:39 am** 4:39 am
- ☽ ⚻ ☿ **10:50 am** 7:50 am
- ☽ ⚺ ♃ **11:15 am** 8:15 am
- ☽ ✶ ♇ **12:45 pm** 9:45 am
- ☿ △ ♃ **6:53 pm** 3:53 pm
- ☽ ☍ ☉ **7:55 pm** 4:55 pm

21 TUESDAY
- ☽ ☍ ♂ **7:03 am** 4:03 am
- ☽ ✶ ♄ **12:43 pm** 9:43 am
- ☽ ⚻ ♀ **11:34 pm** 8:34 pm
- ☽ ⚺ ♅ 11:20 pm

22 WEDNESDAY
- ☽ ⚺ ♅ **2:20 am**
- ☿ □ ♇ **9:12 am** 6:12 am
- ☽ ⚺ ♆ **4:11 pm** 1:11 pm
- ☽ ✶ ♃ **7:42 pm** 4:42 pm
- ☽ □ ♇ **9:37 pm** 6:37 pm
- ☽ ☍ ☿ **10:05 pm** 7:05 pm

23 THURSDAY
- ♀ ☍ ♅ **5:41 am** 2:41 am
- ☽ ⚻ ☉ **10:08 am** 7:08 am
- ☽ ⚻ ♂ **8:07 pm** 5:07 pm
- ☽ □ ♄ **10:40 pm** 7:40 pm

24 FRIDAY
- ☽ ☌ ♅ **12:56 pm** 9:56 am
- ☽ ☍ ♀ **4:16 pm** 1:16 pm

25 SATURDAY
- ☽ ✶ ♆ **3:23 am** 12:23 am
- ☽ □ ♃ **6:49 am** 3:49 am
- ☽ △ ♇ **9:09 am** 6:09 am
- ☽ ⚻ ☿ **11:10 am** 8:10 am
- ♂ △ ♄ **5:50 pm** 2:50 pm

26 SUNDAY
- ☽ △ ☉ **3:35 am** 12:35 am
- ☽ △ ♄ **10:57 am** 7:57 am
- ☽ △ ♂ **11:59 am** 8:59 am
- ☽ ⚺ ♅ 10:32 pm

27 MONDAY
- ☽ ⚺ ♅ **1:32 am**
- ☽ ⚻ ♀ **11:28 am** 8:28 am
- ☽ □ ♆ **4:11 pm** 1:11 pm
- ☽ △ ♃ **7:25 pm** 4:25 pm
- ☽ ⚻ ♇ **10:06 pm** 7:06 pm
- ☽ △ ☿ 9:18 pm

28 TUESDAY
- ☽ △ ☿ **12:18 am**
- ☽ □ ☉ **9:57 pm** 6:57 pm
- ☽ ⚻ ♄ **11:39 pm** 8:39 pm

29 WEDNESDAY
- ☽ □ ♂ **4:17 am** 1:17 am
- ♀ △ ♆ **12:14 pm** 9:14 am
- ☽ ✶ ♅ **1:54 pm** 10:54 am
- ☉ △ ♄ **6:19 pm** 3:19 pm

30 THURSDAY
- ☽ △ ♆ **4:06 am** 1:06 am
- ☽ △ ♀ **5:44 am** 2:44 am
- ☽ ⚻ ♃ **7:02 am** 4:02 am
- ☽ ☍ ♇ **9:54 am** 6:54 am
- ☽ □ ☿ **10:49 am** 7:49 am
- ♀ □ ♃ **7:31 pm** 4:31 pm

SEPTEMBER 2021

DATE	SID.TIME	SUN	MOON	NODE	MERCURY	VENUS	MARS	JUPITER	SATURN	URANUS	NEPTUNE	PLUTO	CERES	PALLAS	JUNO	VESTA	CHIRON
1 W	22 41 30	8♍47 07	27♊17	6♊08℞	2♎30	18♎34	20♍59	25♒41℞	8♒08℞	14♉44℞	22♓09℞	24♑36℞	8♊01	21♓09℞	10♐31	20♎08	12♈01℞
2 Th	22 45 27	9 45 11	9♋21	6 06	3 52	19 44	21 38	25 34	8 05	14 43	22 07	24 35	8 12	20 54	10 40	20 37	11 59
3 F	22 49 24	10 43 17	21 39	6 01	5 13	20 54	22 16	25 26	8 01	14 43	22 06	24 35	8 24	20 39	10 49	21 07	11 57
4 Sa	22 53 20	11 41 26	4♌15	5 53	6 32	22 04	22 55	25 19	7 58	14 42	22 04	24 34	8 36	20 24	10 58	21 37	11 55
5 Su	22 57 17	12 39 36	17 12	5 43	7 50	23 13	23 33	25 12	7 55	14 41	22 03	24 33	8 47	20 09	11 08	22 06	11 53
6 M	23 1 13	13 37 47	0♍31	5 31	9 05	24 23	24 12	25 05	7 51	14 41	22 01	24 32	8 58	19 53	11 18	22 36	11 50
7 T	23 5 10	14 36 01	14 08	5 19	10 20	25 32	24 50	24 58	7 48	14 40	21 59	24 31	9 08	19 38	11 27	23 06	11 48
8 W	23 9 6	15 34 16	28 03	5 07	11 32	26 42	25 29	24 51	7 45	14 39	21 58	24 30	9 19	19 22	11 38	23 36	11 46
9 Th	23 13 3	16 32 33	12♎09	4 58	12 42	27 51	26 07	24 44	7 42	14 38	21 56	24 30	9 29	19 06	11 48	24 06	11 43
10 F	23 16 59	17 30 52	26 23	4 50	13 51	29 00	26 46	24 37	7 39	14 37	21 54	24 29	9 39	18 51	11 59	24 35	11 41
11 Sa	23 20 56	18 29 12	10♏40	4 46	14 57	0♏10	27 25	24 31	7 36	14 36	21 53	24 28	9 48	18 35	12 10	25 06	11 38
12 Su	23 24 53	19 27 34	24 55	4 44D	16 02	1 19	28 03	24 24	7 34	14 35	21 51	24 27	9 58	18 19	12 21	25 36	11 36
13 M	23 28 49	20 25 58	9♐07	4 44℞	17 03	2 28	28 42	24 18	7 31	14 34	21 49	24 27	10 07	18 03	12 32	26 06	11 34
14 T	23 32 46	21 24 23	23 14	4 44	18 03	3 37	29 21	24 12	7 28	14 32	21 48	24 26	10 15	17 47	12 44	26 36	11 31
15 W	23 36 42	22 22 49	7♑15	4 43	19 00	4 45	0♎00	24 06	7 26	14 31	21 46	24 26	10 24	17 32	12 56	27 06	11 29
16 Th	23 40 39	23 21 17	21 09	4 41	19 54	5 54	0 38	24 00	7 24	14 30	21 44	24 25	10 32	17 16	13 08	27 37	11 26
17 F	23 44 35	24 19 47	4♒56	4 35	20 45	7 03	1 17	23 54	7 21	14 29	21 43	24 24	10 40	17 00	13 20	28 07	11 23
18 Sa	23 48 32	25 18 19	18 34	4 27	21 33	8 11	1 56	23 48	7 19	14 27	21 41	24 24	10 47	16 45	13 32	28 37	11 21
19 Su	23 52 28	26 16 52	2♓01	4 17	22 17	9 20	2 35	23 43	7 17	14 26	21 40	24 23	10 55	16 29	13 45	29 08	11 18
20 M	23 56 25	27 15 26	15 16	4 06	22 58	10 28	3 14	23 37	7 15	14 25	21 38	24 23	11 01	16 14	13 58	29 38	11 16
21 T	0 0 22	28 14 03	28 17	3 55	23 34	11 36	3 53	23 32	7 13	14 23	21 36	24 22	11 08	15 58	14 11	0♏09	11 13
22 W	0 4 18	29 12 42	11♈02	3 44	24 06	12 44	4 32	23 27	7 11	14 22	21 35	24 22	11 14	15 43	14 24	0 40	11 10
23 Th	0 8 15	0♎11 22	23 31	3 36	24 33	13 52	5 11	23 22	7 09	14 20	21 33	24 22	11 20	15 28	14 37	1 10	11 08
24 F	0 12 11	1 10 05	5♉46	3 30	24 56	15 00	5 50	23 18	7 07	14 18	21 31	24 21	11 26	15 13	14 51	1 41	11 05
25 Sa	0 16 8	2 08 50	17 49	3 26	25 13	16 07	6 29	23 13	7 06	14 17	21 30	24 21	11 31	14 59	15 05	2 12	11 03
26 Su	0 20 4	3 07 37	29 42	3 25D	25 24	17 15	7 08	23 09	7 04	14 15	21 28	24 21	11 36	14 44	15 19	2 43	11 00
27 M	0 24 1	4 06 26	11♊30	3 25	25 28℞	18 22	7 47	23 04	7 03	14 13	21 26	24 20	11 41	14 30	15 33	3 13	10 57
28 T	0 27 57	5 05 18	23 18	3 26	25 26	19 30	8 26	23 00	7 01	14 12	21 25	24 20	11 45	14 16	15 47	3 44	10 54
29 W	0 31 54	6 04 11	5♋11	3 26℞	25 17	20 37	9 05	22 57	7 00	14 10	21 23	24 20	11 49	14 02	16 01	4 15	10 52
30 Th	0 35 51	7 03 07	17 14	3 26	25 01	21 44	9 44	22 53	6 59	14 08	21 22	24 20	11 53	13 48	16 16	4 46	10 49

EPHEMERIS CALCULATED FOR 12 MIDNIGHT GREENWICH MEAN TIME. ALL OTHER DATA AND FACING ASPECTARIAN PAGE IN **EASTERN TIME (BOLD)** AND PACIFIC TIME (REGULAR).

OCTOBER 2021

☽ Last Aspect day	ET	PT	asp	☽ Ingress sign	day	ET	PT
2	7:43 pm	4:43 pm	□♀	♍	3	4:38 am	1:38 am
5	4:46 am	1:46 am	✶♀	♎	5	8:41 am	5:41 am
6		10:03 pm	□♇	♏	7	10:22 am	7:22 am
7	1:03 am		□♇	♏	7	10:22 am	7:22 am
8		11:05 pm	✶♇	♐	9	11:24 am	8:24 am
9	2:05 am		✶♇	♐	9	11:24 am	8:24 am
10		9:30 pm	✶♃	♑	11	1:15 pm	10:15 am
11	12:30 am		✶♃	♑	11	1:15 pm	10:15 am
13	6:53 am	3:53 am	☌♇	♒	13	4:47 pm	1:47 pm
15	8:33 am	5:33 am	△☉	♓	15	10:22 pm	7:22 pm
17	7:24 pm	4:24 pm	✶♇	♈	18	6:04 am	3:04 am
20	10:57 am	7:57 am	☍☉	♉	20	3:59 pm	12:59 pm
22	4:35 pm	1:35 pm	△♇	♊	23	3:57 am	12:57 am
25	10:11 am	7:11 am	△♂	♋	25	5:00 pm	2:00 pm
27		11:02 pm	□♂	♌	28	5:07 am	2:07 am
28	2:02 am		□♂	♌	28	5:07 am	2:07 am
30	3:05 am	12:05 am	△♀	♍	30	2:09 pm	11:09 am

☽ Phases & Eclipses phase	day	ET	PT
New Moon	6	7:05 am	4:05 am
2nd Quarter	12	11:25 pm	8:25 pm
Full Moon	20	10:57 am	7:57 am
4th Quarter	28	4:05 pm	1:05 pm

Planet Ingress	day	ET	PT
♀ ♐	7	7:21 am	4:21 am
☉ ♏	22		9:51 pm
☉ ♏	23	12:51 am	
♂ ♏	30	10:21 am	7:21 am

Planetary Motion	day	ET	PT
♇ D	6	2:29 pm	11:29 am
⚳ ℞	8	9:31 pm	6:31 pm
♄ D	10	10:17 pm	7:17 pm
♃ D	17		10:30 pm
♃ D	18	1:30 am	
☿ D	18	11:17 am	8:17 am

1 FRIDAY
☽ ☍ ♄ 10:10 am 7:10 am
☿ □ ♇ 10:26 am 7:26 am
☽ ✶ ☉ 1:34 pm 10:34 am
☽ ✶ ♂ 5:46 pm 2:46 pm
☿ ⚺ ♀ 9:56 pm 6:56 pm
☽ □ ♅ 11:32 pm 8:32 pm

2 SATURDAY
♀ ✶ ♇ 3:48 am 12:48 am
☽ ⚻ ♆ 12:51 pm 9:51 am
☽ ☍ ♃ 3:29 pm 12:29 pm
☽ ✶ ☿ 4:57 pm 1:57 pm
☽ ⚻ ♇ 6:22 pm 3:22 pm
☽ □ ♀ 7:43 pm 4:43 pm

3 SUNDAY
☽ ⚻ ♄ 4:56 pm 1:56 pm
☿ △ ♃ 8:05 pm 5:05 pm
☽ ⚺ ☉ 9:23 pm
☽ ⚺ ♂ 11:47 pm

4 MONDAY
☽ ⚺ ☉ 12:23 am
☽ ⚺ ♂ 2:47 am
☽ △ ♅ 5:19 am 2:19 am
☽ ☍ ♆ 5:48 pm 2:48 pm
☽ ⚺ ☿ 6:48 pm 3:48 pm
☽ ⚻ ♃ 8:10 pm 5:10 pm
☽ △ ♇ 11:03 pm 8:03 pm

5 TUESDAY
☽ ✶ ♀ 4:46 am 1:46 am
☿ ⚻ ♆ 9:53 am 6:53 am
☽ △ ♄ 8:16 pm 5:16 pm

6 WEDNESDAY
♂ ⚻ ♅ 5:27 am 2:27 am
☽ ☌ ☉ 7:05 am 4:05 am
☽ ⚻ ♅ 7:56 am 4:56 am
☽ ☌ ♂ 8:04 am 5:04 am
☽ ☌ ☿ 5:40 pm 2:40 pm
☉ ⚻ ♅ 7:11 pm 4:11 pm
☽ ⚻ ♆ 7:54 pm 4:54 pm
☽ △ ♃ 10:08 pm 7:08 pm
☽ □ ♇ 10:03 pm

7 THURSDAY
☽ □ ♇ 1:03 am
☽ ⚺ ♀ 10:37 am 7:37 am
☽ □ ♄ 9:37 pm 6:37 pm
☉ ☌ ♂ 9:01 pm

8 FRIDAY
☉ ☌ ♂ 12:01 am
☽ ☍ ♅ 9:00 am 6:00 am
☽ ⚺ ♂ 11:32 am 8:32 am
☽ ⚺ ☉ 11:49 am 8:49 am
☽ ⚺ ☿ 3:10 pm 12:10 pm
☽ △ ♆ 8:53 pm 5:53 pm
☽ □ ♃ 11:04 pm 8:04 pm
☽ ✶ ♇ 11:05 pm

9 SATURDAY
☽ ✶ ♇ 2:05 am
☉ ☌ ☿ 12:18 pm 9:18 am
☽ ☌ ♀ 3:37 pm 12:37 pm
☿ ☌ ♂ 6:48 pm 3:48 pm
☽ ✶ ♄ 10:43 pm 7:43 pm

10 SUNDAY
☽ ⚻ ♅ 10:08 am 7:08 am
☽ ✶ ☿ 12:49 pm 9:49 am
☽ ✶ ♂ 3:12 pm 12:12 pm
☽ ✶ ☉ 4:45 pm 1:45 pm
☽ □ ♆ 10:17 pm 7:17 pm
☽ ✶ ♃ 9:30 pm

11 MONDAY
☽ ✶ ♃ 12:30 am
☽ ⚺ ♇ 3:42 am 12:42 am
☽ ⚺ ♀ 9:43 pm 6:43 pm
☽ ⚺ ♄ 9:54 pm
☿ ⚻ ♅ 10:29 pm

12 TUESDAY
☽ ⚺ ♄ 12:54 am
☿ ⚻ ♅ 1:29 am
☽ □ ☿ 11:51 am 8:51 am
☽ △ ♅ 12:34 pm 9:34 am
☽ □ ♂ 8:27 pm 5:27 pm
☽ □ ☉ 11:25 pm 8:25 pm
☽ ✶ ♆ 10:11 pm

13 WEDNESDAY
☽ ✶ ♆ 1:11 am
☽ ⚺ ♃ 3:30 am 12:30 am
☽ ☌ ♇ 6:53 am 3:53 am
♀ ✶ ♄ 3:26 pm 12:26 pm
☉ ⚻ ♆ 11:32 pm 3:32 pm

14 THURSDAY
☽ ☌ ♄ 4:54 am 1:54 am
☽ ✶ ♀ 6:03 am 3:03 am
☽ △ ☿ 1:09 pm 10:09 am
☽ □ ♅ 4:52 pm 1:52 pm

15 FRIDAY
☽ △ ♂ 3:58 am 12:58 am
☽ ⚺ ♆ 6:02 am 3:02 am
☉ △ ♃ 7:46 am 4:46 am
☽ ☌ ♃ 8:29 am 5:29 am
☽ △ ☉ 8:33 am 5:33 am
☽ ⚺ ♇ 12:05 pm 9:05 am

16 SATURDAY
☽ ⚺ ♄ 10:59 am 7:59 am
☽ □ ♀ 4:59 pm 1:59 pm
☽ ⚻ ☿ 5:27 pm 2:27 pm
♂ ⚻ ♆ 8:32 pm 5:32 pm
☿ ✶ ♀ 9:24 pm 6:24 pm
☽ ✶ ♅ 11:14 pm 8:14 pm

17 SUNDAY
☉ □ ♇ 8:12 am 5:12 am
☽ ☌ ♆ 1:00 pm 10:00 am
☽ ⚻ ♂ 1:56 pm 10:56 am
☽ ⚺ ♃ 3:37 pm 12:37 pm
☽ ✶ ♇ 7:24 pm 4:24 pm
☽ ⚻ ☉ 8:20 pm 5:20 pm

18 MONDAY
☽ ✶ ♄ 7:15 pm 4:15 pm
♂ △ ♃ 10:36 pm 7:36 pm
☽ ☍ ☿ 10:26 pm

19 TUESDAY
☽ ☍ ☿ 1:26 am
☽ △ ♀ 6:40 am 3:40 am
☽ ⚺ ♅ 7:46 am 4:46 am
♀ ⚻ ♅ 7:15 pm 4:15 pm
☽ ⚺ ♆ 10:09 pm 7:09 pm
☽ ✶ ♃ 9:59 pm
☽ ☍ ♂ 11:28 pm

20 WEDNESDAY
☽ ✶ ♃ 12:59 am
☽ ☍ ♂ 2:28 am
☽ □ ♇ 4:56 am 1:56 am
☽ ☍ ☉ 10:57 am 7:57 am

21 THURSDAY
☽ □ ♄ 5:45 am 2:45 am
☽ ⚻ ☿ 1:44 pm 10:44 am
☽ ☌ ♅ 6:28 pm 3:28 pm
☽ ⚻ ♀ 11:08 pm 8:08 pm
♂ □ ♇ 9:20 pm

22 FRIDAY
♂ □ ♇ 12:20 am
☽ ✶ ♆ 9:26 am 6:26 am
☽ □ ♃ 12:32 pm 9:32 am
☽ △ ♇ 4:35 pm 1:35 pm
☽ ⚻ ♂ 5:33 pm 2:33 pm

23 SATURDAY
☽ ⚻ ☉ 4:14 am 1:14 am
☽ △ ♄ 6:12 pm 3:12 pm

24 SUNDAY
☽ △ ☿ 6:17 am 3:17 am
☽ ⚺ ♅ 6:54 am 3:54 am
☿ ⚻ ♅ 1:45 pm 10:45 am
☽ ☍ ♀ 5:42 pm 2:42 pm
☽ □ ♆ 10:14 pm 7:14 pm
☽ △ ♃ 10:33 pm

25 MONDAY
☽ △ ♃ 1:33 am
☽ ⚻ ♇ 5:36 am 2:36 am
☽ △ ♂ 10:11 am 7:11 am
☽ △ ☉ 10:54 pm 7:54 pm

26 TUESDAY
☽ ⚻ ♄ 7:21 am 4:21 am
☽ ✶ ♅ 7:37 pm 4:37 pm
♀ □ ♆ 9:06 pm 6:06 pm
☽ □ ☿ 10:10 pm

27 WEDNESDAY
☽ □ ☿ 1:10 am
☽ △ ♆ 10:48 am 7:48 am
☽ ⚻ ♀ 12:04 pm 9:04 am
☽ ⚻ ♃ 2:16 pm 11:16 am
☽ ☍ ♇ 6:08 pm 3:08 pm
☽ □ ♂ 11:02 pm

28 THURSDAY
☽ □ ♂ 2:02 am
♀ ✶ ♃ 3:15 pm 12:15 pm
☽ □ ☉ 4:05 pm 1:05 pm
☽ ☍ ♄ 7:03 pm 4:03 pm

29 FRIDAY
☽ □ ♅ 6:25 am 3:25 am
☽ ✶ ☿ 6:32 pm 3:32 pm
☽ ⚻ ♆ 8:53 pm 5:53 pm
☽ ☍ ♃ 9:24 pm

30 SATURDAY
☽ ☍ ♃ 12:24 am
☽ △ ♀ 3:05 am 12:05 am
☽ ⚻ ♇ 3:54 am 12:54 am
☉ □ ♄ 5:53 am 2:53 am
♀ ⚺ ♇ 1:54 pm 10:54 am
☽ ✶ ♂ 2:22 pm 11:22 am
☿ ⚻ ♆ 3:40 pm 12:40 pm

31 SUNDAY
☽ ⚻ ♄ 3:17 am 12:17 am
☽ ✶ ☉ 4:58 am 1:58 am
☽ △ ♅ 1:33 pm 10:33 am
☿ △ ♃ 9:18 pm

Eastern time in bold type
Pacific time in medium type

OCTOBER 2021

DATE	SID.TIME	SUN	MOON	NODE	MERCURY	VENUS	MARS	JUPITER	SATURN	URANUS	NEPTUNE	PLUTO	CERES	PALLAS	JUNO	VESTA	CHIRON
1 F	0 39 47	8♎02 06	29♋32	3♊23℞	24♎37℞	22♏51	10♎24	22♒49℞	6♒58℞	14♉06℞	21♓20℞	24♑19℞	11♊56	13♓34℞	16♐31	5♏17	10♈46℞
2 Sa	0 43 44	9 01 06	12♌11	3 19	24 06	23 58	11 03	22 46	6 57	14 04	21 19	24 19	11 59	13 21	16 46	5 48	10 44
3 Su	0 47 40	10 00 09	25 13	3 12	23 27	25 04	11 42	22 43	6 56	14 03	21 17	24 19	12 01	13 08	17 01	6 20	10 41
4 M	0 51 37	10 59 14	8♍40	3 04	22 40	26 11	12 22	22 40	6 55	14 01	21 15	24 19	12 03	12 55	17 17	6 51	10 38
5 T	0 55 33	11 58 22	22 32	2 55	21 47	27 17	13 01	22 37	6 55	13 59	21 14	24 19	12 05	12 43	17 32	7 22	10 36
6 W	0 59 30	12 57 31	6♎45	2 47	20 47	28 23	13 40	22 35	6 54	13 57	21 12	24 19D	12 06	12 31	17 48	7 53	10 33
7 Th	1 3 26	13 56 42	21 14	2 40	19 43	29 29	14 20	22 32	6 54	13 55	21 11	24 19	12 07	12 19	18 04	8 25	10 30
8 F	1 7 23	14 55 56	5♏54	2 35	18 34	0♐35	14 59	22 30	6 53	13 53	21 09	24 19	12 08	12 07	18 20	8 56	10 27
9 Sa	1 11 19	15 55 11	20 36	2 33D	17 24	1 40	15 39	22 28	6 53	13 50	21 08	24 19	12 08℞	11 56	18 36	9 27	10 25
10 Su	1 15 16	16 54 28	5♐14	2 32	16 13	2 46	16 18	22 27	6 53	13 48	21 07	24 19	12 08	11 45	18 52	9 59	10 22
11 M	1 19 13	17 53 48	19 43	2 33	15 04	3 51	16 58	22 25	6 53D	13 46	21 05	24 19	12 08	11 34	19 08	10 30	10 19
12 T	1 23 9	18 53 08	4♑00	2 34	13 58	4 56	17 37	22 24	6 53	13 44	21 04	24 19	12 07	11 24	19 25	11 02	10 17
13 W	1 27 6	19 52 31	18 02	2 35℞	12 58	6 01	18 17	22 23	6 53	13 42	21 02	24 19	12 05	11 14	19 42	11 33	10 14
14 Th	1 31 2	20 51 56	1♒50	2 35	12 05	7 05	18 57	22 22	6 53	13 40	21 01	24 20	12 04	11 04	19 59	12 05	10 11
15 F	1 34 59	21 51 22	15 23	2 32	11 21	8 10	19 36	22 21	6 53	13 37	20 59	24 20	12 01	10 55	20 16	12 36	10 09
16 Sa	1 38 55	22 50 49	28 42	2 28	10 46	9 14	20 16	22 20	6 54	13 35	20 58	24 20	11 59	10 46	20 33	13 08	10 06
17 Su	1 42 52	23 50 19	11♓48	2 22	10 23	10 18	20 56	22 20	6 54	13 33	20 57	24 20	11 56	10 38	20 50	13 40	10 03
18 M	1 46 48	24 49 50	24 40	2 16	10 10D	11 21	21 36	22 20D	6 55	13 31	20 55	24 21	11 53	10 29	21 08	14 11	10 01
19 T	1 50 45	25 49 23	7♈19	2 09	10 08	12 25	22 16	22 20	6 56	13 28	20 54	24 21	11 49	10 22	21 25	14 43	9 58
20 W	1 54 42	26 48 58	19 47	2 03	10 18	13 28	22 55	22 20	6 57	13 26	20 53	24 21	11 45	10 14	21 43	15 15	9 56
21 Th	1 58 38	27 48 35	2♉02	1 58	10 38	14 31	23 35	22 21	6 58	13 24	20 52	24 22	11 40	10 07	22 01	15 46	9 53
22 F	2 2 35	28 48 14	14 08	1 55	11 08	15 33	24 15	22 21	6 59	13 21	20 50	24 22	11 36	10 00	22 19	16 18	9 51
23 Sa	2 6 31	29 47 56	26 04	1 54D	11 47	16 36	24 55	22 22	7 00	13 19	20 49	24 23	11 30	9 54	22 37	16 50	9 48
24 Su	2 10 28	0♏47 39	7♊54	1 54	12 35	17 38	25 35	22 23	7 01	13 16	20 48	24 23	11 25	9 48	22 55	17 22	9 46
25 M	2 14 24	1 47 25	19 41	1 55	13 30	18 39	26 15	22 24	7 02	13 14	20 47	24 24	11 19	9 42	23 13	17 54	9 43
26 T	2 18 21	2 47 12	1♋29	1 57	14 32	19 41	26 55	22 26	7 04	13 12	20 46	24 24	11 12	9 37	23 32	18 26	9 41
27 W	2 22 17	3 47 02	13 21	1 58	15 40	20 42	27 35	22 27	7 05	13 09	20 45	24 25	11 05	9 32	23 50	18 58	9 38
28 Th	2 26 14	4 46 54	25 22	2 00℞	16 53	21 43	28 16	22 29	7 07	13 07	20 44	24 26	10 58	9 28	24 09	19 30	9 36
29 F	2 30 11	5 46 48	7♌38	2 00	18 10	22 43	28 56	22 31	7 09	13 04	20 43	24 26	10 51	9 24	24 28	20 02	9 33
30 Sa	2 34 7	6 46 45	20 13	1 59	19 32	23 43	29 36	22 34	7 11	13 02	20 41	24 27	10 43	9 20	24 47	20 34	9 31
31 Su	2 38 4	7 46 43	3♍12	1 57	20 56	24 42	0♏16	22 36	7 13	12 59	20 40	24 28	10 35	9 17	25 06	21 06	9 29

EPHEMERIS CALCULATED FOR 12 MIDNIGHT GREENWICH MEAN TIME. ALL OTHER DATA AND FACING ASPECTARIAN PAGE IN **EASTERN TIME (BOLD)** AND PACIFIC TIME (REGULAR).

NOVEMBER 2021

☽ Last Aspect day	ET / hr:mn / PT	asp	☽ Ingress sign day	ET / hr:mn / PT
1	**1:00 pm** 10:00 am	□ ♀	♎ 1	**7:11 pm** 4:11 pm
3	**6:32 pm** 3:32 pm	⚹ ♀	♏ 3	**8:52 pm** 5:52 pm
5	**12:10 pm** 9:10 am	⚹ ♇	♐ 5	**8:52 pm** 5:52 pm
7	**8:44 am** 5:44 am	⚹ ♃	♑ 7	**8:03 pm** 5:03 pm
9	**12:51 pm** 9:51 am	☌ ♇	♒ 9	**10:03 pm** 7:03 pm
11	**2:52 pm** 11:52 am	☌ ♃	♓ 11	11:54 pm
11	**2:52 pm** 11:52 am	☌ ♃	♓ 12	**2:54 am**
13	9:40 pm	⚹ ♇	♈ 14	**10:48 am** 7:48 am
14	**12:40 am**	⚹ ♇	♈ 14	**10:48 am** 7:48 am
16	**10:51 am** 7:51 am	□ ♇	♉ 16	**9:18 pm** 6:18 pm

☽ Last Aspect day	ET / hr:mn / PT	asp	☽ Ingress sign day	ET / hr:mn / PT
19	**3:57 am** 12:57 am	☍ ☉	♊ 19	**9:33 am** 6:33 am
21	**10:52 am** 7:52 am	△ ♃	♋ 21	**10:33 pm** 7:33 pm
23	9:46 pm	☍ ♇	♌ 24	**10:59 am** 7:59 am
24	**12:46 am**	☍ ♇	♌ 24	**10:59 am** 7:59 am
26	**11:24 am** 8:24 am	☍ ♃	♍ 26	**9:12 pm** 6:12 pm
28	**7:02 pm** 4:02 pm	△ ♇	♎ 29	**3:55 am** 12:55 am
30	**11:20 pm** 8:20 pm	△ ♃	♏ 12/1	**6:55 am** 3:55 am

☽ Phases & Eclipses phase	day	ET / hr:mn / PT
New Moon	4	**5:15 pm** 2:15 pm
2nd Quarter	11	**7:46 am** 4:46 am
Full Moon	19	**3:57 am** 12:57 am
☊	19	27° ♉ 14'
4th Quarter	27	**7:28 am** 4:28 am

Planet Ingress	day	ET / hr:mn / PT
♀ ♑	5	**6:44 am** 3:44 am
⚵ ♑	14	**3:23 pm** 12:23 pm
⚶ ♐	16	**9:07 am** 6:07 am
☉ ♐	21	**9:34 pm** 6:34 pm
☿ ♐	24	**10:36 am** 7:36 am

Planetary Motion	day	ET / hr:mn / PT
♀ D	8	**4:23 am** 1:23 am

1 MONDAY
☿ △ ♃ **12:18 am**
☽ ☍ ♆ **3:05 am** 12:05 am
☽ ⚻ ♃ **6:35 am** 3:35 am
☽ ⚺ ☿ **7:18 am** 4:18 am
☽ △ ♇ **9:43 am** 6:43 am
☽ □ ♀ **1:00 pm** 10:00 am
☽ ⚺ ♂ **10:01 pm** 7:01 pm

2 TUESDAY
☿ □ ♇ **5:39 am** 2:39 am
☽ △ ♄ **7:31 am** 4:31 am
☽ ⚺ ☉ **12:51 pm** 9:51 am
☽ ⚻ ♅ **4:50 pm** 1:50 pm

3 WEDNESDAY
☽ ⚻ ♆ **5:36 am** 2:36 am
☽ △ ♃ **9:08 am** 6:08 am
☽ □ ♇ **11:57 am** 8:57 am
☽ ☌ ☿ **3:27 pm** 12:27 pm
☽ ⚹ ♀ **6:32 pm** 3:32 pm
☽ ☌ ♂ 10:55 pm

4 THURSDAY
☽ ☌ ♂ **1:55 am**
☽ □ ♄ **8:46 am** 5:46 am
☽ ☌ ☉ **5:15 pm** 2:15 pm
☽ ☍ ♅ **5:26 pm** 2:26 pm
☉ ☍ ♅ **7:58 pm** 4:58 pm

5 FRIDAY
☽ △ ♆ **5:53 am** 2:53 am
☽ □ ♃ **9:33 am** 6:33 am
☽ ⚹ ♇ **12:10 pm** 9:10 am
☽ ⚺ ☿ **9:09 pm** 6:09 pm
☽ ⚺ ♀ **9:49 pm** 6:49 pm

6 SATURDAY
☽ ⚺ ♂ **4:06 am** 1:06 am
☽ ⚹ ♄ **8:46 am** 5:46 am
☿ ⚹ ♀ **11:59 am** 8:59 am
☽ ⚻ ♅ **5:09 pm** 2:09 pm
☽ ⚺ ☉ **8:32 pm** 5:32 pm

7 SUNDAY
☽ □ ♆ **4:47 am** 1:47 am
☽ ⚹ ♃ **8:44 am** 5:44 am
☽ ⚺ ♇ **11:14 am** 8:14 am
☽ ☌ ♀ 9:19 pm
☽ ⚹ ☿ 11:13 pm

8 MONDAY
☽ ☌ ♀ **12:19 am**
☽ ⚹ ☿ **2:13 am**
☽ ⚹ ♂ **5:49 am** 2:49 am
☽ ⚺ ♄ **8:25 am** 5:25 am
☽ △ ♅ **4:48 pm** 1:48 pm
☽ ⚹ ☉ 9:06 pm

9 TUESDAY
☽ ⚹ ☉ **12:06 am**
☽ ⚹ ♆ **6:01 am** 3:01 am
☽ ⚺ ♃ **10:26 am** 7:26 am
☽ ☌ ♇ **12:51 pm** 9:51 am

10 WEDNESDAY
☽ ⚺ ♀ **6:04 am** 3:04 am
☿ ☌ ♂ **7:57 am** 4:57 am
☽ □ ♂ **10:55 am** 7:55 am
☽ □ ☿ **11:08 am** 8:08 am
☽ ☌ ♄ **11:15 am** 8:15 am
☿ □ ♄ **12:04 pm** 9:04 am
♂ □ ♄ **6:14 pm** 3:14 pm
☽ □ ♅ **7:45 pm** 4:45 pm

11 THURSDAY
☽ □ ☉ **7:46 am** 4:46 am
☽ ⚺ ♆ **9:51 am** 6:51 am
☽ ☌ ♃ **2:52 pm** 11:52 am
☽ ⚺ ♇ **5:13 pm** 2:13 pm

12 FRIDAY
☉ △ ♆ **11:24 am** 8:24 am
☽ ⚹ ♀ **3:18 pm** 12:18 pm
☽ ⚺ ♄ **5:05 pm** 2:05 pm
☽ △ ♂ **7:28 pm** 4:28 pm
☽ △ ☿ 9:23 pm
☽ ⚹ ♅ 10:44 pm

13 SATURDAY
☽ △ ☿ **12:23 am**
☽ ⚹ ♅ **1:44 am**
☿ ☍ ♅ **10:57 am** 7:57 am
☽ ☌ ♆ **4:46 pm** 1:46 pm
☽ △ ☉ **7:19 pm** 4:19 pm
♀ ⚺ ♄ **7:43 pm** 4:43 pm
☽ ⚺ ♃ **10:29 pm** 7:29 pm
☽ ⚹ ♇ 9:40 pm

14 SUNDAY
☽ ⚹ ♇ **12:40 am**
☽ ⚹ ♄ 10:59 pm

15 MONDAY
☽ ⚹ ♄ **1:59 am**
☽ □ ♀ **4:06 am** 1:06 am
☽ ⚻ ♂ **7:32 am** 4:32 am
☽ ⚺ ♅ **10:36 am** 7:36 am
☉ □ ♃ **2:58 pm** 11:58 am
☽ ⚻ ☿ **5:58 pm** 2:58 pm
☽ ⚺ ♆ 11:29 pm

16 TUESDAY
☽ ⚺ ♆ **2:29 am**
☽ ⚹ ♃ **8:55 am** 5:55 am
☽ ⚻ ☉ **10:23 am** 7:23 am
☽ □ ♇ **10:51 am** 7:51 am
☉ ⚹ ♇ **4:01 pm** 1:01 pm

17 WEDNESDAY
♂ ☍ ♅ **12:23 pm** 9:23 am
☽ □ ♄ **1:19 pm** 10:19 am
☽ △ ♀ **7:39 pm** 4:39 pm
☽ ☌ ♅ **9:44 pm** 6:44 pm
☽ ☍ ♂ **10:20 pm** 7:20 pm

18 THURSDAY
☿ △ ♆ **10:38 am** 7:38 am
☽ ⚹ ♆ **2:14 pm** 11:14 am
☽ ☍ ☿ **2:48 pm** 11:48 am
☽ □ ♃ **9:23 pm** 6:23 pm
☽ △ ♇ **10:57 pm** 7:57 pm
♀ △ ♅ 10:08 pm

19 FRIDAY
♀ △ ♅ **1:08 am**
☽ ☍ ☉ **3:57 am** 12:57 am
☽ △ ♄ 11:12 pm

20 SATURDAY
☽ △ ♄ **2:12 am**
☽ ⚺ ♅ **10:14 am** 7:14 am
☽ ⚻ ♀ **12:43 pm** 9:43 am
☽ ⚻ ♂ **2:46 pm** 11:46 am
☿ □ ♃ **6:43 pm** 3:43 pm

21 SUNDAY
☽ □ ♆ **3:05 am** 12:05 am
☿ ⚹ ♇ **4:14 am** 1:14 am
☽ △ ♃ **10:52 am** 7:52 am
☽ ⚻ ♇ **12:01 pm** 9:01 am
☽ ⚻ ☿ **1:13 pm** 10:13 am
☽ ⚻ ☉ **10:38 pm** 7:38 pm

22 MONDAY
☽ ⚻ ♄ **3:32 pm** 12:32 pm
☽ ⚹ ♅ **10:59 pm** 7:59 pm

23 TUESDAY
☽ ☍ ♀ **5:49 am** 2:49 am
☽ △ ♂ **7:24 am** 4:24 am
☽ △ ♆ **3:50 pm** 12:50 pm
☽ ⚻ ♃ 9:06 pm
☽ ☍ ♇ 9:46 pm

24 WEDNESDAY
☽ ⚻ ♃ **12:06 am**
☽ ☍ ♇ **12:46 am**
☽ △ ☿ **11:02 am** 8:02 am
☽ △ ☉ **4:34 pm** 1:34 pm

25 THURSDAY
☽ ☍ ♄ **3:52 am** 12:52 am
☽ □ ♅ **10:32 am** 7:32 am
☽ ⚻ ♀ **8:57 pm** 5:57 pm
☽ □ ♂ **10:19 pm** 7:19 pm
☽ ⚻ ♆ 11:55 pm

26 FRIDAY
☽ ⚻ ♆ **2:55 am**
☽ ☍ ♃ **11:24 am** 8:24 am
☽ ⚻ ♇ **11:35 am** 8:35 am

27 SATURDAY
☽ □ ☿ **5:27 am** 2:27 am
☽ □ ☉ **7:28 am** 4:28 am
♃ ⚺ ♇ **11:16 am** 8:16 am
☽ ⚻ ♄ **1:30 pm** 10:30 am
☽ △ ♅ **7:18 pm** 4:18 pm

28 SUNDAY
☽ △ ♀ **8:15 am** 5:15 am
☽ ⚹ ♂ **9:37 am** 6:37 am
☽ ☍ ♆ **10:50 am** 7:50 am
☽ △ ♇ **7:02 pm** 4:02 pm
☽ ⚻ ♃ **7:17 pm** 4:17 pm
☉ ☌ ☿ **11:39 pm** 8:39 pm

29 MONDAY
♂ △ ♆ **9:10 am** 6:10 am
☽ ⚹ ☉ **5:44 pm** 2:44 pm
☽ ⚹ ☿ **6:33 pm** 3:33 pm
☽ △ ♄ **7:24 pm** 4:24 pm
☽ ⚻ ♅ 9:22 pm
☿ ⚹ ♄ 11:19 pm

30 TUESDAY
☽ ⚻ ♅ **12:22 am**
☿ ⚹ ♄ **2:19 am**
☽ □ ♀ **2:56 pm** 11:56 am
☽ ⚻ ♆ **2:58 pm** 11:58 am
♀ ⚹ ♆ **3:46 pm** 12:46 pm
☽ ⚺ ♂ **4:29 pm** 1:29 pm
☉ ⚹ ♄ **6:14 pm** 3:14 pm
☽ □ ♇ **10:43 pm** 7:43 pm
☽ △ ♃ **11:20 pm** 8:20 pm

Eastern time in bold type
Pacific time in medium type

NOVEMBER 2018

DATE	SID.TIME	SUN	MOON	NODE	MERCURY	VENUS	MARS	JUPITER	SATURN	URANUS	NEPTUNE	PLUTO	CERES	PALLAS	JUNO	VESTA	CHIRON
1 M	2 42 0	8♏46 44	16♍37	1♊55℞	22♎23	25♐42	0♏56	22♒39	7♒15	12♉57℞	20♓39℞	24♑28	10♊26℞	9♓14℞	25♐25	21♏38	9♈27℞
2 T	2 45 57	9 46 47	0♎29	1 51	23 53	26 41	1 37	22 42	7 17	12 54	20 39	24 29	10 17	9 11	25 44	22 10	9 24
3 W	2 49 53	10 46 52	14 47	1 48	25 24	27 39	2 17	22 45	7 19	12 52	20 38	24 30	10 08	9 09	26 03	22 42	9 22
4 Th	2 53 50	11 46 58	29 28	1 46	26 57	28 37	2 58	22 48	7 21	12 50	20 37	24 31	9 58	9 07	26 23	23 14	9 20
5 F	2 57 46	12 47 07	14♏24	1 44	28 31	29 34	3 38	22 51	7 24	12 47	20 36	24 31	9 48	9 06	26 42	23 46	9 18
6 Sa	3 1 43	13 47 18	29 27	1 43D	0♏06	0♑31	4 19	22 55	7 26	12 45	20 35	24 32	9 38	9 04	27 02	24 18	9 16
7 Su	3 5 40	14 47 30	14♐29	1 44	1 41	1 28	4 59	22 59	7 29	12 42	20 34	24 33	9 27	9 04	27 22	24 51	9 13
8 M	3 9 36	15 47 45	29 21	1 45	3 17	2 24	5 40	23 03	7 32	12 40	20 33	24 34	9 16	9 03D	27 41	25 23	9 11
9 T	3 13 33	16 48 00	13♑57	1 46	4 54	3 20	6 20	23 07	7 34	12 37	20 33	24 35	9 05	9 03	28 01	25 55	9 09
10 W	3 17 29	17 48 17	28 13	1 47	6 31	4 15	7 01	23 11	7 37	12 35	20 32	24 36	8 53	9 04	28 21	26 27	9 07
11 Th	3 21 26	18 48 36	12♒06	1 48℞	8 07	5 09	7 42	23 16	7 40	12 32	20 31	24 37	8 42	9 05	28 42	26 59	9 05
12 F	3 25 22	19 48 56	25 38	1 48	9 44	6 03	8 22	23 21	7 43	12 30	20 31	24 38	8 30	9 06	29 02	27 32	9 04
13 Sa	3 29 19	20 49 17	8♓48	1 47	11 21	6 56	9 03	23 25	7 47	12 27	20 30	24 39	8 17	9 07	29 22	28 04	9 02
14 Su	3 33 15	21 49 39	21 41	1 46	12 58	7 48	9 44	23 31	7 50	12 25	20 29	24 40	8 05	9 09	29 43	28 36	9 00
15 M	3 37 12	22 50 03	4♈17	1 45	14 35	8 40	10 25	23 36	7 53	12 22	20 29	24 41	7 52	9 11	0♑03	29 09	8 58
16 T	3 41 9	23 50 28	16 39	1 44	16 12	9 31	11 05	23 41	7 57	12 20	20 28	24 42	7 39	9 14	0 24	29 41	8 56
17 W	3 45 5	24 50 55	28 51	1 43	17 48	10 22	11 46	23 47	8 00	12 18	20 28	24 44	7 26	9 17	0 44	0♐13	8 55
18 Th	3 49 2	25 51 23	10♉53	1 42	19 24	11 11	12 27	23 53	8 04	12 15	20 27	24 45	7 13	9 20	1 05	0 46	8 53
19 F	3 52 58	26 51 53	22 49	1 42D	21 00	12 00	13 08	23 59	8 07	12 13	20 27	24 46	7 00	9 24	1 26	1 18	8 51
20 Sa	3 56 55	27 52 25	4♊40	1 41	22 36	12 48	13 49	24 05	8 11	12 10	20 26	24 47	6 46	9 27	1 47	1 50	8 50
21 Su	4 0 51	28 52 57	16 28	1 42	24 12	13 35	14 30	24 11	8 15	12 08	20 26	24 48	6 32	9 32	2 08	2 23	8 48
22 M	4 4 48	29 53 32	28 15	1 42	25 48	14 21	15 11	24 18	8 19	12 06	20 26	24 50	6 19	9 36	2 29	2 55	8 47
23 T	4 8 44	0♐54 08	10♋05	1 42℞	27 23	15 06	15 52	24 24	8 23	12 03	20 25	24 51	6 05	9 41	2 50	3 28	8 45
24 W	4 12 41	1 54 46	22 00	1 42	28 58	15 50	16 33	24 31	8 27	12 01	20 25	24 52	5 51	9 46	3 11	4 00	8 44
25 Th	4 16 38	2 55 25	4♌03	1 42	0♐33	16 34	17 15	24 38	8 31	11 59	20 25	24 54	5 37	9 52	3 33	4 32	8 43
26 F	4 20 34	3 56 06	16 19	1 42	2 08	17 16	17 56	24 45	8 36	11 57	20 25	24 55	5 23	9 58	3 54	5 05	8 41
27 Sa	4 24 31	4 56 48	28 50	1 42D	3 43	17 57	18 37	24 52	8 40	11 54	20 25	24 56	5 09	10 04	4 15	5 37	8 40
28 Su	4 28 27	5 57 32	11♍42	1 42	5 17	18 37	19 18	25 00	8 44	11 52	20 24	24 58	4 55	10 10	4 37	6 10	8 39
29 M	4 32 24	6 58 18	24 58	1 42	6 52	19 15	20 00	25 07	8 49	11 50	20 24	24 59	4 40	10 17	4 58	6 42	8 38
30 T	4 36 20	7 59 05	8♎40	1 42	8 26	19 53	20 41	25 15	8 53	11 48	20 24	25 01	4 26	10 24	5 20	7 15	8 37

EPHEMERIS CALCULATED FOR 12 MIDNIGHT GREENWICH MEAN TIME. ALL OTHER DATA AND FACING ASPECTARIAN PAGE IN **EASTERN TIME (BOLD)** AND PACIFIC TIME (REGULAR).

DECEMBER 2021

☽ Last Aspect day	ET / hr:mn / PT	asp	☽ Ingress sign	day	ET / hr:mn / PT
11/30	**11:20 pm** 8:20 pm	△ ♃	♏	1	**6:55 am** 3:55 am
2	9:22 pm	□ ♃	♐	3	**7:13 am** 4:13 am
3	**12:22 am**	□ ♃	♐	3	**7:13 am** 4:13 am
4	9:08 pm	⚹ ♃	♑	5	**6:31 am** 3:31 am
5	**12:08 am**	⚹ ♃	♑	5	**6:31 am** 3:31 am
6	**11:42 pm** 8:42 pm	⚹ ♂	♒	7	**6:49 am** 3:49 am
9	**5:00 am** 2:00 am	□ ♂	♓	9	**9:53 am** 6:53 am
11	**2:40 pm** 11:40 am	△ ♂	♈	11	**4:46 pm** 1:46 pm
13	**9:52 pm** 6:52 pm	⚹ ♃	♉	14	**3:11 am** 12:11 am
16	**11:08 am** 8:08 am	□ ♃	♊	16	**3:43 pm** 12:43 pm
18	10:02 pm	△ ♃	♋	19	**4:42 am** 1:42 am
19	**1:02 am**	△ ♃	♋	19	**4:42 am** 1:42 am
21	**9:44 am** 6:44 am	☍ ♀	♌	21	**4:54 pm** 1:54 pm
23	10:39 pm	☍ ♃	♍	24	**3:24 am** 12:24 am
24	**1:39 am**	☍ ♃	♍	24	**3:24 am** 12:24 am
26	**3:39 am** 12:39 am	△ ♇	♎	26	**11:24 am** 8:24 am
28	**4:11 pm** 1:11 pm	△ ♃	♏	28	**4:16 pm** 1:16 pm
30	**12:10 pm** 9:10 am	⚹ ☿	♐	30	**6:08 pm** 3:08 pm

☽ Phases & Eclipses phase	day	ET / hr:mn / PT
New Moon	3	11:43 pm
New Moon	4	**2:43 am**
●	3/4	12° ♐ 22'
2nd Quarter	10	**8:36 pm** 5:36 pm
Full Moon	18	**11:36 pm** 8:36 pm
4th Quarter	26	**9:24 pm** 6:24 pm

Planet Ingress	day	ET / hr:mn / PT
♂ ♐	13	**4:53 am** 1:53 am
☿ ♑	13	**12:52 pm** 9:52 am
⚳ ♉	21	**5:38 am** 2:38 am
☉ ♑	21	**10:59 am** 7:59 am
♃ ♓	28	**11:09 pm** 8:09 pm

Planetary Motion	day	ET / hr:mn / PT
♆ D	1	**8:22 am** 5:22 am
♀ ℞	19	**5:36 am** 2:36 am
⚷ D	19	**11:33 am** 8:33 am

1 WEDNESDAY
☿ ⚻ ♅ **9:15 pm** 6:15 pm
☽ □ ♄ **9:43 pm** 6:43 pm
☽ ⊻ ☉ **11:35 pm** 8:35 pm
☽ ☍ ♅ 11:01 pm
☽ ⊻ ☿ 11:36 pm

2 THURSDAY
☽ ☍ ♅ **2:01 am**
☽ ⊻ ☿ **2:36 am**
☽ △ ♆ **3:58 pm** 12:58 pm
☽ ⚹ ♀ **5:52 pm** 2:52 pm
☽ ☌ ♂ **7:45 pm** 4:45 pm
☽ ⚹ ♇ **11:26 pm** 8:26 pm
☽ □ ♃ 9:22 pm

3 FRIDAY
☽ □ ♃ **12:22 am**
☉ ⚻ ♅ **10:14 am** 7:14 am
☽ ⚹ ♄ **9:46 pm** 6:46 pm
☽ ⚻ ♅ 10:35 pm
☽ ☌ ☉ 11:43 pm

4 SATURDAY
☽ ⚻ ♅ **1:35 am**
☽ ☌ ☉ **2:43 am**
☽ ☌ ☿ **7:43 am** 4:43 am
☽ □ ♆ **3:22 pm** 12:22 pm
☽ ⊻ ♀ **6:55 pm** 3:55 pm
☽ ⊻ ♂ **9:22 pm** 6:22 pm
☽ ⊻ ♇ **10:50 pm** 7:50 pm
☽ ⚹ ♃ 9:08 pm

5 SUNDAY
☽ ⚹ ♃ **12:08 am**
☽ ⊻ ♄ **9:25 pm** 6:25 pm
☽ △ ♅ 9:56 pm

6 MONDAY
☽ △ ♅ **12:56 am**
☽ ⊻ ☉ **5:39 am** 2:39 am
♂ ⚹ ♇ **6:41 am** 3:41 am
☽ ⊻ ☿ **12:53 pm** 9:53 am
☽ ⚹ ♆ **3:09 pm** 12:09 pm
☽ ☌ ♀ **8:21 pm** 5:21 pm
☽ ☌ ♇ **10:56 pm** 7:56 pm
☽ ⚹ ♂ **11:42 pm** 8:42 pm
☽ ⊻ ♃ 9:40 pm

7 TUESDAY
☽ ⊻ ♃ **12:40 am**
☿ □ ♆ **10:16 am** 7:16 am
☽ ☌ ♄ **10:43 pm** 7:43 pm
♂ □ ♃ 10:21 pm
☽ □ ♅ 11:01 pm

8 WEDNESDAY
♂ □ ♃ **1:21 am**
☽ □ ♅ **2:01 am**
☽ ⚹ ☉ **10:57 am** 7:57 am
☽ ⊻ ♆ **5:11 pm** 2:11 pm
☽ ⚹ ☿ **9:07 pm** 6:07 pm
☽ ⊻ ♀ 9:15 pm
☽ ⊻ ♇ 10:34 pm

9 THURSDAY
☽ ⊻ ♀ **12:15 am**
☽ ⊻ ♇ **1:34 am**
☽ ☌ ♃ **3:53 am** 12:53 am
☽ □ ♂ **5:00 am** 2:00 am

10 FRIDAY
☽ ⊻ ♄ **3:18 am** 12:18 am
☽ ⚹ ♅ **6:22 am** 3:22 am
☿ ⊻ ♀ **7:50 am** 4:50 am
☿ ⊻ ♇ **12:56 pm** 9:56 am
☽ □ ☉ **8:36 pm** 5:36 pm
☽ ☌ ♆ **10:50 pm** 7:50 pm

11 SATURDAY
☽ ⚹ ♀ **7:52 am** 4:52 am
☽ ⚹ ♇ **7:56 am** 4:56 am
☽ □ ☿ **10:33 am** 7:33 am
☽ ⊻ ♃ **10:59 am** 7:59 am
♀ ☌ ♇ **11:29 am** 8:29 am
☿ ⚹ ♃ **2:24 pm** 11:24 am
☽ △ ♂ **2:40 pm** 11:40 am
☉ □ ♆ 10:21 pm

12 SUNDAY
☉ □ ♆ **1:21 am**
☽ ⚹ ♄ **11:50 am** 8:50 am
☽ ⊻ ♅ **2:34 pm** 11:34 am

13 MONDAY
☽ ⊻ ♆ **8:16 am** 5:16 am
☽ △ ☉ **11:03 am** 8:03 am
☽ □ ♇ **6:01 pm** 3:01 pm
☽ □ ♀ **7:02 pm** 4:02 pm
☿ ⊻ ♂ **7:16 pm** 4:16 pm
☽ ⚹ ♃ **9:52 pm** 6:52 pm

14 TUESDAY
☽ ⚻ ♂ **4:33 am** 1:33 am
☽ △ ☿ **5:20 am** 2:20 am
☽ □ ♄ **11:36 pm** 8:36 pm
☽ ☌ ♅ 10:51 pm

15 WEDNESDAY
☽ ☌ ♅ **1:51 am**
☽ ⚹ ♆ **8:21 pm** 5:21 pm

16 THURSDAY
☽ ⚻ ☉ **4:50 am** 1:50 am
☽ △ ♇ **6:29 am** 3:29 am
☽ △ ♀ **8:14 am** 5:14 am
☽ □ ♃ **11:08 am** 8:08 am
☽ ☍ ♂ **8:56 pm** 5:56 pm
☉ ⊻ ♇ 9:21 pm

17 FRIDAY
☉ ⊻ ♇ **12:21 am**
☽ ⚻ ☿ **3:14 am** 12:14 am
☽ △ ♄ **12:57 pm** 9:57 am
☽ ⊻ ♅ **2:36 pm** 11:36 am
☉ ⊻ ♀ **11:28 pm** 8:28 pm

18 SATURDAY
☽ □ ♆ **9:24 am** 6:24 am
☽ ⚻ ♇ **7:38 pm** 4:38 pm
☽ ⚻ ♀ **9:35 pm** 6:35 pm
☽ ☍ ☉ **11:36 pm** 8:36 pm
☽ △ ♃ 10:02 pm

19 SUNDAY
☽ △ ♃ **1:02 am**
☽ ⚻ ♂ **1:43 pm** 10:43 am
☉ ⚹ ♃ **7:32 pm** 4:32 pm
☽ ☍ ☿ 10:25 pm
☽ ⚻ ♄ 11:17 pm

20 MONDAY
☽ ☍ ☿ **1:25 am**
☽ ⚻ ♄ **2:17 am**
☽ ⚹ ♅ **3:17 am** 12:17 am
☿ ⊻ ♄ **8:22 am** 5:22 am
☿ △ ♅ **3:18 pm** 12:18 pm
☽ △ ♆ **10:00 pm** 7:00 pm

21 TUESDAY
☽ ☍ ♇ **8:10 am** 5:10 am
☽ ☍ ♀ **9:44 am** 6:44 am
☽ ⚻ ♃ **2:12 pm** 11:12 am
☽ ⚻ ☉ **5:26 pm** 2:26 pm

22 WEDNESDAY
☽ △ ♂ **5:24 am** 2:24 am
☽ ☍ ♄ **2:28 pm** 11:28 am
☽ □ ♅ **2:50 pm** 11:50 am
☽ ⚻ ☿ **9:54 pm** 6:54 pm

23 THURSDAY
☽ ⚻ ♆ **9:12 am** 6:12 am
☽ ⚻ ♇ **7:07 pm** 4:07 pm
☽ ⚻ ♀ **7:50 pm** 4:50 pm
☽ ☍ ♃ 10:39 pm
♄ □ ♅ 11:17 pm

24 FRIDAY
☽ ☍ ♃ **1:39 am**
♄ □ ♅ **2:17 am**
☽ △ ☉ **9:05 am** 6:05 am
☽ □ ♂ **6:52 pm** 3:52 pm
☽ △ ♅ 9:24 pm
☽ ⚻ ♄ 9:37 pm

25 SATURDAY
☽ △ ♅ **12:24 am**
☽ ⚻ ♄ **12:37 am**
♀ ☌ ♇ **7:02 am** 4:02 am
☽ △ ☿ **3:08 pm** 12:08 pm
☽ ☍ ♆ **6:07 pm** 3:07 pm

26 SUNDAY
☽ △ ♀ **3:12 am** 12:12 am
☽ △ ♇ **3:39 am** 12:39 am
☽ ⚻ ♃ **10:32 am** 7:32 am
☿ ⚹ ♆ **4:29 pm** 1:29 pm
☽ □ ☉ **9:24 pm** 6:24 pm

27 MONDAY
☽ ⚹ ♂ **5:07 am** 2:07 am
☽ ⚻ ♅ **7:13 am** 4:13 am
☽ △ ♄ **7:55 am** 4:55 am
☽ ⚻ ♆ 9:04 pm

28 TUESDAY
☽ ⚻ ♆ **12:04 am**
☽ □ ☿ **3:57 am** 12:57 am
☽ □ ♀ **7:19 am** 4:19 am
☽ □ ♇ **9:06 am** 6:06 am
☽ △ ♃ **4:11 pm** 1:11 pm
♂ ⚻ ♅ **8:04 pm** 5:04 pm

29 WEDNESDAY
☿ ☌ ♀ **5:27 am** 2:27 am
☽ ⚹ ☉ **5:43 am** 2:43 am
☽ ☍ ♅ **10:51 am** 7:51 am
☽ ⊻ ♂ **11:38 am** 8:38 am
☽ □ ♄ **11:58 am** 8:58 am
♂ ⚹ ♄ **7:22 pm** 4:22 pm
☽ △ ♆ 11:51 pm

30 THURSDAY
☽ △ ♆ **2:51 am**
☿ ☌ ♇ **4:54 am** 1:54 am
☽ ⚹ ♀ **8:19 am** 5:19 am
☽ ⚹ ♇ **11:27 am** 8:27 am
☽ ⚹ ☿ **12:10 pm** 9:10 am
☽ □ ♃ **6:42 pm** 3:42 pm

31 FRIDAY
☽ ⊻ ☉ **10:31 am** 7:31 am
☽ ⚻ ♅ **11:47 am** 8:47 am
☽ ⚹ ♄ **1:15 pm** 10:15 am
☽ ☌ ♂ **3:01 pm** 12:01 pm

Eastern time in bold type
Pacific time in medium type

DECEMBER 2021

DATE	SID.TIME	SUN	MOON	NODE	MERCURY	VENUS	MARS	JUPITER	SATURN	URANUS	NEPTUNE	PLUTO	CERES	PALLAS	JUNO	VESTA	CHIRON
1 W	4 40 17	8♐59 53	22♎49	1♊43	10♐00	20♑29	21♏23	25♒23	8♒58	11♉46℞	20♓24D	25♑02	4♊12℞	10♓31	5♑42	7♐47	8♈36℞
2 Th	4 44 13	10 00 43	7♏23	1 44	11 35	21 04	22 04	25 31	9 03	11 44	20 24	25 04	3 58	10 39	6 04	8 20	8 35
3 F	4 48 10	11 01 35	22 18	1 44℞	13 09	21 37	22 46	25 39	9 08	11 42	20 24	25 05	3 44	10 47	6 26	8 52	8 34
4 Sa	4 52 7	12 02 27	7♐28	1 44	14 43	22 09	23 27	25 48	9 13	11 39	20 24	25 07	3 31	10 55	6 47	9 25	8 33
5 Su	4 56 3	13 03 21	22 43	1 44	16 17	22 40	24 09	25 56	9 17	11 37	20 24	25 08	3 17	11 04	7 09	9 57	8 32
6 M	5 0 0	14 04 16	7♑52	1 43	17 51	23 08	24 50	26 05	9 23	11 35	20 25	25 10	3 03	11 13	7 32	10 29	8 31
7 T	5 3 56	15 05 12	22 47	1 41	19 25	23 36	25 32	26 13	9 28	11 34	20 25	25 11	2 50	11 22	7 54	11 02	8 31
8 W	5 7 53	16 06 09	7♒21	1 39	20 59	24 01	26 14	26 22	9 33	11 32	20 25	25 13	2 36	11 31	8 16	11 34	8 30
9 Th	5 11 49	17 07 06	21 28	1 37	22 33	24 25	26 55	26 31	9 38	11 30	20 25	25 15	2 23	11 41	8 38	12 07	8 29
10 F	5 15 46	18 08 04	5♓08	1 36	24 07	24 47	27 37	26 41	9 43	11 28	20 25	25 16	2 10	11 50	9 00	12 39	8 29
11 Sa	5 19 43	19 09 03	18 21	1 36D	25 41	25 07	28 19	26 50	9 49	11 26	20 26	25 18	1 58	12 01	9 23	13 12	8 28
12 Su	5 23 39	20 10 02	1♈11	1 36	27 16	25 25	29 01	26 59	9 54	11 24	20 26	25 20	1 45	12 11	9 45	13 44	8 28
13 M	5 27 36	21 11 01	13 40	1 37	28 50	25 40	29 43	27 09	10 00	11 23	20 26	25 21	1 33	12 22	10 08	14 17	8 27
14 T	5 31 32	22 12 01	25 53	1 39	0♑24	25 54	0♐25	27 19	10 05	11 21	20 27	25 23	1 21	12 33	10 30	14 49	8 27
15 W	5 35 29	23 13 02	7♉54	1 41	1 58	26 06	1 07	27 28	10 11	11 19	20 27	25 25	1 09	12 44	10 53	15 22	8 27
16 Th	5 39 25	24 14 03	19 48	1 42	3 33	26 15	1 49	27 38	10 16	11 17	20 28	25 27	0 57	12 55	11 15	15 54	8 27
17 F	5 43 22	25 15 05	1♊37	1 42℞	5 07	26 22	2 31	27 48	10 22	11 16	20 28	25 28	0 46	13 07	11 38	16 26	8 26
18 Sa	5 47 18	26 16 08	13 25	1 42	6 42	26 27	3 13	27 59	10 28	11 14	20 29	25 30	0 35	13 19	12 01	16 59	8 26
19 Su	5 51 15	27 17 11	25 13	1 40	8 16	26 29℞	3 55	28 09	10 34	11 13	20 29	25 32	0 25	13 31	12 23	17 31	8 26D
20 M	5 55 12	28 18 14	7♋05	1 37	9 50	26 29	4 37	28 19	10 40	11 11	20 30	25 34	0 14	13 43	12 46	18 04	8 26
21 T	5 59 8	29 19 19	19 01	1 32	11 25	26 26	5 19	28 30	10 46	11 10	20 31	25 35	0 04	13 56	13 09	18 36	8 26
22 W	6 3 5	0♑20 24	1♌04	1 27	12 59	26 21	6 01	28 41	10 52	11 09	20 31	25 37	29♉55	14 08	13 32	19 08	8 26
23 Th	6 7 1	1 21 29	13 15	1 21	14 33	26 14	6 44	28 51	10 58	11 07	20 32	25 39	29 45	14 21	13 55	19 41	8 26
24 F	6 10 58	2 22 35	25 37	1 16	16 06	26 04	7 26	29 02	11 04	11 06	20 33	25 41	29 36	14 34	14 18	20 13	8 27
25 Sa	6 14 54	3 23 42	8♍12	1 13	17 40	25 51	8 08	29 13	11 10	11 05	20 34	25 43	29 28	14 48	14 41	20 46	8 27
26 Su	6 18 51	4 24 49	21 03	1 10	19 13	25 36	8 51	29 24	11 16	11 03	20 35	25 45	29 19	15 02	15 04	21 18	8 27
27 M	6 22 47	5 25 57	4♎12	1 09D	20 45	25 18	9 33	29 35	11 22	11 02	20 35	25 47	29 12	15 15	15 27	21 50	8 28
28 T	6 26 44	6 27 05	17 43	1 10	22 16	24 59	10 16	29 47	11 29	11 01	20 36	25 48	29 04	15 29	15 50	22 22	8 28
29 W	6 30 41	7 28 14	1♏36	1 11	23 47	24 37	10 58	29 58	11 35	11 00	20 37	25 50	28 57	15 44	16 13	22 55	8 29
30 Th	6 34 37	8 29 24	15 53	1 12	25 17	24 12	11 41	0♓09	11 41	10 59	20 38	25 52	28 50	15 58	16 36	23 27	8 29
31 F	6 38 34	9 30 34	0♐32	1 13℞	26 45	23 46	12 23	0 21	11 48	10 58	20 39	25 54	28 44	16 13	17 00	23 59	8 30

EPHEMERIS CALCULATED FOR 12 MIDNIGHT GREENWICH MEAN TIME. ALL OTHER DATA AND FACING ASPECTARIAN PAGE IN **EASTERN TIME (BOLD)** AND PACIFIC TIME (REGULAR).

Notes